Jasper J. Allen,
402 E. Main St.,
Vevay, In. 47043

March 1, 1977

The Son of God

SWORD OF THE LORD PUBLISHERS
Box 1099, Murfreesboro, Tennessee 37130

The Son of God

A Verse-by-Verse Commentary
on the
GOSPEL ACCORDING TO JOHN

by

John R. Rice, D.D., Litt.D., S.T.D.
Editor, THE SWORD OF THE LORD

SWORD OF THE LORD PUBLISHERS
Box 1099, Murfreesboro, Tennessee 37130

Printed and bound in the United States of America

Table of Contents

JOHN, CHAPTER 5

JOHN, CHAPTER 6

JOHN, CHAPTER 7

TABLE OF CONTENTS   9

Introduction

Many friends, having read my commentaries on Matthew, Luke, Acts, the Corinthian Letters, and Genesis, have asked, "When will you have a commentary on the Gospel of John?" I shrank from writing this commentary, because the Gospel of John is not as much taken up with narrative as are the other Gospels, mentioning only events in about twenty days in the life of Christ on earth, but with a great deal of very serious, weighty discussions by the Saviour Himself. With heavy preaching engagements, with editorial duties to a third of a million homes where THE SWORD OF THE LORD goes weekly, with outside preaching engagements every week, with a weekly radio broadcast on many stations, and heavy mail, I doubted if I could take the time and have the ability to do the work well.

But with very heavy duties there is always the temptation to get to be routine and matter-of-fact in attitude instead of keeping a warm, devotional fervor which one needs in getting out the Gospel. So I earnestly try to regularly keep up my private devotions and Bible study, praying the dear Lord will keep my heart warm.

Once when I felt myself growing a little dull spiritually because of such a heavy preaching schedule, I set out to write a commentary on the Gospel of Matthew. In the early thirties when a group, including Drs. W. B. Riley, T. T. Sheilds, and J. Frank Norris, were dissatisfied with the International Sunday School Lessons, they planned a new schedule of lessons through the whole Bible in a five-year course. I was asked to prepare lesson comments for the more than 300 teachers in the First Baptist Church of Fort Worth and for hundreds of others who took the lessons as a Bible correspondence course week by week.

I labored five years through the whole Bible, with comments on every chapter and every principal verse. Then I went back to my notes on Matthew and with detailed study, enlarged it into the commentary, *The King of the Jews*. Then I found myself full of rich thoughts and Scriptures that pressed upon me to be expounded.

Later, again, I prepared the commentary on Acts, *Filled With the Spirit*; then the commentary on Luke, *The Son of Man*; and on the Corinthian letters, *The Church of God at Corinth*; and then the commentary on Genesis, *"In the Beginning. . . ."*

I had not thought to prepare a commentary on John, but one night the Lord awoke me at 2:00 a.m., and I went to my desk in a motel room and spent two hours in a detailed study of the first chapter. How rich it was! Then it was that I decided I must write a commentary on this Gospel, too.

The Gospel of John was written by the Apostle John who identifies himself as the disciple who leaned on Jesus' breast, the disciple whom Jesus loved. He says, "This is the disciple which testifieth of these things, and wrote these things: and we know that his testimony is true" (John 21:24). It was written long after the Synoptic Gospels: Matthew, Mark and Luke, were written, probably about the year 90. John's brother James was killed by King Herod, as we read in Acts, chapter 12. There are many references in the Church Fathers that indicate John later went to Ephesus and he took Mary with him there. He was exiled to the Island of Patmos under the reign of Emperor Domitian and there he wrote the book of Revelation and was released about the time Emperor Trajan began his reign in the year 98.

Of course, we believe the Gospel of John is verbally inspired: "All scripture is given by inspiration of God," that is, all Scripture is "God-breathed," says II Timothy 3:16. And all the way through, the Gospel of John is written as if it were the very Word of God. John claims to give word for word long quotations from Jesus and from others. John is not the author, he is the penman; God is the author.

The Gospel of John is much different from the Synoptic Gospels. They had been written many years before. They had given more details in the life of Christ. Some of these details were repeated in the Gospel of John but many are not. The Synoptic Gospels had told about a certain woman who had anointed Jesus with ointment shortly before His death, but John 11:2 tells us,

"It was that Mary which anointed the Lord with ointment, and wiped his feet with her hair, whose brother Lazarus was sick." When the story of Lazarus and Mary and Martha is to be told, then the woman is identified. She was not named before in the other Gospels.

The Synoptic Gospels use the Jewish way of counting time. For example, Mark 15:25 tells us that Jesus was crucified about the third hour. That is 9:00 in the morning, three hours from sunrise. Luke 23:44 tells us it was noon: "about the sixth hour" when darkness covered the earth and sky "until the ninth hour," that is, Jesus was crucified at 9:00 in the morning and at noon the sky became dark and that darkness continued until 3:00 in the afternoon by our time.

But John counted time after the Roman method, that is, counting from midnight. Now Jerusalem has been destroyed, Jews have been scattered to all the world and now everybody would count time the accepted Roman way. So John 19:14 tells us that in the early morning, when Jesus was brought before Pilate and he said to them, "Behold your King!" it was "about the sixth hour," that is, it was about 6:00 in the morning counting from midnight, as the Romans did, and as we do.

The emphasis in the Gospel of John is on the deity of Christ. Matthew wrote about Jesus as *King of the Jews*, Mark wrote about Him as the suffering, *Faithful Servant*, Luke wrote about Him as the *Son of Man*, the model Man. John writes about Him as the *Son of God* and all the way through great emphasis is put on the teaching that Jesus is one with the Father, the Father has put all things in His power, there is no way to honor the Father unless one honors the Son, no man comes to the Father but by Jesus, etc.

And so the emphasis on the Holy Spirit in John is more on the Holy Spirit as coming to represent Jesus as "another Comforter," that is, one of the same kind, one called alongside to help. Jesus is going away; the Spirit will come instead and so dwell within the bodies of Christians. And Jesus said in John 14:17 about this Holy Spirit, "For he dwelleth with you" (before the crucifixion), "and shall be in you" (after Christ's resurrection)—the emphasis on the indwelling Saviour. And so in John 20:19-22 we find on the day of His resurrection Jesus comes to breathe on the disciples and tell them, "Receive ye the Holy Ghost." The indwelling of the Holy Spirit came that day Jesus arose from the dead, no doubt.

The same teaching is given in John 7:37-39:

"In the last day, that great day of the feast, Jesus stood and cried, saying, If any man thirst, let him come unto me, and drink. He that believeth on me, as the scripture hath said, out of his belly shall flow rivers of living water. (But this spake he of the Spirit, which they that believe on him should receive: for the Holy Ghost was not yet given; because that Jesus was not yet glorified.)"

Now we know that here it is clearly implied that the Holy Spirit living within ought to be outflowing as a river of power and blessing. And when Jesus breathed on the disciples He said, ". . . as my Father hath sent me, even so send I you."

But the emphasis is primarily on the indwelling of the Holy Spirit and His part as representing Jesus in the Comforter, the Guide, the Teacher, one who reminds us of all Jesus would say; the Holy Spirit as the seal and down payment of our salvation.

In the Gospel of Luke, however, emphasizing Jesus as the model Man, there is much more about the enduement of power from on High. So we are told how John the Baptist was filled with the Holy Spirit, and Elisabeth, and Zacharias. Jesus tells at Nazareth that now Isaiah 61:1 is fulfilled. He is anointed to preach. And Luke 11:13 has the parable about a friend seeking heavenly bread for a friend and there is the promise of Luke 11:11-13, ". . .how much more shall your heavenly Father give the Holy Spirit to them that ask him?" And there is the emphasis in Luke 24:49 that the disciples, starting out to carry out the Great Commission, should "tarry. . .until ye be endued with power from on high."

Oh, we need all the Gospels.

The Gospel of John is written to prove the deity of Christ. As John 20:30,31 says, "And many other signs truly did Jesus in the presence of his disciples, which are not written in this book: But these are written, that ye might believe that Jesus is the Christ, the Son of God; and that believing ye might have life through his name."

I am indebted to and grateful for help from *Bible Lectures on John* by a very dear friend, the late Dr. H. A. Ironside; to the devotional commentary on John by Dr. J. C. Macaulay, my one-time pastor who graciously autographed for me his two-volume set; to Dr. W. B. Riley, a dear friend, and his comments on John, in the 40-volume set of *The Bible of the Expositor and Evangelist*; and Matthew Henry, F. B. Meyer's commentary on John; August Van Ryn's *Meditations in John*; and Dr. Herschel Ford with his *Simple Sermons From the Gospel of John*, which I found warm and helpful. Perhaps a dozen other commentaries on John's Gospel I have sometimes referred to but have not quoted.

I have noted some twenty-six volumes of commentaries on the Gospel of John on my shelves, but this commentary has been written primarily with earnest waiting upon God and continually examining and seeking the fullest meaning from the Word itself.

Oh, may God in mercy smile upon the effort and make this commentary a blessing to many, and may it show forth Christ in His power and might.

But we must remind you that the plan of salvation is mentioned more often and more clearly in the Gospel of John than anywhere else in the Bible, we believe. It is so clearly stated in John 1:12; John 3:15,16,18,36; John 5:24; John 6:37,40,47. Everyone who would win souls must let this repeated emphasis become his own. One who puts his trust in Jesus, relying on Him for salvation, then, has everlasting life, has become a child of God, is born again.

John R. Rice

1976

The Gospel According to John

A Verse-by-Verse Commentary

John 1

VERSES 1,2:

IN the beginning was the Word, and the Word was with God, and the Word was God.

2 The same was in the beginning with God.

Jesus Christ Is Eternal God

"In the beginning" (vs. 1), that is, in the beginning of this universe and before. The first three words in this chapter are the same as the first three words in Genesis; and these first five verses talk about the same time and events as the first chapter of Genesis. Jesus was there Himself and had part in creation. When God said, "Let us make man" (Gen. 1:26), He certainly included Himself, Jesus and the Holy Spirit. Jesus is as old as God the Father. He is deity. So He could say, "Before Abraham was, I am" (8:58). He is "the Ancient of days" of Daniel 7:9,10 with white hair like wool. That Scripture tells of One ruling and judging; and all judgment is given to the Son. When Jesus healed the woman physically older than He, the woman with an issue of blood for twelve years, He addressed her, "Daughter" (Matt. 9:22; Mark 5:34; Luke 8:48). He is older then than any man; He is eternal God. So He *"was in the beginning with God"* (vs. 2). Wherever God was before creation, Christ was there with Him.

Herschel Ford reminds us:

> Look how different is the beginning of John's gospel from the other three gospels. Matthew begins by giving us the genealogy

of Christ, then tells of His conception and birth. Mark begins
by telling of Christ's baptism by John the Baptist at age thirty.
Luke begins his story of Jesus by telling of the announcement
of His birth; then, like the physician he was, gives the details of
that birth. But not so with John. He goes back to the beginning. He goes back into all eternity past and presents Christ,
not as a babe in a manger, but as the second person of the
Trinity, dwelling forever with God the Father.

Christ Is the Word

Three times we have the term *"the Word"* in this first verse. It
is obviously a name for the Lord Jesus Christ. He is *"the Word"*
of God, the Revelation of God, the Manifestation of God. He is
God approaching man by becoming Man. He is God saving man.
So He is the Revelation and Manifestation of God.

Dr. Scofield says, "The Greek term means, (1) a thought or
concept; (2) the expression or utterance of that thought."

It is fitting that the same term is used for Christ and the Bible.
Both Christ and the Scriptures are eternal. Christ was "in the
beginning with God," and of the Word of the Scriptures it is said,
"For ever, O Lord, thy word is settled in heaven." Before God
had men whom He had prepared from before their birth to write
portions of Scripture (Isa. 49:1,2; Jer. 1:4,5), He had it written
down in Heaven. And in every case, God prepared the penman,
his vocabulary, his circumstances, and gave him the very words
already predetermined and written down in Heaven. This
thought is repeated in Psalm 119:152, "Concerning thy
testimonies, I have known of old that thou hast founded them for
ever." It is repeated in verse 160, "Thy word is true from the
beginning: and every one of thy righteous judgments endureth
for ever."

One cannot be saved without Christ, and one cannot be saved
without the Word, the Gospel, whether it be read or heard or
paraphrased. "The gospel. . .is the power of God unto
salvation" (Rom. 1:16).

Paul was inspired to write the Corinthians of "the
gospel. . .by which also ye are saved," that is, ". . .how that
Christ died for our sins according to the scriptures; And that he
was buried, and that he rose again the third day according to the

scriptures" (I Cor. 15:3,4). Psalm 19:7 says, "The law of the Lord is perfect, converting the soul." First Peter 1:23 says, "Being born again, not of corruptible seed, but of incorruptible, by the word of God, which liveth and abideth for ever." And we are asked the plain question in Romans 10:14, ". . .and how shall they believe in him of whom they have not heard?" So Christ and the Gospel about Him are both essential to salvation.

The gospel sower knew that "the seed is the word of God" (Luke 8:11). And that is the meaning of Psalm 126:6, "He that goeth forth and weepeth, bearing precious seed, shall doubtless come again with rejoicing, bringing his sheaves with him." But the Word of the Gospel, received and believed, the "engrafted word" of James 1:21, becomes or produces "Christ in you, the hope of glory" (Col. 1:27).

Christ is human and divine; so is the Bible. But Mary was the passive receiver by faith of the Saviour. She had no choice in making Christ's character or personality. He was wholly God and wholly sinless Man. So those who wrote the Scripture could not choose either word or thought of the Scriptures, for "every word . . .proceedeth out of the mouth of God," Jesus said in Matthew 4:4. And the revelation is given and the Scripture written, ". . . not in the words which man's wisdom teacheth, but which the Holy Ghost teacheth" (I Cor. 2:13).

So Christ and the Word of God stand or fall together. No one who refuses the Bible as God's Word can trust Christ as Saviour. To refuse one is to refuse the other; to be ashamed of one is to be ashamed of the other. Jesus said in Mark 8:38, "Whosoever therefore shall be ashamed of me and of my words in this adulterous and sinful generation; of him also shall the Son of man be ashamed, when he cometh in the glory of his Father with the holy angels."

Ah, wonderful Bible and wonderful Saviour, both eternal and divine!

I may very poorly preach Christ, or I may poorly translate His Word, but the simple truth is, both the Scriptures and Christ are the eternal Word of God.

VERSE 3:

3 All things were made by him; and without him was not any thing made that was made.

Christ, Creator of All Things

All things are made by the Lord Jesus. Actually, all three of the Trinity: Father, Son and Holy Spirit, had part in creation.

Compare verse 3 with Hebrews 1:2, which shows that God made the worlds by Jesus, that is, He seems to have left the details in the hands of the Saviour. It is clear then that Jesus is the Son of God in a sense that no other man can be. He is called "the only begotten Son of God" that is, the only One physically begotten of God (vss. 14,18; 3:16). Compare verse 1 with John 17:5 and John 8:58. In Titus 1:2 we find that eternal life was promised evidently by the Father to Jesus for all those who should trust in Him before the world began. In II Timothy 1:9 we learn that the grace of God was given to us in Christ Jesus "before the world began." In John 10:30 and many other places Jesus claims to be one with the Father.

Genesis 1:1 says, "In the beginning God created the heaven and the earth." And the Hebrew word *Elohim* is a plural form of *El* for God. And then we are told, "And the Spirit of God moved upon the face of the waters" (Gen. 1:2). So the Holy Spirit had part in creation, too. But here we are told that Christ, the Word, had part in the creation of everything that was made. Colossians 1:16,17 says:

"For by him were all things created, that are in heaven, and that are in earth, visible and invisible, whether they be thrones, or dominions, or principalities, or powers: all things were created by him, and for him: And he is before all things, and by him all things consist."

This illustrates the unity of deity. They are one in purpose and one in dealing with people. They are all-knowing, so each would know all the other knows. They are all-perfect in righteousness, so they would never disagree. What one does, all do. In salvation, the Father, Son and Holy Spirit all take part.

God the Father "so loved the world, that he gave his only begotten Son." The Son, our dear Saviour, died for our sins. Then the Holy Spirit works the miracle of regeneration in the believer, so the new convert is "born. . .of the Spirit" (John 3:5).

This perfect unity of Father, Son and Holy Spirit is illustrated by the words of Jesus in John 5:19,21 and 30:

"Then answered Jesus and said unto them, Verily, verily, I say unto you, The Son can do nothing of himself, but what he seeth the Father do: for what things soever he doeth, these also doeth the Son likewise. . . .For as the Father raiseth up the dead, and quickeneth them; even so the Son quickeneth whom he will . . . . I can of mine own self do nothing: as I hear, I judge: and my judgment is just; because I seek not mine own will, but the will of the Father which hath sent me."

That helps to explain how Jesus called Himself "even the Son of man which is in heaven" (3:13). Where one of the Persons of deity is, all others are there. What one does, they all do.

Some would suggest that to pray one must not address the Lord Jesus personally but must address the Father, and perhaps in the name of Jesus. But that is an artificial program the Lord does not require. No, with Jesus on earth, people prayed to Him and were answered; why should we not call upon our Saviour, too? And if I pray to the Father, the Holy Spirit and Christ both hear. If I pray to the Lord Jesus or the Holy Spirit, all hear. There is no jealousy and no competition in the Trinity. What one wants all want; what one of them does, all approve and do.

VERSES 4,5:

4 In him was life; and the life was the light of men.

5 And the light shineth in darkness; and the darkness comprehended it not.

Christ Is Life and Truth

Colossians 1:17 tells us not only did Christ make all things, but "by him all things consist." Does that mean that since all things were made for Jesus Christ and by Him that He has control over every heartbeat of every person, and the life of every beast? We think it does. Christ is God who has the power of life and death. And we are kept alive only by His loving mercy.

And since Christ Himself is the Life, then there is no way anybody in the world can have real life, eternal life, except by coming to Christ. Jesus said, "I am the way, the truth, and the life: no man cometh unto the Father, but by me" (14:6).

Jesus is "the light of the world." Jesus said this again and again. John 8:12 says, "Then spake Jesus again unto them, saying, I am the light of the world: he that followeth me shall not walk in darkness, but shall have the light of life." Then in John 9:5 Jesus said, "As long as I am in the world, I am the light of the world." That is the same meaning, I think, as when Jesus said, "I am the way, the *truth*, and the life." So it is true that the law came by Moses "but grace and truth came by Jesus Christ" (1:17).

light
illuminate

Oh, Christ is the fullness of divine revelation, the fullness of truth, the fullness of light and wisdom.

In I Corinthians 1:24 we are told, "Christ. . .the wisdom of God." In verse 30, ". . .who of God is made unto us wisdom." So, then, "the fear of the Lord is the beginning of wisdom" (Ps. 111:10). A reverential, seeking attitude toward Christ and the Scriptures is the way to wisdom. The term "wisdom" seems to be a personification of Jesus in some of the early proverbs. Proverbs 8:22-30 says:

"The Lord possessed me in the beginning of his way, before his works of old. I was set up from everlasting, from the beginning, or ever the earth was. When there were no depths, I was brought forth; when there were no fountains abounding with water. Before the mountains were settled, before the hills was I brought forth: While as yet he had not made the earth, nor the fields, nor the highest part of the dust of the world. When he prepared the heavens, I was there: when he set a compass upon the face of the depth: When he established the clouds above: when he strengthened the fountains of the deep: When he gave to the sea

his decree, that the waters should not pass his commandment:
when he appointed the foundations of the earth: Then I was by
him, as one brought up with him: and I was daily his delight, re-
joicing always before him."

Christ is the Light of the world.

VERSES 6-8:

6 ¶ There was a man sent from God, whose name *was* John.

7 The same came for a witness, to bear witness of the Light, that all *men* through him might believe.

8 He was not that Light, but *was sent* to bear witness of that Light.

The Ministry of John the Baptist

John was *"a man sent from God"* (vs. 6). His coming was prophesied long ahead of time in Isaiah 40:3,4 and in Malachi 3:1. His life and ministry were foretold by the angel to Zacharias before he was conceived (Luke 1:14-17). So in a very peculiar, unique way he was sent from God.

The birth and life style of John were remarkable, since never was a greater man born of woman, Jesus said in Luke 7:28. We are interested in the elements that made him great.

1. First, he was born after long years of pleading prayer, born miraculously after Elisabeth was long past the child-bearing age. Such a child ought to be greatly blessed and used.

Hannah, long barren, prayed and God gave her the mighty Prophet Samuel.

Sarah and Abraham prayed for long years and Isaac was born when Sarah was ninety years old and Abraham a hundred.

Barren Rachel cried to God long and Joseph was born.

So we judge that the children born after earnest prayer are likely to be more blessed and more used than many others.

2. His rearing was, no doubt, Spartan and Christian. Zacharias and Elisabeth "were both righteous before God" (Luke 1:6 says). It appears that they had prayed about the matter of drunkenness among priests and others and so were assured

by the angle that John should "drink neither wine nor strong drink" (Luke 1:15). The fact that he was "in the deserts till the day of his shewing unto Israel" indicates retirement from this busy and wicked world and waiting on God in self-imposed poverty and discipline. We are reminded of the unworldly sons of Rechab who so lived (Jer. 35:1-10).

3. Most important, John was "filled with the Holy Ghost, even from his mother's womb" (Luke 1:15). That is unique in human history when, still an innocent child, and not conscious of sin, he continued filled with the Spirit. When he came to know himself a sinner, he surely at once turned to God for forgiveness and thus was continually Spirit-filled.

John was about six months older than Jesus (Luke 1:26). We suppose he began to preach at thirty, as did Jesus, and some months before Jesus. Since their mothers were cousins and near in heart interest, no doubt these two knew something of each other though reared somewhat apart.

John had great reverence for the Lord Jesus, that perfect, sinless young Man, and he knew He would be greatly revered in Nazareth where He grew up. There He was asked to do the public reading of the Word of God by those who had known Him long (Luke 4:16).

John did not at first know that Jesus was the promised Messiah until He was baptized and John saw the Holy Spirit come upon Him as a sign (1:32-34).

We are told that John came for a witness. Since he made sure that he was only a witness to Jesus and not a rival, he never worked a miracle (John 10:41). Many Old Testament saints and New Testament apostles had worked miracles, but not John.

The purpose of his coming was "that all men through him might believe." He was to be a soul winner. For this reason he was "filled with the Holy Ghost." That was and is the requirement for soul winning, as we see in Luke 24:49; Acts 1:8; 11:24. Even Jesus never won a soul until He was filled with the Spirit or anointed with the Spirit (Luke 3:21,22; Acts 10:37,38). So John was filled with the Spirit and "many of the children of Israel shall he turn to the Lord their God," promised the angel before his birth (Luke 1:15,16). And so it was.

"That ALL. . .might believe" (vs. 7). The purpose of John's ministry was not for a few specially predestined to be saved, but for ALL. So II Peter 3:9 says, "The Lord is not slack concerning his promise, as some men count slackness; but is longsuffering to us-ward, not willing that any should perish, but that all should come to repentance."

We believe sometimes one may be more used to win children, or youth, or Jews, or prisoners, than some other class of people, but every Christian should have the intent to win everybody possible. God wants them all.

The king who made a marriage for his son so instructed his messengers: "So those servants went out into the highways, and gathered together all as many as they found, both bad and good: and the wedding was furnished with guests" (Matt. 22:10). Alas, some refused the wedding garment, but that is not the intent of the king nor of his messengers. Oh, the Lord wants all saved!

Jesus wept over Jerusalem because they would not come, though He would have saved them.

John was a witness, as we all are. Jesus reveals the Father and is sent from the Father. So Jesus sends us. In John 17:18 Jesus prayed, "As thou hast sent me into the world, even so have I also sent them into the world." And when Jesus arose from the dead, He came to the disciples and breathed on them and said, "Peace be unto you: as my Father hath sent me, even so send I you. And when he had said this, he breathed on them, and saith unto them, Receive ye the Holy Ghost" (20:21,22).

As He is the Light of the world, so are we too, according to Jesus in Matthew 5:14 where He said, "Ye are the light of the world."

VERSES 9,10:

9 *That* was the true Light, which lighteth every man that cometh into the world.

10 He was in the world, and the world was made by him, and the world knew him not.

Christ Lights Every Man

As John intended that "all men through him might believe," so Jesus lights every person in the world. There is a plain statement we dare not dodge nor twist. It is true that man is a sinner, even dead in trespasses and in sin (Eph. 2:1). It is true that "no man can come to me, except the Father which hath sent me draw him," as Jesus said (6:44). It is true—all those indictments about a sinful race in Romans 3:9-18. Every poor sinner should make sure to come, then, when God's Spirit draws him, for he will be drawn.

But here it is plainly said that Christ *"lighteth every man that cometh into the world"* (vs. 9). That is the same promise of Jesus in John 12:32,33, "And I, if I be lifted up from the earth, will draw all men unto me. This he said, signifying what death he should die."

How does God call? Through His creation. Romans 1:19,20 says:

"Because that which may be known of God is manifest in them; for God hath shewed it unto them. For the invisible things of him from the creation of the world are clearly seen, being understood by the things that are made, even his eternal power and Godhead; so that they are without excuse."

God called Heaven and earth to witness against Israel (Deut. 4:26). Acts 14:17 says that God "left not himself without witness." And Psalm 19:1-6 says:

"The heavens declare the glory of God; and the firmament sheweth his handywork. Day unto day uttereth speech, and night unto night sheweth knowledge. There is no speech nor language, where their voice is not heard. Their line is gone out through all the earth, and their words to the end of the world. In them hath he set a tabernacle for the sun, Which is as a bridegroom coming out of his chamber, and rejoiceth as a strong man to run a race. His going forth is from the end of the heaven, and his circuit unto the ends of it: and there is nothing hid from the heat thereof."

And wherever men have the Scriptures, those Scriptures call men to repent. We are told "the law was our schoolmaster to bring us unto Christ" (Gal. 3:24). And that the law is given "that every mouth may be stopped, and all the world may become guilty before God" (Rom. 3:19). Does that mean that even lost men can be and are moved by the Scriptures? Yes. (3)

And where people do not have a Bible, their conscience is the voice of God, too. Romans 2:14-16 says:

"For when the Gentiles, which have not the law, do by nature the things contained in the law, these, having not the law, are a law unto themselves: Which shew the work of the law written in their hearts, their conscience also bearing witness, and their thoughts the mean while accusing or else excusing one another;) In the day when God shall judge the secrets of men by Jesus Christ according to my gospel."

Man's conscience is "the candle of the Lord, searching all the inward parts of the belly" (Prov. 20:27).

That little spark of celestial fire called conscience is of God! A burning conscience in a lost man, whether he ever chooses to be saved or not? Oh, yes. For example, Judas Iscariot was not and never would be saved, yet with a burning conscience he returned the price of his betrayal and cried out, "I have sinned in that I have betrayed the innocent blood." And that conscience led him to kill himself.

Yes, and when Pharisees brought a woman taken in adultery to Jesus, He said, "He that is without sin among you, let him first cast a stone at her." Then "they which heard it, being convicted by their own conscience, went out one by one, beginnning at the eldest, even unto the last: and Jesus was left alone, and the woman standing in the midst" (8:9).

Don't ever try to explain it away. Christ "lighteth every man that cometh into the world." And when He died on the cross, "he is the propitiation for our sins: and not for our's only, but also for the sins of the whole world" (I John 2:2).

So He came into this world that He made. Into this world where He keeps every heartbeat going and breath in every body and sustains all things by His power, He came, and was unknown, unloved and not received.

It is not only wickedness that this world doesn't know Jesus, it is idiocy; it is fatal, wicked blindness; it is willing ignorance.

———————

VERSES 11-13:

11 He came unto his own, and his own received him not.
12 But as many as received him, to them gave he power to become the sons of God, *even* to them that believe on his name:
13 Which were born, not of blood, nor of the will of the flesh, nor of the will of man, but of God.

All Who Receive Him Are Saved

It was Christ's own world He came to, the world He made. But it was particularly to His own people Israel. For Christ was humanly of the seed of Abraham, of the tribe of Judah. It was the wickedness of the human heart that Jews did not receive Him. They had the promises of His coming which God had given, that the Seed of the woman should bruise the serpent's head. They had the promise so clearly pictured in the passover lamb. Christ was pictured in the rock out of which gushed the river of water to fill the thirsting Israelites in the desert. Christ was pictured in the brazen serpent on the pole to which the snakebitten were instructed to "look and live." The offering of Christ, the Suffering Servant, was made so clear in Isaiah 52 and 53. His terrible sufferings on the cross were pictured in Psalm 22. A thousand references would have stirred the heart of any spiritual ones but most Jews did not receive the long promised Saviour, expected by many and rejected by most.

But what about those who received Him? Why, very simply, based on that simple heart reception He gave them authority to become sons of God. There was no question of their merit or character or fitness, just the simple condition that any who wanted the Lord Jesus may have Him. Any who would receive Him may take Him. And those who received Him, "to them gave he power to become the sons of God, even to them that believe on his name."

Will you note that receiving and believing are the same? If any one wants to know what it means to believe on Jesus, it simply means to receive Him. That is the same kind of promise as Revelation 3:20, "Behold, I stand at the door, and knock: if any man hear my voice, and open the door, I will come in to him, and will sup with him, and he with me." That is the same kind of promise of Revelation 22:17, "Let him that is athirst come. And whosoever will, let him take the water of life freely." Instant salvation, undeserved salvation, glorious, eternal salvation to the one who receives Christ in the heart. Oh, simple, beautiful, and marvelous!

We will remember that the Gospel of John was written with a special color intent that people should be saved, and so again and again the sweet plan of salvation is stated, that one who believes on Christ or depends upon Christ, relies on Him for forgiveness and salvation, immediately has everlasting life (3:14, 16, 18, 36; 5:24; 6:40, 47; it is also in Acts 13:38, 39; 16:31; 10:43).

VERSE 14:

14 And the Word was made flesh, and dwelt among us, (and we beheld his glory, the glory as of the only begotten of the Father,) full of grace and truth.

Christ, the Physically Begotten Son of God

Here is a statement of the incarnation of Jesus. What a marvel that God should become Man!

Dr. Herschel Ford reminds us that Bishop Taylor Smith was standing in an open field one day and moved a stone out of its place. Ants began running from under the stone, seeking safety. The bishop asked himself, "How can I make these ants understand that I don't want to hurt them? How can I convey my thoughts to them?" He concluded that in order to do that, he would have to become an ant himself in order to express his love to them. And Dr. Ford says: "That is what Jesus did. He became one of us so that He might understand our needs and express the great love God has toward us."

And the inspired John says here, *"And we beheld his glory, the glory as of the only begotten of the Father."* In other words, Jesus was sinlessly born, physically begotten of God, and there was about Him the glory of perfection, the glory of perfect wisdom, the glory of absolute purity. It was not all immediately manifest, but even John so reverenced Him that he hesitated to baptize the Lord Jesus even before he learned that Christ was the Messiah. It is true that in the perfect sense Christ is glorified after His resurrection. That kind of glory was seen on the Mount of Transfiguration. And Peter reminds us that the apostles

". . .have not followed cunningly devised fables, when we made known unto you the power and coming of our Lord Jesus Christ, but were eyewitnesses of his majesty. For he received from God the Father honour and glory, when there came such a voice to him from the excellent glory, This is my beloved Son, in whom I am well pleased. And this voice which came from heaven we heard, when we were with him in the holy mount."—II Pet. 1:16-18.

Even of a frail and sinful man it is said, "I am fearfully and wonderfully made" (Ps. 139:14). There are marvels in the human body and mind and spirit, but in Christ Jesus these were perfected. So there is some glimmer, some foretaste of all this heavenly glory and majesty which must have appeared daily in the sinless Saviour as He went among the people.

When Lazarus was sick Jesus said, "This sickness is not unto death, but for the glory of God" (11:4). Only after His resurrection was Jesus glorified beyond all question or doubt among the people. John 7:39 says, ". . .for the Holy Ghost was not yet given; because that Jesus was not yet glorified." The night before His crucifixion and before going to Gethsemane, the Lord Jesus said, "Father, the hour is come; glorify thy Son, that thy Son also may glorify thee" (17:1). In verse 5 He said, "And now, O Father, glorify thou me with thine own self with the glory which I had with thee before the world was." So when John saw the Saviour at the time of the revelation, he saw Him in His glory and fell at His feet as one dead (Rev. 1:17).

But the Lord Jesus was "the only begotten of the Father." Here is, I think, a very strong statement of the virgin birth of Christ. The translators of the Revised Standard Version changed John 3:16 from the familiar "God. . .gave his only begotten Son" to "God. . .gave his only Son." That was not scholarly and not theologically correct. Jesus was not the only son of God—all who "received him, to them gave he power to become the sons of God." But here the contrast is, Jesus is the only one *physically* begotten of God. That means that not Joseph but God Himself begat the Baby conceived in the womb of Mary. So in the 2nd Psalm a prophecy says, "Thou art my Son; this day have I begotten thee." The same term is used in John 3:18. God is stressing the fact that Christ was the only Person physically begotten of God. The term is used again in Acts 13:33, quoting from the 2nd Psalm, and again in Hebrews 1:5, quoting the 2nd Psalm.

Those who say that the virgin birth is not told anywhere except in Matthew and in Luke are not only willingly ignorant but are wickedly avoiding what God so clearly stated even here as well as elsewhere.

VERSES 15-18:

15 ¶ John bare witness of him, and cried, saying, This was he of whom I spake, He that cometh after me is preferred before me: for he was before me.

16 And of his fulness have all we received, and grace for grace.

17 For the law was given by Moses, *but* grace and truth came by Jesus Christ.

18 No man hath seen God at any time; the only begotten Son, which is in the bosom of the Father, he hath declared *him*.

The Witness of John the Baptist

John seems to have begun his great ministry with a marvelous revival on the banks of the river Jordan. It was a camp meeting and the crowds were enormous, including, at different times, practically the entire population of Jerusalem and the province of Judaea (Matt. 3:5,6). Multitudes were truly converted and great numbers were baptized in the Jordan river (vs. 28).

John said, *"He that cometh after me is preferred before me: for he was before me"* (vs. 15). Jesus is pre-existent God. As a Baby, He was born six months after John. As God the Son, He was existent from eternity.

Oh, that we might enter into the riches of verse 16, "And of his fulness have all we received." Every heartbeat, every breath of air, every peaceful moment, all the provisions of nature, are from the fullness of Christ and from His grace. Oh, "grace for grace"!

The law was given by Moses. And the law is not wrong but good. God Himself is a holy God and if man had always obeyed God, had always done right, there would be no special manifestation of the grace of God. But even so the ceremonies showed always the need for a Saviour. The Sabbath of the Decalogue was a promise of Heaven for those who earned it, for those who all the six days, representing man's life on earth, had done right, never wrong. They would deserve and get a Sabbath of rest. Alas, man had failed. The law was not wrong, but man has sinned.

So now we need not a Sabbath after six days of labor but the passover Sabbath, where people on the very first day of the passover week have a day of holy convocation and rest and begin that first day of the week to eat the unleavened bread. And then with a lifetime of blessing we enter into the heavenly rest, pictured by that Sabbath on the seventh day, that day of holy convocation (Exod. 12:14-16). And so the law was a schoolmaster to bring us to Christ. Christ Himself has fulfilled all the law and "Christ is the end of the law for righteousness to every one that believeth" (Rom. 10:4).

Ah, but the law was not meant to be only a form. Sacrifices in themselves brought no pleasure to God. One is not circumcised really before God unless he is circumcised in heart (Gal. 5:6 and 6:15). "And if ye be Christ's, then are ye Abraham's seed, and heirs according to the promise" (Gal. 3:29). We who are believers "are circumcised with the circumcision made without hands" (Col. 2:11). And when Israel did not see the spiritual meaning of forgiveness through Christ and the pictured Saviour in all the sacrifices and ceremonies, the Lord cried out to them:

"Hear the word of the Lord, ye rulers of Sodom; give ear unto the law of our God, ye people of Gomorrah. To what purpose is the multitude of your sacrifices unto me? saith the Lord: I am full of the burnt-offerings of rams, and the fat of fed beasts; and I delight not in the blood of bullocks, or of lambs, or of he goats. When ye come to appear before me, who hath required this at your hand, to tread my courts? Bring no more vain oblations; incense is an abomination unto me; the new moons and sabbaths, the calling of assemblies I cannot away with; it is iniquity, even the solemn meeting. Your new moons and your appointed feasts my soul hateth: they are a trouble unto me; I am weary to bear them."—Isa. 1:10-14.

"But grace and truth came by Jesus Christ" (vs. 17). All the pointers pointed this way, and now the Saviour Himself appeared!

Verse 18 says, *"No man hath seen God at any time; the only begotten Son, which is in the bosom of the Father, he hath declared him."*

Scofield says, "The divine essence, God, in His own triune Person, no human being in the flesh has seen. But God, veiled in angelic form, and especially as incarnate in Jesus Christ, has been seen of men (Gen. 18. 2, 22; John 14. 8, 9)."

F. B. Meyers says: "No man hath seen God at any time. Never yet. Not Moses, for he was hidden under the hand of God, and saw not His face. Not Elijah; for God was not in the earthquake or fire. Not the favoured three; for the cloud of glory dazzled them with its splendour. And even in the Apocalyptic vision (in Revelation), the rapt gaze of the seer beheld only the circumambient halo as of the jasper and sardonyx stone."

Jesus is *"in the bosom of the Father"* (vs. 18). Was that while He was here on earth? Yes, as Jesus said in John 3:18, ". . .even the Son of man which is in heaven." Jesus is so at one with the Father that the Father was in Christ on earth, manifested in Him, and Christ was with the Father in Heaven. For remember that although Christ was now in the flesh and all things are His,

created by Him and for Him, He has not lost His oneness with
the Father, nor His place in Heaven.

VERSES 19-27:

19 ¶ And this is the record of John, when the Jews sent priests and Levites from Jerusalem to ask him, Who art thou?

20 And he confessed, and denied not; but confessed, I am not the Christ.

21 And they asked him, What then? Art thou Ē-lī́-ăs? And he saith, I am not. Art thou that prophet? And he answered, No.

22 Then said they unto him, Who art thou? that we may give an answer to them that sent us. What sayest thou of thyself?

23 He said, I *am* the voice of one crying in the wilderness, Make straight the way of the Lord, as said the prophet Ē-śāī́-ăs.

24 And they which were sent were of the Pharisees.

25 And they asked him, and said unto him, Why baptizest thou then, if thou be not that Christ, nor Ē-lī́-ăs, neither that prophet?

26 John answered them, saying, I baptize with water: but there standeth one among you, whom ye know not;

27 He it is, who coming after me is preferred before me, whose shoe's latchet I am not worthy to unloose.

John Explains Himself

Who is this John? He comes baptizing with authority as if he had a new dispensation from God. This is not a ceremony that the Jews had before, though some foolishly have thought so. No, this seemed utterly strange to Jewish leaders, so John was thus claiming some special authority other prophets before him had not had. Why? Who is he?

Two are prophesied to come in the Old Testament. One was Elijah. The last sentence in the Old Testament says:

"Behold, I will send you Elijah the prophet before the coming of the great and dreadful day of the Lord: And he shall turn the heart of the fathers to the children, and the heart of the children to their fathers, lest I come and smite the earth with a curse."— Mal. 4:5,6.

And so they wonder if this is a reappearance of Elijah. We know that later John the Baptist came "in the spirit and power of Elias" (Luke 1:17), and of him Jesus said, "Elias is come already" (Matt. 17:12). Many think, because of this prophecy, Elijah will be one of the two witnesses to come during the tribulation time (Zech. 4:11-14; Rev. 11:3). But John the Baptist said he is not Elijah.

Moses foretold also. God led Moses to prophesy, "The Lord thy God will raise up unto thee a Prophet from the midst of thee, of thy brethren, like unto me; unto him ye shall hearken" (Deut. 18:15).

So here they ask John the Baptist, *"Art thou that prophet? And he answered, No"* (vs. 21). The Prophet Moses foretold it was the Lord Jesus Himself, and John was not that. But who, then, is he? He quotes to them from Isaiah 40:3, *"I am the voice of one crying in the wilderness, Make straight the way of the Lord, as said the prophet Esaias"* (vs. 23). He is the forerunner God had promised for His Son.

Ah, but John does not miss the opportunity—they must meet that Greater One who is coming, the Saviour Himself. John was not worthy to unloose the latchet of His shoes or sandals. Here John knew that the Saviour was already among them, although he did not know that Jesus was the One until he baptized Him and saw the Holy Spirit descending in form like a dove upon Him and abiding upon Him.

VERSES 28-34:

28 These things were done in Bĕth-ăb´-ă-ră beyond Jordan, where John was baptizing.

29 ¶ The next day John seeth Jesus coming unto him, and saith, Behold the Lamb of God, which taketh away the sin of the world.

30 This is he of whom I said, After me cometh a man which is preferred before me: for he was before me.

31 And I knew him not: but that he should be made manifest to Israel, therefore am I come baptizing with water.

32 And John bare record, saying, I saw the Spirit descending from heaven like a dove, and it abode upon him.

33 And I knew him not: but he that sent me to baptize with water, the same said unto me, Upon whom thou shalt see the Spirit descending, and remaining on him, the same is he which baptizeth with the Holy Ghost.

34 And I saw, and bare record that this is the Son of God.

John the Baptist Introduces the Saviour
to the Multitude

John was baptizing at Bethabara beyond Jordan. John has already baptized Jesus, as told in Matthew 3:13-17 and in Luke 3:21,22, and now he introduces Jesus as "the Lamb of God." After he baptized Him, he recognized Him because the Spirit of God descended upon Him and "abode upon him." The sign was to see *"the Spirit descending, and remaining on him"* (vs. 33).

And what a flood of great truth now begins to be announced. Jesus is not only the Saviour; He is the One who will baptize with the Holy Ghost. Christians may have the floodtide of power, the Holy Spirit living within, representing Christ in the Christian and showing the power of Christ in soul winning. And now John the Baptist, who all these years has known that Jesus was a marvelously righteous and godly Man, knows that He is the Son of God.

Why was Jesus baptized? I think He was publicly announcing to the Father and the people that He had given Himself up to die. The Gospel is that "Christ died for our sins according to the scriptures; And that he was buried, and that he rose again the third day according to the scriptures." So Jesus is here announcing Himself the Son of God who will die for the sins of the world and be raised from the dead, proving His deity.

Dr. Scofield, who was a Pedobaptist and so never understood the Bible doctrine of baptism, says about Jesus, "Why one who needed no repentance should insist upon receiving a rite which signified confession (v. 6) and repentance (v. 11) is nowhere directly explained." And he thinks that this is a fulfillment of the Levitical way of washing a priest and then anointing him! But Dr. Scofield was wrong. Baptism, to Jesus, pictured the grave and resurrection, and He freely gave Himself to that.

And when a Christian is buried with Christ in baptism, it is not so much a picture of confession and repentance as a picture of the old man being counted dead and the new man alive and living now a new life, the life of Christ in the power of the Holy Spirit.

One would not understand baptism if he had to put it some

way in the Levitical priesthood. All the way through Dr. Scofield's notes in the fine Scofield Bible he some way seems to rate John the Baptist as an Old Testament character and John's baptism as a Jewish rite. But that is a mistake. John the Baptist was a New Testament prophet and preacher. His Gospel was the Gospel of salvation by faith in Christ. The baptism of John is the same baptism Jesus had and all the apostles had, and the same one New Testament Christians should have today.

The first two verses in the Gospel of Mark say, "The beginning of the gospel of Jesus Christ, the Son of God; As it is written in the prophets, Behold, I send my messenger before thy face, which shall prepare thy way before thee." Here the New Testament begins with the story of John the Baptist.

Dr. Scofield, in his notes on the baptism of Jesus, in Matthew 3, says, "But John's baptism was the voice of God to Israel, and the believing remnant responded (v. 5). It was an act of righteousness on the part of Him who had become, as to the flesh, an Israelite, to take His place with this believing remnant." But here Dr. Scofield gives a dispensational meaning that is not mentioned in Scripture. The message of John the Baptist was not particularly Jewish. The baptism of Jesus was not particularly an example or sign to Jews. It was an example to everybody who would trust Christ for salvation and thus follow Him in baptism.

In Acts 19, where Paul came and found certain disciples and said to them, "Have ye received the Holy Ghost since ye believed?" they had not understood about the fullness of the Spirit. So they were baptized again and Paul laid his hands upon them and the Holy Ghost came on them.

But Dr. Scofield says, "Paul was evidently impressed by the absence of spirituality and power in these so-called disciples. Their answer brought out the fact that they were Jewish proselytes, disciples of John the Baptist, looking forward to a coming King, not Christians looking backward to an accomplished redemption."

Here our Plymouth Brethren friends and Dr. Scofield have erred greatly, we think. A disciple of John the Baptist would be no different from a disciple of Paul or Barnabas or Apollos or Peter or any other New Testament preacher.

In the first place, there never was but one plan of salvation in the Old Testament or New Testament, for in Acts 10:43 Peter was inspired to say, "To him give all the prophets witness, that through his name whosoever believeth in him shall receive remission of sins." So when God calls people "disciples" who have "believed," neither Dr. Scofield nor anybody else has a right to call them "so-called disciples." That is unjustified as well as being irreverent.

In John 3:27-36 John the Baptist is preaching, and he says, "He that believeth on the Son hath everlasting life: and he that believeth not the Son shall not see life; but the wrath of God abideth on him." John's disciples were Christians and they were baptized as Christians should be baptized. All the apostles and Jesus Himself were baptized by John. Christians today ought to be baptized the same way. John was New Testament, not Old Testament; he was Gospel, nor ceremonial, in his preaching and practice.

Remember that baptism was not an Old Testament ordinance. There is no record in the Bible of any such ceremony given by the Lord for Jews. Jesus plainly taught that now new wine must be put into new bottles.

It is clear that the announcement in verse 29, that Jesus is the Lamb of God, is after Jesus had been baptized and recognized as the Son of God.

VERSES 35-42:

35 ¶ Again the next day after John stood, and two of his disciples;

36 And looking upon Jesus as he walked, he saith, Behold the Lamb of God!

37 And the two disciples heard him speak, and they followed Jesus.

38 Then Jesus turned, and saw them following, and saith unto them, What seek ye? They said unto him, Rabbi, (which is to say, being interpreted, Master,) where dwellest thou?

39 He saith unto them, Come and see. They came and saw where he dwelt, and abode with him that day: for it was about the tenth hour.

40 One of the two which heard

John *speak*, and followed him, was Andrew, Simon Peter's brother.

41 He first findeth his own brother Simon, and saith unto him, We have found the Messias, which is, being interpreted, the Christ.

42 And he brought him to Jesus. And when Jesus beheld him, he said, Thou art Simon the son of Jona: thou shalt be called Çĕ-phăs, which is by interpretation, A stone.

The Conversion of Andrew and Peter

As John the Baptist was preaching, "Behold the Lamb of God," two of John's disciples saw Jesus and followed Him. There is a wonderful lesson in verse 39. They wanted to know where Jesus lived and He said to them, "Come and see." So Jesus says the same to every seeking heart. He said to the wayward Israelites in Jeremiah 29:11-13,

"For I know the thoughts that I think toward you, saith the Lord, thoughts of peace, and not of evil, to give you an expected end. Then shall ye call upon me, and ye shall go and pray unto me, and I will hearken unto you. And ye shall seek me, and find me, when ye shall search for me with all your heart."

Jesus said in James 4:8, "Draw nigh to God, and he will draw nigh to you." The Scripture says about wisdom, personifying Jesus, I believe, "Those that seek me early shall find me" (Prov. 8:17).

One of those who heard John speak was Andrew, Simon Peter's brother. It was about 4:00 p.m. The day was well spent and he "abode with him that day" (vs. 39). Jesus was not at home but perhaps was camping out or staying in some home offered Him. His home was at Capernaum, and this is at Bethabara beyond Jordan. And whatever happened there, we think Andrew came to know certainly this was the Saviour, came to put his trust in Him, and now he must find his brother Peter. We suppose Andrew was the younger of the two. He was not as forceful, nor as prominent as Peter, but he immediately went to find his brother. And his message was very simple: *"We have found the Messias, which is, being interpreted, the Christ. And he brought him to Jesus"* (vss. 41,42). Ah, the main thing about soul winning is to go after them. And personal influence is so important that it may not take a profound message or a long explanation, if you let people understand that here is the Saviour for sinners and they may have Him. So Andrew brought Peter to Jesus.

Will you note that here is a young convert just saved, we suppose, last night or in the last few hours, and he goes to find his brother and wins him.

In chapter 4, we learn that when the Samaritan woman knew that Jesus was the Messiah, she left her waterpots and ran to the city to tell the men, "Come, see a man, which told me all things that ever I did: is not this the Christ?" Some were saved there on her testimony, while others came to see for themselves and were saved. Yes, new converts should win souls.

The plain command in Revelation 22:17 is, "Let him that heareth say, Come." And oftentimes the warmth and joy and testimony of a young convert is more effective than the learned discourses of an older Christian. Whoever is saved should win souls.

We note there is no reference here to any profound emotional crisis in the life of Peter. There may have been, or there may not have been. Nor with Andrew. One who trusts in Christ is saved. Sometimes we would like so much to see a great outward display of emotion. We would like to see some of the outward evidences that the miraculous change has taken place within. But that is not promised and not required in the Bible. There is a profound change, but it is an inward change; whether it shows on the outside or not we cannot always tell.

It is true that when one becomes a Christian, all things are new, that is, all things within the real being of the man. There is a new creation. But he still has the old nature and sometimes the old nature dominates. Remember that "man looketh on the outward appearance, but the Lord looketh on the heart." We are plainly warned not to judge by outward appearances who is saved and who is not. That is not our business. Christians ought to live right, though sometimes the seed is choked by cares of this world and deceitfulness of riches and other things, as with the sower of seed in Matthew 13:22. And sometimes a David or a Peter may fall into deepest sins, or sometimes a Demas may forsake a Paul, having loved this present world; but the change is inward, not measurable outwardly, and no one has a right to judge by outward appearance whether one is saved or not. If one has trusted Christ, he is saved.

VERSES 43-51:

43 ¶ The day following Jesus would go forth into Galilee, and findeth Philip, and saith unto him, Follow me.

44 Now Philip was of Bĕth-să′ĭ-dă, the city of Andrew and Peter.

45 Philip findeth Nathanael, and saith unto him, We have found him, of whom Moses in the law, and the prophets, did write, Jesus of Nazareth, the son of Joseph.

46 And Nathanael said unto him, Can there any good thing come out of Nazareth? Philip saith unto him, Come and see.

47 Jesus saw Nathanael coming to him, and saith of him, Behold an Israelite indeed, in whom is no guile!

48 Nathanael saith unto him, Whence knowest thou me? Jesus answered and said unto him, Before that Philip called thee, when thou wast under the fig tree, I saw thee.

49 Nathanael answered and saith unto him, Rabbi, thou art the Son of God; thou art the King of Israel.

50 Jesus answered and said unto him, Because I said unto thee, I saw thee under the fig tree, believest thou? thou shalt see greater things than these.

51 And he saith unto him, Verily, verily, I say unto you, Hereafter ye shall see heaven open, and the angels of God ascending and descending upon the Son of man.

The Salvation of Philip and Nathanael

It is interesting to compare the word *"findeth"* in verses 41, 43 and 45. Andrew findeth Peter; Jesus findeth Philip; Philip findeth Nathanael! The way to win souls is to find them. We may sometimes pray for God to send somebody to us, but already the command is in the Scripture—He hath sent us to go to sinners. There may come a time when, after a great demonstration of God's miraculous power, a jailer may come and fall down before a Paul and Silas and inquire, "What must I do to be saved?" but that is rare. The usual thing is that God sends us out to "go. . .into all the world, and preach the gospel to every creature." He sends us out to get the guests for the wedding feast, to "go out quickly into the streets and lanes of the city, and bring in hither the poor, and the maimed, and the halt, and the blind," and, "Go out into the highways and hedges, and compel them to come in" (Luke 14:21,23).

Andrew was saved and he won Peter.

"The day following Jesus would go forth into Galilee" (vs. 43). He has been across the Jordan River at Bethabara, but now He goes north into the province of Galilee, probably around the lake to His home in Capernaum. And He finds Philip there. We know that Peter and Andrew lived nearby at the city of Bethsaida (vs. 44).

Verse 43 tells how Jesus did personal work, winning Philip. He did not stumble on him by chance, take a liking to him, and invite his company. He had come to seek and to save those who were lost. Yes, Jesus repeatedly did personal work as He did with Nicodemus, and the woman at the well. Philip won his friend Nathanael to the Saviour.

Nathanael soon out-talked Philip, as we see from verse 45. Philip was a very ignorant Christian, not even knowing, we suppose, that Jesus was born of a virgin, supposing that Joseph was His father. So he said, *"We have found him, of whom Moses in the law, and the prophets, did write, Jesus of Nazareth, the son of Joseph."* But Jesus was ordinarily called the Son of Joseph, and Joseph would so have introduced Him, no doubt. He was the adopted Son, a foster Son of Joseph.

(It is not surprising that Jesus is listed in the ancestral line of Matthew, the official line of Davidic kings, as if Jesus had come down through Solomon and through Joseph. That is not the true genealogy but the official one, and is listed as though He came through Joseph who acted in the place of a parent and was responsible as a father, though he was not the Father. The true genealogy is found in Luke 3:23-38.

But we know that Jesus was not the Son of Joseph, although He appeared to be that to the people.)

How happy that God could use even an ignorant Christian like Philip! When Philip had told all he knew, he was wise enough to say, "Come and see." Any infidel in the world can find out today whether Jesus is the Saviour if he will do what Nathanael did— "Come and see."

Nathanael has a serious question: *"Can there any good thing come out of Nazareth?"* (vs. 46). And Philip told him the same thing that Jesus had said to Andrew, *"Come and see."* Jesus is approachable by every honest heart.

John 7:17 says, "If any man will do his will, he shall know of the doctrine, whether it be of God, or whether I speak of myself." And Hosea 6:3 says, "Then shall we know, if we follow on to know the Lord."

Perhaps there are no honest doubters. There are people who do doubt, it is true, but they did not come to that position with an honest, seeking heart. Cornelius, that devout man who prayed and sought God, found Him, for God sent him an Angel Gabriel to tell him where to get a preacher! And the Ethiopian eunuch, reading the Scripture in Isaiah and longing to be saved, found that God sent Philip the evangelist to meet him and explain the Scripture and tell him about Jesus. So if one has a question about Jesus, he need only come to Jesus to see and he will find that Christ is all He claims to be and that the Bible is the Word of God.

This wonderful truth, that those who really seek God can find Him and those who earnestly want to know the truth can know the truth, means if one goes on in unbelief, it is his own fault. Jesus said after His resurrection, "O fools, and slow of heart to believe all that the prophets have spoken" (Luke 24:25). No wonder the psalmist declares, "The fool hath said in his heart, There is no God" (Ps. 14:1). Ah, yes, Nathaniel can know and soon he learns all about Jesus.

Jesus had said, *"Behold an Israelite indeed, in whom is no guile!"* (vs. 47). Nathanael wondered how Jesus could know. Well, Jesus said, "Before that Philip called thee, when thou wast under the fig tree, I saw thee" (vs. 48). Ah, no doubt, under the sheltering leaves of a fig tree Nathanael had been praying, seeking God, and Jesus saw and knew it; now He reveals Himself to Nathanael and Nathanael's doubts are all cured in a moment.

"On such small evidence do you believe Me?" Jesus said. "Ah, then, one day you are going to see Heaven open and the angels of God ascending and descending upon the Son of Man." When is that? At the rapture? No. Probably when Christ returns to reign.

According to Revelation 1:7, "Behold, he cometh with clouds; and every eye shall see him, and they also which pierced him: and all kindreds of the earth shall wail because of him." That is the time discussed in Matthew 24:30,31:

"And then shall appear the sign of the Son of man in heaven: and then shall all the tribes of the earth mourn, and they shall see the Son of man coming in the clouds of heaven with power and great glory. And he shall send his angels with a great sound of a trumpet, and they shall gather together his elect from the four winds, from one end of heaven to the other."

And the wicked high priest who put Jesus on oath, asked, "Tell us whether thou be the Christ, the Son of God. Jesus saith unto him, Thou hast said: NEVERTHELESS I say unto you, Hereafter shall ye see the Son of man sitting on the right hand of power, and coming in the clouds of heaven." That high priest, we suppose, has been in Hell these centuries past. But when Jesus comes, we suppose He will remove the lid of Hell and everybody in Hell will see Him whom they spurned and rejected. For we are plainly told in Philippians 2:9-11:

"Wherefore God also hath highly exalted him, and given him a name which is above every name: That at the name of Jesus every knee should bow, of things in heaven, and things in earth, and things under the earth; And that every tongue should confess that Jesus Christ is Lord, to the glory of God the Father."

The recognition of Jesus as God and honoring Him as Lord and when every knee in Heaven and earth and Hell will bow before Him is coming, when Christ comes back to take up His reign on earth. A like promise is given in Colossians 2:9-11.

Says F. B. Meyer: "This chapter abounds in striking names and titles for our Lord. They are a study in themselves. The Word, the Light, the Life of Men, the Only begotten of the Father, the Christ, the Lamb of God, the Master, Son of God, and King of Israel. But the climax, with which this marvelous enumeration closes, is as wonderful as any: *The Son of Man.* It occurs eighty times in the Gospels, and is always applied by our Lord to Himself."

John 2

AND the third day there was a marriage in Cana of Galilee; and the mother of Jesus was there:

2 And both Jesus was called, and his disciples, to the marriage.

Jesus at a Marriage Feast

Cana was about four miles from Nazareth. Nathanael was of Cana (21:2). The marriage evidently was in the home of some friend or relative either of Jesus or Nathanael.

* * *

This is the first miracle that Jesus ever worked (vs. 11). It is not mentioned in the other Gospels, and neither Matthew nor Luke mentions any miracle of Jesus until the fourth chapters. They do tell about the miraculous conception and birth of the Saviour, but those Gospels were not written so much to stress the deity of Jesus as God's Son as is the book of John. All the Bible agrees on that great doctrine, but this first miracle is here mentioned for the particular purpose to show that Jesus exercised supernatural power, even from the very beginning of His public ministry.

This miracle happened three days after the events mentioned in the previous chapter.

It is interesting that Jesus accepted every invitation honestly given, as far as we can tell. He was a guest at the house of Simon and Andrew and healed Peter's wife's mother. He came willingly to heal the centurion's servant, although the centurion insisted He need not come to the home. He went willingly to the house of a Pharisee, although the Pharisee questioned in his heart whether Jesus were really a "prophet."

When Martha invited Him to her home, He came and greatly loved Mary, Martha and Lazarus. He stopped by the roadside at the cry of blind Bartimaeus. He stopped under the tree where Zacchaeus, the rich publican, had climbed to see Him and announced He would go home with him that day. So we need not be surprised that, when Jesus was invited, He went to the marriage feast.

What kind of ceremony? None is described. They had a feast. In the parable of the ten virgins, we think it was a custom to have the bridegroom come to the bride's house, accompanied by the bridesmaids. The Bible has no requirement about a wedding ceremony. What is an official and legal marriage by law is accepted as marriage. It is well, of course, for Christians to have a religious ceremony and accept reverently the Bible standard of marriage "till death do us part."

We are reminded that Christians ought to be happy, ought to be friendly. We should "rejoice with them that do rejoice, and weep with them that weep" (Rom. 12:15).

VERSES 3-5:

3 And when they wanted wine, the mother of Jesus saith unto him, They have no wine.
4 Jesus saith unto her, Woman, what have I to do with thee? mine hour is not yet come.
5 His mother saith unto the servants, Whatsoever he saith unto you, do it.

Jesus and His Mother

Mary the mother of Jesus knew of a certainty that Jesus was a virgin-born Saviour. She expected miracles, though she had never seen Him work a miracle. According to the announcement of the Angel Gabriel in Luke 1:26-30, she was to have a Son without a human father, called "the Son of the Highest." And when Jesus was born and His birth announced to the shepherds by the angels and the shepherds came to see the Baby Jesus, "Mary kept all these things, and pondered them in her heart" (Luke 2:19). No doubt she remembered the solemn warning of Simeon:

"And Simeon blessed them, and said unto Mary his mother, Behold, this child is set for the fall and rising again of many in Israel; and for a sign which shall be spoken against; (Yea, a sword shall pierce through thy own soul also,) that the thoughts of many hearts may be revealed."—Luke 2:34,35.

And so now she is thinking that Jesus, baptized and filled with the Spirit, will begin His public ministry. But Jesus said, *"Mine hour is not yet come"* (vs. 4).

Jesus knew what was in Mary's heart. Did she expect Him now to set out to rule on David's throne, as the angel had promised? Did she expect the persecution, that was inevitable, to begin now? At any rate, the perfect fulfillment of His ministry was not yet. Jesus now would still have to say, "I have a baptism to be baptized with; and how am I straightened till it be accomplished!" (Luke 12:50). The Lord Jesus must yet say, "Therefore have I set my face like a flint," going on toward the cross and the resurrection (Isa. 50:7). Although it is the time He should begin His miracles and His miraculous ministry, there is a long road ahead before the complete fulfillment of the prophecies and His death and triumphant resurrection and then later His coming back to reign.

Did Jesus address His mother abruptly when He said, *"Woman, what have I to do with thee?"* (vs. 4). I think there was no disrespect here. But it is obvious that Jesus is dealing with His mother as a Christian woman, not setting her apart from other women. Will you remember that all the way through the Gospels Mary is never put above other good women. And after the Gospels, she is mentioned only once, in Acts 1:14, where it said she was one of others who attended that pre-Pentecostal prayer meeting.

So Jesus let it be understood to Mary, but primarily to all of us, that He did not work a miracle at Mary's request because she was His mother but just as He would do it for any woman of faith. In Luke 8:19-21 we are told:

"Then came to him his mother and his brethren, and could not come to him for the press. And it was told him by certain which said, Thy mother and thy brethren stand without, desiring to see thee. And he answered and said unto them, My mother and my brethren are these which hear the word of God, and do it."

There is never a hint in the Bible that Mary was a "perpetual virgin," after the birth of Jesus. Read Matthew 12:46-50 and Mark 3:31-35. Jesus said, "Whosoever shall do the will of my Father which is in heaven, the same is my brother, and sister, and mother." The Lord Jesus loved His mother, but there was no evidence that she was better or more respected than other good women. No one ever prayed to Mary in New Testament times. After Jesus was born, then Mary and Joseph were husband and wife and they had other children, including James, Joses, Simon and Judas and some sisters, perhaps younger (Matt. 13:55,56). This "James the Lord's brother," as Paul calls him in Galatians 1:19, became pastor at Jerusalem, and is called an apostle. James, the brother of John, had been beheaded in Acts 12. This James, brother of Jesus, is the one who seemed to have presided in the Council at Jerusalem (Acts 15) and the one who wrote the book of James. There he calls himself only "a servant of God and of the Lord Jesus Christ."

Judas (Jude) wrote the book of Jude and calls himself "servant of Jesus Christ, and brother of James." Neither claim any merit or standing by being born of Mary.

Psalm 69 is, part of it, prophetic about the Lord Jesus. Verse 9 is quoted as referring to Him: "For the zeal of thine house hath eaten me up." But the preceding verse, also about Jesus, said, "I am become a stranger unto my brethren, and an alien unto my mother's children." So these who are called "brethren" were not cousins, as Catholic authorities claim, but were His mother's children.

And in verse 12 we note that these brothers came with His mother to live with Him in Capernaum. Matthew 4:13 tells that Jesus had moved His home from Nazareth to Capernaum, probably before this.

Let any woman, then, who loves the Lord Jesus and seeks to please Him and loves His Word, know that she has the same right to call on Jesus for help as did Mary, His mother.

$2 \times 4 = 18$ gals
$3 \times 9 = 27$
$6 \times 18 = 108$
$6 \times 27 = 162$

VERSES 6-10:

6 And there were set there six waterpots of stone, after the manner of the purifying of the Jews, containing two or three firkins apiece.

7 Jesus saith unto them, Fill the waterpots with water. And they filled them up to the brim.

8 And he saith unto them, Draw out now, and bear unto the governor of the feast. And they bare *it*.

9 When the ruler of the feast had tasted the water that was made wine, and knew not whence it was: (but the servants which drew the water knew;) the governor of the feast called the bridegroom,

10 And saith unto him, Every man at the beginning doth set forth good wine; and when men have well drunk, then that which is worse: *but* thou hast kept the good wine until now.

The Water Turned to Wine

Jesus turned the water to wine. Here is a miracle of creation. It would be foolish and wicked to try to explain it away. The Lord Jesus who created all things in the beginning could make water into wine as He did here. There were six waterpots of stone, each of them containing "two or three firkins apiece" (one firkin about 9 gallons—Scofield). In the first place, "wine" in the Bible does not necessarily mean intoxicating wine. Proverbs 3:10 says, ". . .and thy presses shall burst out with new wine." Evidently grape juice pressed out is that very moment wine, though it is not fermented. The grape juice was pressed out and put into new wine skins. Eventually, if it was not drunk fresh it would, of course, begin to ferment and have alcoholic content. Canon Farrar in *Smith's Bible Dictionary* says: "The simple wines of anti-

quity were incomparably less deadly than the stupefying and ardent beverages of our western nations. The wines of antiquity were more like sirups; many of them were not intoxicant; many more intoxicant in a small degree; and all of them, as a rule, taken only when largely diluted with water. They contained, even undiluted, but 4 or 5 per cent of alcohol."

Authorities tell us that fruit juice was called wine. Or the fruit might be dried and later it might be mixed with water and made into a drink.

The Bible has strong words against alcoholic liquor. In that sense, "Wine is a mocker, strong drink is raging: and whosoever is deceived thereby is not wise" (Prov. 20:1). And since there was no exact point when one could say the grape juice ceased to be simply grape juice and other fruit juice ceased to be pure fruit juice and had a bit of alcohol in it, the rule about the Nazarites was that they should drink no wine nor even eat grapes (Num. 6:3). And the priests were instructed not to drink wine before going into the sanctuary (Ezek. 44:21; Lev. 10:9).

Leaven is when certain microbes multiply in dough, so leaven has an evil meaning in the ceremonial law. First Corinthians 5:6 warns that "a little leaven leaveneth the whole lump." And verse 7 says, "Purge out therefore the old leaven, that ye may be a new lump, as ye are unleavened. For even Christ our passover is sacrificed for us." But the microbes or decay that takes part in bread are similar to the microbes and decay in grape juice that make it into intoxicating wine. And if leavened bread would not be a suitable picture of the body of Christ, neither would alcoholic fruit juice be a fit picture of the blood of Christ.

The "fruit of the vine" used when Christ gave the Last Supper is not intoxicating wine, and "the cup" which represents the drink at the Lord's Supper in I Corinthians, chapter 11, did not refer to intoxicating wine. You may be sure that Jesus knew well the teaching that "wine is a mocker, strong drink is raging," and He would not go against the teaching of the Scripture of which He Himself was Author and Founder before the world began. The kind of wine which Jesus made is not the kind which is a mocker and, along with strong drink, is raging.

VERSE 11:

11 This beginning of miracles did Jesus in Cana of Galilee, and mani- fested forth his glory; and his disciples believed on him.

Christ's First Miracle

This was the *"beginning of miracles"* for Jesus (vs. 11). Dr. W. B. Riley says:

> The very phrase employed is a promise of marvels to follow. To turn water into wine is wonderful; but greater things shall they see who walk with the Son of God. Tomorrow He will heal the nobleman's son; the next day He will still the tempest; shortly the demoniacs of Gadara shall be dispossessed; Jairus' daughter raised; the paralytic freshly empowered; the leper cleansed; the Centurion's servant healed; Simon's wife's mother recovered from her fever; the widow's son raised from the dead; etc. How many miracles Jesus wrought, no man knows. In addition to the thirty odd, detailed, there are those sweeping sentences, "And he healed all that were sick, and oppressed of the devil."

Jesus is now about thirty years old, and all these years He had never begun His ministry, never preached a sermon, never won a soul, never worked a miracle until now, after He was filled with the Holy Spirit at His baptism. He was baptized, then was led of the Spirit into the wilderness for forty days of fasting and a great time of temptation and then He went to Nazareth and entered a synagogue where He had been brought up and read the Scripture, Isaiah 61:1, "The Spirit of the Lord God is upon me; because the Lord hath anointed me to preach good tidings unto the meek; he hath sent me to bind up the brokenhearted, to proclaim liberty to the captives, and the opening of the prison to them that are bound." Then He said, "This day is this scripture fulfilled in your ears" (Luke 4:21).

Jesus was determined He should be a pattern for other Christians. Other Christians are to carry out the Gospel. Other Christians are to be the "light of the world" when He is gone. Other Christians are to be sent as He is sent. All Christians are to do the same kind of work He does, for He said in John 14:12, "Veri-

ly, verily, I say unto you, He that believeth on me, the works that
I do shall he do also; and greater works than these shall he do;
because I go unto my Father."

So Jesus did not do His miracles in His power as the Son of
God, the second Person of the Trinity, but in the power of the
Holy Spirit which was upon Him, beginning at His baptism. See
again Acts 10:37,38:

*"That word, I say, ye know, which was published throughout
all Judaea, and began from Galilee, after the baptism which
John preached; How God anointed Jesus of Nazareth with the
Holy Ghost and with power: who went about doing good, and
healing all that were oppressed of the devil; for God was with
him."*

Then the miracles of Jesus did not set Him apart from others.
The miracles proved He was a prophet from God, as Nicodemus
recognized in the next chapter, but the miracles did not prove
His deity. Moses worked miracles. There were miracles under the
ministry of many of the judges, and under Joshua. Elijah and
Elisha worked miracles. Later the apostles will work many
miracles. No, miracles did not prove the deity of Christ. They
were simply expressions of His compassion and concern, when
they were needed.

The Pharisees insisted that Jesus work a miracle as a "sign" to
prove His deity. But in Matthew 12:39,40 He said:

*"There shall no sign be given to it, but the sign of the prophet
Jonas: For as Jonas was three days and three nights in the
whale's belly; so shall the Son of man be three days and three
nights in the heart of the earth."*

The resurrection of Jesus is the one miracle that will prove His
deity. Romans 1:4 says, "And declared to be the Son of God with
power, according to the spirit of holiness, by the resurrection
from the dead." And Jesus refers to that in this chapter, verse 19.

People say the day of miracles is passed. The Bible never hints
anything of the kind. Sometimes men look through the Scriptures and they say that God only had miracles in certain times of
great change. However, that is man's interpretation. Did not

Jesus in Mark 11:24 promise miracles? And in many other Scriptures? Miracles were never a plaything of mighty prophets of God. There are not many occasions when a miracle of God would be needed or where men would have faith for a miracle. Every time one is born again, that is a spiritual miracle and it guarantees the future physical miracle of a bodily resurrection for that convert.

VERSE 12:

12 ¶ After this he went down to Că-pĕr-nă-ŭm, he, and his mother, and his brethren, and his disciples: and they continued there not many days.

Jesus and His Family at Capernaum

The Lord Jesus had moved from Galilee where He was brought up, perhaps twelve or fifteen miles away to Capernaum, on the northwest shore of the little Sea of Galilee, as Matthew 4:13 tells us. Dr. Ironside gives us a good thought on Capernaum:

Capernaum is called elsewhere "his own city." It was not His birthplace but the city which He chose as a residence as He began His ministry. He was seldom at home, but if He had a home at all, it was Capernaum. Capernaum, therefore, was one of the most privileged of the Galilean cities. Here He often appeared in the synagogue.

I cannot express the emotion that overwhelmed several of us as we stood in the excavated synagogue in Capernaum and realized we were standing, in all probability, on the very stones where His feet once stood; and as we looked down from that raised platform, we could imagine the healing of the withered arm and the deliverance of the poor woman who had been so crippled that her body was bent together for so many years. We remembered that it was there that He delivered His great discourse—"I am the Bread of Life."

We could look down to the seashore and we knew that there Matthew once had his office as collector of customs, and we noticed the road going by and thought of the Lord Jesus as He raised the daughter of Jairus, after healing the woman who pressed her way through the crowd, crying in faith, "If I may but touch the hem of his garment I shall be healed."

Capernaum, blessed above all places on earth, for Jesus chose it as His home, and there He taught and did His works of power, but, alas, it was of this very city that later on He said, "Thou, Capernaum, which art exalted unto heaven, shalt be brought down to hell," the city so privileged! Do you know, that very city was blotted out of existence?

Notice His mother goes with Jesus to Capernaum, but Joseph is not mentioned. We suppose he had been dead a number of years. The last mention of Joseph was when Jesus was twelve years old, in Luke, chapter 2.

Notice there went with Jesus and His mother *"his brethren."* They were literal brothers of Jesus, and they are named in Matthew 13:55. None of these brothers were converted, we understand, until the death of Jesus and His resurrection. John 7:5 says, "For neither did his brethren believe on him." James became the pastor, we suppose, at Jerusalem. Galatians 1:19 says Paul saw "James the Lord's brother" there.

James, Joses, Simon and Judas are named in Matthew 13:55. Simon and Joses are not mentioned elsewhere, we think. And the sisters are not named. All these were younger than Jesus; probably the sisters much younger.

Our Catholic friends would like to insist on what is the equivalent to deifying Mary. They would teach that she was conceived immaculately without a taint of sin. They would say that she was a perpetual virgin even after the birth of Christ. However, neither is taught in Scripture. The Catholics have sometimes said that these "brethren" were cousins. No, they came with their mother to live with Jesus at Capernaum. And Psalm 69:8 refers to them prophetically, saying, "I am become a stranger unto my brethren, and an alien unto my mother's children." And in the next verse, Psalm 69:9, he is quoted here in John 2:17 as referring to Jesus, so we know that the preceding verse does, too. These "brethren" were His mother's children.

Mary was not born sinless. In her Spirit-filled praises over the announcement that she would bear the Saviour, she said, "And my spirit hath rejoiced in God my Saviour" (Luke 1:47). The only ones who have a Saviour are sinners. Mary was a sinner, and

Christ was her Saviour. She is never referred to in the New Testament after Acts 1:14 where she attended prayer meeting, along with others. She lived with Jesus at Capernaum for a time.

VERSES 13-17:

13 ¶ And the Jews' passover was at hand, and Jesus went up to Jerusalem,

14 And found in the temple those that sold oxen and sheep and doves, and the changers of money sitting:

15 And when he had made a scourge of small cords, he drove them all out of the temple, and the sheep, and the oxen; and poured out the changers' money, and overthrew the tables;

16 And said unto them that sold doves, Take these things hence; make not my Father's house an house of merchandise.

17 And his disciples remembered that it was written, The zeal of thine house hath eaten me up.

The First Cleansing of the Temple

This is the first of three passovers mentioned in John. Here, then again in 6:4, then in 11:55.

Do not confuse this cleansing of the Temple, the first passover where Jesus attended in Jerusalem, with that great cleansing of the Temple in the last week of His life, told in Matthew 21:12,13; Mark 11:15-17; Luke 19:45,46. That cleansing of the Temple was just before His triumphal entry into Jerusalem and, we think, the week of His crucifixion. In that later cleansing of the Temple, He would "cast out all them that sold and bought in the temple, and overthrew the tables of the money-changers, and the seats of them that sold doves." But here in this earlier cleansing of the Temple, in John, chapter 2, we learn that He made a whip of cords or ropes and drove all out of the Temple and the sheep and the oxen "and poured out the changers' money, and overthrew the tables." Some folks do not like sensational preachers, and think preachers ought not fight sin. They would not like what Jesus did with that whip in verse 15!

Malachi 3:1 says, "Behold, I will send my messenger, and he shall prepare the way before me: and the Lord, whom ye seek, shall suddenly come to his temple. . . ." John the Baptist would come to announce Jesus, and Jesus would suddenly come to His

Temple. But the next verse says, "But who may abide the day of his coming? and who shall stand when he appeareth? for he is like a refiner's fire, and like fullers' soap."

Dr. H. A. Ironside says:

> What had, perhaps, begun innocently enough, as an accommodation to supply lambs for visiting passover guests, and the exchanging of money for those from distant lands, had degenerated into a feverish effort to make merchandise of what was needed in order to observe the sacrificial service connected with the passover. Covetousness and over-reaching prevailed to such an extent that God was dishonored and the Temple scandalized. There was the bleating of sheep and the cooing of doves disturbing the worship of the Lord, and these who offered them for sale thought only of enriching themselves. They were commercializing the things of God, and that is always repugnant in His sight. So Jesus asserted Himself as the Lord of the Temple.

Why was Jesus so indignant? The ruling priesthood had made a rule that one had to have special Temple money to offer in the Temple, so they made a profit on the exchange of money. Then people would come from far away and want to buy a sacrifice to offer there and they must pay higher prices, and these who sold the cattle and sheep and doves were profiteering. So the spirit of reverence for holy things and the spiritual lessons picturing Christ and spiritual truths were wholly obscured by the merchandising of these people. They made the house of God a house of merchandise. In the later cleansing of the Temple, He will say, "It is written, My house shall be called the house of prayer; but ye have made it a den of thieves."

This is the indignation such as God has always for those who hold to the outward form without any heart for the central meaning. See with what indignation God assails unspiritual, unbelieving Jews in Isaiah 1:10-15:

"Hear the word of the Lord, ye rulers of Sodom; give ear unto the law of our God, ye people of Gomorrah. To what purpose is the multitude of your sacrifices unto me? saith the Lord: I am full of the burnt-offerings of rams, and the fat of fed beasts; and I delight not in the blood of bullocks, or of lambs, or of he goats. When ye come to appear before me, who hath required this at your hand, to tread my courts? Bring no more vain oblations; incense is an abomination unto me; the new moons and sabbaths, the calling of assemblies, I cannot away with; it is iniquity, even the solemn meeting. Your new moons and your appointed feasts my soul hateth: they are a trouble unto me; I am weary to bear them. And when ye spread forth your hands, I will hide mine eyes from you: yea, when ye make many prayers, I will not hear: your hands are full of blood."

To the Jews in Jesus' time He said, "Woe unto you, scribes and Pharisees, hypocrites! for ye pay tithe of mint and anise and cummin, and have omitted the weightier matters of the law, judgment, mercy, and faith: these ought ye to have done, and not to leave the other undone" (Matt. 23:23). Jesus later plainly told the Jews that all the law of God is summed up in two great commandments, that man should love God with all his heart, mind, soul and strength and his neighbor as himself (Matt. 22:35-40; Mark 12:28-34; Luke 10:25-28). So really one is not a Jew who is merely a Jew outwardly but one who is a Jew inwardly (Rom. 2:28).

Galatians 5:6 tells us, "For in Jesus Christ neither circumcision availeth any thing, nor uncircumcision; but faith which worketh by love." The real circumcision God wants is circumcision of the heart. Without that, the outward form of circumcision is meaningless and pagan. And the sweet promise of Galatians

3:29 is, "And if ye be Christ's, then are ye Abraham's seed, and heirs according to the promise."

How would it please God for people to kill the lamb if it did not picture the Lamb of God? How would it please God for a Jew to rigorously keep the Jewish Sabbath if he did not recognize that it pictured a Heaven in the future?

And the sacrifices at Jerusalem were no better than the worship at Mount Gerizim, except as each was worship from loving, believing hearts. So Jesus told the Samaritan woman:

"Woman, believe me, the hour cometh, when ye shall neither in this mountain, nor yet at Jerusalem, worship the Father. Ye worship ye know not what: we know what we worship: for salvation is of the Jews. But the hour cometh, and now is, when the true worshippers shall worship the Father in spirit and in truth: for the Father seeketh such to worship him."—4:21-23.

And so the angry, indignant Saviour cleaned out the Temple with its empty mockery of ceremonies that to many Jewish leaders did not have any spiritual meaning, and where worldly men were making merchandise of the forms and ceremonies.

The words in verse 17, "The zeal of thine house hath eaten me up," are from Psalm 69:9 which shows that Psalm is partly a prophecy about the Saviour.

VERSES 18-22:

18 ¶ Then answered the Jews and said unto him, What sign shewest thou unto us, seeing that thou doest these things?

19 Jesus answered and said unto them, Destroy this temple, and in three days I will raise it up.

20 Then said the Jews, Forty and six years was this temple in building, and wilt thou rear it up in three days?

21 But he spake of the temple of his body.

22 When therefore he was risen from the dead, his disciples remembered that he had said this unto them; and they believed the scripture, and the word which Jesus had said.

Jesus Promises a Sign of His Deity

The Jews naturally were shocked at the astonishing action of

Jesus and asked Him what authority He had and what sign He had to prove it.

Jesus worked no miracles to prove His deity to unbelievers. The one sign on which the deity of Christ and the plan of salvation and the authority of the Bible all depend is the bodily resurrection of Christ from the dead. They would destroy that temple of His body, that is, they would nail Him to a cross and watch Him die. And then Jesus would, in three days, rise from the dead. Then Jesus would "shew himself alive after his passion by many infallible proofs," as Acts 1:3 says. That literal, bodily resurrection of Jesus from the dead is of such importance that the evidence is given in detail in I Corinthians 15:3-8:

"For I delivered unto you first of all that which I also received, how that Christ died for our sins according to the scriptures; And that he was buried, and that he rose again the third day according to the scriptures: And that he was seen of Cephas, then of the twelve: After that, he was seen of above five hundred brethren at once; of whom the greater part remain unto this present, but some are fallen asleep. After that, he was seen of James; then of all the apostles. And last of all he was seen of me also, as of one born out of due time."

Note how many people literally saw Jesus, talked with Him, put their hands upon Him, saw Him eat, heard Him talk. There was Peter, then all the twelve, then more than five hundred Christians saw Him at one time, and long years later over half of them were still alive. Then He was seen of James, then again of all the apostles, and last of all Paul himself, "as. . .one born out of due time," saw Jesus personally.

The disciples themselves found it hard to believe that Christ was risen from the dead. And so to doubting Thomas Jesus said, "Reach hither thy finger, and behold my hands; and reach hither thy hand, and thrust it into my side: and be not faithless, but believing" (John 20:27). Oh, and Thomas was convinced!

How He convinced the doubts of the disciples themselves is told again in Luke 24:38-43:

"And he said unto them, Why are ye troubled? and why do

*thoughts arise in your hearts? Behold my hands and my feet,
that it is I myself: handle me, and see; for a spirit hath not flesh
and bones, as ye see me have. And when he had thus spoken, he
shewed them his hands and his feet. And while they yet believed
not for joy, and wondered, he said unto them, Have ye here any
meat? And they gave him a piece of a broiled fish, and of an
honeycomb. And he took it, and did eat before them."*

In the nature of the case, any unbelief about the deity of Christ
and the inspiration of the Bible will lead men to question the actual, literal, bodily resurrection of Christ. Silly, unscholarly and
wicked men have said that there are "conflicting accounts of the
crucifixion." No, they are not conflicting. And the resurrection of
Christ is one of the most thoroughly manifested and proven facts
of all the events of history.

The body of Jesus was gone. He appeared bodily to people who
saw Him and knew Him and put their hands upon Him. They
saw Him eat and drink. They heard Him speak. And that went
on for forty days—from the resurrection of Christ until His
ascension. So the sign, the miracle, the evidence of the deity of
Christ is His resurrection, as Romans 1:4 says, "And declared to
be the Son of God with power, according to the spirit of holiness,
by the resurrection from the dead." And that resurrection is the
guarantee of a resurrection for those of us who know Him and
love Him and are born of God.

About His resurrection body, Jesus said, ". . .I will raise it
up" (vs. 19). But Romans 8:11 says, "But if the Spirit of him that
raised up Jesus from the dead dwell in you, he that raised up
Christ from the dead shall also quicken your mortal bodies by his
Spirit that dwelleth in you." Christ will raise Himself up from
the dead, but the Holy Spirit will have part in raising Him also.
But Romans 6:4 says that "Christ was raised up from the dead
by the glory of the Father." So the Son, the Holy Spirit, the
Father—all were united in the resurrection of Jesus. His resurrection did prove His deity.

VERSES 23-25:

23 ¶ Now when he was in Jerusalem at the passover, in the feast *day*, many believed in his name, when they saw the miracles which he did.

24 But Jesus did not commit him-self unto them, because he knew all *men*,

25 And needed not that any should testify of man: for he knew what was in man.

Miracles and Believers in Jerusalem

Verse 23 shows that Jesus had now performed other miracles and that many people were converted. These miracles that Jesus performed in Jerusalem at this time are not told us. But they were known throughout all that country. Those are the miracles to which Nicodemus referred in John 3:2.

Many now believed on Christ and trusted Him when they saw the miracles. The miracles did attest that God was with Him, and so they could believe His word when He claimed to be the Son of God.

"But Jesus did not commit himself unto them" (vs. 24). That is, He knew the frailty of human character. Some of these would forsake Him when enemies rose up against Him. And this made them no different from mankind the world over. He knew, no doubt, that the time would come when many of these would follow Him no more when the pressure was too great, when it would involve the scorn and hatred of the Pharisees. He knew that even in the Garden of Gethsemane the disciples would go to sleep, and when He was arrested, the disciples would forsake Him and flee. Then at the house of Caiaphas, Peter would deny Him.

He knew that when the gospel seed is sown, some of it, sown among thorns, will spring up, but among thorns the converted people will not bear much fruit for God, since "the cares of this world, and the deceitfulness of riches, and the lusts of other things entering in, choke the word, and it becometh unfruitful" (Mark 4:19). No doubt Jesus knew that after all these people who are converted and baptized under John the Baptist and those converted and baptized under Jesus' preaching and that of His disciples, there would only be 120 faithful ones gathered together in the pre-Pentecostal prayer meeting. He knew how

David had fallen into adultery and murder, how Peter would
curse and deny Him. He knew how Demas would forsake Paul (II
Tim. 3:10).

Does that mean that one cannot wholly rely upon born-again
Christians? That is exactly right. When persecution arises, many
will not stand fast. When there is pressure from friends or the cry
of popularity, and when it costs a great deal to stand up for
Jesus, as it eventually will, many of God's own people do not stay
true. But we must remember that nobody is saved by being true.
We are saved only by personally trusting Christ. Poor and weak
as we are, we are beloved of Christ and are kept by the Father.

John 3

THERE was a man of the ✝Phari-
sees, named Nicodemus, a ruler
╷of the Jews:

Nicodemus, a Ruler of the Jews

Nicodemus was a ruler of the Jews, that is, we understand a member of the body of seventy-one men who made up the Sanhedrin, religious rulers over Israel and allowed by the Romans also to judge in many civil matters. In John, chapter 7, these rulers derided the common people and said, "Have any of the rulers or of the Pharisees believed on him?" (vs. 48). And the common people said, "Do the rulers know indeed that this is the very Christ?" (7:26).

These rulers will, most of them, ardently hate the Lord Jesus and try to kill Him. They will send officers to arrest Him (7:32). They will try to trap Him in His words. They will hire Judas to betray Him. Their plans to put Jesus to death are told in John 11:47-53. The chief priests among them even "consulted that they might put Lazarus also to death; Because that by reason of him many of the Jews went away, and believed on Jesus" (John 12:10,11). These rulers will condemn Jesus to death and will insist before Pilate that He be crucified.

Then when Jesus hung on a cross, Luke 23:35 says, "And the people stood beholding. And the rulers also with them derided him, saying, He saved others; let him save himself, if he be Christ, the chosen of God." The chief priests, among these rulers, had Pilate to seal the tomb of Jesus lest the disciples should steal His body away (Matt. 27:62-66). And the same chief priests, when it was learned that Jesus was risen from the dead, gave money to the soldiers and bribed them to lie about it. How they hated Jesus!

But there was a stirring among these rulers, and some of them were greatly convicted.

And a "rich young ruler" came to Jesus deeply troubled and saying, "Good Master, what good thing shall I do, that I may have eternal life?" (Matt. 19:16). He had great riches so he went away loving his riches, unsaved.

Joseph of Arimathaea was a "counsellor" (Mark 15:43), which means he was a member of the Sanhedrin and so one of the rulers. And he was "a disciple of Jesus, but secretly for fear of the Jews." John 12:42 says, "Among the chief rulers also many believed on him" [Jesus]. But of the seventy-one in the Sanhedrin and the chief priests, many, led by the high priest, were bitter enemies of Jesus.

But Nicodemus did not hate Jesus, and we have some reason to believe that he later did trust Christ and claim Him as Saviour. In a meeting of the Sanhedrin one time he spoke up to claim Jesus had a right to defend Himself (7:50,51). And when Jesus died on the cross, he went with Joseph of Arimathaea to bury the body of Jesus and Nicodemus bought the hundred pounds of spices and the fine linen to wrap the poor body in as they put it in Joseph's new tomb (19:38-42).

But Nicodemus came to Jesus *"by night."* One might think that he did that in order to have privacy for discussion. Possibly so. Or it may be that he did not want to be publicly known as a disciple of Jesus. At any rate, Nicodemus is mentioned three times in the Gospel and in each case we are reminded that he is the man who came to Jesus by night! But if he were a secret

disciple, now he did not continue so, for he helped to bury the body of Jesus, openly taking the body down from the cross.

Nicodemus was *"a Pharisee."* There were two principal parties or "denominations" we might say, among the Jews. The Pharisees believed in miracles, in spirits, in the resurrection. They were not Christian and they depended largely on traditions they had added to the Scriptures. But at least they did claim to believe the Bible. They seem to have been more numerous than the Sadducees.

On the other hand, the Sadducees did not believe in spirits or angels, nor in the resurrection (Acts 23:8). They were openly liberals or modernists in their day. Jesus warned Christians to "beware of the leaven of the Pharisees and of the Sadducees" (Matt. 16:6-12).

It is sadly true that one can be orthodox in doctrine and unconverted and wicked in his heart. "Devils also believe, and tremble" (Jas. 2:19).

The Pharisee is the best possible picture of a moral and religious man—without Christ. The Pharisees had such a strict moral code of living, were such devout believers and students of the Bible, were frequent in prayer, and held such a place of religious leadership that surely a Pharisee could come as close to Heaven as any man could come without Christ. Read Philippians 3:5 and Luke 18:11,12 to see what kind of men were the Pharisees. Paul still said, "I am a Pharisee," after his conversion (Acts 23:6). Nicodemus was evidently a man as moral as Paul or as the Pharisee who went in the Temple to pray. Yet Jesus plainly told him that he had utterly no hope for salvation unless he should be born again. Notice the repetition in verses 3, 5 and 7. If Nicodemus must be born again, then so must every other man.

VERSES 2-7:

2 The same came to Jesus by night, and said unto him, Rabbi, we know that thou art a teacher come from God: for no man can do these mir-

acles that thou doest, except God be with him.

3 Jesus answered and said unto him, Verily, verily, I say unto thee, Except a man be born again, he cannot see the kingdom of God.

4 Nicodemus saith unto him, How can a man be born when he is old? can he enter the second time into his mother's womb, and be born?

5 Jesus answered, Verily, verily, I say unto thee, Except a man be born of water and *of* the Spirit, he cannot enter into the kingdom of God.

6 That which is born of the flesh is flesh; and that which is born of the Spirit is spirit.

7 Marvel not that I said unto thee, Ye must be born again.

"Ye Must Be Born Again"

Nicodemus addressed Jesus, *"Rabbi,"* a term of respect. *"Thou art a teacher come from God"* (vs. 2). He was a recognized teacher, leader, a man of great authority and learning, it was supposed, in the Scriptures. But it is noticeable that Jesus was not pleased by the compliments of Nicodemus. It was no honor to Jesus Christ, Son of God, Maker of Heaven and earth, to be called "Rabbi" or "Professor" by an ordinary lost sinner. If Jesus were only "a teacher come from God," then He was no more than Elijah or Moses or Paul, for they too did miracles. Jesus was abrupt in His answer, as He needed to be, for men must take Him as a Saviour, the Son of God, if they are to be saved.

This passage must settle the question that there is no way to live good enough to be saved; that one cannot be saved by being prayerful, religious, a church member, etc. "The heart is deceitful above all things, and desperately wicked: who can know it?" (Jer. 17:9). People are born wrong the first time, with a nature full of sin. The human heart has inherited a tendency toward sin, as David said, "Behold I was shapen in iniquity; and in sin did my mother conceive me" (Ps. 51:5). Christ died for all of our inherited sinful nature, but after people become accountable, we then become deliberate sinners, and must have a new birth from God.

So Nicodemus came to inquire and to meet Him. Whether Nicodemus before knew that He was God's Son, we are not sure. He simply knew that Jesus was "a teacher come from God." He was convinced by the miracles mentioned in John 2:23. Miracles authenticate a prophet of God.

But Jesus made clear that He would not simply teach doctrine. He came to demand repentance and a new heart. *"Except a man be born again, he cannot see the kingdom of God"* (vs. 3). That word "again" is Greek *anothen,* and it should be "born from *above."* It is so translated "from above" in John 3:31; 19:11; James 1:17; 3:15,17. It is the same word used in Luke 1:3 where the King James Version says, "It seemed good to me also, having had perfect understanding of all things *from the very first,* to write unto thee in order, most excellent Theophilus." But "from the very first" is not a good translation. It should be literally "from above" for that is the translation of this word *anothen* again.

Jesus is insisting on not just a new dedication, a new course of action, but one should be born miraculously "from above," born of God. One is thus to become literally "a son of God" when he receives Christ, trusting Him, and so he is "born . . . of God." That miraculous birth means that one is made "partaker of the divine nature" (II Pet. 1:4).

Second Corinthians 5:17 says, "Therefore if any man be in Christ, he is a new creature: old things are passed away; behold, all things are become new." Literally that verse says so that if anyone is in Christ, *a new creation* the literal Greek says, "the old things are passed away, lo, all things have become new." So, one who comes to trust actually becomes miraculously a new creation.

Do not misunderstand that verse. The part that is changed is not the physical but the spiritual. One still has the old nature, but the part that is created is new, and so one needs daily to "put on the new man" (Eph. 4:24). Still "the flesh lusteth against the Spirit, and the Spirit against the flesh" (Gal. 5:17). And so Paul found that "with the mind I myself serve the law of God; but with the flesh the law of sin" (Rom. 7:25).

So, being born again means that one who was before a child of the Devil has now become actually a child of God.

It is in this sense we understand that the term "sons of God" is used in Genesis 6:2. But in Job 2:1, "The sons of God" refers evidently to the angels who belong to God by creation but who

had not sinned and who did not need to be born again, though
Satan came that day to appear before God also.

And in Acts 17:29 Paul said, "Forasmuch then as we are the
offspring of God . . . ," meaning not spiritual birth but made by
the hand of God and thus accountable to Him.

The Lord here is speaking about a miracle that God works
when one is born again, and it does not necessarily involve any
particular emotional experience. It is by choice that a man turns
from sin to trust Christ, but whether one is in tears or not,
whether one waits long upon God—that is not involved in being
born again. So it is not wise to speak of "experiencing the new
birth," for that experience means a certain feeling, emotion, etc.,
that *may* or may not accompany salvation and may be the result
but not necessarily a part of salvation.

The song is wrong which says,

> **Then at last by faith I touched Him,**
> **And, like sparks from smitten steel,**
> **Just so quick salvation reached me,**
> **Oh, bless God, I know it's real!**

That puts the emphasis on man and man's feeling, as if one
struggled long and hard to reach God. But the simple truth is
that anyone may "take the water of life freely," may "call upon
the name of the Lord" and be saved.

"Born of Water and of the Spirit"

Verse 3 has troubled many souls. It says nothing about
baptism and does not mean baptism.

Some have thought that *"born of water"* here refers to the first
physical birth. No, the Lord would not tell Nicodemus, already
born, that he must be born in a new fleshly birth.

The most frequent misinterpretation is to make the water here
mean baptism, but it could not be. Because we are told
repeatedly again and again that when one believes on Christ or
trusts in Him that he "hath everlasting life," that he is "not
condemned."

One who trusts Christ already has salvation. He is not
condemned. He is passed from death to life.

And we are told that this is the same plan of salvation all the prophets preached (Acts 10:43)—yes, the Old Testament prophets preached the same plan of salvation but it did not have baptism in it.

And all the sweet Scriptures that invite to salvation make it clear it does not involve human righteousness or works or ceremonies. Isaiah 55:6,7 says, "Seek ye the Lord while he may be found, call ye upon him while he is near: Let the wicked forsake his way, and the unrighteous man his thoughts: and let him return unto the Lord, and he will have mercy upon him; and to our God, for he will abundantly pardon".

The wicked who forsakes his way and returns to the Lord has abundant pardon.

One who calls upon the Lord is saved. One who will may simply "take the water of life freely" (Rev. 22:17). That leaves no room for baptism as part of the plan of salvation.

We do well to remember that Nicodemus was "a ruler of the Jews," a prominent man in the religious ceremonies and traditions and teaching of the ceremonial law. So he was accustomed to passover lambs picturing Christ and the high priest picturing the priesthood of Christ and the golden candlestick picturing Christ as the Light of the world, burning the oil of the Holy Spirit and the table of shewbread picturing Christ as the Manna from Heaven. So he would know certainly, as we ought to know, that this was figurative language picturing something else besides baptism. What does it picture?

We think Titus 3:5 explains John 3:5: "Not by works of righteousness which we have done, but according to his mercy he saved us, by the washing of regeneration, and renewing of the Holy Ghost." That washing is a heart washing. And Ephesians 5:26 says, ". . . with the washing of water by the word." Ah, so the blessed Word of God has a part in bringing men to repentance and so to being saved. "Born of water" means born of the Gospel, the Word of God. The Gospel is "the power of God unto salvation to every one that believeth." Psalm 19:7 says, "The law of the Lord is perfect, converting the soul." And I Peter 1:23 says, "Being born again, not of corruptible seed, but of incorruptible, by the word of God, which liveth and abideth for ever."

So there are two great factors in getting man saved. One is the Word of God, the Gospel. Paul spoke of "the gospel . . . By which also ye are saved" (I Cor. 15:1,2). No one is ever saved until he hears the Gospel. Then as one hears the Word of God, the Holy Spirit brings conviction and works a miracle of regeneration. So "born of water and of the Spirit" means that one is led by the Gospel to repent and trust Christ; then the Spirit of God works the miracle of regeneration.

VERSE 8:

8 The wind bloweth where it listeth, and thou hearest the sound thereof, but canst not tell whence it cometh, and whither it goeth: so is every one that is born of the Spirit.

Regeneration Is Like the Unseen Wind

Wind and spirit are the same Greek word *pneuma*. So wind can be a symbol of the Holy Spirit. On the day of Pentecost, "suddenly there came a sound from heaven as of a rushing mighty wind, and it filled all the house where they were sitting" (Acts 2:2). That symbolized the pouring out of the Holy Spirit upon the disciples, the "enduement of power from on high."

Wind is unseen but real. So the new birth is miraculous and a literal miracle, but it cannot be explained logically. There is no visible manifestation of the new birth. One does not automatically weep or shout or tremble or fall when saved. So the new birth is, like the wind, unseen though powerful, literal, real.

VERSES 9-12:

9 Nicodemus answered and said unto him, How can these things be?

10 Jesus answered and said unto him, Art thou a master of Israel, and

knowest not these things?
11 Verily, verily, I say unto thee, We speak that we do know, and testify that we have seen; and ye receive not our witness.

12 If I have told you earthly things, and ye believe not, how shall ye believe, if I tell you *of* heavenly things?

A Master or Teacher of the Old Testament in Israel Should Have Known This

Many professed religious people slip over the Bible teaching of the new birth, and that is strange considering how carefully and how often it is taught in the Bible. People may think of the new birth as simply a figure of speech for baptism or for dedication and blindly do not take it to heart that the wicked heart must be changed, born of God, in order for one to be saved.

Did not Nicodemus know that a slain lamb on the altar pictured the Messiah and that we must have an atonement for sin? Abraham knew that and so did Abel (Gen. 15:6; Heb. 11:4). Why did not Nicodemus know that, when he read that God gave Saul "another heart" (I Sam. 10:9)? Would he not see that that was necessary? When in Deuteronomy 30:3 God said that when He should return and regather Israel, then "the Lord thy God will circumcise thine heart, and the heart of thy seed, to love the Lord thy God with all thine heart, and with all thy soul, that thou mayest live" (vs. 6), surely a spiritual mind should know it meant a radical conversion, a new heart.

Of the regathered Israel of literal Jews to be in Palestine, God had Ezekiel to say:

"A new heart also will I give you, and a new spirit will I put within you: and I will take away the stony heart out of your flesh, and I will give you an heart of flesh. And I will put my spirit within you, and cause you to walk in my statutes, and ye shall keep my judgments, and do them."—Ezek. 36:26,27.

Psalm 19:7 says, "The law of the Lord is perfect, converting the soul." Why be surprised that Jesus demands a new heart? Any ruler of Israel ought to know that.

In Psalm 119, eight times the psalmist pleads, ". . . quicken thou me according to thy word," in verses 25, 37, 40, 88, 107, 149, 154, 156. And then once he praises, "I will never forget thy precepts: for with them thou hast quickened me" (vs. 93). To be made spiritually alive or quickened required one to be born again. Nicodemus should have known it.

And how many times do the psalmist and the prophets speak to God of "thy salvation" and "the joy of thy salvation"! To Abraham God revealed that his descendants, some literal Israelites, should be "as the dust of the earth: so that if a man can number the dust of the earth, then shall thy seed also be numbered" (Gen. 13:16), to inherit Canaan. But He also brought Abraham out to see the stars and said, "Look now toward heaven, and tell the stars, if thou be able to number them: and he said unto him, So shall thy seed be" (Gen. 15:5). Surely God spoke of spiritual seed, born of the Spirit, heavenly seed. And Abraham so understood it as a promise of salvation through the coming Greater Seed, Christ, and the next verse then tells us, "And he believed in the Lord; and he counted it to him for righteousness."

How could one understand all the Scriptures about bloody sacrifices and atonement and God's righteousness and mercy without seeing that the wicked heart must be changed, must be forgiven? Nicodemus was wrong not to have found all that in the Old Testament.

Galatians 3:24 says, "Wherefore the law was our schoolmaster to bring us unto Christ." So all the Old Testament points to salvation through Christ. The Apostle Peter understood that and said by divine revelation, "To him give all the prophets witness, that through his name whosoever believeth in him shall receive remission of sins" (Acts 10:43). So every prophet was teaching the new birth by faith in Christ. And the Scripture is in the Old Testament that first said, "The just shall live [or have everlasting life] by his faith" (Hab. 2:4). So millions believed like Abraham and David and found Christ and salvation through the Old Testament Scriptures and were born again. Nicodemus was not excusable in claiming a position as a religious leader and ruler and not knowing one must be born again to enter the kingdom.

A French war bride in my meeting in Spearman, Texas, years

ago, night after night held her hand, claiming to be a "Christian." But when I preached on "ye must be born again," she was overwhelmed with conviction and ran home from the service. Coming to me to be saved the next day she said, "There are so many, many churches in Paris. Why did they not tell me I must be born again?"

Oh, the sinful tragedy for any pastor, preacher or teacher to fail to see and teach this eternal truth, that one must be born from above, miraculously made a child of God, to know God in Heaven.

It is inexcusable blindness and neglect.

We do not wonder that Jesus said in Matthew 7:21-23:

"Not every one that saith unto me, Lord, Lord, shall enter into the kingdom of heaven; but he that doeth the will of my Father which is in heaven. Many will say to me in that day, Lord, Lord, have we not prophesied in thy name? and in thy name have cast out devils? and in thy name done many wonderful works? And then will I profess unto them, I never knew you: depart from me, ye that work iniquity."

No religious conviction or practice or character is satisfactory to God without the new birth.

No one is adequate to teach any spiritual truth unless he knows "heavenly things," that is, the supernatural, miraculous nature of the new birth.

VERSE 13:

13 And no man hath ascended up to heaven, but he that came down | from heaven, *even* the Son of man which is in heaven.

"The Son of Man Which Is in Heaven"

Jesus on earth is called *"the Son of man which is in heaven."* John 1:18 says He was "the only begotten Son, which is in the bosom of the Father." Remember Jesus could say, "I and my Father are one" (10:30). Remember that Christ is not only the

Creator, for "all things were created by him, and for him" (Col. 1:16), but also, ". . . by him all things consist" (Col. 1:17).

Can you see how Christ Jesus could control the planets and keep all hearts beating, sustain all things in this creation of His, while He was on earth in a human body? Well, Colossians 1:19 says, "For it pleased the Father that in him should all fulness dwell." Jesus, even in the flesh, had all the fullness of God. He laid aside the outward appearance of deity but not the substance of deity.

So Jesus, on earth, was "that . . . true Light, which lighteth every man that cometh into the world" (1:9).

It pleased the Lord Jesus to take on the form of man, to be a Man, to limit His actions as a man, but He still had all the fullness of God; He knew what God knew. He saw what God saw. He was present wherever God the Father was present, so says this verse.

Note again the whole verse: *"And no man hath ascended up to heaven, but he that came down from heaven, even the Son of man which is in heaven."* There can be no doubt that Enoch and Elijah went immediately to be with the Lord, but not after death for they did not die. Both went alive into Heaven, that is, were translated, physical body and all. "And Enoch walked with God: and he was not; for God took him" (Gen. 5:24). And Hebrews 11:5 says, "By faith Enoch was translated that he should not see death; and was not found, because God had translated him: for before his translation he had this testimony, that he pleased God." And II Kings 2:11 and 12, "And Elijah went up by a whirlwind into heaven. And Elisha saw it . . . ." Elijah and Enoch both went to Heaven.

Then what does Jesus mean in verse 13? Read verses 12 and 13 together, and it will make it easier to understand.

I believe the point is that Jesus has come down from Heaven, and has authority to tell men how to get to Heaven. He means that if Nicodemus will not believe Him, the Son of God, who came down from Heaven, then there is no one he can believe on this question. Literally no man on earth was there to tell Nicodemus how to be saved who had ascended up to Heaven.

Enoch and Elijah stayed in Heaven and could not help Nicodemus. The only person on earth at that time who had been to Heaven and knew all about it was Jesus. I believe that *"no man"* in verse 13 means that there was no man then on earth, no man that Nicodemus knew, no man who could tell sinners how to get to Heaven except Jesus, that is, speaking from personal knowledge and experience, having been in Heaven.

In John 5:19 Jesus said, "The Son can do nothing of himself, but what he seeth the Father do: for what things soever he doeth, these also doeth the Son likewise." Then we are amazed to see there is no isolation of any Person in the Godhead. What one can do, all can do; what one approves, all approve.

On the earth, then, God's Son, the Lord Jesus, shared God's omnipotence, God's omniscience, except as He chose to empty Himself and limit Self to be a model Man. So He chose it that He "increased in wisdom and stature, and in favour with God and man" (Luke 2:52), allowing Himself to be limited and to grow out of His self-imposed limitations. So "the Son of man" was "in heaven" while on earth. He was "in the bosom of the Father" while in a peasant home in Nazareth, or walking the dusty roads of Judaea, or preaching in the Temple at Jerusalem (1:18 and 3:13).

VERSES 14-18:

14 ¶ And as Moses lifted up the serpent in the wilderness, even so must the Son of man be lifted up:

15 That whosoever believeth in him should not perish, but have eternal life.

16 ¶ For God so loved the world, that he gave his only begotten Son, that whosoever believeth in him should not perish, but have ever-lasting life.

17 For God sent not his Son into the world to condemn the world; but that the world through him might be saved.

18 ¶ He that believeth on him is not condemned: but he that believeth not is condemned already, because he hath not believed in the name of the only begotten Son of God.

Everlasting Life by Faith

Here are the grandest words ever written or spoken! It is as easy to be saved as it was for an Israelite to be healed of snake bites by simply looking to the brass serpent on a pole.

A young evangelist said, "I want to win souls, so I always preach from the New Testament." Oh, but here the Lord Jesus preaches to the ruler of Israel, Nicodemus, from the Old Testament! And it is the same Gospel, whether from Numbers 21:5-9, where the sinning, snake-bitten Israelites had simply to look to a brazen snake on a pole and be healed, or here in John 3:16 where one is simply to believe on Christ and be saved.

We remember that Philip preached the Gospel to the Ethiopian eunuch from Isaiah 53 which he was reading. And that eunuch was saved. Make no mistake, the same Jesus, the same plan of salvation, was preached by every Old Testament prophet just as it was preached all through the New Testament. In Acts 10:43 Peter said, "To him give all the prophets witness, that through his name whosoever believeth in him shall receive remission of sins."

Seeking a friendly approach to a strange man on a plane I asked, "Do you know the one sentence printed more often, read by more people, known by heart and quoted by more people than any other sentence ever written in the world?" He was interested and I showed him John 3:16. The marvel of the verse is beyond description.

The love of God is greater far than tongue or pen
  can ever tell,
It goes beyond the highest star and reaches to the
  lowest Hell;
The guilty pair, bowed down with care, God gave His
  Son to win,
His erring child He reconciled and pardoned from his sin.

When hoary time shall pass away, and earthly thrones
  and kingdoms fall,
When men who here refuse to pray on rocks and hills
  and mountains call;
God's love, so sure, shall still endure, all
  measureless and strong,
Redeeming grace to Adam's race, the saints' and
  angels' song.

Could we with ink the ocean fill, and were the skies
of parchment made,
Were ev'ry stalk on earth a quill, and ev'ry man a
scribe by trade;
To write the love of God above, would drain the
ocean dry,
Nor could the scroll contain the whole, though stretched
from sky to sky.

O love of God, how rich and pure! How measureless
and strong!
It shall forevermore endure, The saints' and angels'
song.

One has outlined this verse thus:

GOD—the greatest Person.

SO LOVED—the greatest love.

THE WORLD—the greatest number ever loved.

THAT HE GAVE HIS ONLY BEGOTTEN SON—the greatest Gift ever given.

THAT WHOSOEVER BELIEVETH IN HIM—the simplest requirement possible.

SHOULD NOT PERISH—the most awful destiny avoided.

BUT HAVE EVERLASTING LIFE—the greatest gift for all eternity.

Dr. R. A. Torrey preached on John 3:16 as "The Greatest Sentence Ever Written."

Martin Luther called verse 16 the "Miniature Gospel" because it represents all the great truth of the Gospel and the meaning of Christ's coming.

Dr. H. A. Ironside tells the story of a little girl in Martin Luther's day, when the first edition of the Bible came out.

She had a terrible fear of God. God had been presented in such a way that it filled her heart with dread when she thought of Him. She brooded over the awfulness of the character of God and of some day having to meet this angry Judge.

But one day she came running to her mother, holding a scrap of paper in her hand. She cried out, "Mother! Mother! I am not afraid of God any more."

Her mother said, "Why are you not?"

"Why, look, Mother," she said, "this bit of paper I found in the print shop, and it is torn out of the Bible." It was so torn as to be almost illegible except about two lines. On the one line it said, "God so loved," and on the other line it said, "that he gave." "See, Mother," she said, "that makes it all right."

Her mother read it and said, "God so loved that he gave." "But," she said, "it does not say what He gave."

"O Mother," exclaimed the child, "if He loved us enough to give anything, it is all right."

Then the mother said, "But, let me tell you what He gave." She read, "God so loved the world, that he gave his only begotten Son, that whosoever believeth in him should not perish, but have everlasting life." Then she told how we can have peace and eternal life through trusting Him.

Note, the believer, one who simply trusts Christ for salvation—

1. He "shall not perish."
2. He "has everlasting life."
3. He "is not condemned."

Other Scriptures restate this truth, or illustrate it, or state corollaries to it but never limit it, never contradict it, not a breath of it! No one has a right to limit God's love to all, or His desire to save all. He has offered mercy to all "the world." If so-called "sovereign grace" means a limited atonement, thus meaning limited love and God's limited concern for sinners and His limited offer of mercy, then that so-called "sovereign grace" is not the simple grace so called in the Bible and offered here.

If one makes "believeth in him" to include also things not stated here, such as confessing to a priest, or baptism, or holding out faithful, then he slanders, misuses this great passage and it is wrong.

If "everlasting life" is explained away as less than everlasting so that one who got saved found it didn't last forever, then that is heresy contradicting this central passage in the Bible, this greatest truth of the Gospel.

Condemnation only if one does not believe on the only begotten Son of God. Not the murderer, not the drunkard, not the lewd, the vile, the wretched, but the one who does not trust in

Christ is condemned! Oh, trusting in Christ will change the other things, but salvation is settled on that simple point of trusting Christ.

"Condemned already" (vs. 18). You do not have to wait 'til the judgment day to find that out. Not that one will be condemned when he dies but he is living now under condemnation. "God is angry with the wicked every day" (Ps. 7:11). "The wrath of God abideth on him," says verse 36.

One crosses the Rubicon, from death to life; he comes out of darkness into light. Instead of a child of Satan, he becomes transformed into a child of God. He is miraculously born instantly when he trusts in Jesus Christ!

Have you said,

"Jesus, I will trust Thee, trust Thee with my soul,
Weary, worn and helpless, Thou canst make me whole.
There is none in Heaven, or on earth like Thee;
Thou hast died for sinners; therefore, Lord, for me."

VERSES 19-21:

19 And this is the condemnation, that light is come into the world, and men loved darkness rather than light, because their deeds were evil.
20 For every one that doeth evil hateth the light, neither cometh to the light, lest his deeds should be reproved.
21 But he that doeth truth cometh to the light, that his deeds may be made manifest, that they are wrought in God.

The Unbeliever Chooses Darkness

Notice that there is only one reason why men go to Hell. They love their sins and hold on to them, rejecting Christ. Everyone who turns down Christ does it because of his wicked heart, which he does not want Jesus to change. He loves his sin, loves and clings to Satan and his ways.

There is a moral wickedness in unbelief. Those who do not come to Christ refuse to come because *"their deeds are evil."* They "hate the light." They do not want to acknowledge their sinful, lost state. No one who follows what light he has will be lost, for the seeking soul will find God. God will see to that.

The praying, devout Cornelius will have an angel come tell him where to find Peter, who will tell him how to be saved! (Acts 10). The seeking Ethiopian eunuch will find God pulls Philip away from a great revival to meet him on the road to Gaza and explain the Scriptures that he studied so he can be saved (Acts 8).

Jesus said in John 7:17, "If any man will do his will, he shall know of the doctrine, whether it be of God, or whether I speak of myself."

That passage was explained by a simple gospel preacher that one who is willing to do the will of God will be led to the truth, to B. H. Carroll. He was crippled from the Civil War, and broken over a personal tragedy, an infidel who had tasted the bitterness of finding that all the roads of unbelief led only to "the jumping-off place," as he said, and to failure. But he agreed to follow all the light God would give him. Then a sweet hymn, sung by country women around a little organ, so sweetly opened his heart to see the Lord Jesus and to be saved. (Read his "My Infidelity and What Became of It," from *The Sword Book of Treasures.*) So that willingness of heart routed infidelity, and Dr. Carroll became the great theologian, the mighty preacher, the founder of Southwestern Baptist Theological Seminary.

How often the Scripture says this truth, "Those that seek me early shall find me" (Prov. 8:17). "Draw nigh to God, and he will draw nigh to you" (Jas. 4:8).

Only "the fool hath said in his heart, There is no God" (Ps. 14:1; 53:1). Really that infidel is not saying that "there is no God," but he is saying, "No God for me. I don't want any God. I won't have any God."

The sin of the Pharisees who said Jesus cast out devils only by the power of devils (Matt. 12:24-32), may have been the unpardonable sin. That sin was their determination not to accept Jesus, for, convinced in their heads, they still hated Him in their hearts and would not acknowledge His deity.

Light fully understood and rejected means that some day the

door is closed. One may harden his heart until it is too late to be saved.

On the cross Jesus said, "Father, forgive them; for they know not what they do." One may for a time reject salvation without knowing all he does. But those who go on knowingly and deliberately against the full light of God pass the point where they might be led to repentance.

Jesus said to the two doubting disciples on the road to Emmaus, "O fools, and slow of heart to believe all that the prophets have spoken" (Luke 24:25). Those who do not believe the Bible are wrong; not first in the head but first in the heart. They are subjective, not objective. They do not accept the truth because of a sinful attitude.

Intelligence, education, science—these do not make unbelievers and infidels. Infidelity is the product of the wicked heart which rejects Christ first, then rejects His Word. So Jesus said in Mark 8:38, "Whosoever therefore shall be ashamed of me and of my words in this adulterous and sinful generation; of him also shall the Son of man be ashamed, when he cometh in the glory of his Father with the holy angels." People turn their hearts away from the light and so they do not believe the Bible and do not receive Christ.

We need to preach to the unbeliever, "Repent," then he can believe. The trouble with the Christ-rejecter, the unbeliever in the Bible, the evolutionist who rejects direct creation, is heart trouble, not head trouble.

Why do evolutionists talk of billions of years, uncounted ages, through natural process making fossils, without God and without the flood? Second Peter 3:4-6 says,

"And saying, Where is the promise of his coming? for since the fathers fell asleep, all things continue as they were from the beginning of the creation. For this they willingly are ignorant of, that by the word of God the heavens were of old, and the earth standing out of the water and in the water: Whereby the world that then was, being overflowed with water, perished."

Oh, the sin of being "willingly ignorant"! Why? Because of the sinful rejection of Christ and sin against God.

---

22 ¶ After these things came Jesus and his disciples into the land of Judæa; and there he tarried with them, and baptized.

23 ¶ And John also was baptizing in Ænŏn near to Salim, because there was much water there: and they came, and were baptized.

24 For John was not yet cast into prison.

John the Baptist Baptizing

It is probable that Jesus was baptized in the lower reaches of the Jordan River, and that now He and His disciples go there and baptize many, many converts.

John the Baptist was still baptizing great numbers at Aenon, further north, west of the Jordan River. Notice the reason that he chose that place, mentioned in verse 23. Bible baptism requires enough water for a burial (Rom. 6:45; Col. 2:12; Acts 8:38). Notice that Jesus also was having a revival meeting and that many were being baptized (vs. 26). From John 4:1,2 it is clear that Jesus Himself was not doing the actual baptizing, but that it was being done for Him by His disciples.

Baptism of a convert scripturally involves the following:

1. **Believing on Christ.** To the Ethiopian eunuch who wanted to be baptized, Philip said, "If thou believest with all thine heart, thou mayest" (Acts 8:37).

Dr. Bob Gray at Jacksonville, Florida, said that a woman called him asking, "Will you baptize my baby?" At first he was flustered, then he said, "I would be glad to talk with you about it. If he can meet the Bible requirement, I will baptize him."

She said, "What is the Bible requirement?"

"Do you have a Bible? Then find the 8th chapter of Acts."

She did. He pointed to this verse and said, "Now, if your baby meets this requirement, 'If thou believest with all thine heart, thou mayest.' Has your baby believed in Christ with all his heart?"

She was startled. She had never seen that before! She saw that the baby did not need to be baptized.

2. **Much water.** Not a cupful and not a well but some body of

water like at Aenon or the Jordan.

3. **Going down into the water.** The Scripture says about Philip and the eunuch, ". . . and they went down both into the water, both Philip and the eunuch; and he baptized him" (Acts 8:38). I have seen what is called Philip's Fountain near Bethlehem, but that present little fountain is not the one of the Scripture. It may well be that over 1900 years ago there was a fountain built to hold the water that ran from that spring, and it may well be that there was at one time a fountain deep enough for immersion and there Philip and the eunuch both walked down into the water and he was baptized, but not as that little place is now. It may be that then there was a larger basin and that spring of water filled it and kept it full. But it takes *going down into the water* for Bible baptism.

4. **A burial.** Romans 6:4 says, "Therefore we are buried with him by baptism into death."

5. **A raising up from the burial.** Romans 6:4 says, ". . . like as Christ was raised up from the dead by the glory of the Father, even so we also should walk in newness of life." And the following verse says that that baptism means "if we have been planted . . . in the likeness of his death, we shall be also in the likeness of his resurrection."

6. **Coming up out of the water.** So Matthew 3:16 says, "And Jesus, when he was baptized, went up straightway out of the water."

7. **Pictures the burial and resurrection of Christ** and that the new believer now counts the old sinner he once was as dead, and rises up to walk in newness of life.

We understand the baptism of John the Baptist was New Testament baptism. It was the baptism Jesus had. We understand that John baptized all the apostles, too, because when they must elect another man to take the place of Judas they said, "Wherefore of these men which have companied with us all the time that the Lord Jesus went in and out among us, Beginning from the baptism of John, unto that same day that he was taken up from us, must one be ordained to be a witness with us of his resurrection" (Acts 1:21,22). So John's baptism was New Testa-

ment baptism. It had exactly the same meaning as the baptism
of people today who follow the Bible.

VERSES 25-30:

25 ¶ Then there arose a question between *some* of John's disciples and the Jews about purifying.

26 And they came unto John, and said unto him, Rabbi, he that was with thee beyond Jordan, to whom thou barest witness, behold, the same baptizeth, and all *men* come to him.

27 John answered and said, A man can receive nothing, except it be given him from heaven.

28 Ye yourselves bear me witness, that I said, I am not the Christ, but that I am sent before him.

29 He that hath the bride is the bridegroom: but the friend of the bridegroom, which standeth and heareth him, rejoiceth greatly because of the bridegroom's voice: this my joy therefore is fulfilled.

30 He must increase, but I *must* decrease.

The Last Testimony of John the Baptist

John was a national figure. Matthew 3:5,6 says that "Jerusalem, and all Judaea, and all the region round about Jordan" went out to the Jordan River to be baptized of John." And in Luke 1:15 and 16 the angel announcing his birth had foretold that "many of the children of Israel shall he turn to the Lord their God." Nationally known and heard, he was loved or hated, accepted or feared. He had boldly rebuked King Herod for taking his brother's wife. Now, will John be jealous that more people hear Jesus than heard him? And that the Lord Jesus, by His disciples, baptized more converts than John? His disciples came to tell him about the tremendous crowd that flocked to Jesus, probably thinking so. They may have been distressed because this mighty evangelist they followed was being superseded by Jesus, *"and all men come to him"* (vs. 26).

But John knew his calling and ministry. He was a forerunner, not a peer or equal, not with a parallel ministry. He was an announcer, not a competitor, of Jesus. His main work now is done. Now the disciples of Jesus will be trained to follow Jesus and go out to work miracles and win souls, many of them, but John alone, as a swift meteor soon to disappear, had announced His coming. There was never a greater born of woman than John, said Jesus in Matthew 11:11. But he was to finish his work soon after the Lord began His ministry. He was to be arrested, jailed, then beheaded by Herod (Matt. 14:1-12; Mark 6:14-29).

John had made the greatest impact on Israel of any prophet now for hundreds of years, but from the beginning he had insisted he was not the Messiah, not Christ, the Light of the world, the Saviour, but only a witness, a marvelous witness but always lesser than Jesus. No, he was *"sent before him"* (vs. 28).

John said, *"He must increase, but I must decrease"* (vs. 30). Did John have some impression, some intimation of his coming imprisonment and death? We think so.

When William Carey was dying, he turned to a friend and said, "When I am gone, don't talk about William Carey; talk about William Carey's Saviour. I desire that Christ alone might be magnified." And so with John here: "He must increase, but I must decrease."

And how can this man, one of the greatest ever born, best leave the scene? By prison and a martyr's death! For his is the most blessed of the Beatitudes:

"Blessed are ye, when men shall revile you, and persecute you, and shall say all manner of evil against you falsely, for my sake. Rejoice, and be exceeding glad: for great is your reward in heaven: for so persecuted they the prophets which were before you."—Matt. 5:11,12.

You will note, perhaps with surprise, that while others of the Beatitudes took from nine words to fifteen, this one takes forty-six. Oh, blessed was John who had great reward in Heaven!

We are told that "John did no miracle" (10:41). In this, too, he must be no rival to Jesus in the attention of the multitudes.

Since one great ministry of John was to introduce Jesus, the ultradispensationalists entirely miss the point of his ministry when they think his baptism was a Jewish ceremony of the Old Testament and that his disciples were simply "Jewish proselytes . . . looking forward to a coming King, not Christians looking

backward to an accomplished redemption," as the Scofield note
wrongly says on Acts 19:2. He perfectly represented the Gospel.
His baptism was New Testament baptism. His ministry fitly introduced the ministry of Jesus.

VERSES 31-36:

31 He that cometh from above is
above all: he that is of the earth is
earthly, and speaketh of the earth: he
that cometh from heaven is above
all.
32 And what he hath seen and
heard, that he testifieth; and no man
receiveth his testimony.
33 He that hath received his testimony hath set to his seal that God is
true.

34 For he whom God hath sent
speaketh the words of God: for God
giveth not the   Spirit by measure
unto him.
35 The Father loveth the Son, and
hath given all things into his hand.
36 He that believeth on the Son hath
everlasting life: and he that believeth
not the Son shall not see life; but the
wrath of God abideth on him.

The Gospel of John the Baptist

We understand these verses are a continuation of the statement of John the Baptist. A distinguished translator recently put
these verses in quotation marks as part of the statement of John.

"He that cometh from above is above all" (vs. 31) declares
the deity of Christ, and is equivalent to affirming again the
virgin birth. In John 8:23,24 we read: "And he said unto them,
Ye are from beneath; I am from above: ye are of this world; I am
not of this world. I said therefore unto you, that ye shall die in
your sins: for if ye believe not that I am he, ye shall die in your
sins."

Jesus *"cometh from heaven,"* we are told in verse 31.

The purpose of John's Gospel is: "But these are written, that
ye might believe that Jesus is the Christ, the Son of God; and
that believing ye might have life through his name" (20:31).

So the theme is repeated often.

Verse 31 then means that Jesus Christ was from above, born
without sin, God come in the flesh in a way that no one else ever
was. Everybody else that is born of earthly parentage is sinful

with Adam's taint of sin. Hence, the Scripture says here one ought to receive the witness of Jesus Christ because He was sent from God and speaks the words of God and had the Spirit without measure.

John continues to exalt the Lord Jesus. *"No man receiveth his testimony"* (vs. 32)—like John 1:11 and John 3:11. This foreshadows the rejection of Christ and His crucifixion. Oh, He was born to die.

My Christmas song, "Jesus, Baby Jesus," says:

> **Jesus, Baby Jesus,**
> **There's a cross along the way.**
> **Born to die for sinners,**
> **Born for crucifixion day!**

Jesus is *"the Word,"* and so every word of His is God's Word (vs. 34). Others filled with the Spirit, are speaking for God, but all of us preachers are limited, imperfect. We do not seek perfectly nor receive all the mighty power and wisdom of God when we speak for Him. But the anointing of Jesus at His baptism and continuing after that (Luke 3:21,22; Matt. 3:13-17) was perfect and unlimited. God did not give Jesus that Holy Spirit "by measure"! Since He is God the Son, His power was completely— all of it—the power of the Holy Spirit.

Note the anointing of Aaron the high priest mentioned in Psalm 133:1,2:

"Behold, how good and how pleasant it is for brethren to dwell together in unity! It is like the precious ointment upon the head, that ran down upon the beard, even Aaron's beard: that went down to the skirts of his garments."

That abundant anointing of Aaron, with oil running down on his beard and down to the skirt of his garment, symbolizes the Holy Spirit poured out without measure on Jesus (vs. 34).

God loves the Son. How often He wants to say it! No praise is enough for Jesus. The Father has put all salvation, all judgment, all His Word in the hands of Jesus (vs. 35).

What Gospel did John preach? Verse 36 states it: *"He that believeth on the Son hath everlasting life: and he that believeth not the Son shall not see life; but the wrath of God abideth on him."* His Gospel was exactly like that stated in John 3:16; 5:24; 6:40,47; Acts 10:43; 13:38,39; 16:31. Yes, John was a New Testament preacher. And the same Gospel he preached, like all Old Testament prophets, was the Gospel of faith in Christ for salvation.

This verse once gave to me, a twelve-year-old boy who had gone three years doubting about my salvation, the perfect assurance that I was saved, that I was a child of God. Oh, thus on this we can rest our souls: one who believes in Christ, trusts in Christ, already has everlasting life and he may know it, not because he feels this or that but because God's Word has plainly said it.

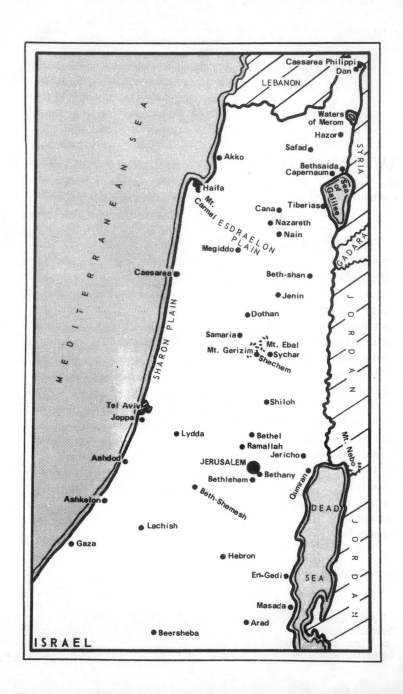

John 4

VERSES 1-3:

WHEN therefore the Lord knew how the Pharisees had heard that Jesus made and baptized more disciples than John,

2 (Though Jesus himself baptized not, but his disciples,)

3 He left Judæa, and departed again into Galilee.

Jesus Leaves Judaea Thinking of John

The disciples of John had reported that Jesus, through His disciples, had baptized more converts than John (3:26). The Pharisees heard the same and perhaps there were remarks made that compared John unfavorably with Jesus. When Jesus heard that, He left the area, going north to Galilee. Doubtless He was anxious that no one belittle John whom He greatly loved. The ministry of Jesus would be beyond compare with any other, with wondrous miracles when John had none, and Jesus speaking as "never man spake" (7:46). But Jesus did not want odious comparison with John's work, so He decided He must leave the area.

The tender love for John was evident when Jesus heard later of his death: "When Jesus heard of it, he departed thence by ship into a desert place apart: and when the people had heard thereof, they followed him on foot out of the cities" (Matt. 14:13). He intended then to rest and perhaps to mourn and said to His disciples, when He received that news, "Come ye yourselves apart into a desert place, and rest a while" (Mark 6:31). We think John the Baptist held a place in the human affection of Jesus beyond that of any others.

VERSES 4-12:

4 And he must needs go through Samaria.

5 Then cometh he to a city of Samaria, which is called Sȳ́-chär,

near | to the parcel of ground that Jacob gave to his son Joseph.

6 Now Jacob's well was there. Jesus therefore, being wearied with

his journey, sat thus on the well: *and it was about the sixth hour.*

7 There cometh a woman of Samaria to draw water: Jesus saith unto her, Give me to drink.

8 (For his disciples were gone away unto the city to buy meat.)

9 Then saith the woman of Samaria unto him, How is it that thou, being a Jew, askest drink of me, which am a woman of Samaria? for the Jews have no dealings with the · Samaritans.

10 Jesus answered and said unto her, If thou knewest the gift of God, and who it is that saith to thee, Give me to drink; thou wouldest have asked of him, and he would have given thee living water.

11 The woman saith unto him, Sir, thou hast nothing to draw with, and the well is deep: from whence then hast thou that living water?

12 Art thou greater than our father Jacob, which gave us the well, and drank thereof himself, and his children, and his cattle?

Jesus at Jacob's Well

There were two routes between Jerusalem and the province of Galilee. The route down the Jordan valley from the Sea of Galilee to Jericho, then up the hills to Jerusalem, may have been an earlier route. It was mostly water-level walking. We know Jesus took that route on His last trip to Jerusalem before His death. He announced His departure to Jerusalem and foretold His arrest, His punishment in death, and the next verse tells that He came to Jericho. And the next chapter tells of His winning of Zacchaeus at Jericho. And Luke 19:28,29 tells us that He was "ascending up to Jerusalem" from Jericho, approaching Jerusalem by the Mount of Olives.

But this time *"he must needs go through Samaria"* (vs. 4). Why? Doubtless because he knew with word from God about the woman there and other hungry hearts He must win! H. A. Ironside said, "Long before the creation of the world it had been settled in the counsels of eternity that He was to meet a poor, sinful, Samaritan woman that day. He could not forgo that appointment."

It may be that the other trip later, when He returned to Jerusalem by the other route, He took because He must save Bartimaeus and Zacchaeus. But now He would go up that route I have traveled by bus several times, up hill and down with switchbacks and hairpin turns, a most arduous trip. So we are not surprised that *"Jesus therefore, being wearied with his journey, sat thus on the well"* (vs. 6).

Jacob's Well at Sychar is thirty miles or more from Jerusalem by the map, but with crooks and turns around and over the mountains, the road was doubtless considerably longer. When Jesus sat on the well "about the sixth hour," they had journeyed at least a day and a half from Jerusalem, and Jesus was weary.

Sychar was near the ancient Shechem and now the city of Nablus is nearby. The Greek Orthodox church of Russia started a church building over the area of the well, but the rise of communism in Russia stopped the flow of missionary funds and so the building was never completed.

The land is that *"parcel of ground that Jacob gave to his son Joseph"* (vs. 5). The parcel was evidently purchased by Jacob "of the children of Hamor" (Gen. 33:19). Jacob there built an altar and we suppose he dug this well. And Shechem was later an important center.

Samaria, named for the hill Samaria, was purchased by King Omri, the father of King Ahab of the northern kingdom. When Jeroboam had rebelled against Solomon's son Rehoboam and had taken ten tribes to make up the northern kingdom, Israel, then Jeroboam had built Shechem. But Omri and Ahab built Samaria as the capital city and the area became known as Samaria.

But the people of Samaria were a mixed people, mixed in race and religion. The Assyrian king had besieged and taken the city of Samaria and then carried the northern tribes away in captivity (II Kings 17:4-6). The Assyrian king then sent in some of his people to fill the empty land and then after lions killed many, sent some Israelites to be priests, so the land would tolerate this alien people. Then the Assyrians and the Israelites mingled and became the Samaritan people. They had the Pentateuch but no other books of the Bible. They still have a very ancient copy of the books of Moses in the synagogue there at Nablus, shown to visitors by their high priest. He calls it "the oldest book in the vorld." They think the center of religion should be on Mount Gerizim, near Nablus, instead of at Jerusalem.

This woman was astonished at the friendliness of Jesus. *"How is it that thou, being a Jew, askest drink of me, which am a woman of Samaria?"* the woman said in verse 9, *"for* [as the Apostle John explains] *the Jews have no dealings with the Samaritans."* The Samaritans were despised because they were partly Gentiles and heathens, and Samaritans hated the Jews. At one time when the Lord Jesus was coming to Jerusalem with His disciples, the Samaritans would not even give them lodging since they were headed toward Jerusalem. Then James and John suggested they call down fire from Heaven and destroy them! But Jesus rebuked them (Luke 9:51-56).

There are now, I think, only a few hundred Samaritans living in two localities—Nablus and another.

The Heathen Woman Was Won at Jacob's Well

In arid Palestine the wells are usually deep and in old times dug by hand, with much labor. Usually one well would water a whole community or several families. If this well was dug by Jacob, as tradition says it was, it was over a thousand years old when Jesus sat there, and some three thousand years old now. And the water is good.

Let us look at the great contrasts in this chapter. We are reminded that Jesus was weary, yet He promises rest to all who are heavy laden. He was thirsty, yet He offers to give us the water which quenches every thirst. He was hungry, yet He gives us the bread of life. He asked for a cup of water, yet He can give us Heaven and earth. He was a stranger, yet His name is better known than that of any man who ever lived.

Jesus sat alone resting. They had walked some thirty miles or more from Jerusalem, probably taking a long day. At least it was now the sixth hour, 6:00 p.m. Roman time (vs. 6). The disciples had gone into the city to buy food. When the Samaritan woman came, Jesus asked her, *"Give me to drink"* (vs. 7). The question of water is a common, everyday matter and a point of contact. So Jesus can then talk of the Water of Life. One thirsts physically for water, but this frustrated woman has a spiritual thirst and need.

How skillfully, gently, Jesus led her to see her need, to see she was a guilty sinner needing salvation! She needed peace for her guilt and for the sense of failure in all these five marriages, and the living now in adultery.

Jesus regularly, with parables, spoke to farmers of sowing and reaping, spoke to renters about money or property they must account for. He spoke of the lost sheep, of lost money, of prodigal boys, of weddings, and of fishing. But here He presses straight to the sin issue and leads to conviction and then toward salvation. He first leads to recognition of sin.

She asks how He can draw water—the well is deep, He has no rope or bucket. (The guides say the well is over 70 feet deep.)

But Jesus does not offer water from this well. This well, like all other earthly satisfactions, gives only temporary comfort. She will thirst again; so all will find that they "thirst again." This world's good times end in heartache. This world's wells are dry, its clouds without rain, its cisterns broken cisterns that can hold no water. All Satan's apples have worms. "There is a way which seemeth right unto a man, but the end thereof are the ways of death" (Prov. 14:12).

She had been married five times and each time love had faded. What was it? Drunkenness? Cruelty? Neglect? Had any of these broken her heart and caused love to be lost? Vexation, emptiness and loneliness followed. No doubt each time she had thought, "This time it is forever. Now I have found a true love." But it never worked out. "Whosoever drinketh of this water shall thirst again."

Jesus offers her better water than that found in Jacob's Well
(vs. 12). Oh, yes, better than all the wells of this world!

VERSES 13,14:

13 Jesus answered and said unto her, Whosoever drinketh of this water shall thirst again:
14 But whosoever drinketh of the water that I shall give him shall never thirst; but the water that I shall give him shall be in him a well of water springing up into everlasting life.

The Living Water

How often the Scriptures speak of salvation as a living well of water!

In Isaiah 44:3 the Lord promises, "I will pour water upon him that is thirsty, and floods upon the dry ground: I will pour my spirit upon thy seed, and my blessing upon thine offspring." It is promised that Christ shall be "as rivers of water in a dry place" (Isa. 32:2). In Isaiah 12:3 the prophet exclaims, "Therefore with joy shall ye draw water out of the wells of salvation."

That great rock in Mount Horeb which Moses was commanded to smite with a rod and from which there came out a river of water that watered all the three and a half million people and their livestock, was a picture of Christ smitten (Exod. 17:5-7). As Christ the Bread of Life was pictured by the manna from Heaven, so Christ the Water of Life is pictured in that rock. And since He was once smitten, and Christ died but once now Moses should only speak to the rock to get water again, and he was rebuked for smiting the rock (Num. 20:11,12).

First Corinthians 10:4, speaking of Israel, says the "Rock that followed them . . . was Christ."

Isaiah cries out, "Ho, every one that thirsteth, come ye to the waters, and he that hath no money; come ye, buy, and eat; yea, come, buy wine and milk without money and without price" (55:1).

And the last sweet invitation in the Bible says, "And

whosoever will, let him take the water of life freely" (Rev. 22:17). In some of the Scriptures, as in Isaiah 44:3, the water pictures the pouring out of the Spirit. So it is in John 7:37-39:

"In the last day, that great day of the feast, Jesus stood and cried, saying, If any man thirst, let him come unto me, and drink. He that believeth on me, as the scripture hath said, out of his belly shall flow rivers of living water. (But this spake he of the Spirit, which they that believe on him should receive: for the Holy Ghost was not yet given; because that Jesus was not yet glorified.)"

Do not be surprised if Christ and the Holy Spirit are so closely related that the same picture may represent either or both.

But Jesus does not offer water from this well, but *"a well of water springing up into everlasting life"* (vs. 14). Living water means a spring that does not run dry. The promise of Jesus in verse 14 proves that salvation is everlasting, and the one who drinks of this water shall never thirst again. Oh, the water of life is not merely a washing; it is a fountain set up inside that flows continually. Christ, who is Himself the Light of the world, said, "Ye are the light of the world." It is not simply that one reflects the light from outside, but a Christian has the Light inside. Jesus speaks of a changed life and a dwelling of Christ within through the Spirit and everlasting life.

VERSES 15-27:

15 The woman saith unto him, Sir, give me this water, that I thirst not, neither come hither to draw.

16 Jesus saith unto her, Go, call thy husband, and come hither.

17 The woman answered and said, I have no husband. Jesus said unto her, Thou hast well said, I have no husband:

18 For thou hast had five husbands; and he whom thou now hast is not thy husband: in that saidst thou truly.

19 The woman saith unto him, Sir, I perceive that thou art a prophet.

20 Our fathers worshipped in this mountain; and ye say, that in Jerusalem is the place where men ought to worship.

21 Jesus saith unto her, Woman, believe me, the hour cometh, when ye shall neither in this mountain, nor yet at Jerusalem, worship the Father.

22 Ye worship ye know not what: we know what we worship: for salva-

tion is of the Jews.

23 But the hour cometh, and now is, when the true worshippers shall worship the Father in spirit and in truth: for the Father seeketh such to worship him.

24 God *is* a Spirit: and they that worship him must worship *him* in spirit and in truth.

25 The woman saith unto him, I know that *Messias cometh, which is called Christ: when he is come, he will tell us all things.

26 Jesus saith unto her, I that speak unto thee am *he*.

27 ¶ And upon this came his disciples, and marvelled that he talked with the woman: yet no man said, What seekest thou? or, Why talkest thou with her?

The Samaritan Woman Saved

Now the woman is interested. She asked, *"Sir, give me this water, that I thirst not, neither come hither to draw"* (vs. 15). But Jesus said, *"Go, call thy husband, and come hither."* F. B. Meyer says:

> What a train of memory that word evoked! Beneath its spell, she was back long years; again an innocent girl, courted by him in the sunny vineyards of Gerizim; going with him to his home as his loving wife. Then perhaps there came a growing coldness, leading to alienation and dislike, ending in infidelity. That husband might have died of a broken heart. She had tried to banish his memory and his face, though they would haunt her. What a spasm of remorse and fear seized her, as she remembered that grave within her heart, where her first love lay buried, trampled down by the unholy crew of wilder later passions!
>
> But why awake such memories? Why open the cupboard-door and bid that skeleton step down? Why unsod that grave? Why lay bare that life-secret? It could not be otherwise. The wound must be probed to the bottom and cleansed, ere it could be healed. There must be confession before forgiveness. . . . .This woman must judge her past sins in the light of those pure eyes, ere she could know the bliss of the fountain opened within the soul.

Jesus had never before seen this woman, but He knew she had had five husbands and was then living in sin with a man to whom she was not married.

Let us remember that if we want people saved, they must be told that they are sinners.

It was for her and the others who were to be saved that John said, "He must needs go through Samaria." The woman's eyes opened wide! "Ah, so He knows all about me!" She was so startled, so convicted, that later she told others, "He told me all things that ever I did!" (vs. 29). Well, He did not need to tell her everything she did, but He knew it all. And she said, *"Sir, I perceive that thou art a prophet"* (vs. 19).

But now if Jesus is a Jewish prophet, she has a controversy with Him: "We Samaritans think it is perfectly satisfactory to worship God in the synagogue on Mount Gerizim here. Our religion satisfies us, and we don't need Your Jewish religion."

Ah, but Jesus tells her that what God is wanting now is not the ceremonial sacrifices of the Jews nor anybody else's ceremonies; these were only pictures pointing to Christ. Not any one place now is the place to be saved. Not any one set of circumstances and ceremonies now is necessary. What God insists upon is a heart turned to God to worship in Spirit and in truth.

The Jews will have just as much trouble receiving this truth as she will, but it was true. Nobody was ever saved by circumcision, or animal sacrifices, or the priestly ceremonies. And circumcision was no good except as it pointed toward circumcision of heart. And all the time what God was seeking was that the law would be a schoolmaster to bring people to Christ. So Jesus said, *"God is a Spirit: and they that worship him must worship him in spirit and in truth"* (vs. 24).

But although this woman had rejected the Jewish ceremonies and was not interested in the Temple at Jerusalem, she knew about the coming Messiah, the promised Saviour; so with concern and penitence she said, "I know that Messias cometh, which is called Christ: when he is come, he will tell us all things" (vs. 25).

Now her hungry heart is penitent and ready, and Jesus tells her, *"I that speak unto thee am he"* (vs. 26).

The disciples had gone to town to buy food. They were not too patient with Jesus spending time talking to this shabby woman! In town they didn't whisper a word that out at the well was the Messiah, the Son of God! How careless and worldly-minded and thoughtless are we about souls around us undone, unsaved!

Once on a Sante Fe train going from Chicago to Newton,

Kansas, I ate breakfast with three other men in the diner. I did have my Bible along; I did bow my head silently to thank God; but I did not talk to them about Christ. Instead, we talked about the war, about the crowded conditions of the trains, etc.

Then I paid for my breakfast and went up to sit in the chair car. One man hastily followed me. There were no seats in two chair cars and I went back to the lounge car, and he followed me. I sat down, and he sat beside me. Then with troubled face he said, "Mister, are you a minister?"

I answered that I was.

He said, "I hope you won't mind my bothering you, but I am in awful trouble!" Then he told me that his wife had died and her body was on this train, going back out to Los Angeles for burial. He was an executive of General Motors. General Motors had sent two men with him to bury his wife. Then he said, "I wasn't a very good husband. Do you think she has forgiven me?" He said she was the best Christian he had ever known. He knew she loved him.

I told him then that he might be sure that she had forgiven him.

Then he said sadly, and almost desperately, "Well, how am I ever going to see her again?"

I told him how to be saved. Then when we prayed, he prayed right out loud as the other workers from General Motors sat across the aisle from us and listened reverently.

He trusted Christ.

He went on to Los Angeles and buried his wife, the daughter of a good preacher. That father-in-law wrote me a glad letter telling how his beloved Bill had claimed the Lord. When I saw him two years later, he was still an active, happy, useful Christian in a good church in Rochester, Michigan.

I am saying, how shamed I was to find one must seek me out and beg me to tell him how to be saved!

These disciples were like the rest of us here—very careless and unaccountable.

Oh, if we are openhearted, eager and in touch with God, surely sometime we will find out when there is a Samaritan woman with a hungry heart, a centurion Cornelius crying, fasting, praying and begging to be saved, as Peter did. Or we will find out there is an Ethiopian eunuch on the way back to Africa unsatisfied, unsaved, and reading without comprehension the 53rd chapter of Isaiah, as Philip found him and won him.

VERSES 28-42:

28 The woman then left her waterpot, and went her way into the city, and saith to the men,

29 Come, see a man, which told me all things that ever I did: is not this the Christ?

30 Then they went out of the city, and came unto him.

31 ¶ In the mean while his disciples prayed him, saying, Master, eat.

32 But he said unto them, I have meat to eat that ye know not of.

33 Therefore said the disciples one to another, Hath any man brought him *ought* to eat?

34 Jesus saith unto them, My meat is to do the will of him that sent me, and to finish his work.

35 Say not ye, There are yet four months, and *then* cometh harvest? behold, I say unto you, Lift up your eyes, and look on the fields; for they are white already to harvest.

36 And he that reapeth receiveth wages, and gathereth fruit unto life eternal: that both he that soweth and he that reapeth may rejoice together.

37 And herein is that saying true, One soweth, and another reapeth.

38 I sent you to reap that whereon ye bestowed no labour: other men laboured, and ye are entered into their labours.

39 ¶ And many of the Samaritans of that city believed on him for the saying of the woman, which testified, He told me all that ever I did.

40 So when the Samaritans were come unto him, they besought him that he would tarry with them: and he abode there two days.

41 And many more believed because of his own word;

42 And said unto the woman, Now we believe, not because of thy saying: for we have heard *him* ourselves, and know that this is indeed the Christ, the Saviour of the world.

The Blessed Harvest Ready

Should a new convert set out immediately to win souls? Oh, yes. This woman did. Within ten minutes after she found the Messiah, she was telling others, *"Come, see a man, which told me all things that ever I did: is not this the Christ?"* (vs. 29). And they came. Some were saved on her testimony; others came to hear Him.

In John 1:41,42 Andrew was saved and "he first findeth his own brother Simon, and saith unto him, We have found the

Messias, which is, being interpreted, the Christ. And he brought
him to Jesus." Then Jesus found Philip and Philip "findeth
Nathanael."

When that poor man possessed of a legion of devils whom Jesus
found over in the country of the Gadarenes was saved, he wanted
to go with Jesus, but Jesus sent him away saying, "Return to
thine own house, and shew how great things God hath done unto
thee. And he went his way, and published throughout the whole
city how great things Jesus had done unto him" (Luke 8:38,39).

Oh, yes, new converts ought to start at once to tell what God
has done for them. You should learn to win souls.

Oh, but one might well think Samaria would be a hard place to
win souls. Those mixed breed in race hated the Jews. They were
all mixed up in their religion. They were not friendly nor
receptive. But the Lord Jesus found a hungry heart who was
saved, and she found others she could win.

The disciples settled down to eat the food they had brought,
but when they said unto Him, *"Master, eat,"* Jesus said unto
them, *"I have meat to eat that ye know not of"* (vs. 32). Jesus
had been very weary (vs. 6). Now, however, He was refreshed and
so anxious for the salvation of the people of Samaria, that He
would not eat! Read verse 32 again and remember that the joy of
Jesus on earth or in Heaven now is to see sinners saved.

Winning a soul to Christ is a joy unspeakable. We learn how
the Lord feels about it when He tells us about the shepherd who
found the lost sheep and laid it on his shoulder rejoicing. And the
woman who found her lost coin, called her friends and neighbors
and said, "Rejoice with me; for I have found the piece which I
had lost." And the father, when the prodigal son came home, had
a feast and rejoiced, "For this my son was dead, and is alive
again; he was lost, and is found" (Luke 15:3-24).

A harvest field here in Samaria? Yes, and everywhere else. Oh,
Jesus said it more than once! In Matthew 9, speaking to the
twelve disciples, Jesus, moved with compassion on the people
who fainted and were scattered abroad like sheep having no
shepherd, said, "The harvest truly is plenteous, but the
labourers are few; Pray ye therefore the Lord of the harvest, that

he will send forth labourers into his harvest" (vss. 37,38).

Then Jesus said it again to the seventy new workers He had recruited:

"After these things the Lord appointed other seventy also, and sent them two and two before his face into every city and place, whither he himself would come. Therefore said he unto them, The harvest truly is great, but the labourers are few: pray ye therefore the Lord of the harvest, that he would send forth labourers into his harvest."—Luke 10:1,2.

You will notice that again in another situation and with another crowd Jesus states this same truth—the harvest always is plenteous. The trouble is always to have laborers, Spirit-filled, burdened, earnest laborers, to get out the Gospel, to get people saved. In this case He said, "Behold, I send you forth as lambs among wolves." They are not great Christians, they are not mature, they are only young converts, they are only lambs, but Jesus sends them forth to win souls.

Yes, the harvest is always white.

In I Kings 18, Elijah, when he prayed down the fire of God to burn up the sacrifice, found the people fell on their faces and cried out, "The Lord, he is the God; the Lord, he is the God" (I Kings 18:39).

In Nineveh, when God got Jonah to go at last and give strict warning, there was a mighty repenting and thousands were saved and the city was spared.

In wicked Jerusalem, the Jerusalem where the scribes and Pharisees and chief priests hated Jesus and slew Him, the Jerusalem where Jesus was mocked by the multitude while He died on the cross, the Jerusalem where one of His disciples sold Jesus for thirty pieces of silver, then betrayed Him with a kiss, where Peter, the main preacher, cursed and swore and denied Jesus and quit the ministry, and where the rest of the disciples forsook Him and fled—oh, even there, when the people prayed and had the power of God, they could win three thousand souls in a day at Pentecost!

"The harvest truly is plenteous, but the labourers are few." Don't say harvesttime is not here yet. Don't say another place is the place to harvest. The fields everywhere are white to harvest.

In verse 35 here Jesus is urging the disciples to stop looking at their food, stop thinking about other things and see the white harvest field around them. And Jesus promised them wages of rejoicing. *"And he that reapeth receiveth wages, and gathereth fruit unto life eternal: that both he that soweth and he that reapeth may rejoice together"* (vs. 36).

It is true that one can go forth and sow, even among strangers, and win souls. But whether he knows it or not, he is sowing in ground that some other has plowed. He is reaping where someone else has sowed.

After John the Baptist and others had preached the Gospel and throughout all this country the Word had gone, now others are winning souls. In this country where even this woman knew about the Messiah and where they had the Pentateuch and the promise of a great Prophet who would come, there were people hungry-hearted.

We remember that when Jesus was born in Bethlehem, old Simeon was looking forward to His coming and rejoiced to hold the Baby Jesus in his arms. And Anna the prophetess gave witness to redemption there when Jesus was brought to the Temple. All of us are reaping where others have sowed.

That does not mean that anyone must do only sowing; everyone must do reaping also. But with continual gratitude we ought to recognize that God has had a thousand reapers and we can rejoice and capitalize on the work they did and bring to fruition in many cases the seed they planted.

Some of these Samaritans had been saved in town without seeing Jesus, when the woman told her story. Oh, can you see how hungry-hearted many of them must have been? How open to the Gospel? Now others come out to hear Jesus and are saved and they tell the woman, "Now we believe, not because of thy saying: for we have heard him ourselves, and know that this is indeed the Christ, the Saviour of the world" (vs. 42).

Two short days Jesus stayed there and had such a reaping. Ah, this is why "he must needs go through Samaria"!

VERSES 43-45:

43 ¶ Now after two days he departed thence, and went into Galilee.

44 For Jesus himself testified, that a prophet hath no honour in his own country.

45 Then when he was come into Galilee, the Galilæans received him, having seen all the things that he did at Jerusalem at the feast: for they also went unto the feast.

Jesus Goes to Galilee Again

"A prophet hath no honour in his own country" (vs. 44). Jesus twice visited Nazareth where He was brought up. He had moved from there to Capernaum (Matt. 4:13). Then He visited Nazareth immediately after His baptism and His temptation, and taught in the synagogue (Luke 4). There He said, "Verily I say unto you, No prophet is accepted in his own country" (Luke 4:24). Here in John 4:44 the Lord Jesus, about to go up to Galilee again, spake this truth again. And after His teaching again in the synagogue at Nazareth, He will find the people saying, "Is not this the carpenter's son?" He will say again, "A prophet is not without honour, save in his own country, and in his own house" (Matt. 13:57; Mark 6:4). In His own house! Yes, for even His brothers who lived in the house with Him believed not (7:5).

"The Galileans received him" (vs. 45). It is not that they "believed on him." No, they were interested in seeing and hearing Jesus. He had become famous. How in the world did He get this wisdom and power! And they allowed Him to teach in the synagogue, but they still insisted He was only the carpenter's son "and they were offended at him." Jesus repeated this saying of a prophet without honor (Mark 6:3,4).

These Galileans had been to Jerusalem at the feast. There they had seen many miracles (John 2:23). Those miracles had impressed Nicodemus (John 3:2); now these Galileans, although they do not trust Him as Saviour and are offended at Him, they receive Him.

Mark 6:5,6 says, "And he could there do no mighty work, save that he laid his hands upon a few sick folk, and healed them. And

he marvelled because of their unbelief. And he went round about the villages, teaching."

VERSES 46-54:

46 So Jesus came again into Cana of Galilee, where he made the water wine. And there was a certain nobleman, whose son was sick at Că-pĕr̓-nă-ŭm.

47 When he heard that Jesus was come out of Judæa into Galilee, he went unto him, and besought him that he would come down, and heal his son: for he was at the point of death.

48 Then said Jesus unto him, Except ye see signs and wonders, ye

49 The nobleman saith unto him, Sir, come down ere my child die.

50 Jesus saith unto him, Go thy way; thy son liveth. And the man believed the word that Jesus had spoken unto him, and he went his way.

51 And as he was now going down, his servants met him, and told him, saying, Thy son liveth.

52 Then enquired he of them the hour when he began to amend. And they said unto him, Yesterday at the seventh hour the fever left him.

53 So the father knew that it was at the same hour, in the which Jesus said unto him, Thy son liveth: and himself believed, and his whole house.

54 This is again the second miracle that Jesus did, when he was come out of Judæa into Galilee.

A Nobleman's Son Healed

"Jesus came AGAIN into Cana" (vs. 46). He had been there at the wedding in John, chapter 2. A few miles away from Cana, at Capernaum, a nobleman had a son desperately sick. He heard that Jesus was come out of Judaea into Galilee for Jesus was famous and it was noised abroad everywhere He went. Now the nobleman came beseeching Him to come and heal the son at the point of death.

Jesus tested his faith: *"Except ye see signs and wonders, ye will not believe"* (vs. 48).

But the urgent nobleman had no time to trifle. He said, "Sir, come down ere my child die" (vs. 49). That nobleman knew that Jesus could do something if he could only get Him to come in time to where his son was.

That is so often a question with us. If Jesus would only hurry up! We try to hurry the Lord up when we pray for the salvation of a loved one. How troubled were Mary and Martha when Lazarus was so sick. These women thought that Jesus would drop everything if He only knew His friend Lazarus was sick. But four days went by and Jesus had not come to Bethany. But when He did arrive, those sisters thought it was too late. But Jesus had already told His disciples that He was glad He had not come earlier. You might have expected Him to say, "I am sorry I was not there." Rather, He said, "I am glad I wasn't there." We do not need to try to hurry God.

But this dear father knew that his son was tossing with a high fever and that any moment it might be too late, so he wanted the Lord not to waste any time.

He did not know that Jesus did not need to go down to Capernaum to raise up his beloved son.

So Jesus simply told him, *"Go thy way; thy son liveth"* (vs. 50). He went home and found the child restored and that he had been healed at the very time Jesus spoke the words. "And himself believed, and his whole house"—they were converted.

This was the second miracle Jesus did in the province of Galilee; the first had been at Cana, but He had done other miracles in Jerusalem.

We can understand how the Lord Jesus, who had been poorly received in Galilee, at Nazareth, would scoff at those who would not believe without signs and wonders. But this nobleman believed and trusted Him immediately, both with the healing of his boy and then for the saving of his soul, and the whole family was saved.

John 5

VERSES 1-9:

AFTER this there was a feast of the Jews; and Jesus went up to Jerusalem.

2 Now there is at Jerusalem by the sheep *market* a pool, which is called in the Hebrew tongue Bethesda, having five porches.

3 In these lay a great multitude of impotent folk, of blind, halt, withered, waiting for the moving of the water.

4 For an angel went down at a certain season into the pool, and troubled the water: whosoever then first after the troubling of the water stepped in was made whole of whatsoever disease he had.

5 And a certain man was there, which had an infirmity thirty and eight years.

6 When Jesus saw him lie, and knew that he had been now a long time *in that case*, he saith unto him, Wilt thou be made whole?

7 The impotent man answered him, Sir, I have no man, when the water is troubled, to put me into the pool: but while I am coming, another steppeth down before me.

8 Jesus saith unto him, Rise, take up thy bed, and walk.

9 And immediately the man was made whole, and took up his bed, and walked: and on the same day was the ⁝sabbath.

At Jerusalem Impotent Man Healed

"A feast of the Jews" (vs. 1), not a passover, we think, for that most important of all the feasts would probably have been named, as it is in John 2:13, John 6:4 and John 11:55.

The Feasts which the Jews observed in Jesus' day were: Passover in April; Pentecost in June; Tabernacles in October; Dedication in December; Purim, shortly before Passover. Dr. Scofield and most of the older commentaries think it was the Feast of Pentecost that would be fifty days after the passover of John 2:13, according to Deuteronomy 16:9-12. There were seven weeks between the two. This was one of the "three times in a year" when all the males should appear before God at Jerusalem, "the place which the Lord thy God shall choose," he said in Deuteronomy.

The pool of Bethesda, with five porches, has now been excavated and identified; it is inside the wall of Old Jerusalem, near the church of St. Anne. One source says on the wall of the pool is a faded fresco which shows an angel troubling the water. There Jesus found an "impotent man," that is, helpless and paralyzed. Many other sick were there also.

"An angel . . . troubled the water" (vs. 4). Our English Bible is translated from ancient manuscripts into English. There are hundreds of these manuscripts, those of the Old Testament, or different parts of the Old Testament, being written in Hebrew while manuscripts of the New Testament are written in Greek. These manuscripts are copies of the original ones and there are so many of them, and they are so nearly exactly alike, that we can be sure the copies in the main are just like the manuscripts which John, Matthew, Paul and others originally wrote down, directed by the Holy Spirit.

However, there are some small differences caused by the copyists. Some manuscripts have a verse or two which other manuscripts do not have. However, there are only a few such cases in the Bible.

We are told that in the oldest manuscripts, the words *"waiting for the moving of the water"* (vs. 3) and that all of verse 4 are omitted. But it is written that an angel did go down in a certain season and troubled the water and that the Lord miraculously healed the first one to go in. Why not? Certainly the people thought so. It is also certain that if one trusted the Lord for healing, he got it.

If in John 9:6,7 Christ used mud to restore sight to a man's eyes and had him wash at the pool of Siloam and that washing restored his sight, why could God not at certain seasons send an angel to trouble the waters and heal someone there? It would be no greater miracle for the man to be healed by faith, stepping into the water, than for Jesus to heal the man as He did. I believe in all the miracles mentioned by the Bible. If Jesus could not work miracles, then He would not be God.

On request, the elders are to pray for the sick, anointing them with oil in the name of the Lord, "and the prayer of faith shall save the sick," says James 5:14-16. Why not faith when dipped in Bethesda? If God chose to heal Naaman's leprosy by having him dip in the Jordan seven times, why not heal some by having them dip in this pool?

Acts 19:11,12 says:

"And God wrought special miracles by the hands of Paul: So that from his body were brought unto the sick handkerchiefs or aprons, and the diseases departed from them, and the evil spirits went out of them."

There were "special miracles." The fact that some have, without authority and without power, sent out handkerchiefs to radio listeners, does not change the fact that in Paul's case, God used "special miracles," that is, miracles of healing, in unusual ways.

God does work "special miracles" sometimes, as He did for Paul.

God raised the body of a dead man when he was hastily put in upon the bones of Elisha! (II Kings 13:21). Why do some want to leave out or explain away all the miracles? Let God do things in the way He chooses.

But a helpless man lay frustrated and powerless while someone else always got the healing at first entrance to the pool.

How old was the man? We do not know, but he had been paralyzed for thirty-eight years! We are reminded that there are no hard cases with God.

Dr. H. A. Ironside says on this passage:

> Why did Jesus wait so long? That the man might come to the
> end of himself. You and I would not have come to Christ if we
> had not been brought to see our insufficiency.
> You have heard of the poor man who fell into the water.

Unable to swim, he went down once and came up again, and went down again. A strong swimmer stood on the pier, looking on, and the people cried, "Why don't you leap in and save that man?" He said nothing, but let the man go down again, and then he threw off his coat and plunged in and brought him safely to shore. They said, "Why did you wait so long before you went in to save him?" He answered, "He was too strong before. I had to wait till his strength was gone. I had to wait till he could do nothing himself, till he was helpless."

I think Jesus was waiting for that. When the man was brought to the pool first he had high hopes, "It won't be long till I can get in," he thinks, and then someone else got in before him. Over and over again he had gone through this disappointing experience, and now he is ready to give up in despair. It is the despairing soul that Jesus loves to meet in grace. He saves the one who admits, "I cannot do anything to deliver myself."

On Mount Carmel, against 450 prophets of Baal, Elijah prayed down the fire of God. It was no trouble to God that the wood was wet with twelve barrels of water.

God Loves to Show His Power
for Needy Souls

On the cross Jesus saved a vile criminal who admitted he was justly condemned. Hard cases are easy cases with God.

Thank God, I have seen in major campaigns all over America dope addicts, harlots, drunkards, infidels, murderers, false cultists, Gentiles and Jews saved and transformed. I have seen Muslems saved in Arab countries; Muslems, Parsee fire-worshippers, Buddhists in Japan and Korea saved under the Gospel.

Healing? I saw my father, when two consulting physicians agreed he would not live till morning, restored to health in answer to our prayers. I saw my daughter with diphtheria and a fever of 105 healed completely in a few hours, as Mrs. Rice and I knelt by her bed to pray until we had assurance. How astonished the county health officers were the next morning! With Grace well, they took down the quarantine sign!

After two years in a state TB sanitarium in Kerrville, Texas, a woman had wasted away from 140 to only 90 pounds. She could speak only in a whisper, and the doctors said one more hemorrhage and she would die. She was sent home to her husband and two children to die. The home had been sold; the two children given away to relatives, waiting her death. But she was completely healed in answer to prayer, and in two weeks was doing all her own housework and washing. The sale of the house was stopped, the children returned. She has lived over thirty years since, with no tuberculosis.

It is not always God's will to heal. Paul did not have his thorn in the flesh removed. Healers die, too. But God can and often does heal the most difficult diseases in answer to prayer when God gives the faith.

Psalm 81:10 says, "I am the Lord thy God which brought thee out of the land of Egypt: open thy mouth wide, and I will fill it."

So let all who are as helpless as this impotent man, all who are as utterly sinful in heart, trust in God's mercy. It is freely offered to the tottering gray head and to the beardless youth.

A year ago there was a shortage of paper in the publishing field. An enormous increase in the use of paper and cartons, with strikes in Canada in the paper mills, cut down the supply. In publishing THE SWORD OF THE LORD, we use about thirty-five 1,000-pound rolls of newsprint paper weekly.

Our contract with the supplier was for 250,000 copies of a 16-page SWORD OF THE LORD each week. We had been printing some 300,000 weekly. They could not supply that much paper without taking some from contracts with other publishers. So we were told we must cut down the number of papers or reduce the number to 8 or 12 pages weekly.

We contacted other nationwide paper supply houses. No more paper was available beyond our contract! We tried the smaller size for two weeks.

We went to the Lord insistently. We prayed, "Lord, YOU have no paper shortage: others may, YOU do not. YOU are not controlled by strikes and limited supply! YOU have no paper shortage!"

A paper supplier called us on the phone, saying, "I am in a tight. We have cut and put in rolls 250,000 pounds of newsprint—about your paper size. Now the man cannot take it. What will we do?"

Well, to help the man out, we said we would take it! And we laughed for joy! We have no shortage now.

Christ could heal this impotent man, and with a word He did. Jesus said to him, *"Rise, take up thy bed, and walk"* (vs. 8). The man wanted to be healed. He believed Jesus and simply arose, perfectly well, and took up his bed! We don't even know if the man had a chance to thank Jesus properly for healing him.

Note, in Acts 3 Peter and John took the lame man at the Temple by the hand. Jesus sometimes touched blind eyes. A woman who touched the hem of His garment was healed, and so were others who touched Him. Sometimes the apostles anointed with oil as they prayed (as a symbol of Holy Spirit power), and the people were healed (Mark 6:13). It is God who heals, not the method or means. He can do it with or without doctors. He can do it with spittle and mix mud on the eyes and washing in the pool of Siloam or dipping in Bethesda when the water is troubled or at a word. Faith is often given to the afflicted to claim the blessing.

VERSES 10-18:

10 ¶ The Jews therefore said unto him that was cured, It is the sabbath day: it is not lawful for thee to carry *thy* bed.

11 He answered them, He that made me whole, the same said unto me, Take up thy bed, and walk.

12 Then asked they him, What man is that which said unto thee, Take up thy bed, and walk?

13 And he that was healed wist not who it was: for Jesus had conveyed himself away, a multitude being in *that* place.

14 Afterward Jesus findeth him in the temple, and said unto him, Behold, thou art made whole: sin no more, lest a worse thing come unto thee.

15 The man departed, and told the Jews that it was Jesus, which had made him whole.

16 And therefore did the Jews persecute Jesus, and sought to slay him, because he had done these things on the sabbath day.

17 ¶ But Jesus answered them, My Father worketh hitherto, and I work.

18 Therefore the Jews sought the more to kill him, because he not only had broken the sabbath, but said also that God was his Father, making himself equal with God.

Healing on the Sabbath Day Offended the Jews

"It is not lawful for thee to carry thy bed" (vs. 10), the Jews said to the blind man Jesus had healed. They didn't rejoice that he had been healed after so many years. And surely they knew the man. They just saw him carrying his mattress on the Sabbath!

The law in Exodus 20:8-11 says:

"Remember the sabbath day, to keep it holy. Six days shalt thou labour, and do all thy work: But the seventh day is the sabbath of the Lord thy God: in it thou shalt not do any work, thou, nor thy son, nor thy daughter, thy manservant, nor thy maidservant, nor thy cattle, nor thy stranger that is within thy gates: For in six days the Lord made heaven and earth, the sea, and all that in them is, and rested the seventh day: wherefore the Lord blessed the sabbath day, and hallowed it."

In Exodus 35:3 the Jews were forbidden even to light a fire in their houses on the Sabbath day. Enough manna was given the multitude in the wilderness on Friday to last through Saturday. They were not to gather any on that day.

Nehemiah straightly threatened men who tread winepresses; who on the Sabbath sold wood and vegetables. He forbade those gathering outside the gates of Jerusalem to come in until the Sabbath closed at sundown (Neh. 13:15-22).

It was true that Israel was strictly commanded and often reminded that they should keep the Sabbath, that they should not do any of their regular labor on that day of rest nor should their servants or animals.

But Jewish leaders had added a thousand details of instruction as to how to keep the Sabbath. The *International Standard Bible Encyclopaedia* says:

It was during the period between Ezra and the Christian era that the spirit of Jewish legalism flourished. Innumerable restrictions and rules were formulated for the conduct of life under the law. Great principles were lost to sight in the mass of petty details. Two entire treatises of the Mish, *Shabbath* and *Erubhin,* are devoted to the details of Sabbath observance. The subject is touched upon in other parts of the Mish; and in the

Gemara there are extended discussions, with citations of the often divergent opinions of the rabbis (In the Mish *(Shabbath,* vii. 2) there are 39 classes of prohibited actions with regard to the Sabbath, and there is much hair-splitting in working out the details.)—Vol. IV, p. 2631.

The *International Standard Bible Encyclopaedia* continues that Jesus

> . . . set Himself squarely against the current rabbinic restrictions as contrary to the spirit of the original law of the Sabbath. The rabbis seemed to think that the Sabbath was an end in itself, an institution to which the pious Israelite must subject all his personal interests; in other words, that man was made for the Sabbath: man might suffer hardship, but the institution must be preserved inviolate. Jesus, on the contrary, taught that the Sabbath was made for man's benefit. If there should arise a conflict between man's needs and the letter of the Law, man's higher interests and needs must take precedence over the law of the Sabbath (Mt 12:1-14; Mk 2:23-3:6; Lk 6:1-11; also Jn 5:1-18; Lk 13:10-17; 14:1-6).

These many, many detailed rules and interpretations were handed down in oral form and became the Talmud and were held by many Pharisees and others as having as much authority as the Scripture itself.

Jesus seems to have made a special issue of the Sabbath day and of some of the hair-splitting interpretations Jewish leaders had made.

There are seven recorded healings on the Sabbath: A demoniac in Capernaum (Mark 1:21-27); Peter's mother-in-law in Capernaum (Mark 1:29-31); an impotent man in Jerusalem (mentioned here); the man with the withered hand (Mark 3:1-6); the woman bowed together (Luke 13:10-17); the man with dropsy (Luke 14:1-6); and the man born blind (John 9:1-14).

Again and again He healed people on the Sabbath day. He must have had three purposes in mind.

First, the Sabbath Was Made for Man, for Man's Good, for Man's Comfort

Man needed to rest one day in the week. His servant, his ox and ass needed rest. Even about that "high sabbath" (John

19:31), the annual Sabbath which began with the feast of unleavened bread, the eating of the passover, it is commanded that
"no manner of work shall be done in them, save that which every
man must eat, that only may be done of you" (Exod. 12:16). The
Sabbath was not to interfere with serving meals. When His
hungry disciples rubbed out some grain in their hands and ate on
the Sabbath day, Jesus reminded the Pharisees of this and said:

*"Have ye not read what David did, when he was an hungred,
and they that were with him; How he entered into the house of
God, and did eat the shewbread, which was not lawful for him to
eat, neither for them which were with him, but only for the
priests? Or have ye not read in the law, how that on the sabbath
days the priests in the temple profane the sabbath, and are
blameless?"—Matt. 12:3-5.*

In other words, He is saying that the Sabbath was made for the
good of man, and man was not made for the Sabbath.

And when He healed the man with the withered hand, Jesus
pressed this matter upon the Pharisees again:

*"And he said unto them, What man shall there be among you,
that shall have one sheep, and if it fall into a pit on the sabbath
day, will he not lay hold on it, and lift it out? How much then is a
man better than a sheep? Wherefore it is lawful to do well on the
sabbath days. Then saith he to the man, Stretch forth thine
hand. And he stretched it forth; and it was restored whole, like as
the other."—Matt. 12:11-13.*

Second, Christ, the Creator, Is Lord
of the Sabbath

Surely Jesus meant it should be known that "therefore the Son
of man is Lord also of the sabbath" (Mark 2:28; Matt. 12:8). And
Jesus expressed it in Matthew 12:6, "But I say unto you, That in
this place is one greater than the temple." Jesus Christ is the
God who gave the Sabbath. He had the right to interpret it and
to end it. And in that connection He said, "But if ye had known
what this meaneth, I will have mercy and not sacrifice, ye would
not have condemned the guiltless." Oh, God meant the Sabbath

for good and not to be burdensome and hard.

Third, the Sabbath Command Is Ceremonial Law, Not for Us

I think Jesus is clearly showing the end of the Sabbath and the binding ceremonial law. The Sabbath is distinctly a part of the ceremonial law. It is included in the Ten Commandments. But if the Ten Commandments are to represent all the law for the Jews, it is proper there would be some reference to ceremonies. If "six days shalt thou labour" pictures human perfection, with all duty done, then the Sabbath would picture Heaven gained by good works. And the Jews were continually to be reminded by the law as a schoolmaster, to be thinking about Heaven. Yes, and since men had sinned and thus the Heaven to be attained by good works is no more a possibility, then God gave the passover lamb, and Sabbath, picturing a *Sabbath on the first day of the week,* as well as one on the seventh day, picturing that one has rest in Christ and Heaven assured on the very first day of his life as a Christian (Exod. 12:15,16), and a Heaven of rest after life, pictured by six days.

So Hebrews 4:9,10 says, "There remaineth therefore a rest [Greek *sabbatismas*, Sabbath rest] to the people of God. For he that is entered into his rest, he also hath ceased from his own works, as God did from his."

Thus the passover Sabbath pictures salvation before works.

Note the following facts about the Sabbath.

It was made known at Mount Sinai. Nehemiah 9:13,14 says:

"Thou camest down also upon mount Sinai, and spakest with them from heaven, and gavest them right judgments, and true laws, good statutes and commandments: And madest known unto them thy holy sabbath, and commandedst them precepts, statutes, and laws, by the hand of Moses thy servant."

Nobody before the ceremonial law was given ever heard of the Sabbath—not Adam, nor Abraham, nor Jacob. The Lord had set aside the Sabbath in His own mind, but it was not made known until Mount Sinai. Even the statement of creation in Genesis and God's rest on the seventh day was not recorded before Moses.

But the Sabbath was given as a special covenant with Israel. "Moreover also I gave them my sabbaths, to be a sign between me and them, that they might know that I am the Lord that sanctify them" (Ezek. 20:12).

The Lord said the same thing when the Sabbath was given.

"And the Lord spake unto Moses, saying, Speak thou also unto the children of Israel, saying, Verily my sabbaths ye shall keep: for it is a sign between me and you throughout your generations; that ye may know that I am the Lord that doth sanctify you."— Exod. 31:12,13.

Again verse 17 there says, "It is a sign between me and the children of Israel for ever: for in six days the Lord made heaven and earth, and on the seventh day he rested, and was refreshed."

The Sabbath was ceremonial law given to Israel, and given until the time of Christ, when the ceremonial law should be done away.

Jews, for example, are commanded, "Ye shall kindle no fire throughout your habitations upon the sabbath day" (Exod. 35:3). That would do in Palestine, but not in Canada nor Alaska nor for people living in temperate or Arctic zones. It was not intended to be.

Sabbath Is Not Commanded for New Testament Christians

New Testament Christians are plainly commanded not to be judged concerning a Sabbath.

"In whom also ye are circumcised with the circumcision made without hands, in putting off the body of the sins of the flesh by the circumcision of Christ: Buried with him in baptism, wherein also ye are risen with him through the faith of the operation of God, who hath raised him from the dead. And you, being dead in your sins and the uncircumcision of your flesh, hath he quickened together with him, having forgiven you all trespasses; Blotting out the handwriting of ordinances that was against us, which was contrary to us, and took it out of the way, nailing it to

*his cross; And having spoiled principalities and powers, he made a shew of them openly, triumphing over them in it. Let no man therefore judge you in meat, or in drink, or in respect of an holyday, or of the new moon, or of the sabbath days: Which are a shadow of things to come; but the body is of Christ."—*Col. 2:11-17.

Note that the Sabbath is part of that ceremonial law "which are a shadow of things to come; but the body is of Christ."

Other commands of the Ten Commandments are repeated in the New Testament; the command of the Sabbath is not. There is not a single command in the New Testament to keep the Sabbath. Sabbath-breaking as a sin is never mentioned in the New Testament. Just as circumcision, the offering of animal sacrifices, the Levitical priesthood are no more required, so the Sabbath, one of the ceremonies, is done away with, is now fulfilled.

The other commandments involve moral law, written in the heart. A heathen who never saw a Bible knows it is wrong to murder, to commit adultery with another man's wife, to steal his property. A heathen, if he had no calendar and if he had never heard the command about the Sabbath, would not know instinctively that it was wrong to work on the Sabbath day, just as he would not instinctively know it was wrong to eat pork or catfish—part of the same ceremonial laws; and just as a heathen would have no special impulse in heart that he must go to Jerusalem to worship. All those ceremonial laws had their time and place for Jews; they are not now in force for us.

Sunday is not a Sabbath day. It is voluntary. It is a time set apart for worship and rest, and that is proper. But the law of the Sabbath does not apply.

But the Pharisees were more concerned about the little details they had added to the law and interpretations of the law than they were about mercy and righteousness. They hated Jesus and persecuted Him *"and sought to slay him, because he had done these things on the sabbath day"* (vs. 16), and again, "Therefore the Jews sought the more to kill him, because he not only had broken the sabbath, but said also that God was his Father, making himself equal with God" (vs. 18).

Yes, Jesus "broke the sabbath" in the sense of those interpretations of the Pharisees, but He, the Creator and the Maker of the law and greater than the Temple, was Lord of the Sabbath and had a right to change it. He was also thus picturing the end of the ceremonial law, the fulfillment in Christ Himself.

VERSES 19-27:

19 Then answered Jesus and said unto them, Verily, verily, I say unto you, The Son can do nothing of himself, but what he seeth the Father do: for what things soever he doeth, these also doeth the Son likewise.

20 For the Father loveth the Son, and sheweth him all things that himself doeth: and he will shew him greater works than these, that ye may marvel.

21 For as the Father raiseth up the dead, and quickeneth *them;* even so the Son quickeneth whom he will.

22 For the Father judgeth no man, but hath committed all judgment unto the Son:

23 That all *men* should honour the Son, even as they honour the Father. He that honoureth not the Son hon-

oureth not the Father which hath sent him.

24 Verily, verily, I say unto you, He that heareth my word, and believeth on him that sent me, hath everlasting life, and shall not come into condemnation; but is passed from death unto life.

25 Verily, verily, I say unto you, The hour is coming, and now is, when the dead shall hear the voice of the Son of God: and they that hear shall live.

26 For as the Father hath life in himself; so hath he given to the Son to have life in himself;

27 And hath given him authority to execute judgment also, because he is the Son of man.

Jesus Is God Equal With the Father

The Jews wanted to kill Jesus because He had *"said . . . that God was his Father, making himself equal with God"* (vs. 18). He had claimed to be "Lord . . . of the sabbath" (Mark 2:28; Matt. 12:8), and had affirmed boldly, "But I say unto you, That in this place is one greater than the temple" (Matt. 12:6).

And now He insists on His place as equal with the Father. What Jesus did, the Father did. The Father showed the Son everything that He did. Christ had emptied Himself of the outward manifestation of His glory, but the Father showed Him all things the Father would do. When Jesus acted, God was acting.

God the Father could raise the dead, and Jesus could raise the dead (vs. 21). The great God Almighty had turned "all judgment unto the Son" (vs. 22).

So in the judgment seat of Christ, Christians in Heaven will be judged before the Son Himself (I Cor. 3:10-15; II Cor. 5:9,10). So in the judgment of the Gentiles who are to be alive after the tribulation time, Christ will go back to Jerusalem. It will be "when the Son of man shall come in his glory, and all the holy angels with him, then shall he sit upon the throne of his glory: And before him shall be gathered all nations" (Matt. 25:31,32).

And the last judgment of the unsaved dead in Revelation 20:11 where John said, "And I saw a great white throne, and him that sat on it, from whose face the earth and the heaven fled away; and there was found no place for them"—that holy and mighty One in judgment will be the Son Himself, the Lord Jesus Christ. All judgment is given to the Son.

Salvation is given to the Son also. Verse 24 tells us, *"Verily, verily, I say unto you, He that heareth my word, and believeth on him that sent me, hath everlasting life, and shall not come into condemnation; but is passed from death unto life."* But previously in John 3:15,16,18,36, salvation is promised to one who "believeth on the Son." Here the language is different and Jesus is saying that if one hears His Word and believes in the Father who sent Him, he has this everlasting life. In other words, to trust Christ is to trust the Father. The words Jesus gave are the words of the Father. The salvation God gives, Jesus gives. There is no distinction. Christ is identifying Himself with the Father.

"The hour is coming . . . ." (vs. 25). The hour mentioned here has lasted already these nineteen hundred years. Compare "the hour" in verse 25 to verses 28 and 29. The first refers to all this period of time since Jesus spoke, when sinners who hear the voice of Christ, trust Him and have everlasting life. The second hour is one thousand years long, for it involves both the first and second resurrections, with the one thousand years' reign of Christ on earth between them (Rev. 20:1-6).

The first resurrection is of the saved only. It begins at the rapture of the saints (I Thess. 4:14-17) and is finished seven years later at the close of the tribulation, with the resurrection of other Christians slain by the Antichrist who will be raised to reign with Christ (Rev. 20:4). Evidently living saints will be changed, as a part of the first resurrection, both before and after the tribulation. The second resurrection consists altogether of the unsaved dead and comes at the end of Christ's one thousand years' reign on earth, as told in Revelation 20:5,12,13.

It is no harder to believe that "the hour" in verses 28 and 29 should be over one thousand years than to believe that the hour in verse 25 has been over nineteen hundred years. Do not let anybody deceive you into thinking that there is only one general resurrection. (For other verses on the resurrection, see 6:39,40; 11:24-26; I Cor. 15; Dan. 12:2,3).

So in the resurrection of the dead, Christ Himself will speak the word and at *"the voice of the Son of God . . . they that hear shall live"* (vs. 25). Ah, the Father has life in Himself, and Jesus has life in Himself. Jesus would say in John 14:6, "I am the way, the truth, and the life." At the grave of Lazarus, Jesus said to Martha, "I am the resurrection, and the life: he that believeth in me, though he were dead, yet shall he live: And whosoever liveth and believeth in me shall never die." And in proof of what Jesus is claiming, He Himself said the word and Lazarus came out of the grave, as everyone who ever rises from the dead will come at His command.

This is a strong, emphatic and detailed declaration that Christ is God and has all the power, wisdom and authority that God the Father has.

VERSES 28,29:

28 Marvel not at this: for the hour is coming, in the which all that are in the graves shall hear his voice, 29 And shall come forth; they that have done good, unto the resurrection of life; and they that have done evil, unto the resurrection of damnation.

The Two Resurrections

Since all power is given into the hands of Christ and He Himself has the power of life and death, to save whom He will, to condemn whom He will, Christ will be the one who calls people out of the grave (vs. 25). But there are two resurrections: one of the unsaved dead and one of the Christian dead. Those resurrections are mentioned in Daniel 12:2,3:

"And many of them that sleep in the dust of the earth shall awake, some to everlasting life, and some to shame and everlasting contempt. And they that be wise shall shine as the brightness of the firmament; and they that turn many to righteousness as the stars for ever and ever."

Those two resurrections are: one, the resurrection of life; the other, the resurrection of damnation. That a thousand years separates these two resurrections is made clear in Revelation 20:4-6:

"And I saw thrones, and they sat upon them, and judgment was given unto them: and I saw the souls of them that were beheaded for the witness of Jesus, and for the word of God, and which had not worshipped the beast, neither his image, neither had received his mark upon their foreheads, or in their hands; and they lived and reigned with Christ a thousand years. But the rest of the dead lived not again until the thousand years were finished. This is the first resurrection. Blessed and holy is he that hath part in the first resurrection: on such the second death hath no power, but they shall be priests of God and of Christ, and shall reign with him a thousand years."

Then that chapter tells of a thousand years of the millennial reign of Christ on the earth, and of the last rebellion put down, then the last judgment of the unsaved dead is told in Revelation 20:11-15. No saved person will be judged in this judgment. We understand that the saved will be witnesses of the judgment. For when the Christian living are changed and the Christian dead shall rise to meet Christ in the air, then shall "we ever be with the Lord." Where He goes, we will go. Christians will see that judgment of the unsaved dead. Jesus said, "The men of Nineveh shall rise in judgment with this generation, and shall condemn it: because they repented at the preaching of Jonas; and, behold, a greater than Jonas is here" (Matt. 12:41). So Christians will bear witness against lost people. But the two resurrections are a thousand years apart and the Lord Jesus controls both times.

The first resurrection is identified with Christ's coming to receive His own into the air.

"For the Lord himself shall descend from heaven with a shout, with the voice of the archangel, and with the trump of God: and the dead in Christ shall rise first: Then we which are alive and remain shall be caught up together with them in the clouds, to meet the Lord in the air: and so shall we ever be with the Lord."—I Thess. 4:16,17.

The same truth is given in I Corinthians 15:51,52. Then there follows the wedding feast in Heaven during the time of the tribulation on earth, and Christians return to reign with Christ a thousand years and then the unsaved dead will be raised and caught up to meet the Lord in a judgment scene out in space. That will be when this world is being purged with fire "against the day of judgment and perdition of ungodly men" (II Pet. 3:7).

VERSES 30-47:

30 I can of mine own self do nothing: as I hear, I judge: and my judgment is just; because I seek not mine own will, but the will of the Father which hath sent me.

31 If I bear witness of myself, my witness is not true.

32 ¶ There is another that beareth witness of me; and I know that the witness which he witnesseth of me is true.

33 Ye sent unto John, and he bare witness unto the truth.

34 But I receive not testimony from man: but these things I say, that ye might be saved.

35 He was a burning and a shining light: and ye were willing for a season to rejoice in his light.

36 ¶ But I have greater witness than *that* of John: for the works which the Father hath given me to finish, the same works that I do, bear witness of me, that the Father hath sent me.

37 And the Father himself, which hath sent me, hath borne witness of me. Ye have neither heard his voice at any time, nor seen his shape.

38 And ye have not his word abiding in you: for whom he hath sent, him ye believe not.

39 ¶ Search the scriptures; for in

them ye think ye have eternal life: and they are they which testify of me.

40 And ye will not come to me, that ye might have life.

41 I receive not honour from men.

42 But I know you, that ye have not the love of God in you.

43 I am come in my Father's name, and ye receive me not: if another shall come in his own name, him ye will receive.

44 How can ye believe, which re-ceive honour one of another, and seek not the honour that *cometh* from God only?

45 Do not think that I will accuse you to the Father: there is *one* that accuseth you, *even* Moses, in whom ye trust.

46 For had ye believed Moses, ye would have believed me: for he wrote of me.

47 But if ye believe not his writings, how shall ye believe my words?

Witnesses to Jesus

The Lord Jesus says that His judgment is the judgment of the Father. His decision is the Father's decision. Jesus did nothing separate from God the Father.

In verse 31 He said, *"If I bear witness of myself, my witness is not true."* That is, by the laws of evidence not necessarily true. Of course, the Lord Jesus would always tell the truth, but as Dr. Scofield says: "Our Lord, defending His Messianic claims before Jews who denied those claims, accepts the biblical rule of evidence, which required 'two witnesses' (John 8.17; Num. 35.30; Deut. 17.6)." But besides Jesus, there are other witnesses as to His deity and power.

1. There was John the Baptist, as verses 33 to 35 say. Jesus did not need the testimony of any man, but the greatest quibbler, the greatest scoffer, could not deny these witnesses. And how the crowds went to hear this John the Baptist, *"a burning and a shining light"* (vs. 35). He was burning with the power of the Holy Spirit (Luke 1:15,16). He said, "Behold the Lamb of God!" (1:36). He said, "I saw, and bare record that this is the Son of God" (1:34).

2. Jesus had the witness of His works. The miracles of Jesus did not prove His deity, but they proved He was from God, and His word about His deity could be believed.

3. The Father bore witness of the Son. In a voice from Heaven, audible to multitudes, He said, "This is my beloved Son, in whom I am well pleased" (Matt. 3:17), and, "Thou art my beloved Son; in thee I am well pleased" (Luke 3:22).

Not only then, but on the Mount of Transfiguration, once more the Father said, "This is my beloved Son . . .hear ye him" (Matt. 17:5). And later on when Jesus lifted up His voice and said, "Father, glorify thy name," a voice was heard from Heaven saying, "I have both glorified it, and will glorify it again" (12:28).

And not only that word from Heaven, but God's Word abiding in the heart of saved people would bear witness that Jesus was the Messiah, the Son of God, as verse 38 tells us.

4. The Scriptures bear witness to Jesus. The Jews thought that by keeping the law they would be saved. Paul said later, "They being ignorant of God's righteousness, and going about to establish their own righteousness, have not submitted themselves unto the righteousness of God" (Rom. 10:3).

"Search the Scriptures . . . They Testify of Me"

Paul reminded them, "Christ is the end of the law for righteousness to every one that believeth" (Rom. 10:4). One who pretended to love the Scriptures and follow the Scriptures was foolish and with some arrogant, spiritual blindness did not see the Lord Jesus in those Old Testament Scriptures.

By faith righteous Abel had recognized Christ in the bloody sacrifice he offered. Why should not other Jews have seen it? All the way through, the Mosaic Law pictured Christ in the Levitical priesthood, in the sacrifices, in the tabernacle itself—its colors, its boards, its sockets; in the golden candlestick, in the table of shewbread, in the altar of incense. Christ was pictured in the smitten rock out of which gushed the stream of water which saved the thirsty nation in the wilderness. Christ is pictured in the brazen serpent so that those bitten by the fiery serpents could turn to the snake on a pole, look and be healed.

Every prophet in the Old Testament preached salvation by faith in Christ. "To him give all the prophets witness, that through his name whosoever believeth in him shall receive remission of sins," says Acts 10:43.

How Jesus rebuked those disciples who did not believe He was risen from the dead!

"Then he said unto them, O fools, and slow of heart to believe

all that the prophets have spoken: Ought not Christ to have suf-
fered these things, and to enter into his glory? And beginning at
Moses and all the prophets, he expounded unto them in all the
scriptures the things concerning himself.''—Luke 24:25-27.

One who reads the Old Testament and doesn't see Christ there is a fool in his heart, with a perversion of heart and will which keeps him from seeing the truth. Christ and His death are pictured so well in Isaiah 53, in Psalm 22. The Scriptures witness to Christ.

Since the Pharisees doted on the laws of Moses, that is, in keeping rules and commands, like the rich young ruler who said about the commandments, "All these have I kept from my youth up," so they depended on salvation by keeping the law. But Jesus said that Moses, who witnessed to the coming Messiah so strongly, will witness against them, for "Moses . . . wrote of me," He said.

This also proves that the Pentateuch was written by Moses, and that the Graff-Wellhausen theory is not only foolish, and unscholarly, but it scoffs at the clear statement of Jesus.

Again we remind you that Christ and the Bible stand or fall together. And Mark 8:38 says, "Whosoever therefore shall be ashamed of me and of my words in this adulterous and sinful generation; of him also shall the Son of man be ashamed, when he cometh in the glory of his Father with the holy angels."

Summing up: We have these witnesses. There is His own testimony; there is John the Baptist's testimony; the miracles He performed; the witness of His Father's voice; and there is the Word of God. All agree that Jesus is the Son of God, which should come into the world.

John 6

AFTER these things Jesus went over the sea of Galilee, which is *the sea* of Tiberias.

2 And a great multitude followed him, because they saw his miracles which he did on them that were diseased.

3 And Jesus went up into a mountain, and there he sat with his disciples.

4 And the passover, a feast of the Jews, was nigh.

The Feeding of the Five Thousand

Nowhere is the use of the four different Gospels better shown than in this passage. The four Gospel writers, Matthew, Mark, Luke and John, inspired of God, all tell about the feeding of the 5,000, which is rather unusual since, aside from the crucifixion, most of the instances are not mentioned by all the writers.

This account is found in Matthew 14, Mark 6, Luke 9. The accounts are alike, yet each one adds details, under divine inspiration, which the others do not give.

John tells the time of year—"near the passover" (vs. 4), therefore, in the month of April. Mark says that the grass was green, as you would expect in the spring (Mark 6:39).

The other accounts say that it was a desert place, that is, where no one lived; and John says it was a mountain (vs. 3).

We speak of this as "The Feeding of the 5,000" but there were about 5,000 men, besides the women and children (Matt. 14:21).

John gives the word about Philip and Andrew (vss. 7,8) and tells that there was a little boy who had five barley loaves and two small fishes. The other Gospels do not tell where the food came from.

"The sea of Galilee, which is the sea of Tiberias" (vs. 1)— named for the town Tiberias on the west middle side. The sea is also the sea of Chinnereth or Chinneroth (Num. 34:11; Josh. 12:3) and lake Gennesaret (Luke 5:1). It is more lake than sea,

only 7 or 8 miles wide, and 15 miles long. It is fresh water, fed by the Jordan River, which branches from the foot of Mount Hermon on the north and flows through the Sea of Galilee down to the Dead Sea some 60 miles south. The Dead Sea, or Salt Sea, has no outlet but evaporation. It is the saltiest sea water known.

The Sea of Galilee is over 600 feet below sea level, and the Jordan descends to about 1300 feet below sea level at the Dead Sea.

The place "over the sea of Galilee" from where He was evidently meant Jesus came from further south by boat on over to the west side of Galilee, for the place was "a desert place belonging to the city called Bethsaida" (Luke 9:10). Bethsaida is thought to have been at the north end of the sea, a short distance east from Capernaum, but the place is not certain. Mark 1:29 says of Jesus, "Forthwith, when they were come out of the synagogue [in Capernaum], they entered into the house of Simon and Andrew . . ." (1:44). It was "a desert place," not sandy and barren but simply uninhabited, near Bethsaida. There was "green grass" there (Mark 6:39), "much grass," John 6:10 tells us.

"The passover, a feast of the Jews, was nigh" (vs. 4). It has been a year since the passover and the events of John 2:13. *Halley's Handbook* says verse 4 was "one year before Jesus' death . . ·. . Jesus Himself did not go to Jerusalem this Passover, because on His previous visit they had formed a plot to kill him (5:1,18). It was probably the first Passover He had missed going to Jerusalem since He was twelve. He celebrated it by working one of His most marvelous miracles for the Passover-bound multitudes."

VERSES 5,6:

5 ¶ When Jesus then lifted up *his* eyes, and saw a great company come unto him, he saith unto Philip, Whence shall we buy bread, that these may eat?

6 And this he said to prove him: for he himself knew what he would do.

The Compassion of Jesus Would Feed the Multitude

The feeding of the five thousand is the only miracle told in all the four Gospels, so it is intended to have special attention. Here in John the crowd is called *"a great company"* (vs. 5). But Matthew 14:21 says, "And they that had eaten were about five thousand men, beside women and children." Mark 6:44 says, ". . . about five thousand men," as does Luke 9:14.

Why did Jesus feed the multitude miraculously? Because He "was moved with compassion toward them, because they were as sheep not having a shepherd" (Mark 6:34). There we are told that because of His compassion He "began to teach them many things." Matthew 14:14 says that Jesus "was moved with compassion toward them, and he healed their sick." But the account of the feeding of the five thousand is immediately following and we know that Jesus had compassion not only for their ignorance and their sickness but for the hunger of the weary bodies of those who had stayed to hear Him. The apostles cared about this and pleaded that Jesus would "send them away" to buy food. Well, the heart of the Lord Jesus is more concerned about their needs than anyone else!

How many provisions God makes about food for us! So we should pray, "Give us day by day our daily bread" (Luke 11:3). We should remember to bless the Lord "who satisfieth thy mouth with good things; so that thy youth is renewed like the eagle's" (Ps. 103:5). The liberal giver will be blessed with barns filled with plenty and presses bursting out with grape juice (Prov. 3:10). Psalm 107:9 reminds us, "He . . . filleth the hungry soul." And blessed are those who give food to the poor (Isa. 58:7; Ezek. 18:7). God gave manna faithfully to Israel for forty years in the wilderness. And the angel prepared food and drink for desolate Elijah as he fled for his life (I Kings 19:5-8).

God cares, and Jesus cares, for our daily provision. In truth, all animal-kind as well as human beings are dependent upon His remembering (Ps. 136:25; Ps. 104:10-22). We must remember that Christ the Creator is the Sustainer of all things (Col. 1:17).

How good it is to remember that the compassionate heart of the Lord Jesus cares about our food and our comfort!

The disciples thought of there having passed many hours since these thousands had eaten and they suggested He send them away to nearby villages to buy food (Matt. 14:15; Mark 6:36; Luke 9:12), but Jesus would not send them away hungry.

The Unbelief of These Disciples

The Synoptic Gospels (Matthew, Mark and Luke) all add what is omitted here in John. Jesus said, "They need not depart; give ye them to eat" (Matt. 14:16; Mark 6:37; Luke 9:13). This would be a miracle of creation and Christ would have them do it, but they could not because of unbelief!

Elisha could say the word and the widow's oil would be multiplied (II Kings 4:1-7). He made a small gift of bread feed a hundred hungry men (II Kings 4:42,44). Those were miracles of actually creating food. So with Elijah when the widow's barrel of meal and cruse of oil did not fail but continually produced more while Elijah was with her in the famine (I Kings 17:8-16).

So these disciples could have, at Christ's command, fed the multitudes miraculously. Remember, the nine disciples left at the foot of the Mount of Transfiguration could not heal the demon-possessed boy, but Jesus said it was because of their unbelief (Mark 9:28,29; Matt. 17:19,20). The disciples had been given power over unclean spirits, and Jesus was greatly vexed that they could not cast out the demons. He said, "O faithless and perverse generation, how long shall I be with you, and suffer you?" (Luke 9:41).

Our carnal minds shrink from this teaching, but the promise of Jesus to all of us in John 14:12 is, "Verily, verily, I say unto you, He that believeth on me, the works that I do shall he do also; and greater works than these shall he do; because I go unto my Father." And surely the command and promise of Mark 11:22-24, given at the incident of the cursed and withered fig tree, is for us:

"And Jesus answering saith unto them, Have faith in God. For verily I say unto you, That whosoever shall say unto this mountain, Be thou removed, and be thou cast into the sea; and shall not doubt in his heart, but shall believe that those things which

he saith shall come to pass; he shall have whatsoever he saith. Therefore I say unto you, What things soever ye desire, when ye pray, believe that ye receive them, and ye shall have them."

The promise of Mark 9:23, in connection with the healing of the devil-possessed boy, is for us, too: "If thou canst believe, all things are possible to him that believeth."

Miracles are not playthings. They are rare. They can come only in the will of God. But they are available when God gives the faith for them. Jesus knew what He would do here. Often our unbelief is because we are not close enough to Him to know His will.

VERSES 7-9:

7 Philip answered him, Two hundred pennyworth of bread is not sufficient for them, that every one of them may take a little.

8 One of his disciples, Andrew, Simon Peter's brother, saith unto him,

9 There is a lad here, which hath five barley loaves, and two small fishes: but what are they among so many?

One Boy's Lunch Feeds Five Thousand

"Five barley loaves"! (vs. 9). Flat, tough, pancake-like loaves such as Arab people eat today, perhaps. Enough for a boy's lunch

with *"two small fishes."* But no more are available, so these must do. But when you add Jesus to what the boy had, there was plenty for everybody. "God and one are always a majority." Friend, whatever you have is enough if it is all given to the Lord Jesus and if He blesses it.

A rod in the hand of Moses was enough to open the Red Sea, to bring a river of water enough for three and a half million people and their cattle. There was no power in the rod but God's power was available to faith.

With one stone and a sling, David conquered the giant Goliath, though armed and armored as he was. God did it.

The small pot of oil in a widow's home was enough to free her boys from slavery and enough to live on when the oil was multiplied.

Pitchers and lamps in the hands of Gideon's three hundred brought victory over multitudes of Midianites.

It is pleasing to God that

". . . not many wise men after the flesh, not many mighty, not many noble, are called: But God hath chosen the foolish things of the world to confound the wise; and God hath chosen the weak things of the world to confound the things which are mighty; And base things of the world, and things which are despised, hath God chosen, yea, and things which are not, to bring to nought things that are: That no flesh should glory in his presence."—I Cor. 1:26-29.

God could better use Paul with a thorn in the flesh than without it. What we need is not great human strength, not great human learning but all we have wholly given over to God in faith, that He may use us and ours. It is God's work, not ours; God's strength, not ours; God's wisdom, not ours. With God, 'one can chase a thousand and two can put ten thousand to flight.'

I am certain that the lad did not go hungry after giving Jesus his lunch.

———

VERSES 10-14:

10 And Jesus said, Make the men sit down. Now there was much grass in the place. So the men sat down, in number about five thousand.

11 And Jesus took the loaves; and when he had given thanks, he distributed to the disciples, and the disciples to them that were set down; and likewise of the fishes as much as they would.

12 When they were filled, he said unto his disciples, Gather up the fragments that remain, that nothing be lost.

13 Therefore they gathered *them* together, and filled twelve baskets with the fragments of the five barley loaves, which remained over and above unto them that had eaten.

14 Then those men, when they had seen the miracle that Jesus did, said, This is of a truth that prophet that should come into the world.

Orderliness Pleases God

Shall we have here a crowding about, to grab food, leaving debris on all the ground? No. First, all must be seated on the grass. They were to sit in groups, in ranks "by fifties in a company" (Luke 9:14). "Let all things be done decently and in order" (I Cor. 14:40). So Jesus broke and multiplied the food; the twelve apostles, with baskets of bread and fish, passed through and served the seated people. And when all had eaten all they wanted, there were twelve baskets of the fish and bread left over. Notice here Jesus' love of order, and that He was not wasteful.

God uses human instruments to bring men to Christ. This means if some soul doesn't know about Christ, hasn't heard the Gospel, we are to blame. Oh, what a tremendous responsibility it is to be a Christian! So there is reason to plan a special time or times for house-to-house soul winning, and have detailed oversight for better work. We suppose Jesus would have divided people into age groups for Sunday school teaching. He would have planned adequate seating for great crowds in revival services.

Save the leftovers! The food they ate was for the hungry people there, but the twelve baskets were for us, showing that had there been a million people, there would have been provision for them, too, and showing that Jesus has concern for us as much as for them.

Thrift, careful use of money and things, reliability in all our church work, is taught here. If something is worth doing, it is worth enough attention to make sure it is done well.

Once a young man living in my home (now a seminary president) was asked to do a small task. He did not seem to do it as well as some would think he should. So one of my daughters, nine or ten years old, protested. "There are just two ways of doing things—the John R. Rice way and the wrong way." She is to be forgiven for her filial loyalty to her father; but we were all reminded that every task, no matter how small or secular it might seem, should be done well for Christ's sake.

All that multitude were quiet and orderly. Look at Jesus standing there with the bread in hand. He gave thanks, then He gave to the disciples and they distributed to the people who sat on the grass in orderly groups (vs. 11). Our Lord gave thanks. We think He always did. By His thanks, the two disciples on the road to Emmaus after His resurrection recognized Him when they sat to eat with that poor stranger who had called them "fools, and slow of heart" to believe the resurrection. Their hearts burned so within them as He expounded to them the Scriptures about Himself, but they suddenly knew Him when they saw the sweet, familiar way He broke the bread and blessed it (Luke 24:13-32).

How shameful ever to eat without openly and sincerely thanking God for our food. We need to, and those who see us, need it.

At Seattle, Washington, where I was engaged in a citywide revival campaign, my wife, daughter and I ate at a cafeteria. When we bowed our heads for thanksgiving quietly, without ostentation but without embarrassment, a man wrote this note and left it at our table as he left: "I was greatly moved to see your family pray at the table. That is the first time I have ever seen that in thirty years. Please pray for me." I ran to the entrance to meet him, but he had disappeared.

On a train from Chicago to Los Angeles, I had my Bible with

me in the diner and put it under my seat at a table. I bowed my head silently to thank God for the food. A man in the diner, an executive of General Motors, en route to bury his dead wife in Los Angeles, followed me through the car, back to my seat, to ask me how to be saved. I showed him and he trusted Christ. His father-in-law then wrote me that he had immediately claimed the Lord openly and two years later he attended my revival campaign in Pontiac, Michigan, and brought his pastor to meet me.

Oh, is our heart always habitually thanking God as we are commanded to do? "In every thing give thanks: for this is the will of God in Christ Jesus concerning you" (I Thess. 5:18).

The miracle convinced many that Jesus was the "Prophet" that Moses had promised in Deuteronomy 18:15,18, the "Prophet" that the people asked John about in John 1:21. Miracles are sometimes greatly used to convict and to save those who know of them. It was so when Elijah called down fire from Heaven in I Kings 18:36-39, and the people, long backslidden, cried out, "The Lord, he is the God." It was so when Peter and John saw the crippled man healed at the Beautiful gate of the Temple in Acts 3, and when Lazarus was raised from the dead many believed on Him (John 12:9-11).

The disciples in Acts 4:29,30 prayed, "Lord, behold their threatenings: and grant unto thy servants, that with all boldness they may speak thy word, By stretching forth thine hand to heal; and that signs and wonders may be done by the name of thy holy child Jesus." We need miracles to give us boldness in preaching and in winning souls. One can boldly represent a God who proves Himself for us.

The miracle here made a great impression so that people wanted immediately to enthrone Jesus (vss. 14,15).

VERSES 15-17:

15 ¶ When Jesus therefore perceived that they would come and take him by force, to make him a king, he departed again into a mountain him-

self alone.
16 And when even was *now* come, his disciples went down unto the sea, 17 And entered into a ship, and went over the sea toward Că-pĕr'-nă-ŭm. And it was now dark, and Jesus was not come to them.

After Great Weariness, Jesus Spends Night in Prayer

Matthew and Mark tell this story also, but Luke does not. Jesus *"departed again into a mountain himself alone"* (vs. 15). Why? He knew some wanted to make Him king by force and He was troubled about it. He would be sad that some would rather have a king who provided food and healing for them, than to have Him as their Saviour! (See vss. 26 and 27.) But Matthew 14:23, like Mark 6:46, says that "he went up into a mountain apart *to pray."* Were the people so weary that they were in distress after listening to Jesus' teaching so long? Then what about the weary Lord Jesus? He had come apart to this place to rest but was crowded by the people. Now after a prolonged day, He must go up into the mountain to spend most of the night in prayer!

Oh, but weariness must not keep Him from long prayer. With lovingkindness He urged the disciples to get into a boat and leave, but He must pray. And there in the mountain in prayer Jesus stayed from the evening until "the fourth watch of the night" (after 3:00 a.m.) and came to the help of the laboring disciples (Matt. 14:25).

Before the feeding of the five thousand, Jesus and the apostles had been pressed by the people that "they had no leisure so much as to eat" (Mark 6:31). And Jesus had said to the disciples, "Come ye yourselves apart into a desert place, and rest a while." But the rushing crowds had followed them, surrounded them, and Jesus thought more of the needs of the hungry people than of His own utter weariness. And now, concerned about His disciples, He sent them away, not pressing on them to pray in their exhaustion, but He Himself must pray nearly all night.

We know that at other times Jesus "went out into a mountain to pray, and continued all night in prayer to God" (Luke 6:12). And when Jesus went up on the Mount of Transfiguration, He "went up into a mountain to pray" (Luke 9:28). He must have prayed all night then, because Luke 9:37 says, "And it came to pass, that on the next day, when they were come down from the hill, much people met him."

We need to learn from Jesus:

1. The urgent need to pray, to continue to pray, as Scriptures command in Luke 18:1; Romans 12:12; Colossians 4:2; Ephesians 6:18 and I Thessalonians 5:17.

2. We need sometimes to withdraw to a lonely place where we will not be disturbed nor distracted from long, private prayer.

3. Often we should give up sleep to pray in the night, as did Jesus, and as does the model man in the parable of Luke 11:5-8, "at midnight" and with "importunity."

VERSES 18-21:

18 And the sea arose by reason of a great wind that blew.

19 So when they had rowed about five and twenty or thirty furlongs, they see Jesus walking on the sea, and drawing nigh unto the ship: and they were afraid.

20 But he saith unto them, It is I; be not afraid.

21 Then they willingly received him into the ship: and immediately the ship was at the land whither they went.

Jesus Walks on the Water

In the night a great wind arose. The disciples were rowing in tempestuous waves. They had rowed *"about five and twenty or thirty furlongs"* (vs. 19). With eight furlongs to a mile, they had rowed four or five miles. They took, we suppose, eight or more hours since sunset to this time "in the fourth watch," past 3:00 a.m. Jesus "saw them toiling in rowing; for the wind was contrary unto them" (Mark 6:48). The feeding of the five thousand was in "a desert place belonging to the city called Bethsaida" (Luke 9:10). Now the disciples are rowing against the wind to go "unto Bethsaida," and it should not have been far but the wind had blown them, we understand, "in the midst of the sea" (Mark

6:45,47). And they had rowed four or five miles without getting to their intended landing!

Now, after hours of toiling, Jesus came to them in the night, walking on the water (vs. 19). They needed Him. Yes, and they needed the miracle to comfort and assure them.

"They were afraid" (vs. 19). Both Matthew and Mark tell that they thought Jesus was "a spirit," a ghost. Jesus said, *"It is I; be not afraid"* (vs. 20). We poor mortals, so alien from the supernatural, are somewhat like Adam, who found himself naked and ran from God. God appeared to Ezekiel: "And when I saw it, I fell upon my face." When Isaiah saw the vision of God in the Temple and heard the seraphims cry, "Holy, holy, holy, is the Lord of hosts," he cried out, "Woe is me! for I am undone; because I am a man of unclean lips . . . ."

When John saw the glorified Jesus, he "fell at his feet as dead." When the angel appeared to Zacharias and to Mary and to the shepherds, he must always say, "Fear not," because they were so troubled. So these disciples were afraid but Jesus said, "Be not afraid."

Really, the disciples had not needed to be troubled during these bitter hours of fighting the waves. Jesus knew where they were and had good reason to let them wait for His help and deliverance.

The disciples had not considered the marvelous feeding of the five thousand, so now they were amazed at the miracle. Later Jesus miraculously fed the four thousand with seven loaves and a few fishes, and there again the disciples said in unbelief, "From whence can a man satisfy these men with bread here in the wilderness" (Mark 8:4). And afterward, crossing Galilee again, they were greatly distressed because they had brought no bread. Jesus must remind them of those two tremendous miracles of creating bread. So the disciples, like us, had "the sin which doth so easily beset us," the sin of unbelief (Heb. 12:1). Now these disciples needed the miraculous deliverance, and Jesus meant it for their good.

The wind ceased when Jesus came into the boat and immediately they were at land.

The unbelief of the disciples was more noticeable because in a storm on Galilee once before Jesus had calmed the wind and waves by a word.

Peter Walks on the Water, Too

John does not tell us, but Matthew does, that Peter, seeing it was Jesus walking on the water, asked if he might come to Him. Dear, lovable, impetuous Peter!

"And when Peter was come down out of the ship, he walked on the water, to go to Jesus. But when he saw the wind boisterous, he was afraid; and beginning to sink, he cried, saying, Lord, save me. And immediately Jesus stretched forth his hand, and caught him, and said unto him, O thou of little faith, wherefore didst thou doubt?"—Matt. 14:29-31.

That was remarkable faith for a time. It took faith to even try it. A great preacher had a favorite sermon titled, "Peter, Stay in the Boat." He thought it was presumptuous for Peter to want to walk on the water, but the Bible does not hint at that. In fact, Jesus bade Peter come, and he went. When his faith failed, Jesus rebuked him for his little faith, saying, "Wherefore didst thou doubt?" At least he had more faith than the other disciples had. God never rebukes people for big prayers or big faith but only for little faith.

VERSES 22-27:

22 ¶ The day following, when the people which stood on the other side of the sea saw that there was none other boat there, save that one where-into his disciples were entered, and that Jesus went not with his disciples into the boat, but *that* his disciples were gone away alone;

23 (Howbeit there came other boats from Tiberias nigh unto the place where they did eat bread, after that the Lord had given thanks:)

24 When the people therefore saw that Jesus was not there, neither his disciples, they also took shipping, and came to Că-pĕr-́nă-ŭm, seeking for Jesus.

25 And when they had found him on the other side of the sea, they said unto him, Rabbi, when camest thou hither?

26 Jesus answered them and said, Verily, verily, I say unto you, Ye seek me, not because ye saw the miracles, but because ye did eat of the loaves, and were filled.

27 Labour not for the meat which perisheth, but for that meat which endureth unto everlasting life, which the Son of man shall give unto you: for him hath God the Father sealed.

Crowds Follow Jesus

The crowd, fed and content, saw the disciples leave in a boat without Jesus. He had slipped away into the mountain to pray, and they could not find Him. Perhaps they thought He had some way gone back to His home in Capernaum. So they "took shipping," and went to Capernaum, we suppose, and landed at Bethsaida and the home of Peter and Andrew. And Jesus went to Capernaum nearby. They wanted Jesus, but how had He come? They had seen the disciples leave without Him.

Jesus knew their hearts. He knew and had compassion on these poor sinful people, as sheep without a shepherd. But He knew their aim. They wanted Him for a King (vs. 15 above). What a king it would be who could feed them without work!

They were not awed by the miracle, did not feel their sinful un-worthiness. When they should be seeking a Saviour, they sought the easy, lazy life. They wanted to be filled with bread, not blessed in soul.

It is true Jesus had great compassion on the thoughtless, un-reliable, worldly and self-seeking crowd. He was concerned when they were hungry and weary. But He did not want to be a worldly king who would feed them without work and leave them in their sins.

Mercy and compassion for the needy are great motives. How often the Scripture teaches us to give to the needy, to love the unworthy, to provide for those who have not!

"He that hath pity upon the poor lendeth unto the Lord; and that which he hath given will he pay him again" (Prov. 19:17), He said.

"Give, and it shall be given unto you," Jesus said (Luke 6:38).

"The liberal soul shall be made fat," says Proverbs 11:25.

James 2:15,16 reminds us: "If a brother or sister be naked, and destitute of daily food, And one of you say unto them, Depart in peace, be ye warmed and filled; notwithstanding ye give them not those things which are needful to the body; what doth it profit?"

James 1:27 says, "pure religion and undefiled" is "to visit the fatherless and widows in their affliction, and to keep himself unspotted from the world." And the Lord gave specific instructions, "When thou doest thine alms . . ." (Matt. 6:2). But in Christ this compassion is balanced by concern for the best things for everybody.

If God willed it, could He not make earth a paradise of plenty, with food and drink without labor, without thrift or character? But God does not want to do that. No, God cursed the ground for man's sake and for man's good (Gen. 3:17). Work is a great blessing. If a man were a millionaire, he still should have good, hard work to do for the good of himself and others. It is not only a crime to be useless but a great sorrow not to be needed.

To give when it erodes character and promotes laziness is wrong. Jesus would have us care for all who need help but not to make them dependent and irresponsible. The rulers at Rome, with conquering armies bringing in riches from enslaved countries, set out to feed the rabble, the mass of people, giving bread without cost. They intended to keep the restless people satisfied with great spectacles in the Colosseum and in Circus Maximus with their gladiatorial combats, but food and entertainment without moral responsibility meant decay and ruin to Rome. With early thrift and character now destroyed within, they fell easy prey to invaders.

Karl Marx and the socialist program say, "From each according to his ability and to each according to his need." But that is not the same as the Bible principle, that "whatsoever a man soweth, that shall he also reap." People who earn more should get more. People who earn less should get less.

In the church at Thessalonica, some ate at the church tables but worked not at all. And Paul was inspired of God to command, ". . . that if any would not work, neither should he eat." He reminded them that when he was among them, "neither did we eat any man's bread for nought; but wrought with labour and travail night and day, that we might not be chargeable to any of you" (II Thess. 3:6-10).

American labor unions have insisted that no one work for less than a specified union wage, and they cry for shorter hours, more pay, more retirement pay. Now our economy cannot balance itself by competition, by the law of supply and demand. Half the population in America is supported by taxation, either of those who are employees of some area of government or who are on welfare, supported by heavier and heavier taxes in county, state and nation.

So we have continued inflation, and billions of dollars in unpaid and unpayable deficits and debts. It is no longer thought a disgrace to live off others, without work. We "owe everybody a living" say the politicians who cater to the votes of those who would ride free! The increase in crime and godlessness is surely tied on to the decrease in moral responsibility for hard work and earned respectability.

We are commanded to "love thy neighbour as thyself" (Matt. 19:19). But we are also commanded, "Let love be without dissimulation. Abhor that which is evil; cleave to that which is good" (Rom. 12:9).

The love and compassion of Jesus that brought Him to die for sinners and moved Him to feed the multitude did not lead Him to turn from saving souls to feeding bodies indiscriminately.

Should helpless and needy widows be supported by the church? Yes, if such widows are "widows indeed," but not if she have children or nephews to care for her, says I Timothy 5:3. The Scripture continues:

"Let not a widow be taken into the number under threescore years old, having been the wife of one man, Well reported of for good works; if she have brought up children, if she have lodged strangers, if she have washed the saints' feet, if she have relieved the afflicted, if she have diligently followed every good work. But the younger widows refuse: for when they have begun to wax wanton against Christ, they will marry; Having damnation, because they have cast off their first faith. And withal they learn to be idle, wandering about from house to house; and not only idle, but tattlers also and busybodies, speaking things which they ought not. I will therefore that the younger women marry, bear children, guide the house, give none occasion to the adversary to speak reproachfully. For some are already turned aside after Satan. If any man or woman that believeth have widows, let them relieve them, and let not the church be charged; that it may relieve them that are widows indeed."—I Tim. 5:9-16.

Then we are commanded to give certain elders double honor (support) if they deserve it: "Let the elders that rule well be counted worthy of double honour, especially they who labour in the word and doctrine." Why? Because "the labourer is worthy of his reward" (I Tim. 5:17,18). And we are commanded, "But seek ye first the kingdom of God, and his righteousness; and all these things shall be added unto you" (Matt. 6:33). And all are commanded in verse 27 here in John 6, *"Labour not for the meat which perisheth, but for that meat which endureth unto everlasting life, which the Son of man shall give unto you: for him hath God the Father sealed."*

All of us are to labor, to seek for the meat of the Word of God, the teaching of Jesus, which leads to everlasting life.

Jeremiah 15:16 says, "Thy words were found, and I did eat them; and thy word was unto me the joy and rejoicing of mine heart: for I am called by thy name, O Lord God of hosts."

How Jesus stressed this truth! In Matthew 4:4 Jesus quoted from Deuteronomy 8:3, "Man shall not live [or be nourished] by bread alone, but by every word that proceedeth out of the mouth of God."

Matthew 6:24-34 stresses that one "cannot serve God and mammon" (money). The sparrows are fed, the wild flowers are beautifully clothed; so we should not be anxious for food and raiment but seek first the kingdom of God.

VERSES 28-36:

28 Then said they unto him, What shall we do, that we might work the works of God?

29 Jesus answered and said unto them, This is the work of God, that ye believe on him whom he hath sent.

30 They said therefore unto him, What sign shewest thou then, that we may see, and believe thee? what dost thou work?

31 Our fathers did eat manna in the desert; as it is written, He gave them bread from heaven to eat.

32 Then Jesus said unto them, Verily, verily, I say unto you, Moses gave you not that bread from heaven; but my Father giveth you the true bread from heaven.

33 For the bread of God is he which cometh down from heaven, and giveth life unto the world.

34 Then said they unto him, Lord, evermore give us this bread.

35 And Jesus said unto them, I am the bread of life: he that cometh to me shall never hunger; and he that believeth on me shall never thirst.

36 But I said unto you, That ye also have seen me, and believe not.

Christ Is the Bread From Heaven

The only way to please God is to put your trust in Jesus Christ for salvation. Verses 28 and 29 are the vital key to all the discussion from verses 27 through 59.

1. Works that please God? Trust the Saviour whom He has sent! There is no righteousness for sinful, fallen man, but the freely offered righteousness of Christ. That is what Romans 10:1-4 says:

"Brethren, my heart's desire and prayer to God for Israel is, that they might be saved. For I bear them record that they have a zeal of God, but not according to knowledge. For they being ignorant of God's righteousness, and going about to establish their own righteousness, have not submitted themselves unto the righteousness of God. For Christ is the end of the law for

righteousness to every one that believeth."

2. The only food to provide life for the sinful, dying soul must come from Heaven, not from man. Christ is the Manna from Heaven. Nothing of human goodness or human wisdom, of human ceremonies can offer life and salvation. It must be from God, not man; God's righteousness, freely put to man's account, not his own limited, faulty, corrupt righteousness. It must be Bread from Heaven.

3. The manna Israel fed on for forty years in the wilderness was not from Moses; it was from God. It had no saving power, but it pictures Christ, the Heavenly Manna, who gives everlasting life, not only food for the belly for a day at a time, but the manna was free, as salvation is free, only one must take the manna to have it, and one must "take the cup of salvation" as "whosoever will" is invited to do (Rev. 22:17).

4. One who trusts in Christ for salvation shall never hunger nor thirst for spiritual life. He has Christ forever.

The big word all the way through is "BELIEVE." This is a statement of John 1:12; 3:14,16,36; 5:24; 6:40; 6:47; of Acts 10:43; 13: 38,39 and 16:31.   *12 times*

"What sign shewest thou then, that we may see, and believe thee?" (vs. 30). A foolish and insincere question. They had seen Him feed five thousand men besides women and children, with bread literally created before their eyes, a miracle similar to the manna that fell in the wilderness. Yet they wanted a "sign," a miraculous manifestation to prove His deity! The one miracle clearly given to prove Christ's deity was to be His resurrection from the dead (John 2:19,21; Matt. 12:38-40; Rom. 1:4; Acts 2:22-36; 17:31).

But the proof of the insincerity of many of these who pretended they sought proof of Christ as God's Manna from Heaven, God's Son, is that when He arose from the dead, they bribed soldiers to say His body was stolen, and they went on in wicked intellectual unbelief. So even now the Lord Jesus could properly accuse them, *"Ye also have seen me, and believe not"* (vs. 36).

VERSES 37-40:

37 All that the Father giveth me shall come to me; and him that cometh to me I will in no wise cast out.

38 For I came down from heaven, not to do mine own will, but the will of him that sent me.

39 And this is the Father's will which hath sent me, that of all which he hath given me I should lose nothing, but should raise it up again at the last day.

40 And this is the will of him that sent me, that every one which seeth the Son, and believeth on him, may have everlasting life: and I will raise him up at the last day.

One Coming to Jesus Is Never Cast Out

In verse 37 are three great truths expressed.

1. Those whom God gives to Jesus come to Him! When any poor sinner wants forgiveness and salvation, he is assured that the Father and Son have already an agreement about him. He is given to Jesus, and Jesus will not turn him away. The price for sin has been paid. Both Father and Son are satisfied with it. One need not argue or plead to get what the Lord has offered so freely. The call in heart is God's call, so come boldly to receive this salvation.

2. One coming to Christ is never rejected, never cast out. How often God says it! "Draw nigh to God, and he will draw nigh to you" (Jas. 4:8).

Again, "Come now, and let us reason together, saith the Lord: though your sins be as scarlet, they shall be as white as snow; though they be red like crimson, they shall be as wool" (Isa. 1:18).

Is one unsure about it? Then come and God will make it sure, for "then shall we know, if we follow on to know the Lord: his going forth is prepared as the morning; and he shall come unto us as the rain, as the latter and former rain unto the earth" (Hosea 6:3).

And in the next chapter, in John 7:17 Jesus says, "If any man will do his will, he shall know of the doctrine, whether it be of God, or whether I speak of myself."

Cornelius, seeking God, will find Him, for God will send an angel to tell him to get Simon Peter who will give the way of salvation.

The hungry-hearted Ethiopian eunuch, reading from Isaiah 53 as he traveled (disappointed, we think, that he did not find peace and salvation at Jerusalem), will find/God sends Philip to explain the Scriptures to him and show him how to trust Jesus Christ.

One who comes in heart is not cast out. One who calls on the Lord is saved (Rom. 10:12,13).

3. Here is stated the eternal salvation of one who trusts Christ: He ". . . should not perish, but have everlasting life" (3:16); he "hath everlasting life" (3:36); he "hath everlasting life, and shall not come into condemnation; but is passed from death unto life" (5:24). Ah, so one who trusts in Christ is not condemned (3:18).

To Christ's sheep He says, "I give unto them eternal life; and they shall never perish, neither shall any man pluck them out of my hand" (John 10:28). The word *"man"* in the verse is in italics, because it was not in the Greek text. So Jesus said, "Neither shall any [man, devil, circumstance, human failure] pluck them out of my hand."

This statement is so clearly stated, so often repeated in Scripture. It is not very honest to ignore or try to explain it away. The doctrine of salvation wholly by faith, without works or merit, means that one who is saved has everlasting life.

"Him that cometh to me. . . ." (vs. 37). There are a number of words for the heart turning to Christ for salvation. One believes, or receives Christ, or repents, or calls on the Lord, or obeys the Gospel, or takes the cup of salvation, or comes to Christ. But all these statements refer to the simple turning of heart from sin to trust in Christ for salvation. Come to Christ is the way it is said in Isaiah 1:18; Isaiah 55:1,2; Matthew 19:14. It is the word God uses in II Peter 3:9; in Revelation 22:17. How simple! Just "come"!

Thank God for such an assurance as that! Moody was right when he said, "the 'whosoever wills' are the elect and the 'whosoever won't's,' the non-elect."

There it is—we cannot get around it: "All that the Father giveth me shall come to me; and him that cometh to me I will in no wise cast out."

VERSES 41-47:

41 The Jews then murmured at him, because he said, I am the bread which came down from heaven.

42 And they said, Is not this Jesus, the son of Joseph, whose father and mother we know? how is it then that he saith, I came down from heaven?

43 Jesus therefore answered and said unto them, Murmur not among yourselves.

44 No man can come to me, except the Father which hath sent me draw him: and I will raise him up at the last day.

45 It is written in the prophets, And they shall be all taught of God. Every man therefore that hath heard, and hath learned of the Father, cometh unto me.

46 Not that any man hath seen the Father, save he which is of God, he hath seen the Father.

47 Verily, verily, I say unto you, He that believeth on me hath everlasting life.

No One Comes to Christ Except Drawn of God

Why did not these unbelieving Jews trust in Christ? Because they did not respond to the call of God.

A sinner may say, "I can get saved any time I want to." Ah, but that is a foolish statement. Because one holding on to sin, hardened in his deliberate rejection of Christ, cannot even want to come except the Spirit of God keeps calling. Then how sinful and foolish to reject when God calls! No one has a guarantee that tomorrow he will feel convicted or will want to be saved. When your day comes, you may find that God has withdrawn Himself. When you at last come to knock on the door, you may find that it has been shut and a voice will say, "Depart from me; I never knew you."

Oh, preacher, man of God, how we should resolve to seek and plead for the power of the Holy Spirit to convict and draw sinners! The letter, even of the Scriptures, is dead of saving results without the work of the Holy Spirit.

But remember, no one can say he is not called, for Jesus is "that . . . Light, which lighteth every man that cometh into the world" (John 1:9). He said, "And I, if I be lifted up from the earth, will draw all men unto me. This he said, signifying what death he should die" (John 12:32,33).

Every sinner is without excuse because God has called him through the creation about him, says Romans 1:19,20.

Every sinner has a call of conscience even if he does not hear the Word of God (Rom. 2:11-16). Cornelius felt the call of God, though he probably had never heard a verse of Scripture. Since God commanded all men everywhere to repent, all men could, and it is sinful rebellion against God when they do not repent.

In verse 45 Jesus reminds the unbelieving of the Scripture, *"And they shall be all taught of God"* (Isa. 54:13). All are taught of God, called of God, warned of God. They are without excuse. Those who choose to hear, hear and come to Christ.

Again Christ states a great truth in verse 47, *"He that believeth on me hath everlasting life."*

VERSES 48-59:

48 I am that bread of life.

49 Your fathers did eat manna in the wilderness, and are dead.

50 This is the bread which cometh down from heaven, that a man may eat thereof, and not die.

51 I am the living bread which came down from heaven: if any man eat of this bread, he shall live for ever: and the bread that I will give is my flesh, which I will give for the life of the world.

52 The Jews therefore strove among themselves, saying, How can this man give us *his* flesh to eat?

53 Then Jesus said unto them, Verily, verily, I say unto you, Except ye eat the flesh of the Son of man, and drink his blood, ye have no life in you.

54 Whoso eateth my flesh, and drinketh my blood, hath eternal life; and I will raise him up at the last day.

55 For my flesh is meat indeed, and my blood is drink indeed.

56 He that eateth my flesh, and drinketh my blood, dwelleth in me, and I in him.

57 As the living Father hath sent me, and I live by the Father: so he that eateth me, even he shall live by me.

58 This is that bread which came down from heaven: not as your fathers did eat manna, and are dead: he that eateth of this bread shall live for ever.

59 These things said he in the synagogue, as he taught in Că-pĕr'-nă-ŭm.

What It Means to Eat Christ's Flesh and Drink His Blood

Again Jesus explains that He is the Bread of Life, the Bread from Heaven. And Jews should have known the meaning of the shewbread, those twelve loaves put fresh on the table in the Holy Place in the Tabernacle each week. And as the candlestick or lampstand with seven lights pictured Christ, the Light of the world, burning with the power of the Holy Spirit, so the shewbread, like the manna from Heaven, pictured Christ as the Bread of Life. Jesus states it again in word picture as eating His flesh and drinking His blood.

Rome teaches that this refers to the mass, that the bread of the memorial supper, blessed by the priest, actually becomes the body of Jesus and the wine actually becomes the blood of Christ. And they teach that there is saving power in this Eucharist. They say it is a continual bloody sacrifice of Christ. So it is given to the dying. But that is a sinful perversion of the Gospel.

In this same passage, Jesus had said to them three times that to take the Bread of Life simply meant to believe on Christ, to trust in Him. In verse 29 He said, *"This is the work of God, that ye believe on him whom he hath sent."* In verse 40 He said, *"And this is the will of him that sent me, that every one which seeth the Son, and believeth on him, may have everlasting life: and I will raise him up at the last day."*

In verse 47 He said it again, *"Verily, verily, I say unto you, He that believeth on me hath everlasting life."*

So it is inexcusable to teach that Jesus meant salvation is in the mass presided over by a Roman priest. No, salvation is in personally coming to know Christ and trusting Him for salvation.

Rome teaches the mass is a repeated sacrifice of Jesus, but that ignores the plain statement of Hebrews 10:16-18:

"This is the covenant that I will make with them after those days, saith the Lord, I will put my laws into their hearts, and in their minds will I write them; And their sins and iniquities will I remember no more. Now where remission of these is, there is no more offering for sin."

The one offering of Christ on the cross was final, complete, eternally effective. Before He gave up the ghost He cried out, "It is finished" (19:30). It is blasphemous, then, to claim to offer

Christ as a bloody Sacrifice again or to depend on the mass for mercy.

To eat the flesh and drink the blood of Jesus is simply to trust in Him for salvation. Eating is appropriating faith. Have you done that?

You will remember that Jesus spoke to Jews who all their lives had been saturated with the symbols, the illustrations, the ceremonial pictures of the Old Testament ceremonial law. How strange that they did not understand this pictorial language of Jesus, similar to the pictures in all the ceremonies of sacrifices and priesthood.

VERSES 60-66:

60 Many therefore of his disciples, when they had heard *this*, said, This is an hard saying; who can hear it?

61 When Jesus knew in himself that his disciples murmured at it, he said unto them, Doth this offend you?

62 *What* and if ye shall see the Son of man ascend up where he was before?

63 It is the spirit that quickeneth; the flesh profiteth nothing: the words that I speak unto you, *they* are spirit, and *they* are life.

64 But there are some of you that believe not. For Jesus knew from the beginning who they were that believed not, and who should betray him.

65 And he said, Therefore said I unto you, that no man can come unto me, except it were given unto him of my Father.

66 ¶ From that *time* many of his disciples went back, and walked no more with him.

Halfhearted Disciples Turn Away

The insistence of the Lord Jesus that He is God, and equal with the Father, not only offended the unbelieving Jews but it troubled His declared disciples.

The word "disciple" here does not apply only to the twelve but to others who followed Jesus. A disciple is a follower, a learner, not necessarily a believer. Judas was a "disciple" but not a Christian. Some of the "disciples" turned back (vs. 66), which means they no longer followed Him about.

"This is an hard saying" (vs. 60), they commented. Must they give up all the dependence on the ceremonies of the law, the

priesthood, the sacrifices, the keeping of the commandments? That was hard for a Jew. It is hard for a Romanist who depends on the mass and prayers to Mary, on confessions to a priest, on the authority of pope and church to give up all reliance on them. People who want to be known as Christians often do not want to accept Christ's sinless deity, His absolute intolerance of any rival.

But Jesus promises the disciples they shall see Him ascend bodily to Heaven, as later they did (Luke 24:50-52; Acts 1:9,10). But some of these did not accept the absolute deity of Jesus Christ because they were not "quickened" or born again of the Spirit.

The understanding of the unregenerate mind and the flesh does not profit the unbelieving hearer. But the words of Jesus are living, eternal words by which men are born again. First Peter 1:23 says, "Being born again, not of corruptible seed, but of incorruptible, by the word of God, which liveth and abideth for ever." Psalm 19:7 says, "The law of the Lord is perfect, converting the soul: the testimony of the Lord is sure, making wise the simple." The Gospel is "the power of God unto salvation" (Rom. 1:16).

We need to be reminded that one is never saved except through the two elements of the Gospel and the Holy Spirit. If it is no inspired Bible, then there is no divine Saviour. Christ and the Scriptures are both called "the word of God"; both are true or false together. One cannot have one without the other. Jesus said, "Whosoever therefore shall be ashamed of me and of my words in this adulterous and sinful generation; of him also shall the Son of man be ashamed, when he cometh in the glory of his Father with the holy angels" (Mark 8:38).

Some of the professed disciples turned away; they had not trusted Christ and were not saved. And Jesus knew who they were. He even knew Judas was an unbeliever and would betray Him.

It may be that some saved people did not openly follow Jesus after this. Joseph of Arimathaea was "a disciple of Jesus, but secretly for fear of the Jews" (John 19:38). Some seed that sprang up among the thorns were so choked with the cares of this world and the deceitfulness of riches and other things that they "bring no fruit to perfection." With Christians, always "the flesh lusteth against the Spirit." Even in Gethsemane, we are told that "all the disciples forsook him, and fled."

VERSES 67-71:

67 Then said Jesus unto the twelve, Will ye also go away?

68 Then Simon Peter answered him, Lord, to whom shall we go? thou hast the words of eternal life.

69 And we believe and are sure that thou art that Christ, the Son of the living God.

70 Jesus answered them, Have not I chosen you twelve, and one of you is a devil?

71 He spake of Judas Iscariot *the son* of Simon: for he it was that should betray him, being one of the twelve.

An Unsaved Pretender

Here Simon Peter answers for the saved and loyal disciples, that there is no one else to whom they can go; only Jesus has the way of eternal life. Later in Acts 4:12 Peter will say, "Neither is there salvation in any other: for there is none other name under heaven given among men, whereby we must be saved." Here he makes the bold assertion that *"we believe and are sure that thou art that Christ, the Son of the living God"* (vs. 69). Yes, Peter, you are sure and you will affirm again, "Thou art the Christ, the Son of the living God" (Matt. 16:16). Or it is possible that here John's account is of the same occasion of Peter's affirmation.

But Peter, not all of the little crowd that went away, not all of the twelve even are saved! For Jesus *"knew from the beginning"* that Judas had never trusted Him (vs. 64). He was still a devil, a child of his father Satan.

Someone says that Judas fell from grace and lost his salvation. No, he was never saved. His covetous heart will lead him to thievery, then to betray Jesus for thirty pieces of silver. Remember, preachers are not all saved. Only God knows the heart. Judas was not saved, so he did not lose his salvation; he lost his place of ministry, to go to his own place, as we read in Acts 1:25.

John 7

AFTER these things Jesus walked in Galilee: for he would not walk in Jewry, because the Jews sought to kill him.

2 Now the Jews' feast of tabernacles was at hand.

3 His brethren therefore said unto him, Depart hence, and go into Judæa, that thy disciples also may see the works that thou doest.

4 For *there is* no man *that* doeth any thing in secret, and he himself seeketh to be known openly. If thou do these things, shew thyself to the world.

5 For neither did his brethren believe in him.

6 Then Jesus said unto them, My time is not yet come: but your time is alway ready.

7 The world cannot hate you; but me it hateth, because I testify of it, that the works thereof are evil.

8 Go ye up unto this feast: I go not up yet unto this feast; for my time is not yet full come.

9 When he had said these words unto them, he abode *still* in Galilee.

The Mounting Hatred of the Jews: They Would Kill Jesus

The term "Jews" probably arose from the name of Jerusalem but it later became the name for all Israel. Jewry here refers to Jerusalem Jews in that area. Those who were still rulers, members of the Sanhedrin, the chief priests, opposed Jesus bitterly. Their authority as teachers and leaders of the Jewish religion was questioned. All the traditions they had added to the law of Moses, all their treasured interpretations, their government, their power to arrest, to jail and to punish in all but the death penalty, allowed by the Romans, was at stake.

How could they compel people to observe their interpretation of the Sabbath when Jesus kept healing people on the Sabbath and when the disciples disregarded their rule and were encouraged to rub out handfuls of grain in their hands on the Sabbath and eat it while walking through the fields on the Sabbath (Mark 2:23). How could they keep up their tremendous extra income by selling sacrifices and changing money at a rich discount, when Jesus called them "a den of thieves" (Matt. 21:13)? And when He denounced their tradition that sons could

call it "Corban" and give all the support God had commanded
for parents to the priests instead, that was great loss. And loss of
face! Jesus publicly denounced these leaders, "Woe unto you,
scribes and Pharisees, hypocrites!" (Matt. 23:13-15). So Jewish
leaders of Jerusalem hated Jesus and schemed to kill Him
(11:47,48). And Jesus avoided coming publicly to Jerusalem at
this time.

"The Jews' feast of tabernacles was at hand" (vs. 2). It began
the fifteenth day of the seventh month and lasted seven days
(Lev. 23:34), and so it was six months from the passover and the
feast of unleavened bread which began on the fourteenth day of
the first month (Exod. 12:18). The feast of tabernacles had been
celebrated by building brush booths or arbors and living under
them for seven days in remembrance of their camping in the
wilderness for forty years (Lev. 23:40-43). The dwelling in booths
is not mentioned in the New Testament and we suppose was not
generally observed, if at all, after the captivity. This is one of the
three feasts each year which all the males were to attend (Deut.
16:16).

Jesus had *"walked in Galilee"* (vs. 1) most of His ministry;
now most of the last six months before His death He will be in
the area of Jerusalem. But He was not ready to go when the
crowd went, and left some days earlier, we suppose, for the
journey of four or five days from Capernaum to Jerusalem.

The brothers of Jesus—James, Joses, Simon and Judas (Matt.
13:55)—born of Mary and Joseph after Jesus was born of the
Virgin Mary, were not saved before the crucifixion (vs. 5). So
perhaps with a sneer in their rejection of His claim to be the
Messiah, they insist He go to Jerusalem and do some more
miracles to please His disciples.

We remember the complaint of Psalm 69:8, surely prophesying
the sorrowful word of Jesus, "I am become a stranger unto my
brethren, and an alien unto my mother's children." We suppose
these brothers were not saved when Jesus, on the cross, left His
mother to the care of John (19:25-27). But they were Christians
and were among the 120 pleading with God for an enduement of
power from on High, before Pentecost (Acts 1:14). Probably in

the glory and joy of Christ's resurrectioh and the witnessing about it, they had been saved between the resurrection and Christ's ascension.

Says verse 7: *"The world cannot hate you: but me it hateth, because I testify of it, that the works thereof are evil."* The world cannot hate the unsaved. It does hate Jesus and those who fervently follow Him. Bishop Ryle reminds us that Erasmus used to say that Luther might have had an easy life if he had not touched the pope's crown, and the monks' bellies. Bengel observes, "Those who please all men, at all times, ought deservedly to look on themselves with suspicion."

But Jesus, knowing His crucifixion was coming, knew *"my time is not yet full come"* (vs. 8).

"Christ our passover is sacrificed for us," says I Corinthians 5:7. So Jesus must die (as the passover type had indicated for the past fifteen hundred years) on the afternoon when passover lambs were being slain, and that was months ahead. So He must not precipitate His arrest and murder before that time. He will go quietly *"as it were in secret"* (vs. 10) some days after the crowd has departed for Jerusalem.

VERSES 10-13:

10 ¶ But when his brethren were gone up, then went he also up unto the feast, not openly, but as it were in secret.

11 Then the Jews sought him at the feast, and said, Where is he?

12 And there was much murmuring among the people concerning him: for some said, He is a good man: others said, Nay; but he deceiveth the people.

13 Howbeit no man spake openly of him for fear of the Jews.

Jesus Goes Quietly to Jerusalem

Jesus is here leaving Galilee for the last time before His crucifixion. Compare this passage with Luke 9:51-62. Jesus did not go with His brothers, but after they were gone, He went up secretly with His disciples. From Matthew 28:7,10 and 16, we see that Jesus came back to Galilee after His resurrection and met the disciples there.

The amazing miracles of the Lord Jesus—healing, raising the dead, feeding the five thousand and the four thousand—had made Him a topic of intense interest wherever Jews gathered. At Jerusalem, the Jewish leaders sought Him. Some argued, "He is a good man." Others, "Nay; but he deceiveth the people."

He made no ordinary claim, but actually He claimed deity— that He and the Father were equal! Those who have loved Jesus and believed in Him could not say so openly. The hate that would have killed Lazarus again because his resurrection led people to believe in Jesus, would brook no praise and no propaganda for Jesus. The man born blind, when he later had been healed, was cast out of the Temple because he defended Jesus (9:34).

The tension was so great and the spirit of the people so aroused that chief priests must hire Judas to lead them to Jesus at night, away from the crowds they feared.

VERSES 14-24:

14 ¶ Now about the midst of the feast Jesus went up into the temple, and taught.

15 And the Jews marvelled, saying, How knoweth this man letters, having never learned?

16 Jesus answered them, and said, My doctrine is not mine, but his that sent me.

17 If any man will do his will, he shall know of the doctrine, whether it be of God, or *whether* I speak of myself.

18 He that speaketh of himself seeketh his own glory: but he that seeketh his glory that sent him, the same is true, and no unrighteousness is in him.

19 Did not Moses give you the law, and *yet* none of you keepeth the law? Why go ye about to kill me?

20 The people answered and said, Thou hast a devil: who goeth about to kill thee?

21 Jesus answered and said unto them, I have done one work, and ye all marvel.

22 Moses therefore gave unto you circumcision; (not because it is of Moses, but of the fathers;) and ye on the sabbath day circumcise a man.

23 If a man on the sabbath day receive circumcision, that the law of Moses should not be broken; are ye angry at me, because I have made a man every whit whole on the sabbath day?

24 Judge not according to the appearance, but judge righteous judgment.

Jesus Teaching at the Feast of Tabernacles

The first excitement—people looking for Jesus, wanting to see more miracles, Jewish leaders fearing His teaching and wishing to kill Him—is calmer by the middle of the week in the feast of tabernacles. So Jesus enters the Temple (the Temple area, not the Holy Place or the Most Holy Place reserved for priests in the Temple service). It was the outer area where they sold animals for sacrifices and changed money. Here people assembled to see celebrities and to hear teaching.

It was the large Temple area where Christians later assembled after Pentecost. "And they continuing daily with one accord in the temple . . ." (Acts 2:46). It was "at the Beautiful gate of the temple . . . in the porch that is called Solomon's," where Peter preached to the people after the healing of the lame man (Acts 3:10,11). It seems that Christians assembled here in Solomon's porch of the Temple regularly (Acts 5:12). Peter and John, released from prison by an angel, "entered into the temple early in the morning, and taught" (Acts 5:21) So Jesus addressed the crowds assembled in this public park of the Temple for observing the feast of tabernacles.

Verse 15 means that Jesus had never been trained in the school of the Talmud and had not had the scribes to interpret the Scriptures for Him. He learned from God.

The wisdom of the Lord Jesus is shown in the certainty and authority with which He dealt with the doctrines and ceremonies of the law and the Pharisees' interpretations. And the sure way of dealing with right and wrong could not but hold and amaze those who heard Him. He had "never learned," that is, He had never been a long-time student of the learned rabbis as had Paul, "brought up . . . at the feet of Gamaliel" (Acts 22:3). But the officers said of Jesus, "Never man spake like this man" (7:46). Jesus explained His teaching was *not mine, but his that sent me* (vs. 16).

First, it was not human wisdom but God-given, faultless wisdom of eternal truth. Second, Jesus surely meant that all this ministry was not simply His own, but as the perfect Man, He spake in the power of the Holy Spirit: "How God anointed Jesus of Nazareth with the Holy Ghost and with power: who went about doing good, and healing all that were oppressed of the devil; for God was with him" (Acts 10:38).

But His truth is verifiable. *"If any man will do his will* [or be willing to do His will], *he shall know of the doctrine, whether it be of God, or whether I speak of myself"* (vs. 17). The words "will do his will" are better translated "willeth to do his will." This verse means that if any man chooses to do God's will, God will reveal to him the truth.

Those who followed on to know the Lord would find Him. All who drew nigh to God were assured God would draw nigh to them. That means there is a moral guilt in unbelief and in false doctrine. Only those who "hath ears to hear" may be sure to learn the truth. Those who are determined to please a loved one, or to hold a popular doctrine, or to follow a loved leader, or those who get their living from a sect or group holding false doctrine are usually not open to learn the truth.

No wonder people "were astonished at his doctrine: For he taught them as one having authority, and not as the scribes" (Matt. 7:28,29). Jesus can be believed, He is saying, because He is not selfishly teaching some private heresy but speaking for God the Father.

Any man who builds a personal empire or wealth out of a doctrine or denomination or institution may be false in doctrine, whether a Father Divine, or a Herbert Armstrong, or a Mary Baker Eddy, or the Church of Rome. One who teaches sprinkling babies for baptism because it is the official position of his church often does not want to learn about the baptism of a believer as the Bible teaches it.

One who believes the world and life and man came by evolution is "willingly . . . ignorant," says II Peter 3:4-7 of creation, the worldwide flood, the return of Christ and eventual world judgment.

Those who want the truth can find it. Those who seek God can find Him. Jeremiah 29:12,13 says, "Then shall ye call upon me, and ye shall go and pray unto me, and I will hearken unto you. And ye shall seek me, and find me, when ye shall search for me with all your heart." Now, one who seeks for God with all his heart will find Him.

It is wicked for one to avoid Bible truth and not find it. It is wicked to stay away from Christ in unbelief. Some are "fools, and slow of heart to believe all that the prophets have spoken." Unbelief is not intelligent. It is not the result of learning or of honest seeking. Rather, it is the turning of the heart away from the light.

Note the insincerity shown in verse 20, *"Who goeth about to kill thee?"* and then, *"Is not this he, whom they seek to kill?"* (vs. 25). The leaders and their deputies were still angry with Jesus over His healing people on the Sabbath day.

Jesus determined not to put His approval on the rabbinical tradition. He must put new wine in new bottles (Matt. 9:17). He made an issue of healing on the Sabbath as being within the true spirit of the commandments—it was lawful to do good on the Sabbath. Priests worked in the Tabernacle on the Sabbath (Matt. 12:5). Babies are circumcised on the Sabbath (vs. 23). In an emergency, David and his men, fleeing from King Saul, ate the shewbread not lawful ordinarily for any but the priests (Matt. 12:3,4). They would rescue an animal falling in a ditch, or lead the way to water on the Sabbath (Matt. 12:11).

Since all the commandments are summed up in loving God and loving one's neighbor, and since loving our neighbor is the royal law and always good, then it is in the spirit of Sabbath-keeping to heal, to help, to do good, for "the sabbath was made for man, and not man for the sabbath." Besides, Jesus is God, Creator, and is Lord of the Sabbath (Mark 2:28).

One is not to judge by incidental circumstances or appearances but "righteous judgment," according to scriptural principles, by the spirit and not only the letter of the law.

VERSES 25-35:

25 Then said some of them of Jerusalem, Is not this he, whom they seek to kill?

26 But, lo, he speaketh boldly, and

they say nothing unto him. Do the rulers know indeed that this is the very Christ?

27 Howbeit we know this man whence he is: but when Christ cometh, no man knoweth whence he is.

28 Then cried Jesus in the temple as he taught, saying, Ye both know me, and ye know whence I am: and I am not come of myself, but he that sent me is true, whom ye know not.

29 But I know him: for I am from him, and he hath sent me.

30 Then they sought to take him: but no man laid hands on him, because his hour was not yet come.

31 And many of the people believed on him, and said, When Christ cometh, will he do more miracles than these which this *man* hath done?

32 ¶ The Pharisees heard that the people murmured such things concerning him; and the Pharisees and the chief priests sent officers to take him.

33 Then said Jesus unto them, Yet a little while am I with you, and *then* I go unto him that sent me.

34 Ye shall seek me, and shall not find *me:* and where I am, *thither* ye cannot come.

35 Then said the Jews among themselves, Whither will he go, that we shall not find him? will he go unto the dispersed among the Gentiles, and teach the Gentiles?

Christ Boldly Claims His Deity

"We know this man whence he is" (vs. 27), they said. But they thought He was born in Galilee, not knowing He had been born at Bethlehem which was fulfilling the prophecy of Micah 5:2. Nathanael made the same mistake (1:46). Jewish leaders knew the Saviour was promised to come from Bethlehem (vss. 41,42). But willing not to believe, they did not inquire. Others, without inquiry, quickly accepted Jesus.

Most who come to know Jesus as Saviour do not need to ask if all the Scriptures have been fulfilled in His coming, or all the "infallible proofs" of His resurrection. Always, one who needs to know and find out about Jesus can know and find Him.

The very humanity of Jesus made some slow to receive Him as God. He was known as Joseph's Son. His unsaved brothers were known. He had grown up in the small and ordinary town of Nazareth. "A prophet is not without honour, save in his own country." Yet, the wonderful fact that Jesus took the place of the poorest, knew all the sorrow and temptation of men, and enters into the most intimate detail of our lives, makes Him Son of Man, our Elder Brother. "Wherefore in all things it behoved him to be made like unto his brethren"; and "he is not ashamed to call them brethren" (Heb. 2:11,17).

But Jesus plainly said, *"Ye both know me, and ye know*

whence I am" (vs. 28). So surely they not only knew He was from Nazareth and was regarded as Joseph's Son or foster Son, but some of them knew what they denied, that He was all He claimed to be—the Son of God. Jesus gave these unbelieving Jews that awful warning that "whosoever speaketh against the Holy Ghost, it shall not be forgiven him, neither in this world, neither in the world to come" (Matt. 12:32).

I am sure it was not the words they spoke to which Christ referred in Matthew 12:31, that is, that Christ "cast out devils . . . by . . . the prince of devils," that was unpardonable. No, their heart rejection after great light of the overwhelming truth that Jesus was the Messiah was their sin. But the warning of Jesus was prefaced by the statement, "And Jesus knew their thoughts, and said unto them . . . ." He answered not their untrue words, but He answered their determined rebellion of heart. In their hearts they said, "He works miracles, so He must be the Messiah, but we still hate Him and we will oppose Him and kill Him if we can." They determine to do away with Jesus despite all the evidence that He is God.

VERSE 36:

36 What *manner of* saying is this that he said, Ye shall seek me, and | shall not find *me:* and where I am, *thither* ye cannot come?

Christ Warns: Opportunity Passes

His "time is not yet full come." It was not time for Jesus to die, as He had said in verse 8. "They sought to take him" (vs. 30) and "the chief priests sent officers to take him" (vs. 32).

Miracles prove a prophet's message. So many, seeing the miracles, believed on Christ. It was a fair question; if Jesus were not the Christ, what greater miracle could Christ do? But the Lord Jesus had said that the final proof of His deity would be His resurrection.

Now Jesus gives solemn warning. He would be with them only a little time. Men would seek Him when He was gone. He knew

His foretold and certain death was in His and the Father's plan. But worldly and wicked hearers did not take it to heart then, as they often ignore such warnings of passing opportunities now.

Would Jesus *"go unto the dispersed among the Gentiles"?* that is, to Jews outside Palestine? They were conscious of the millions of Israelites left in Babylon in the Babylonian Empire when Ezra and Nehemiah built again the Temple in Jerusalem and the nation Israel.

Peter would go there to evangelize these dispersed Jews, and his two epistles were traditionally labeled as from Babylon. The book of James is addressed to "the twelve tribes which are scattered abroad"; but Jesus is to go back to Heaven, not to a foreign country.

VERSES 37-39:

37 In the last day, that great *day* of the feast, Jesus stood and cried, saying, If any man thirst, let him come unto me, and drink.
38 He that believeth on me, as the scripture hath said, out of his belly shall flow rivers of living water.
39 (But this spake he of the Spirit, which they that believe on him should receive: for the Holy Ghost was not yet *given;* because that Jesus was not yet glorified.)

The Christian's Artesian Well

Water in Scripture is often a symbol of the Holy Spirit. A number of places it pictures the Holy Spirit in salvation or receiving Christ, being born again by the Spirit.

For examples, the thirsty nation in the wilderness was watered from a mighty fountain opened from a rock in Horeb, when Moses was instructed to smite the rock (Exod. 17:5,6). Again they thirsted:

"And the Lord spake unto Moses, saying, Take the rod, and gather thou the assembly together, thou, and Aaron thy brother, and speak ye unto the rock before their eyes; and it shall give forth his water, and thou shalt bring forth to them water out of the rock: so thou shalt give the congregation and their beasts

drink. And Moses took the rod from before the Lord, as he commanded him. And Moses and Aaron gathered the congregation together before the rock, and he said unto them, Hear now, ye rebels; must we fetch you water out of this rock? And Moses lifted up his hand, and with his rod he smote the rock twice: and the water came out abundantly, and the congregation drank, and their beasts also." —Num. 20:7-11

Paul was inspired to say that Israel in the wilderness ". . . did all eat the same spiritual meat; And did all drink the same spiritual drink: for they drank of that spiritual Rock that followed them: and that Rock was Christ" (I Cor. 10:3,4).

First, Moses was to smite the rock, picturing Jesus smitten for us and so giving the Water of Life. In the second occasion Moses was instructed to speak to the rock, because once Jesus has paid for sin, "there is no more offering for sin" (Heb. 10:18).

Now one simply comes to the Saviour and takes salvation or takes the daily drink. The rock pictured Christ and the Holy Spirit regeneration and fullness coming from Christ.

Isaiah 12:3 says, "Therefore with joy shall ye draw water out of the wells of salvation." Salvation and comfort and daily blessings are inferred here. And again Isaiah 55:1 says, "Ho, every one that thirsteth, come ye to the waters . . . ." And the drink and the food are "without money and without price." And the promise is, ". . . and your soul shall live."

To the woman of Samaria Jesus promised "living water," flowing water. He said that with other waters in this world one would thirst again, but "the water that I shall give him shall be in him a well of water springing up into everlasting life" (4:10-14). Not just life but everlasting life; not just salvation but overflowing Water of Life so one need never thirst again. Surely Jesus meant that one who has this fountain of Living Water by drinking once would never lose this abiding Holy Spirit within; he "shall never thirst" in the sense of needing salvation again.

The last invitation in the Bible has a sweet picture of the water of salvation, "And the Spirit and the bride say, Come. And let him that heareth say, Come. And let him that is athirst come.

And whosoever will, let him take the water of life freely" (Rev.
22:17).

Isaiah 44:3 promises the outpouring of Holy Spirit power, pictured by floods of water: "For I will pour water upon him that is
thirsty, and floods upon the dry ground: I will pour my spirit
upon thy seed, and my blessing upon thine offspring."

So here in John 7:37-39 we have a wonderful picture of the in-
coming Spirit at salvation and the fountain within the Christian
(the indwelling Holy Spirit) and His marvelous outflow of blessing and salvation.

Note these verses carefully.

1. *"If any man thirst . . ."* (vs. 39). Is anyone dissatisfied
with this world? Is there some sense of guilt, some fear of death,
some hunger of heart? Then come! That is the same invitation of
Isaiah 55:1, "Ho, every one that thirsteth." That is the same as,
"And let him that heareth say, Come. And let him that is athirst
come. And whosoever will, let him take the water of life freely"
(Rev. 22:17).

> **Let not conscience make you linger,**
> **Nor of fitness fondly dream;**
> **All the fitness He requireth**
> **Is to feel your need of Him.**

"If any man . . . ." So this is a universal invitation. Any
person in the world has a right to claim it.

Says Bishop Ryle:

> "If any thirst." "Any!" Those who are grimed with sin.
> "Any!" Those who have no claim but their exceeding need.
> "Any!" Those whom all the world and the church spurn.
> "Any!" Publicans and sinners; outcasts and dying malefactors;
> persecutors and procrastinators. Richard Baxter used to say
> that, if his name had stood on this page, he would have feared
> that it referred to some other who bore it; but, since the Lord
> said *any,* he knew that even he was welcome. The one and only
> qualification is *thirst.*

2. *". . . let him COME UNTO ME"* (vs. 37). Not to the
church for salvation, not to baptism for salvation, not moral
reform—but to Jesus. That is the same sweet intent of Matthew

11:28, "Come unto me, all ye that labour and are heavy laden, and I will give you rest."

3. *". . . and drink"* (vs. 37). Help yourself at the spring! Just "take the cup of salvation," says Psalm 116:13.

4. *"He that believeth on me . . ."* (vs. 38). That is what drinking means; that is what receiving Him means (1:12). Believing is a way to receive the Water of Life.

5. *"Out of his belly shall flow . . ."* (vs. 38). Not only does one by faith have water for himself (salvation), but he becomes a fountain of Holy Spirit power flowing out from him. Note the Holy Spirit living within is intended to be flowing out in rivers of blessing for others, salvation for others.

6. *"But this spake he of the Spirit, which they that believe on him SHOULD receive"* (vs. 39). That is in the future.

7. *". . . for the Holy Ghost was not yet given"* (vs. 39). That is, not given in the sense of a fountain within, the Christian's body becoming a temple of the Holy Spirit and flowing out from the Christian's body as headquarters, *"because that Jesus was not yet glorified"* (vs. 39). In John 15:26,27 Jesus made this same promise:

"But when the Comforter is come whom I will send unto you from the Father, even the Spirit of truth, which proceedeth from the Father, he shall testify of me: And ye also shall bear witness, because ye have been with me from the beginning."

The Holy Spirit was "WITH" the disciples the night before the crucifixion. He was "IN" the disciples after Christ's resurrection.

The Holy Spirit now, after moving into the body of a Christian to dwell, will never leave him. Bishop Ryle made this comment: "In regeneration the Holy Spirit does literally indwell the believer. His life may be stunted, dwarfed, repressed, as plants in a sickly atmosphere, and as streams choked with the debris brought down from the hills; but it can never again be lost. 'He abides for ever.' "

John 20:19-22 tells how the Holy Spirit was received into the bodies of Christians the day Jesus rose from the dead:

"Then the same day at evening, being the first day of the

week, when the doors were shut where the disciples were as-
sembled for fear of the Jews, came Jesus and stood in the midst,
and saith unto them, Peace be unto you. And when he had so
said, he shewed unto them his hands and his side. Then were the
disciples glad, when they saw the Lord. Then said Jesus to them
again, Peace be unto you: as my Father hath sent me, even so
send I you. And when he had said this, he breathed on them, and
saith unto them, Receive ye the Holy Ghost.''

The indwelling of the Holy Spirit did not come at Pentecost
but on the day of the resurrection of Christ. Pentecost was the
day of the enduement of power. The indwelling of the Holy Spirit
in the bodies of Christians began the day Jesus rose from the
dead. Now the Holy Spirit comes to save a penitent, trusting sinner and he will be "born of the Spirit." The Holy Spirit might
say, "I will just bring all My baggage and hang up My clothes for
I am going to live here always!" So I Corinthians 6:19,20 tells us:

"What? know ye not that your body is the temple of the Holy
Ghost which is in you, which ye have of God, and ye are not your
own? For ye are bought with a price: therefore glorify God in your
body, and in your spirit, which are God's.''

And Romans 8:9 says, "Now if any man have not the Spirit of
Christ he is none of his." Do not confuse the indwelling of the
Spirit, which began the day of Christ's resurrection, with the enduement of power from on High for soul winning, which came on
the day of Pentecost to those who waited for power.

They were "filled with the Holy Ghost," as in Acts 2:4. And
that should be repeated again and again as in Acts 4:31 and
Ephesians 5:18. But the indwelling of the Spirit begins the moment one believes on Christ, and that is a fact for every Christian. Dr. F. B. Meyer said:

> If the Spirit of Christ be in us, Christ Himself is in us. It is a
> mistake to dis-sever these two. They are one.
> This, then, is the sum of the whole matter. When weary,
> thirsty souls go to Jesus. He gives them instant relief by giving
> them His Holy Spirit, and in that most blessed of all gifts, He
> Himself glides into the eager nature. He does not strive nor cry;
> there is no sound as of a rushing storm of wind, no coronet of

flame; whilst men are watching at the front door to welcome Him with blare of trumpet, He steals in at the rear, unnoticed; but, in any case, He suddenly comes to His temple, and sits in its inner shrine as a refiner and purifier of the sons of Levi.

Oh, the Power That Should Flow From a Christian!

At the Beautiful gate of the Temple Peter and John said to the lame man, "Silver and gold have I none; but such as I have give I thee: In the name of Jesus Christ of Nazareth rise up and walk," and he did (Acts 3:6).

Peter was so baptized or surrounded or filled with the Spirit "insomuch that they brought forth the sick into the streets, and laid them on beds and couches, that at the least the shadow of Peter passing by might overshadow some of them. There came also a multitude out of the cities round about unto Jerusalem, bringing sick folks, and them which were vexed with unclean spirits: and they were healed every one" (Acts 5:15,16).

Paul had such power of the Holy Spirit that when he laid his ordaining hands on Timothy, the young preacher received a mighty gift of the Holy Spirit power. "Stir it up, Timothy," Paul said.

Some godly teachers fasted and prayed and laid their hands on Paul and Barnabas. We are told, "So they, being sent forth by the Holy Ghost, departed unto Seleucia . . . ," and the great missionary journeys of Paul were begun.

So Elijah could raise a boy from the dead. So Elisha could promise a child to a barren woman, or heal the poison water of Jericho and that fountain still runs. Today at Jericho I saw again the fresh water still flowing from Elisha's fountain. Oh, God gave Elisha much more than that!

So Peter could, at a word, see Ananias and Sapphira fall dead for lying to God.

So Paul could have God strike Elymas the sorcerer blind. But this wonderful artesian well of Holy Spirit power is not only for apostles and prophets and great men, it is "if *any* man thirst." It is "he that believeth on me." So any Christian who drinks for himself and believes and seeks the Holy Spirit power may have it to use as God leads and gives it.

In John 14:12 Jesus said, "Verily, verily, I say unto you, He that believeth on me, the works that I do shall he do also; and greater works than these shall he do; because I go unto my Father." Yes, we are to do the very works Jesus did. We are to have the Holy Spirit power as He had it.

Do not Mark 9:23; 11:24; 16:17 and John 15:7 say about the same? In answer to prayer I have seen rain within a day in the midst of a great drouth; I have known a dying woman miraculously raised up to live more than thirty years; I have known perhaps a dozen barren women conceive children in answer to our prayers; have known a brain cancer labeled "terminal" healed so that one who was not expected to live more than a few months has now lived over seven years and is still strong and well in God's service.

Because of his devotion to a modernistic denominational program, a stubborn deacon declared that this evangelist could not come to the large church where we were announced. "Only over my dead body!" he said. I saw his funeral there within two days, with the casket resting below a great banner announcing my coming. Oh, God still has power for those who trust Him.

A river of blessing! Each Christian ought to be! God make it burn in every heart that reads this!

"As the scripture hath said . . ." (vs. 38). That may refer to Isaiah 44:3. It may refer to Proverbs 11:30, "The fruit of the righteous is a tree of life; and he that winneth souls is wise." But, oh, certainly it refers to Joel 2:28-32 which Peter quoted at Pentecost in these words:

"But Peter, standing up with the eleven, lifted up his voice, and said unto them, Ye men of Judaea, and all ye that dwell at Jerusalem, be this known unto you, and hearken to my words: For these are not drunken, as ye suppose, seeing it is but the third hour of the day. But this is that which was spoken by the prophet Joel; And it shall come to pass in the last days, saith God, I will pour out of my Spirit upon all flesh: and your sons and your daughters shall prophesy, and your young men shall see

visions, and your old men shall dream dreams: And on my servants and on my handmaidens I will pour out in those days of my Spirit; and they shall prophesy: And I will shew wonders in heaven above, and signs in the earth beneath; blood, and fire, and vapour of smoke: The sun shall be turned into darkness, and the moon into blood, before that great and notable day of the Lord come: And it shall come to pass, that whosoever shall call on the name of the Lord shall be saved."—Acts 2:14-21.

We think the general teaching of the flood waters from the rock, first smitten and repeated later, is referred to here. Daniel 12:3 says at the resurrection, ". . . they that be wise shall shine as the brightness of the firmament; and they that turn many to righteousness as the stars for ever and ever."

Let us say a general trend of all Old Testament Scripture justifies the teaching that the Holy Spirit power should pour out from our Christian bodies.

Would not the examples of Elijah and Elisha illustrate the river of blessing to those they met and touched?

One does not read the Old Testament aright who doesn't find the teaching that Holy Spirit power would be given to Christians.

VERSES 40-53:

40 ¶ Many of the people therefore, when they heard this saying, said, Of a truth this is the Prophet.

41 Others said, This is the Christ. But some said, Shall Christ come out of Galilee?

42 Hath not the scripture said, That Christ cometh of the seed of David, and out of the town of Bethlehem, where David was?

43 So there was a division among the people because of him.

44 And some of them would have taken him; but no man laid hands on him.

45 ¶ Then came the officers to the chief priests and Pharisees; and they said unto them, Why have ye not brought him?

46 The officers answered, Never man spake like this man.

47 Then answered them the Pharisees, Are ye also deceived?

48 Have any of the rulers or of the Pharisees believed on him?

49 But this people who knoweth not the law are cursed.

50 Nicodemus saith unto them, (he that came to Jesus by night, being one of them,)

51 Doth our law judge *any* man, before it hear him, and know what he doeth?
52 They answered and said unto him, Art thou also of Galilee? Search, and look: for out of Galilee ariseth no prophet.
53 And every man went unto his own house.

Divided Opinions: Chief Rulers and People

The people argued—most of the common people, perhaps, convinced that Jesus was "the Prophet" that Moses promised (Deut. 18:15,18), that He was "the Christ" (Greek for the Hebrew word *Messiah,* anointed, of Isaiah 42:1 and Isaiah 61:1). That does not mean they were all converted, trusting Him as Saviour, but generally accepting the fact of His deity. But they found the problem—not knowing Jesus was born at Bethlehem, as Micah 5:2 had foretold.

The high priest *"would have taken him,"* having a police force and servants (see "officers" in vs. 45 and Matt. 26:47), *"but no man laid hands on him"* (vs. 44). They could not take Jesus to die until the appointed time. The officers sent to arrest Jesus were confounded. They could not do it since *"never man spake like this man"* (vs. 46).

The foolish question of verse 48 shows the arrogance of the intelligentsia. The university professors with little spiritual light, with no study of Scripture, who "willingly are ignorant" of the truth of direct creation, of a worldwide flood, and coming judgment, think themselves very wise with their denial of God and direct creation. And with their false religion of humanism they scoff at common people who know that a Creator proves a creation. So the wise become fools.

Dr. Harry Emerson Fosdick, noted religious liberal and unbeliever, wrote, "I do not believe in the virgin birth of Christ, and I do not know any intelligent man who does."

For a man of popular following but very ordinary intellectual attainment to so deny the intelligence of Gresham Machen, Robert Dick Wilson, R. A. Torrey, B. H. Carroll, George W. Truett, C. I. Scofield and a host of other mighty men, shows he was dishonest and irresponsible. No wonder about such Jesus said, "O fools, and slow of heart to believe all that the prophets have spoken" (Luke 24:25). Only a fool says in his heart, "There is no God" (Ps. 14:1), or is slow to believe the Bible. We should never take seriously the so-called intellectuals who, with darkened minds and unregenerate hearts, doubt Christ or the Bible.

Nicodemus Speaks: Was He Saved?

Nicodemus was a ruler of the Jews, a member of the 71-member Sanhedrin which will condemn Jesus to death. Here he speaks mildly, perhaps timidly, or it may be with political motive. Should they wait and hear Jesus out before condemning Him? And should they see how events turn out? We do not know that Nicodemus was saved. He did team up with Joseph of Arimathaea, a timid believer, in burying Jesus (John 19:38-42). We hope that timid Nicodemus, who came to Jesus by night, was saved.

"And every man went to his own house" (vs. 53). The meeting broke up in confusion. The Sanhedrin had made a mess of things so far. So they went home. But there will be another day. They will be back. The conflict with our Lord will go on until the bitter end.

John 8

JESUS went unto the mount of Olives.

2 And early in the morning he came again into the temple, and all the people came unto him; and he sat down, and taught them.

Jesus Sleeping on the Ground

The chapter division here between chapters 7 and 8 may be misleading. Read the last verse of chapter 7 with the first verse here.

"And every man went unto his own house. Jesus went unto the mount of Olives."—John 7:53, John 8:1.

Others went to their homes, to their comforts and families. Jesus had neither. Where on the Mount of Olives did Jesus go? To the Garden of Gethsemane, no doubt, where He slept on the ground. There is indication that Jesus often slept there. When Judas betrayed Jesus, he knew, though the chief priests did not, that it would be in the Garden of Gethsemane, and he took the arresting company there (Matt. 26:14-16, 47).

We must take literally the statement of Jesus to a would-be follower who meant well but did not perhaps realize what discipleship would mean: "And Jesus said unto him, Foxes have holes, and birds of the air have nests; but the Son of man hath not where to lay his head" (Luke 9:58).

We know that the disciples once, at least, were so hungry that passing a wheat field they rubbed out raw grain in their hands and ate it. Since Paul suffered "fastings often," do you suppose Jesus, Paul's pattern, would not have been without food often, and without a bed?

God put this inspired information in the Bible, so surely He wants us to take it to heart. Often poverty in ordinary comfort and always poverty of popularity and the esteem of this world, is to be the part of a good Christian. If Jesus would turn away a would-be disciple until he could face privation and want, does He not want us likewise to be ready to suffer, to be poor, to be despised for Him?

The late Dr. H. A. Ironside told me that when Dr. R. A. Torrey first started the Bible conference at Montrose, Pennsylvania, they had few buildings and few comforts. There were yet no comfortable quarters for the speakers, so he and Dr. Torrey slept in a farmhouse on folding canvass cots. In the night he heard Dr. Torrey turning restlessly his big frame on the narrow, temporary bed in the next room.

Dr. Ironside called: "Dr. Torrey, are you comfortable?" He said Dr. Torrey answered, "I am more comfortable than my Saviour ever was!"

Dr. Ironside himself, as a traveling Salvation Army evangelist, had slept on the ground in a city park. Once when I had him to lunch (not expensive but good food), he exclaimed, "Too good for sinners!"

Christ, with no place to lay His head, once sleeping in a boat in a storm, rejecting any disciple who did not face poverty and hardship, gives us some light on the case of the rich young ruler who wanted to do some good thing to inherit eternal life (Matt. 19:16-30; Mark 10:17-31; Luke 18:18-30). Certainly Jesus was teaching the man who claimed to keep all the commandments that his love of money and possessions was sin; and when He commanded the young man to sell all his goods and give to the poor in order to be a disciple, He was commanding repentance of that sin. Was not Jesus showing also that love of money, possessions, comfort, position, are snares that ruin discipleship?

Jesus said there, "How hardly shall they that have riches enter into the kingdom of God!" (Luke 18:24). He then added that those who leave "house, or parents, or brethren, or wife, or children, for the kingdom of God's sake" would surely receive a reward.

The Christian worker who must have a fine new car, must have a luxurious home, who feel they must eat as well and dress as expensively as other successful men, is likely to be greatly hindered in God's work. Oh, to find kinship with the Lord Jesus sleeping on the ground in Gethsemane!

We need to take to heart Paul's description of his life in II Corinthians 4:8-12 and his instruction for "approving ourselves as the ministers of God." He said it included "afflictions, in necessities, in distresses, In stripes, in imprisonments, in tumults, in labours, in watchings [to stay awake in the night watches], in fastings [doing without food]."

VERSES 3-11:

3 And the scribes and Pharisees brought unto him a woman taken in adultery; and when they had set her in the midst,

4 They say unto him, Master, this woman was taken in adultery, in the very act.

5 Now Moses in the law commanded us, that such should be stoned: but what sayest thou?

6 This they said, tempting him, that they might have to accuse him. But Jesus stooped down, and with *his* finger wrote on the ground, *as though he heard them not.*

7 So when they continued asking him, he lifted up himself, and said unto them, He that is without sin among you, let him first cast a stone at her.

8 And again he stooped down, and wrote on the ground.

9 And they which heard *it,* being convicted by *their own* conscience, went out one by one, beginning at the eldest, *even* unto the last: and Jesus was left alone, and the woman standing in the midst.

10 When Jesus had lifted up himself, and saw none but the woman, he said unto her, Woman, where are those thine accusers? hath no man condemned thee?

11 She said, No man, Lord. And Jesus said unto her, Neither do I condemn thee: go, and sin no more.

Jesus Forgives an Adulterous Woman

Dr. Scofield has a note here:

John 7.53-8.1-11 is not found in some of the most ancient manuscripts. Augustine declares that it was stricken from many copies of the sacred story because of a prudish fear that it might teach immorality! But the immediate context (vs. 12-46), beginning with Christ's declaration, "I am the light of the world," seems clearly to have its occasion in the conviction wrought in the hearts of the Pharisees as recorded in verse 9; as, also, it explains the peculiar virulence of the Pharisees' words (vs. 41).

There are three instances of Jesus dealing with women who had made a misstep: This one; the sinful woman of Luke 7; and the Samaritan woman of John 4.

Note the intent of the scribes and Pharisees. They hated Jesus, so they wanted an occasion to say He was not true to the Mosaic law. They were murderers at heart who would bribe Judas to betray Jesus so they could have Him crucified. We cannot feel they were great moral characters trying to teach morality. Any charges they made against this woman were suspect. They did not mean well. They were only trying to trap Jesus.

They said the woman should be stoned according to Mosaic law. No doubt they referred to Leviticus 20:10, "And the man that committeth adultery with another man's wife, even he that committeth adultery with his neighbour's wife, the adulterer and the adulteress shall surely be put to death."

Again the law says in Deuteronomy 22:22, "If a man be found lying with a woman married to an husband, then they shall both of them die, both the man that lay with the woman, and the woman: so shalt thou put away evil from Israel."

But these Scriptures insist that both the man and the woman be executed! Where, then, was the man? If the woman was taken "in the very act" of adultery, then they knew the man. Why shield him? Obviously they were not simply trying to do right. If they knew what was done and its penalty, why did they not do it without bringing the matter to Jesus and trying to trap Him? Or, since they really were not allowed now by Roman law to put the woman to death (18:31), why insist that Jesus should go against the law of Rome? They were not sincere.

But we cannot trust these wicked men. Possibly they had had some man seduce this woman and planned to come upon the scene just to let the man go and to tempt Jesus to say, "Stone her." Or it is possible the woman was raped and so according to Deuteronomy 22:25-29 she would be held blameless.

At any rate, note that these wicked men who broke God's law so easily were not fit to judge in this case. It was not their business nor right to stone anyone, and their witness was not trustworthy.

What did Jesus write on the ground? We do not know, but He waited for the wicked hearts of these men to accuse them, and soon conscience had its work. Jesus said, "He that is without sin among you, let him first cast a stone at her." He stooped again and wrote on the ground. Beginning with the oldest, the guilty men left Jesus and the woman alone.

Jesus said, *"Neither do I condemn thee: go, and sin no more"* (vs. 11). Dear Dr. Ironside comments so sweetly on this verse: "Oh, I should like to have heard Him speak that day. I am sure there was a tenderness, compassion and pity such as that poor woman had never heard in the voice of any man with whom she had held conversation . . . . To how many poor sinners, to how many adulterers and adulteresses, has it brought a message of hope and peace and blessing when they came to the feet of Jesus and trusted Him as Saviour!"

Jesus did not condone the woman's sin. He had no authority to stone her, but He did have a right to forgive her. We think the woman here was saved. If she was guilty, she knew it, and as the consciences of the wicked accusers were burning, do you suppose hers was not? All of us alike are sinful, but she did not go away without wanting to love and trust Christ and be assured of His forgiveness.

VERSE 12:

12 ¶ Then spake Jesus again unto them, saying, I am the light of the world: he that followeth me shall not walk in darkness, but shall have the light of life.

Jesus, the Light of the World

Jesus is not "*a* light" but "*the* Light of the world."

"By him were all things created, that are in heaven, and that are in earth, visible and invisible, whether they be thrones, or dominions, or principalities, or powers: all things were created by him, and for him: And he is before all things, and by him all things consist. And he is the head of the body, the church: who is the beginning, the firstborn from the dead; that in all things he might have the preeminence. For it pleased the Father that in him should all fulness dwell."—Col. 1:16-19.

Christ is absolute without rival or peer. All the light, all the truth is in Jesus. So "the fear of the Lord is the beginning of wisdom" (Ps. 111:10). He is the "Light, which lighteth every man that cometh into the world" (1:9). But God is pleased that in Him *all fullness dwells.*

"In whom are hid all the treasures of wisdom and knowledge" (Col. 2:3). He is "the way, the truth, and the life" (14:6). How absolute, how final, how completely unique is the Lord Jesus! He is the living Bread "which came down from heaven" (6:58). No other living bread gives everlasting life.

He is the "water of life" (Rev. 22:17) which one may drink and live forever; and "whosoever drinketh of the water that I shall give him shall never thirst," He said (4:14). But of all other waters, comforts, hopes and satisfactions in the world, it is true, as He said to the woman of Samaria, "Whosoever drinketh of this water shall thirst again." Jesus is "the way," the only Way. "Neither is there salvation in any other: for there is none other name under heaven given among men, whereby we must be saved" (Acts 4:12).

The moral man, the chaste woman, can be saved only by coming to Jesus. The Hindu can be saved only by coming to Jesus. The Moslem can be saved only by coming to Jesus. The Buddhist can be saved only by coming to Jesus. The modern humanist can be saved only by taking Jesus alone as his atoning Saviour.

Every person in the Old Testament or New who gets to Heaven must come through Jesus, "the . . . Light of the world." Abraham, David, Noah, Abel, all saw that Light by faith and were saved.

Jesus, the Light "of the world," not just a part of it. He "lighteth every man that cometh into the world" (1:9). "And he is the propitiation for our sins: and not for our's only, but also for the sins of the whole world" (I John 2:2). We are told that He is "not willing that any should perish, but that all should come to repentance" (II Pet. 3:9). He was lifted up on the cross. As He said, He would "draw all men unto me" (12:32). To offer less love and less atonement, less invitation than to the whole world, is a false doctrine. To make grace less than that and call it "sovereign grace" is not the grace of the Bible. "Where sin abounded, grace did much more abound" (Rom. 5:20). So grace is freely offered to "the world," not less than that. He is the Lamb of God who taketh away the sin of "THE WORLD."

VERSES 13-24:

13 The Pharisees therefore said unto him, Thou bearest record of thyself; thy record is not true.

14 Jesus answered and said unto them, Though I bear record of myself, *yet* my record is true: for I know whence I came, and whither I go; but ye cannot tell whence I come, and whither I go.

15 Ye judge after the flesh; I judge no man.

16 And yet if I judge, my judgment is true: for I am not alone, but I and the Father that sent me.

17 It is also written in your law, that the testimony of two men is true.

18 I am one that bear witness of myself, and the Father that sent me beareth witness of me.

19 Then said they unto him, Where is thy Father? Jesus answered, Ye neither know me, nor my Father: if ye had known me, ye should have known my Father also.

20 These words spake Jesus in the treasury, as he taught in the temple: and no man laid hands on him; for his hour was not yet come.

21 Then said Jesus again unto them, I go my way, and ye shall seek me, and shall die in your sins: whither I go, ye cannot come.

22 Then said the Jews, Will he kill himself? because he saith, Whither

I go, ye cannot come.

23 And he said unto them, Ye are from beneath; I am from above: ye are of this world; I am not of this world.

24 I said therefore unto you, that ye shall die in your sins: for if ye believe not that I am *he*, ye shall die in your sins.

It Is Jesus or Hell

Jesus gave record that He is the Son of God. The Father witnessed at Christ's baptism with a voice from Heaven, "Thou art my beloved Son; in thee I am well pleased" (Luke 3:21,22). So the requirement of the law that there be two witnesses was fulfilled (Deut. 19:15). The evidence was overwhelming that Jesus is the Son of God.

Why, then, the continued rebellion of the Jewish leaders against Christ? Because they knew not God. "He that knoweth God heareth us" (I John 4:6). They had no ear to hear, no heart to seek. They were unconverted, so they were set against God and Christ and against the evidence.

Note verse 20. Hatred plots seethe against Christ, but He cannot be killed yet because *"his hour was not yet come."*

They were "from beneath," were "of this world," so alien from Christ who is from above, and not a product of nature or a native of this world. So these would die in their sins because they did not believe in Christ and trust and love Him as Saviour.

As for all of us, it is Jesus or Hell. Here again the teaching that without being born again (literally from above), no man can see the kingdom of God.

VERSES 25-32:

25 Then said they unto him, Who art thou? And Jesus saith unto them, Even *the same* that I said unto you from the beginning.

26 I have many things to say and to judge of you: but he that sent me is true; and I speak to the world those things which I have heard of him.

27 They understood not that he spake to them of the Father.

28 Then said Jesus unto them, When ye have lifted up the Son of man, then shall ye know that I am *he*, and *that* I do nothing of myself; but as my Father hath taught me, I speak these things.

29 And he that sent me is with me: the Father hath not left me alone;

for I do always those things that please him.

30 As he spake these words, many believed on him.

31 Then said Jesus to those Jews which believed on him, If ye continue in my word, *then* are ye my disciples indeed;

32 And ye shall know the truth, and the truth shall make you free.

When Christ Is Crucified, Then They Will Know Who He Is

Who is Jesus? (vs. 25). With persistent unbelief they faced Him and again and again Jesus told them. But when Jesus is crucified later, they will know that "I am he," Jesus said. That must mean two things.

First, many of these would be saved. Acts 6:7 says, "And the word of God increased; and the number of the disciples multiplied in Jerusalem greatly; and a great company of the priests were obedient to the faith." And before that, John 12:42 says, "Nevertheless among the chief rulers also many believed on him; but because of the Pharisees they did not confess him, lest they should be put out of the synagogue." Yes, some of these elders of the Jews would be saved.

For these and others Jesus prayed on the cross, "Father, forgive them; for they know not what they do" (Luke 23:34). How wonderful that after years of wickedness, rebellion and sin, lost men sometimes may be saved! ". . . for they know not what they do." Those who later will be saved did not fully understand all that was involved in rejecting Christ, so they could be saved.

But if they did know what they did, then they committed the unpardonable sin of finally, knowingly turning against the full light and against Christ. How sweet the words of Jesus in verse 29, *"And he that sent me is with me: the Father hath not left me alone."* So Jesus would say to the Father, *"I knew that thou hearest me always"* (11:42). But we, the born-again ones, are God's little children, too, and the same sweet comfort is for us. For we are told:

"Let your conversation be without covetousness; and be content with such things as ye have: for he hath said, I will never leave thee, nor forsake thee. So that we may boldly say, The

Lord is my helper, and I will not fear what man shall do unto me."—Heb. 13:5,6.

So poorly do our half-blinded eyes see, we are not always conscious of God's presence. Jacob said, "Surely the Lord is in this place; and I knew it not" (Gen. 28:16).

Desolate Hagar, with her boy near death, did not know that God saw her distress and heard the cry of the lad and had a well in the wilderness (Gen. 21:14-20).

Moses, on the back side of the wilderness of Midian, you, with eighty frustrated years behind you and your dream of freeing Israel almost faded and gone, draw near to that burning bush! God is there, for He has heard the groaning of His enslaved people (Exod. 2:24).

Oh, Elijah, mighty prophet of God, are you alone the only witness, and now they seek to kill you? Must you flee to the wilderness and pray to die? No, God has an angel to prepare food and comfort with a time to sleep and restore you after almost impossible strain and exertion. And God sweetly answers that there are seven thousand unknown to Elijah who, like him, have not yet bowed their knee to Baal. God has work for Elijah yet, and instructions are given. Oh, God never forsakes His own! "I have been young, and now am old; yet have I not seen the righteous forsaken, nor his seed begging bread" (Ps. 37:25).

The Father was with Jesus always, and we, too, are loved and protected and cherished children of God. And with the Great Commission Jesus said, "Lo, I am with you alway, even unto the end of the world" (Matt. 28:20).

VERSES 33-45:

33 ¶ They answered him, We be Abraham's seed, and were never in bondage to any man: how sayest thou, Ye shall be made free?

34 Jesus answered them, Verily, verily, I say unto you, Whosoever committeth sin is the servant of sin.

35 And the servant abideth not in the house for ever: *but* the Son abideth ever.

36 If the Son therefore shall make you free, ye shall be free indeed.

37 I know that ye are Abraham's seed; but ye seek to kill me, because

my word hath no place in you.

38 I speak that which I have seen with my Father: and ye do that which ye have seen with your father.

39 They answered and said unto him, Abraham is our father. Jesus saith unto them, If ye were Abraham's children, ye would do the works of Abraham.

40 But now ye seek to kill me, a man that hath told you the truth, which I have heard of God: this did not Abraham.

41 Ye do the deeds of your father. Then said they to him, We be not born of fornication; we have one Father, *even* God.

42 Jesus said unto them, If God were your Father, ye would love me: for I proceeded forth and came from God; neither came I of myself, but he sent me.

43 Why do ye not understand my speech? *even* because ye cannot hear my word.

44 Ye are of *your* father the devil, and the lusts of your father ye will do. He was a murderer from the beginning, and abode not in the truth, because there is no truth in him. When he speaketh a lie, he speaketh of his own: for he is a liar, and the father of it.

45 And because I tell *you* the truth, ye believe me not.

Children of Abraham or of Satan?

Yes, they were "Abraham's seed" physically but not spiritually. They were Abraham's seed, like the dust of the earth, physical descendants (Gen. 13:16) but they were not his seed as the stars (Gen. 15:5). You see, the Ishmaelites and the Edomites were all Abraham's seed physically, too, but one is not a Jew (spiritually), "which is one outwardly; neither is that circumcision, which is outward in the flesh" (Rom. 2:28). But "know ye therefore that they which are of faith, the same are the children of Abraham" (Gal. 3:7). And again, "If ye be Christ's, then are ye Abraham's seed, and heirs according to the promise" (Gal. 3:29). The circumcision of the flesh is not true circumcision, but that of the heart (Rom. 2:28,29).

The Jews said, *"We be Abraham's seed, and were never in bondage to any man"* (vs. 33). But F. B. Meyer reminds us:

Never did men utter a more barefaced lie than when those Jews exclaimed: "We . . . were never in bondage to any man." Never in bondage! Had they forgotten the long and bitter bondage of Egypt, commemorated annually by the Passover? Or the dreary captivity of seventy years in Babylon, the memory of which lingered in the most plaintive odes of the Psalter? From that very Temple court, could they not see the Roman standard floating over the ancient palace of their kings, and hear the bugle-call regulating the movements of the victorious

Roman soldiery, while Roman officials met them at every turn? They could not have forgotten all this; but, in their pride, they wilfully shut their eyes to distasteful truths. Thus prejudice blinds men. "The eyes of their understanding are darkened."

Jesus could say, *"I know that ye are Abraham's seed"* (vs. 37), that is, actual, physical descendants but spiritually not the children of Abraham, having no part in the Abrahamic covenant. Jesus would say if they were in spirit Abraham's seed (vss. 39,40), they would, like Abraham, believe in Christ and be saved (Gen. 15:6).

A Jew now is not under special covenant with God except he be born again. The little nation Israel, now assembled in war and unbelief but no repentance, no turning to God, nor to Christ, are not God's people any more than unsaved Gentiles. The nation is still under the curse that caused its destruction and its dispersion in A. D. 70. Only in Christ can any Jew or Gentile inherit Abraham's covenant or be spiritually a child of Abraham.

Jewish mission boards love to quote the phrase, "To the Jew first," as if God had some special intent and blessing for Jews and wanted Jews saved more than others; but that is not true. Historically and chronologically the Gospel came to the Jews first. But the same Scripture says, "For there is no respect of persons with God" (Rom. 2:11). So a Jew can have no favor with God except turning to trust in Christ, just like a Gentile must do.

Jesus said, *"Ye are of your father the devil"* (vs. 44). Yes, Paul said to Elymas the sorcerer, "Thou child of the devil, thou enemy of all righteousness . . ." (Acts 13:10). A lost person has an evil heart and nature and he is in bondage to sin. He has Satan as his master. In that sense, every unconverted person is a child of Satan.

Some may say all people are children of God. No, only those born of God are God's children. We are all the creation of God and, like animals and all created things are, in that general sense "the offspring of God" or creatures of God. But unconverted people are not children of God but children of Satan.

And the deeds of the Jews who rejected Christ were *"the deeds of your father"* (vs. 41), the Devil. Murder and lying are the works of Satan. Satan is the father of lies. How sensitive ought Christians to be to speak and think the exact truth.

VERSES 46-50:

46 Which of you convinceth me of sin? And if I say the truth, why do ye not believe me?

47 He that is of God heareth God's words: ye therefore hear *them* not, because ye are not of God.

48 Then answered the Jews, and said unto him, Say we not well that thou art a Samaritan, and hast a devil?

49 Jesus answered, I have not a devil; but I honour my Father, and ye do dishonour me.

50 And I seek not mine own glory: there is one that seeketh and judgeth.

The Sinless Christ Is Called Bad Names

Who ever faced Christ openly and accused Him of sin? Even infidels, going on in their unbelief, have praised Jesus as the fairest, greatest moral character who ever lived. Calling Him only a man, they admit His superiority to all other men, but thus they show their own insincerity, for if Jesus were not God, He was either the greatest liar and deceiver ever to live or He was insane and unaccountable.

As Jesus said to the rich young ruler, "Why callest thou me good? there is none good but one, that is, God" (Matt. 19:17). In other words, if Jesus be good, He is God and deserves to be addressed not simply as "Master" or "Rabbi" but "Lord." To deny the sinless purity of Jesus would prove one a biased fool. To admit His sinlessness and deny His claim to deity is the height of folly and insincerity.

These Jews are not of God, so they cannot hear spiritual truth. How sin in the heart perverts judgment and blinds the mind and coerces the will!

They cannot convince or convict Jesus of sin, so they use slanderous, foolish accusations: *"Thou art a Samaritan"* (vs. 46). How they hated the Samaritans, these half-breeds in blood and half-breeds in religion. They thought to be called a Samaritan would be about as disgraceful a lie as they could manufacture about Jesus. Wicked men in heresy do not face the truth. They accuse the righteous and slander the good men they cannot meet. Harry Emerson Fosdick would say that he did not know a single intelligent man who believed in the virgin birth. Liberals say fundamentalists, Bible believers, are "anti-intellectual" or "uncharitable." They said, *"Thou . . . hast a devil"* (vs. 48). In other words, they say that Jesus is not accountable but beside Himself or unbalanced and demon-possessed. That is irresponsible, childish, wicked name-calling. It is not intelligent argument.

In this connection see verse 41 again. They said, "We be not born of fornication." No doubt they said it with a sneer—as if to say, "Like some people we know here," referring, no doubt, to the fact that Mary was with child before she was married. If the blameless Lord Jesus suffered slander and abuse, "The servant is not greater than his lord." We should not be discouraged if we suffer wrongfully.

First Peter 4:12-16 tells us:

"Beloved, think it not strange concerning the fiery trial which is to try you, as though some strange thing happened unto you: But rejoice, inasmuch as ye are partakers of Christ's sufferings; that, when his glory shall be revealed, ye may be glad also with exceeding joy. If ye be reproached for the name of Christ, happy are ye; for the spirit of glory and of God resteth upon you: on their part he is evil spoken of, but on your part he is glorified. But let none of you suffer as a murderer, or as a thief, or as an evildoer, or as a busybody in other men's matters. Yet if any man suffer as a Christian, let him not be ashamed; but let him glorify God on this behalf."

The Lord Jesus knew He was blameless, and He was glad to leave the verdict with God His Father.

VERSES 51-59:

51 Verily, verily, I say unto you, If a man keep my saying, he shall never see death.

52 Then said the Jews unto him, Now we know that thou hast a devil. Abraham is dead, and the prophets;

and thou sayest, If a man keep my saying, he shall never taste of death.
53 Art thou greater than our father Abraham, which is dead? and the prophets are dead: whom makest thou thyself?
54 Jesus answered, If I honour myself, my honour is nothing: it is my Father that honoureth me; of whom ye say, that he is your God:
55 Yet ye have not known him; but I know him: and if I should say, I know him not, I shall be a liar like unto you: but I know him, and keep his saying.

56 Your father Abraham rejoiced to see my day: and he saw *it*, and was glad.
57 Then said the Jews unto him, Thou art not yet fifty years old, and hast thou seen Abraham?
58 Jesus said unto them, Verily, verily, I say unto you, Before Abraham was, I am.
59 Then took they up stones to cast at him: but Jesus hid himself, and went out of the temple, going through the midst of them, and so passed by.

Christ, Conqueror of Death

Since Jesus is God, He is master of death. He said to Martha, "I am the resurrection, and the life." And one who believes in Christ already has everlasting life. So, fittingly, Jesus could say, "Lazarus sleepeth." When for a bit we lay aside this mortal body, the Christian is not dead but the body only sleeps to be made perfect and raised up again.

Asleep in Jesus! blessed sleep!
From which none ever wakes to weep . . . .

"Verily, verily, I say unto you, If a man keep my saying, he shall never see death" (vs. 51). Said beloved Dr. Ironside: "Then what does he see? He sees the entrance into the Father's house. Death, we are told, is our servant. How does death serve us? By ushering us into the presence of God."

When Mrs. William Booth of the Salvation Army was dying, she looked up and said, "Is this death? Why, this is glorious!" Somebody said, "But you are suffering." She said, "O yes; the waters are rising; but so am I."

Yes, death for a Christian is only the means of entrance into eternal blessing—with Christ. But, oh, what a sad thing if one does not know Christ! That will mean eternal banishment from God.

"Abraham is dead, and the prophets" (vs. 52), they said, but "God is not the God of the dead, but of the living" (Matt. 22:32). So Abraham must be alive. Yes, if you think only of mortal life,

of a few troubled years, Abraham and the prophets' lives are over. Ah, but they never died; they just laid aside these mortal bodies but lived on, and even the sleeping bodies of the Christians will be raised up.

"Abraham rejoiced to see my day: and he saw it, and was glad" (vs. 56), Jesus said. Yes, when Abraham came to know of the starry host of the saved seed through his greater Seed, Jesus Christ, Abraham saw through all the sacrifices to the atoning Saviour and Abraham "believed in the Lord; and he counted it to him for righteousness" (Gen. 15:6).

When Abraham climbed Mount Moriah and the lad Isaac beside him carried the wood and asked, "Behold the fire and the wood: but where is the lamb for a burnt-offering?" Abraham could answer in faith, "My son, God will provide himself a lamb for a burnt-offering" (Gen. 22:7,8).

How guilty are all who, with manyfold more evidence than Abraham had, do not believe in Christ and rejoice!

Had Jesus seen Abraham? Yes, He was before Abraham. And in rage they would have stoned Him, but no, His time is not yet, and He hid Himself and slipped away from their unseeing eyes.

John 9

AND as *Jesus* passed by, he saw a man which was blind from *his* birth.

2 And his disciples asked him, saying, Master, who did sin, this man, or his parents, that he was born blind?

3 Jesus answered, Neither hath this man sinned, nor his parents: but that the works of God should be made manifest in him.

4 I must work the works of him that sent me, while it is day: the night cometh, when no man can work.

5 As long as I am in the world, I am the light of the world.

6 When he had thus spoken, he spat on the ground, and made clay of the spittle, and he anointed the eyes of the blind man with the clay,

7 And said unto him, Go, wash in the pool of Siloam, (which is by interpretation, Sent.) He went his way therefore, and washed, and came seeing.

"As Jesus Passed By"

The book of John is an inspired revelation of one "sign" after another which are meant to show that Jesus is the Son of God and cause people to trust Him and be saved (20:30-34). This healing of the man blind from birth was clearly a miracle. It was not a case where one had seen for a long time and then had a cataract over the eye which could be removed, nor anything of the kind. Bear in mind the purpose, then, of this miracle and the purpose which God had in having the record written for us.

Was Jesus frightened about the threatened stoning in the last chapter? No, He avoided it easily because it was not in the will of God. Jesus was not distracted from duty: He must work the works of God now; the great day of His ministry will soon be gone. He must heal those blind eyes, must have John write it down by divine inspiration for all the millions who will read the Bible.

"I must work the works of him that sent me, while it is day: the night cometh when no man can work."—Vs. 4.

Herschel Ford illustrates this verse this way:

It is said of Michelangelo that while he was working on his great statue of Moses, he slept in his clothes, kept some food at his side, and ate a bite from time to time.

It is said of John Milton that he arose at four o'clock in the morning in order to write his poetry when his mind was fresh.

It is said that when the churches were closed to John Wesley, he went to the cemetery and used his father's tombstone as a pulpit. Oh, that we were just as zealous in our work for the Lord! Just a few years now, then the night will come when we can work no more.

On the cross Jesus will cry, "It is finished," and this miracle and souls won are part of the finished job.

Hiding from those who took up stones to stone Him, slipping out of the Temple, He yet sees a poor man *"blind from his birth"* (vs. 1). The man did not appeal for help. No one interceded for him as far as we know, but Jesus knew this man was in the plan of God *"that the works of God should be made manifest in him"* (vs. 3). His blindness was not because of the sins of his parents nor of his own sins, but allowed of God for a glorious hour when Jesus will show His power and defy the Pharisees' tradition and opposition about the Sabbath healings.

". . .he saw a man" (vs. 1). He saw more about that man than anybody else ever saw. We are told, "And needed not that any should testify of man: for he knew what was in man" (2:25). And, oh, the compassion Jesus had on this blind man! Jesus would give this man more than he ever hoped for or thought of. It is true that he is able to do exceeding abundantly above all that we ask or think; and so this man will get more than he ever thought of. He may have wished that he could see, but he gets eternal life as well.

We are reminded that God said to the children of Israel, desolate, captives in Babylon, discouraged and punished, "For I know the thoughts that I think toward you. . .thoughts of peace, and not of evil, to give you an expected end" (Jer. 29:11). God has better thoughts for us than we have for ourselves!

Verse 2 has a remarkable question: *"Master, who did sin, this man, or his parents, that he was born blind?"* The disciples seemed to think it possible that the man had sinned before he was born. It may be that the disciples believed the heathen idea of reincarnation, that is, that before a child is born, that soul has lived in some other body on this earth. Jesus plainly said that that was not true of this man.

Nothing in the Scripture indicates that anybody ever sinned before he was born. In this particular case, as you see from verse 3, the affliction on the child was not blamed on the parents: *"Neither hath this man sinned, nor his parents. . . ."*

The Bible teaches that sometimes children do suffer because of the parents' sins. In Exodus 20:5 that is clearly taught. We know that in modern days, often children are blind from birth, the eyes having been infected by a disease which the mother or father acquired in sin. Oftentimes drunkenness on the part of the parents is responsible for the birth of feeble-minded children. But in this case, the Saviour plainly stated that the blindness of this man was not caused by the parents' sin, nor his own, *"but that the works of God should be made manifest in him"* (vs. 3). It had been in the plan of God when this child was born, that he should be healed by the Saviour, and that this should be a sign of the deity of Christ.

Verses 4 and 5 mean that the work of Jesus was planned out long beforehand by the Father and Son together and that day by day Jesus carried out that plan.

"When he had thus spoken, he spat on the ground, and made clay of the spittle, and he anointed the eyes of the blind man with the clay" (vs. 6). A good many miracles of Jesus were instantaneous. Compare the healing of the blind man in Luke 18

with the healing of this blind man. Both were supernatural miracles, contrary to the laws of nature. In this one case, the Lord chose to use mud; in the other case, He did not. There was no difference in the power used. There was no special virtue in the mud, nor in the pool of Siloam. It seems certain that the man was sent to the pool of Siloam to wash to show his faith in Jesus. He believed that he could be made whole and did what Jesus said. Blind Bartimaeus had already shown his faith by calling out to Jesus, "Jesus, thou son of David, have mercy on me" (Mark 10:46-52 and Luke 18:35-43 tells the same story, and the man's name is given in Mark).

Why Mud to Cure Blind Eyes?

It would seem unnatural that mud made from dirt under foot would cure blind eyes! But this is not natural; it is supernatural. God has no limitation on means He can use. He can use Moses' rod to open the Red Sea, or bring a river of water out of the rock in the wilderness. Under Gideon, He can use pitchers and lamps of three hundred to set to flight and defeat multiplied thousands of these Midianites. He can use a boy's lunch to feed five thousand! He can use "unlearned and ignorant men" to move multitudes, work miracles, astonish the Jewish leaders, and save many at Jerusalem. But God has chosen "the foolish things of the world to confound the wise, and God hath chosen the weak things of the world to confound the things which are mighty; And base things of the world, and things which are despised, hath God chosen, yea, and things which are not, to bring to nought things that are" (I Cor. 1:27,28).

Let us remember that in healing, as in teaching, preaching, and winning souls, God uses means. He can heal without physicians and medicine, but He more often uses them. Ordinarily, God's people have food, clothes and money because they work and earn it. We pray for daily bread, but usually we are asking God to help us earn it. We pray for the healing of the sick, but usually we intend that God will bless whatever means we are able to use—the physician's skill, the nurse's care, the remedies God has put into the hands of doctors and people. That does not mean we must limit our faith to what doctors and medicines can do. God can and often does heal wonderfully beyond any human means or expectation.

Dr. J. C. Macaulay comments:

> There is a danger that we become book-learned in holy things, and go out to apply indiscriminately the methods taught in the textbooks. Our Lord was a great individualist, and He treated men as individuals, not as pieces of machinery rolled off the assembly line.
>
> Other blind men were given sight, but not by the same method. When God makes a man, He breaks the mould. When God treats an individual, He scraps the method. We do not find our Lord using the same method twice, because He deals with men as men, not as "cases." He uses invariable and fixed principles, and applies these in an infinite variety of methods.

The main thing is, God has compassion on sick and troubled people. When it can honor God best, He is glad to heal them.

But here we learn that "all things work together for good" for us (Rom. 8:28). God had not forgotten that poor man. He had good things and salvation ahead for the blind man! Thorns and trials are part of life, but none are without God's planning and care.

When Israel was carried away and was in Babylon, the Lord said these comforting words:

> *"For I know the thoughts that I think toward you, saith the Lord, thoughts of peace, and not of evil, to give you an expected end. Then shall ye call upon me, and ye shall go and pray unto me, and I will hearken unto you. And ye shall seek me, and find me, when ye shall search for me with all your heart."*—Jer. 29:11-13.

VERSES 8-15:

8 ¶ The neighbours therefore, and they which before had seen him that he was blind, said, Is not this he that sat and begged?

9 Some said, This is he: others *said,* He is like him: *but* he said, I am *he*.

10 Therefore said they unto him, How were thine eyes opened?

11 He answered and said, A man that is called Jesus made clay, and

anointed mine eyes, and said unto me, Go to the pool of Siloam, and wash: and I went and washed, and I received sight.

12 Then said they unto him, Where is he? He said, I know not.

13 ¶ They brought to the Pharisees him that aforetime was blind.

14 And it was the sabbath day when Jesus made the clay, and opened his eyes.

15 Then again the Pharisees also asked him how he had received his sight. He said unto them, He put clay upon mine eyes, and I washed, and do see.

Great Discussion Over the Healing of the Blind Man

Is this the man who was blind? How astonished were the neighbors and those who had seen him so long utterly blind; and now he sees, is physically normal! The miracle could not escape notice. Someone, no doubt, had helped the blind man from the Temple area down the Vale of Cedron, to the pool of Siloam, perhaps a half mile away, and now he got about well, and the change astonished those who knew him!

So they took him to the Pharisees. To them he told the story again—yes, he is the same man. And a Man named Jesus had anointed his eyes. He washed in Siloam's pool and now sees!

Why the concern of the Pharisees? This Jesus had healed on the Sabbath, had made an issue of His right to do so. He had challenged the authority and the traditions of the Pharisees. He claims the authority of God.

Jesus seems to have deliberately made an issue of His right to heal on the Sabbath day, or to put it another way, His right to ignore the ceremonial law as they interpreted it. Jesus in Luke 6 in Mark 2 and in Matthew 12 had plainly claimed that He was the Lord of the Sabbath. By that Jesus meant to claim that He was one with the God who set apart the seventh day following the creation in Genesis 2; therefore, that He Himself was the Creator as well as was God the Father.

In Luke 6 is a very clear case where Jesus deliberately chose to go against the belief of these Pharisees about the Sabbath, knowing that it would offend them.

In the book of John, the record of the controversy between Jesus and the Jews about the Sabbath begins in the 5th chapter and in the 18th verse there we see that the Jews planned to kill Him on that score. In John 7:23 we see that the Jews still were angry about the same thing; and throughout the 6th chapter they were seeking to kill Him. In chapter 9, then, Jesus forces the issue by healing another man on the Sabbath. Had the Jews accepted Jesus as the Son of God, the promised Messiah, they would have had to admit that He was the Lord of the Sabbath. The Sabbath is used many places as a type of all the ceremonial law. It is the only part of the ceremonial law which is in the Ten Commandments. It is especially mentioned in Colossians 2:16,17 as representative of those ceremonial laws which were a shadow, or type, which was fulfilled in the coming of Christ.

The meaning of the Old Testament Sabbath was this: six days of labor represents man perfectly keeping the law through human power, and so earning his peace with God, and entering that great Sabbath of rest, the kingdom of Christ. Remember, the Sabbath was a part of the Mosaic law, was never made known until Mount Sinai, and was a special sign between God and Israel concerning that law. So when Jesus came to bring grace and truth in opposition to the law given by Moses (1:17), necessarily He must set aside the old shadow. He seems to have healed people publicly on the Sabbath again and again; had His disciples pluck grain on the Sabbath (Luke 6:1), and deliberately forced them either to accept or reject Him as the very Son of God.

VERSES 16-34:

16 Therefore said some of the Pharisees, This man is not of God, because he keepeth not the sabbath day. Others said, How can a man that is a sinner do such miracles? And there was a division among them.

17 They say unto the blind man again, What sayest thou of him, that he hath opened thine eyes? He said, He is a prophet.

18 But the Jews did not believe concerning him, that he had been blind, and received his sight, until they called the parents of him that had received his sight.

19 And they asked them, saying, Is this your son, who ye say was born blind? how then doth he now see?

20 His parents answered them and said, We know that this is our son, and that he was born blind:

21 But by what means he now seeth, we know not; or who hath opened his eyes, we know not: he is of age; ask him: he shall speak for himself.

22 These *words* spake his parents, because they feared the Jews: for the Jews had agreed already, that if any man did confess that he was Christ, he should be put out of the synagogue.
23 Therefore said his parents, He is of age; ask him.
24 Then again called they the man that was blind, and said unto him, Give God the praise: we know that this man is a sinner.
25 He answered and said, Whether he be a sinner *or no*, I know not: one thing I know, that, whereas I was blind, now I see.
26 Then said they to him again, What did he to thee? how opened he thine eyes?
27 He answered them, I have told you already, and ye did not hear: wherefore would ye hear *it* again? will ye also be his disciples?
28 Then they reviled him, and said,

Thou art his disciple; but we are Moses' disciples.
29 We know that God spake unto Moses: *as for* this *fellow*, we know not from whence he is.
30 The man answered and said unto them, Why herein is a marvellous thing, that ye know not from whence he is, and *yet* he hath opened mine eyes.
31 Now we know that God heareth not sinners: but if any man be a worshipper of God, and doeth his will, him he heareth.
32 Since the world began was it not heard that any man opened the eyes of one that was born blind.
33 If this man were not of God, he could do nothing.
34 They answered and said unto him, Thou wast altogether born in sins, and dost thou teach us? And they cast him out.

The Blind Man Defends; the Pharisees Accuse

The Pharisees say, *"This man is not of God, because he keepeth not the sabbath day"* (vs. 16). But very sensibly, the man healed knows He is "a prophet," that is, one acting or speaking in the power of God. This man's heart approved the evidence that Jesus was from God.

His father and mother refused to commit themselves about Jesus. "Yes," they said, "this is our son, who was born blind. He now sees but we do not know how. You ask him." They feared the Jews who had threatened to cast out of the synagogue any who admitted Jesus was the Christ.

Can the Jews convince the man who was healed? No. The Pharisees say He is a sinner (vs. 16), but the man who was blind said, "But He opened my eyes!" That was evidence enough. Then more boldly he argues, "God couldn't hear Jesus if He were a sinner!"

The healed man was right in principle. If Jesus had not been from God and speaking for God, He would not have had that miracle. But it is not necessarily literally true that *"God heareth not sinners"* (vs. 31). The record is inspired; the words of the blind man not necessarily inspired.

<u>God does sometimes in mercy hear sinners</u>. He heard those men on the ship in the storm at sea when Jonah, fleeing from God, was the cause of the trouble (Jonah 1:15). So God in mercy hears people who do not deserve it, and He loves and blesses people who do not love Him.

Many an unconverted man has good health, has a job, a loving wife, healthy children, by God's mercy. So God in mercy sometimes hears the cry of the unconverted sinner. But the sense is that God is not committed nor obligated to hear the wicked as He is to hear His children who love and trust Him. Even God's children may block their prayers by unconfessed, unrepented sin, as many, many Scriptures clearly indicate (Isa. 59:1,2; II Chron. 7:14; Prov. 28:13; Ps. 66:18; Matt. 5:23,24; Mark 11:25; I Pet. 3:7,12).

"I have told you already, and ye did not hear" (vs. 27).

Men make out of what they hear what they prefer to believe. The good Dr. Guthrie once said, "Objects take their color from the eyes that look at them; the very sun, as well as the sky and sea and mountains, appear yellow to the jaundiced eye. The brightest prospect wears an air of gloom to a gloomy mind."

When men do not wish to see the truth, they misinterpret it to make of it a lie. *". . .wherefore would ye hear it again"* (vs. 27). Good Dr. W. B. Riley, in commenting on this verse, tells us this about Mrs. Wesley:

"Mrs. Wesley was giving John a lesson one day. She had repeated a single sentence about 19 times, and was ready to add the 20th repetition, when a neighbor lady said, 'Why do you tell him that over so often and often?' 'Because,' answered Mrs. Wesley, 'he is dull of understanding, and if I did not tell him the 20th time, I should have had all my pains of 19 repetitions for nothing.' "

Dr. James M. Gray was a very systematic and disciplined Bible student and teacher. He said that he had a rule: Before he would preach on a passage of Scripture or before writing comments on it, he would read the passage over carefully seven times to make sure to imprint it all upon his mind.

Moses' disciple or a disciple of Jesus (vs. 28)? The Jewish leaders were not lovers of God and of Christ but of Moses. They did not depend on the Lamb of God sacrificed for us and pictured in the passover but depended on the animal sacrifices themselves. They loved the law and ceremonies but these were not regarded as a schoolmaster to lead us to Christ. They loved the letter, not the spirit. "For they being ignorant of God's righteousness, and going about to establish their own righteousness, have not submitted themselves unto the righteousness of God" (Rom. 10:3).

Some weeks ago I left a plane at O'Hare Field in Chicago and as I walked along the corridor toward the terminal, a man approached me, looked on one side, went to the other side, then joyfully called my name, "You are Dr. Rice! I know from THE SWORD OF THE LORD! Praise the Lord! I have been so blessed by THE SWORD! I am Greek Orthodox but I am ecumenical. Once I knew the Lord here (pointing to his forehead), but now, praise God, I know Him here" (pointing to his heart)!

Oh, yes, that is it! To know Him in the head is not enough, but to know Him in the heart is right. Unashamed, that good man cried aloud, "Praise the Lord!" in one of the largest airport terminals in the world. He knew the Lord in His heart! Those Jews who hated Jesus only knew God superficially in the head.

Many Christians have a tendency to trust in Moses or in the law or ceremonies. On the Mount of Transfiguration, Peter would put Moses and Elijah on a par with Jesus, suggesting that tabernacles be set for Moses and Elijah and Jesus alike. But God rebuked the thought, covering them all with a cloud, then with Moses and Elijah gone, God said from Heaven, "This is my beloved Son, in whom I am well pleased; hear ye him" (Matt. 17:5).

Jesus will have no rivalry, not of Moses, not of a church, not of baptism, or any ceremony, or any doctrine, or leader, or faith. Christ Himself alone is the way to Heaven. He said, "I am the way, the truth, and the life: no man cometh unto the Father, but by me" (14:6).

VERSES 35-41:

35 Jesus heard that they had cast him out; and when he had found him, he said unto him, Dost thou believe on the Son of God?

36 He answered and said, Who is he, Lord, that I might believe on him?

37 And Jesus said unto him, Thou hast both seen him, and it is he that talketh with thee.

38 And he said, Lord, I believe. And he worshipped him.

39 ¶ And Jesus said, For judgment I am come into this world, that they which see not might see; and that they which see might be made blind.

40 And *some* of the Pharisees which were with him heard these words, and said unto him, Are we blind also?

41 Jesus said unto them, If ye were blind, ye should have no sin: but now ye say, We see; therefore your sin remaineth.

"Do You Believe on the Son of God?"

Was the man healed before he was saved? Yes, we think he was, but his heart was ready. As soon as he knew Jesus was the Son of God, he gladly trusted Him for salvation. He said, *"Who is he, Lord, that I might believe on him?"* (vs. 36). Or perhaps in his heart he was seeking long for salvation. Maybe, conscious of what a wonderful thing God had done for him, his heart went out in grateful love to God and wanted God.

In Shamrock, Texas, a young couple came to the pastor's home for a wedding, along with relatives. I took the young couple apart to ask them each if they knew they had trusted in Christ, knew Him as their own Saviour. The young man answered eagerly, "Yes, that is why I wanted you to perform the ceremony." They had driven miles for that. I saw the young, beautiful girl was deeply in love, so happy. I called her attention to the great gift God had given in a morally clean, a godly young husband with a good name and a good job and who loved her sincerely. Well, did she not want the Lord Jesus to lead in her home and make her a Christian wife? With grateful heart and tears she trusted the Lord Jesus and we proceeded with the wedding ceremony.

"The goodness of God leadeth thee to repentance," says Romans 2:4. Oh, for a heart of gratitude for all God's mercies, so others, too, as soon as they know who Jesus is, will turn to Him.

Note the words: ". . .on the Son of God" (vs. 35), not to believe about Him. Devils also believe that way and tremble (Jas. 2:19). Only trusting in Christ, personally depending on Him for salvation, relying on Him, is saving faith.

For the Unseeing to See; for the Seeing to Be Blinded!

What a strange doctrine is this! It is a strong statement of Jesus in verse 39. Jesus came *"that they which see not might see."* He has just made a blind man see. That is symbolic for the blinded hearts who do not know God. Jesus cares for you. He wants the blind to see, the far-away to draw nigh, the poor to be made rich. Isaiah 61:1 foretold about Jesus, "The Spirit of the Lord God is upon me; because the Lord hath anointed me to preach good tidings unto the meek; he hath sent me to bind up the brokenhearted, to proclaim liberty to the captives, and the opening of the prison to them that are bound." No one is too blind but that he may see, if his heart wants to see truth and right and meet God.

But Jesus came also, He said, *"that they which see might be made blind"* (vs. 39). What a strange saying! Does not Jesus want to give the truth and everlasting life to all? Yes. But only if they want it and are open to it.

If these Jews knew much Old Testament Scripture, does not Jesus want to reveal the meaning to them? Only if their hearts are open to the spiritual offer and are hungry for God's righteousness! God is under no obligation to give truth to the mind of one whose heart is set against following it. Again we remind you of the great principle Jesus stated in John 3:19-21:

"And this is the condemnation, that light is come into the world, and men loved darkness rather than light, because their deeds were evil. For every one that doeth evil hateth the light, neither cometh to the light, lest his deeds should be reproved. But he that doeth truth cometh to the light, that his deeds may be made manifest, that they are wrought in God."

Jesus often spake in parables, not in plain didactic statements. Why? So only those with a heart for it, and ears for it, would get the truth. He explained in Matthew 13:10-15:

"And the disciples came, and said unto him, Why speakest thou unto them in parables? He answered and said unto them, Because it is given unto you to know the mysteries of the kingdom of heaven, but to them it is not given. For whosoever hath, to him shall be given, and he shall have more abundance: but whosoever hath not, from him shall be taken away even that he hath. Therefore speak I to them in parables: because they seeing see not; and hearing they hear not, neither do they understand. And in them is fulfilled the prophecy of Esaias, which saith, By hearing ye shall hear, and shall not understand; and seeing ye shall see, and shall not perceive: For this people's heart is waxed gross, and their ears are dull of hearing, and their eyes they have closed; lest at any time they should see with their eyes and hear with their ears, and should understand with their heart, and should be converted, and I should heal them."

Why do people go on in heresies, explaining Scriptures to prove their false teaching? Because, having a heart unwilling to follow God, He allows them to be blinded. Those after the flood "did not like to retain God in their knowledge," so "God gave them up to uncleanness." He "gave them up unto vile affections." He "gave them over to a reprobate mind."

"Because that, when they knew God, they glorified him not as God, neither were thankful; but became vain in their imaginations, and their foolish heart was darkened. Professing themselves to be wise, they became fools, And changed the glory of the uncorruptible God into an image made like to corruptible man, and to birds, and fourfooted beasts, and creeping things. Wherefore God also gave them up to uncleanness through the lusts of their own hearts, to dishonour their own bodies between themselves: Who changed the truth of God into a lie, and worshipped and served the creature more than the Creator, who is blessed for ever. Amen.

"For this cause God gave them up unto vile affections: for even

*their women did change the natural use into that which is
against nature: And likewise also the men, leaving the natural
use of the woman, burned in their lust one toward another; men
with men working that which is unseemly, and receiving in
themselves that recompence of their error which was meet. And
even as they did not like to retain God in their knowledge, God
gave them over to a reprobate mind, to do those things which are
not convenient."*—Rom. 1:21-28.

The Bible is not open to the brilliant mind that goes with a
hardened, unbelieving heart.

"Are we blind also?" the Jews asked (vs. 40). They saw what
Jesus meant, but if they were innocently blind to the truth about
Jesus, it would be no sin. He would have shown Himself clearly
to them as He did to the blind man who was healed and was so
anxious to know that he might believe on Him. But, in truth,
they must have realized that Jesus is the Christ of God, all He
claimed to be. If so, they now saw so much their rejecting Him
was willful sin. If they had complete knowledge and still rejected
Him, it would be unpardonable. On the cross Jesus said,
"Father, forgive them; for they know not what they do" (Luke
23:34).

John 10

VERILY, verily, I say unto you, He that entereth not by the door into the sheepfold, but climbeth up some other way, the same is a thief and a robber.

2 But he that entereth in by the door is the shepherd of the sheep.

3 To him the porter openeth; and the sheep hear his voice; and he calleth his own sheep by name, and leadeth them out.

4 And when he putteth forth his own sheep, he goeth before them, and the sheep follow him: for they know his voice.

5 And a stranger will they not follow, but will flee from him: for they know not the voice of strangers.

6 This parable spake Jesus unto them: but they understood not what things they were which he spake unto them.

7 Then said Jesus unto them again, Verily, verily, I say unto you, I am the door of the sheep.

8 All that ever came before me are thieves and robbers: but the sheep did not hear them.

9 I am the door: by me if any man enter in, he shall be saved, and shall go in and out, and find pasture.

10 The thief cometh not, but for to steal, and to kill, and to destroy: I am come that they might have life, and that they might have *it* more abundantly.

Born-Again Ones Are God's Sheep

The Scriptures often liken people to sheep. The parable of the lost sheep (Matt. 18:11-14; Luke 15:3-7) speaks of one saved as a lost sheep found. Jesus said He came "unto the lost sheep of the house of Israel" (Matt. 15:24). To backslidden Peter, Jesus commands, "Feed my sheep" and "Feed my lambs" (21:15-17). All these inferences, I think, look to lost people who should be won, but Jesus said false prophets are wolves in sheep's clothing, pretending to be Christians when they are not (Matt. 7:15). In the great judgment of living Gentiles still alive when Jesus will return to reign after the Great Tribulation, the saved are pictured as sheep and the lost as goats.

Psalm 95:7 and 100:3 say that "we are . . . the sheep of his hand" and "the sheep of his pasture." The dear Lord was moved with compassion on the multitude for they were "as sheep having no shepherd." Christians are especially God's sheep and that is the symbolization of this 10th chapter of John. So it is in Psalm 23, "The Lord is my shepherd."

"... *the shepherd of the sheep*" (vs. 2).

"*I am the door of the sheep*" (vs. 7).

"*I am the door*" (vs. 9).

Dr. Ironside says on these verses:

> Now He seems to change the figure here. Before He said, "I am the Shepherd, and I entered in by the door." Now He says, "I am the door." Is it contradictory? Not at all.
>
> You may have heard a little incident told by Dr. Piazzi Smith. On one occasion he saw a shepherd leading his flock up the hill. He led them into the fold and made them comfortable, and then Dr. Smith said, "Do you leave the sheep in this fold all night?" "Yes." "But aren't there wild beasts around?" "Yes." "Won't they try to get the sheep?" "Yes." "Well, you have no door here; how can you keep the wild beasts out?" But the Arab shepherd lay down on his side, and as he settled himself in that entry way, he looked up and smiled and said, "I am the door." You see, no wild beast could enter without awakening him, and no sheep would go out over his body.

Dr. J. H. Jowett, speaking on this passage, said: "The door to what? Into everything where we ought to go. The door into the central rooms of everything. The way into the Holy Place is not through the synagogue, but through the Christ; not through an organization, but through the Christ; not through any mode of ecclesiastical procedure, but through the Christ . . . . He is the Door from the wilderness of guilt into the rich pastures of grace."

Who is the thief and robber? Anyone who would deal with the sheep or lead Christians in spiritual matters without coming in through Christ, the Door. The Moslem, the spiritist, the Christian Scientist, the Buddhist, the humanist, the modernist all claim a religion without relying on Christ the Son of God as an atoning Sacrifice and Saviour, so all are thieves and robbers.

There is a personal relationship, a oneness between Christ and His own. This is not true with those who follow any other religion or hope of Heaven.

Strangely, sheep who seem to be such dumb creatures are strongly attached to their shepherd. In the Holy Land we saw that sheep are not driven but they follow. If two shepherds meet for greeting, the flocks may mix but immediately when one shepherd starts away and calls, his sheep "know his voice" and follow him. And lambs make the most loving and dependent pets, more so than dogs or cats.

In Nathan's story to David the "one little ewe lamb" slept in his master's bosom, ate of his meat and drank of his cup and "was unto him as a daughter" (II Sam. 12:3). So the affection and dependence of a sheep on the shepherd is very close. Remember,

> **"Mary had a little lamb . . .**
> **And everywhere that Mary went,**
> **The lamb was sure to go."**

We know that sheep are ignorant, sometimes willful, carelessly straying. Christians, too, are not blameless nor sinless. But one who is born again has an inward turn toward Christ and in some sense, in heart follows Him, although never perfectly as far as outward life is concerned.

Christian David may sin terribly and did, but in Psalm 51 we hear his heart-cry, ". . . my sin is ever before me," and a plea, "Restore unto me the joy of thy salvation"!

Peter, saved and an apostle, in a time of great temptation did deny Jesus. He cursed and swore and lied and quit the ministry. Oh, but when he heard the cock crow and remembered Jesus' warning and looked and saw His face, Peter "went out, and wept bitterly" (Matt. 26:75).

Being one of God's sheep does not make one perfect, but it does make one a child of God, a partaker of the divine nature (II Pet. 1:4). It does make one the temple of the Holy Ghost and subject to His rebuke and His reminding.

What is the difference between the Lord Jesus and all other religious leaders who do not come by way of Christ, the Door? He comes to save; they cannot save. False prophets "through covetousness shall . . . with feigned words make merchandise of you: whose judgment now of a long time lingereth not, and their damnation slumbereth not" (II Pet. 2:3). Deniers of Christ's deity and the saving Gospel are not good men; they do not have good hearts or good natures. It is the enemy of Christ who sows tares in the field.

Heresy has always a moral guilt, a self-will, a bias, a willing ignorance (II Pet. 3:5).

VERSES 11-15:

11 I am the good shepherd: the good shepherd giveth his life for the sheep.
12 But he that is an hireling, and not the shepherd, whose own the sheep are not, seeth the wolf coming, and leaveth the sheep, and fleeth: and the wolf catcheth them, and scattereth the sheep.
13 The hireling fleeth, because he is an hireling, and careth not for the sheep.
14 I am the good shepherd, and know my *sheep*, and am known of mine.
15 As the Father knoweth me, even so know I the Father: and I lay down my life for the sheep.

Christ, the Good Shepherd

Christ said, "I am the good shepherd." Good because in devotion He gives His life for us, His sheep. The Scriptures often remind us that He is our Shepherd: "the Shepherd and Bishop of your souls" (I Pet. 2:25), "the chief Shepherd" (I Pet. 5:4). Very tender is this in Isaiah 40:11, "He shall feed his flock like a shepherd: he shall gather the lambs with his arm, and carry them in his bosom, and shall gently lead those that are with young."

And Psalm 23 has been the voice of millions who have this good Shepherd, who leads them "beside the still waters" and makes them to "lie down in . . . pastures" of plenty.

But God's loving care comes after the mercy of forgiveness. Christ died for our sins. No leader or hero can do man any good without personal salvation. Christ died for His sheep.

". . . *the good shepherd giveth his life for the sheep*" (vs. 11). When He gives His life for us, it is that ours might be saved. Dr. W. B. Riley illustrates this verse so beautifully:

> I read a story awhile ago of a man in the far West who came upon a grizzly bear. A vigorous fight ensued. The man, equipped with a knife, drove it to the bear's vitals as they contested

in strength. Torn and bleeding he dragged himself aside to die, and in a little note that they found at his side was written, "The bear killed me, but I also killed him."

It has its kinship in the sacrifice of Christ. Satan nailed Him to the cross, but in the hour and article of death, He, Christ, killed the adversary and then, in turn, "conquered over death itself and the grave."

Someone has said that we are nowhere and never safe for a single minute without God. But is not the opposite true, namely, that everywhere, and at all times we are safe, the Lord with us?

You have heard that tender little story of the lad who became frightened in the night, and, quitting his own bed, crept into that of his father; but as the storm increased, the lightning flashes grew in number and the thunder peals shook the building. He was restless, and leaped up from his pillow again and again, with fear evidently upon him. Finally he said to his father, "Father, have you got your face turned toward me?" "Yes, my lad." "Can I put my hand in yours?" Accorded that privilege, he laid his head snuggly into the pillow against his father's forehead and slept—a sleep of perfect quiet. The peace of broad day was in his soul since Father was present and was watching over him.

Our Great Shepherd neither slumbers nor sleeps! His face is toward us! Our protection is adequate!

The hireling, priests like those who rejected Jesus, ministers and professors who do not believe the Bible but desire to have the prestige and salaries of religious workers, or just professional ministers, cannot be trusted to care for Christ's sheep. They leave them to the wolves or false prophets, to their ruin.

VERSE 16:

16 And other sheep I have, which are not of this fold: them also I must bring, and they shall hear my voice; and there shall be one fold, *and* one shepherd.

Christ's Other Sheep

Do you love all of Christ's sheep? Do you face it that many others of other lands, of other denominational names, are

Christ's sheep, also? I do not mean liberal, unbelieving, unconverted modernists or false cultists who deny the deity of Christ and His virgin birth, the blood atonement. They are not saved; are not Christ's sheep.

Second John, verses 9 to 11, says:

"Whosoever transgresseth, and abideth not in the doctrine of Christ, hath not God. He that abideth in the doctrine of Christ, he hath both the Father and the Son. If there come any unto you, and bring not this doctrine, receive him not into your house, neither bid him God speed: For he that biddeth him God speed is partaker of his evil deeds."

We are not to call infidels Christians. They are not Christ's sheep.

Some who believe the Bible are not saved. Devils believe, too, and those who still expect to earn salvation by ceremonies, or by masses, or by confessions to priests, or by morality, are not saved, so are not Christ's sheep.

But the more we stress the fundamentals of the Faith and preach separation from unbelievers, the more some carnal Christians separate from those who are godly, believing, converted people, differing on baptism or the security of a believer, or over healing, or tongues, or on the Second Coming, for example. That is wrong. Those other sheep are Christ's sheep and so as dear to Him as we are. Are we like the priest and Levite who passed by on the other side of the wounded, robbed man on the road to Jericho? The Samaritan was different in religion, but he loved the wounded man and rescued him.

My book, *I Am a Fundamentalist,* deals carefully with this, and the book on separation from unbelievers, *Come Out or Stay In?* goes into more detail than we have room for here. Oh, but we ought to love Christ's other sheep.

But the best soul winners: Moody, Torrey, Chapman, Finney, Sam Jones, Bob Jones, Ham, Earle, Gipsy Smith—all had sweet fellowship and cooperation with born-again Christians from many denominations who were glad to join in the emphasis on saving sinners and on the great fundamentals of the Faith, leaving the lesser distinctive differences to be preached in their own churches.

In a united, cooperative campaign in an Ohio city, an old Englishman, greatly blessed, sought me out. He was a graduate of Spurgeon's Pastors' College and told me how Spurgeon and two Anglican bishops had gone together and united in a blessed soul-winning effort. He urged me to follow that pattern still.

I do not mean any church should slack up on teaching the whole counsel of God. I can work with godly Presbyterians if they make no division or strife about teaching sprinkling as baptism and baptizing babies. They know what I believe, and I feel free, at proper times, to lovingly correct any false doctrine. I have had Pentecostal and Nazarene pastors and churches cooperate in blessed revivals, but it was understood they would not in that revival effort make an issue on tongues or on entire sanctification.

Romans 14:1 says, "Him that is weak in the faith receive ye, but not to doubtful disputations." We ought to have fellowship, but we should avoid "doubtful disputations." There are times and places for preaching everything we ought to preach, and we can differ with people and say so but still love them and appreciate them and work with them where possible.

Nor do we teach that all God's people should unite in one colossal, superchurch, with no doctrinal distinctives. No, let each Christian and each group hold faithfully to honest convictions and hold to what they understand are scriptural standards for church membership, standards in doctrine and practice, but let us love other Christians and count them God's sheep, too.

F. B. Meyer says: "There may be, and there will be, many folds. By the very constitution of our minds we are sure to have different views of truth, of church government, and of the best methods of expressing our love and worship. And there are many who would have us believe that if we do not belong to their special fold, we have no right to assume that we belong to the flock. But it is not so . . . . There may be many folds, yet one flock; even as there is one Shepherd . . . . Whatever may be your special fold, the one question is: Do you hear and obey the

Shepherd's voice? If so, you belong to the one flock."

What a joy when human barriers are all torn down, when all misunderstandings will be corrected, and when all of Christ's sheep are openly known to be in the one fold with one Shepherd! That time will come in Heaven.

VERSES 17-21:

17 Therefore doth my Father love me, because I lay down my life, that I might take it again.
18 No man taketh it from me, but I lay it down of myself. I have power to lay it down, and I have power to take it again. This commandment have I received of my Father.
19 ¶ There was a division therefore again among the Jews for these sayings.
20 And many of them said, He hath a devil, and is mad; why hear ye him?
21 Others said, These are not the words of him that hath a devil. Can a devil open the eyes of the blind?

How the Father Loves Jesus!

Why does the Father love Jesus? Verse 17 tells why: ". . . *because I lay down my life, that I might take it again.*" There must be thousands of other reasons, but the tender mercy of Jesus in giving up His life for the sinner seems to be the most lovely thing about Jesus in the eyes of the Father, who also loved the world enough to give up His Son for that death on the cross. I remind you of John 3:35 and John 5:20.

Can you imagine how the Father loves the Son? It is an amazing, infinite, eternal love. "God so loved the world"—yes; well, as we see the miraculous compassion of God toward sinful men, how must the Father glory in His perfect and infinite and sinless Son, beautiful in character beyond expression, that He gave Himself to die for those the Father loves and He loves. Jesus is a perfection of all that is holy and righteous and good and all that an all-wise God could delight in.

My father and mother gave me to God to be a preacher of the Gospel the day I was born. After I learned of this twenty-four years later and became a preacher, I went to my father's home town to conduct an extended big tent revival campaign. My father, a state Senator, hitched his car to block and tackle to raise the 800-pound center poles. Then night after night he brought his cane-bottom chair and leaned it against a tent pole. With eyes shining with unshed tears, he heard me preach. And at the invitation he would soon have his arm around some sinner man he knew, to lead him to Christ and bring him down the aisle to confess Christ openly.

I know how his heart burned! I found in an old, old Bible of his after his death heavily underlined, "His name is John," the words of Zacharias naming his son John the Baptist, as a "man sent from God." I felt sure my father marked those words when he named me John. My preaching was the culmination of long years of prayers and dreams. He delighted in it.

But this is such a frail picture of the delight of God the Father in His obedient Son. How strange that "it pleased the Lord to bruise him" (Isa. 53:10)! If God could weep, He might have wept when Jesus suffered on the cross. Instead, God was pleased. "It pleased the Lord to bruise him." He could have said, "I laid it on my dear Son! He delights to do My will. He was the only way an honest God could forgive sin and save sinners. He gladly does it for Me, and He loves men as I do. How glad I am!"

You need not wonder that all the Father has He gives to the Son. All judgment is turned over to Him. No one took Jesus' life—He laid it down Himself (vs. 18). When the time was not yet, He simply evaded those who would kill Him. On the cross when He could say, "It is finished," then only He "gave up the ghost" (19:30).

At Pentecost Peter preached this: "Therefore being by the right hand of God exalted, and having received of the Father the promise of the Holy Ghost, he hath shed forth this, which ye now see and hear." So God the Father and Christ Jesus the Son were thoroughly agreed and of one heart as Jesus lovingly went to the cross for sinners.

In deliberate blindness, those who hated Him said, "He hath a devil" (vs. 20). But sensible people said, "These are not the words of him that hath a devil. Can a devil open the eyes of the blind?" (vs. 21).

VERSES 22-26:

22 ¶ And it was at Jerusalem the feast of the dedication, and it was winter.
23 And Jesus walked in the temple in Solomon's porch.
24 Then came the Jews round about him, and said unto him, How long dost thou make us to doubt? If thou be the Christ, tell us plainly.
25 Jesus answered them, I told you, and ye believed not: the works that I do in my Father's name, they bear witness of me.
26 But ye believe not, because ye are not of my sheep, as I said unto you.

Willful Unbelievers Asked More Proof of Christ's Deity

"How long dost thou make us to doubt? If thou be the Christ, tell us plainly" (vs. 24). He has told them many times, but their ears were deaf, were set and determined to rejection.

Scoffers, supposed scholars, as blind and as willful as these, have said that only Matthew and Luke of the four Gospels claim the virgin birth, that John did not. But the very term, "only begotten Son" (1:18; 3:16,18), is a claim to virgin birth. It is not a claim that Jesus is the only *son* of God; it is a claim that Jesus is the only Son physically begotten of God, not of man.

When Jesus said in John 8:23,24, "Ye are from beneath; I am from above: ye are of this world; I am not of this world. I said therefore unto you, that ye shall die in your sins: for if ye believe not that I am he, ye shall die in your sins," He was clearly claiming supernatural origin from above. He was not conceived "of this world" but from above.

He claims that He was before Abraham, that He did the work of the Father in perfection. All His claims are of deity. And they are recorded more in detail in John than in the other Gospels because John's Gospel is written "that ye might believe that Jesus is the Christ, the Son of God; and that believing ye might have life through his name" (20:31). And the work of Christ, verse 25 says, bears witness that Jesus is all He claims.

But these wicked men are not of Christ's sheep. They are not turned toward Christ and with their heart attitude they will not receive any evidence.

VERSES 27-30:

27 My sheep hear my voice, and I know them, and they follow me:

28 And I give unto them eternal life; and they shall never perish, neither shall any *man* pluck them out of my hand.

29 My Father, which gave *them* me, is greater than all; and no *man* is able to pluck *them* out of my Father's hand.

30 I and *my* Father are one.

Christ's Sheep Shall Never Perish

Verse 27 simply restates that a born-again person has had a miraculous change. It is not outward but inward. It is not always apparent, even to the one who is saved.

Once a giant of a man, a drunken fighter, rough and tough, was saved in Shamrock, Texas. He eagerly began to read the Bible and would often come to me, his pastor, for answers to Bible questions.

One day he came, eyes bright with tears, to tell how some old cronies had determined to get him to drink again. One arrogant young man had thrown beer in his face thinking the smell would draw him to drink with them.

He said he told the man, "I am not mad at you. I am just sorry for you. You know I could break you in two with my two hands, and once I would have done it. But now I am not mad at all. I will pray for you." Then, turning to me, this big fellow who had had so many fights, said, "Brother Rice, something sure has happened to me!"

The results of the new birth are not always so quickly seen, but they are there, as Romans 8:14 says, "For as many as are led by the Spirit of God, they are the sons of God." The leading is not compelling and the hearing of Christ's voice is not plain to all bystanders. "Man looketh on the outward appearance, but the

Lord looketh on the heart." The *following* of verse 27 is a heart action. Saved people are changed inside.

"And I give unto them eternal life" (vs. 28). It is not purchased, it is not earned, it is not bargained for. "For the wages of sin is death; but the gift of God is eternal life through Jesus Christ our Lord" (Rom. 6:23). Not only does God give the life; He gives the "eternal" also. It is foolish and not an honest use of language to claim that eternal life is just a name of the quality of life without any reference to how long it lasts. Some think one may have a bit of eternal life and it lasts until he does wrong and forgets to pray, or doesn't "hold out faithful." No, every honest heart will have to say that what God gives is eternal life, and so it lasts forever.

That is what John 3:15,16,36; 5:24; 6:40; 6:47; Acts 10:43; 13:38 and 16:31 says. How foolish and irresponsible is the heart that is not impressed with the repeated statement that Jesus made again and again and again—that the believer has already everlasting life. The Christian may say, ". . . we have now received the atonement" (Rom. 5:11). The believer is already "born of God." His sins—past, present and future—are paid for on the cross. The Spirit of God already has moved in to dwell in the temple of his body.

And here the Lord plainly says, ". . . *and they shall never perish . . .*" (vs. 28). A child of God may be chastened, for God chastens every son whom he receiveth. He may lose fellowship and weep, as did David, praying that God will "restore unto me the joy of thy salvation" (Ps. 51:12).

And salvation has to be eternal, because it is what God does, not what man does. It is salvation by grace, not of works, lest any man should boast. Therefore since "where sin abounded, grace did much more abound" (Rom. 5:20) salvation by grace must be eternal salvation.

And Jesus continues about His sheep: ". . . *neither shall any man pluck them out of my hand"* (vs. 28). But "man" is in italics here in the King James Version and was not in the original Greek New Testament. What Jesus really said was, ". . . neither shall any pluck them out of my hand"—no man, no circumstances, no devil, not even the believer himself can pluck a Christian from the hand of Christ.

But we are in the dear hands of the Father also, and none shall pluck us from the Father's hand.

Dr. H. A. Ironside tells this experience:

> A lady came to me in San Francisco and she said, "I agree with everything you said tonight except that doctrine, once saved, always saved. I have never found that in the Bible."
>
> I said, "Don't you believe the words of the Lord Jesus? Let me show you what He said."
>
> She replied, "I know where you are going to turn: John 10:28,29."
>
> "Well," I said, "you do know. But let me read the verses: 'And I give unto them eternal life; and they shall never perish, neither shall any man pluck them out of My hand. My Father, which gave them Me, is greater than all; and no man is able to pluck them out of My Father's hand.' " I inquired, "Do you believe that?"
>
> She said, "Not in your way."
>
> I said, "What is my way?"
>
> "Well," she said, "you believe that if a person is once saved, he can never be lost."
>
> I read it again: "My sheep hear My voice, and I know them, and they follow Me: and I give unto them eternal life, and they shall never perish, neither shall any man pluck them out of My hand. My Father, which gave them Me, is greater than all; and no man is able to pluck them out of My Father's hand." I said, "Do you believe that?"
>
> "Not in your way."
>
> "But I am not telling you my way. I have not explained it at all. Do you not believe what the Son of God has said?"
>
> "Not the way you do."
>
> "Well, let me read it again." And I read it through once more, except for one change. I put "ten years" in place of "eternal life." I inquired, "What does that mean?"
>
> She answered, "Well, it would mean that if a person once got saved, he would be saved for ten years."
>
> "Exactly; now let us stretch it a bit. 'I give unto them life for forty years.' What does it mean now?"
>
> She admitted it would imply that one thus saved would be secure for forty years.
>
> "Suppose it read, 'I give unto them life as long as they are faithful.' "

"That is what I believe," she replied.

"But that is not what it says. It says, 'My sheep hear My voice, and I know them, and they follow Me: and I give unto them eternal life; and they shall never perish, neither shall any man pluck them out of My Father's hand.' How long does that mean?"

She said, "As long as they remain His sheep." And she went out.

She did not want light, so turned her back upon it. If one would only take God's Word at its face value. "I give unto them eternal life." It could not be eternal if it could ever come to an end, and He said, "They shall never perish." "No man can pluck them out of My hand." There could not be a stronger statement. His sheep are safe in the hands of the Father and the Son. There is no power in earth or hell that can pluck us out, and there is no power in heaven that would want to do so.

"I defy the world," wrote Alexander Peden to the prisoners in Dunottar Castle, when Scotsmen were suffering for their faith, "I defy the world to steal one lamb out of Christ's flock unmissed." While Paul gives us this: "I am persuaded that neither death, nor life, nor angels, nor principalities, nor powers, nor things present, nor things to come, nor height, nor depth, nor any other creature, shall be able to separate us from the love of God, which is in Christ Jesus our Lord."

Some say this doctrine encourages sin. No, on the contrary. It tends to shut every boasting mouth. For this kind of salvation is wholly unmerited, is the free gift of God.

I have a covenant with the Angel Gabriel that when we get to Heaven, if we hear any person bragging, "I made it! I paid the price! I held out faithful! For holding out faithful, I got to Heaven!"—then Gabriel and I plan to pitch that arrogant boaster over the bannisters of Heaven.

VERSES 31-39:

31 Then the Jews took up stones again to stone him.
32 Jesus answered them, Many good works have I shewed you from my Father; for which of those works do ye stone me?

33 The Jews answered him, saying, For a good work we stone thee not; but for blasphemy; and because that thou, being a man, makest thyself God.

34 Jesus answered them, Is it not written in your law, I said, Ye are gods?

35 If he called them gods, unto whom the word of God came, and the scripture cannot be broken;

36 Say ye of him, whom the Father hath sanctified, and sent into the world, Thou blasphemest; because I said, I am the Son of God?

37 If I do not the works of my Father, believe me not.

38 But if I do, though ye believe not me, believe the works: that ye may know, and believe, that the Father is in me, and I in him.

39 Therefore they sought again to take him: but he escaped out of their hand,

Jesus Further Confounds His Critics

Here the persistent refrain comes again: *"Then the Jews took up stones again to stone him"* (vs. 31). Jesus had said before, "Which of you convinceth me of sin" (8:46). Now He makes him face again his good works: *". . . for which of those works do ye stone me?"* (vs. 32). Not an evil word had He ever spoken.

A prominent Jewish woman, daughter of a rabbi whose husband owned the largest Kosher market in a Canadian province, wept as I told her the story of Calvary which, alas, seems so commonplace to many of us. With choked voice she said, "That was wicked! Jesus had never harmed anybody. The Jews will surely have to pay for their sin!" I told her that not only Jews but all of us had crucified the Saviour. And any unbiased heart would have to say, as she did, that Jesus never did harm anybody.

They accused Him of blasphemy because He said He was the Son of God (vs. 33). And Jesus insisted they must face and evaluate the works He did. Every honest, open heart looking on Jesus is bound to accept His deity as quickly as did the man born blind who said, "Who is he, Lord, that I might believe on him?"

What was the blasphemy? *"Because that thou, being a man, makest thyself God"* (vs. 33). Well, the truth is that He was Man in all perfection, but He was also God—as truly Man as though He had never been God, and as truly God as though He had never become Man, says H. A. Ironside.

Jesus persistently told the Jews that He was the Son of God. He could have had their love and fellowship on any other basis, but the Lord Jesus will not take the allegiance of any man in the world unless He be received as very God. Jesus was not pleased when Nicodemus said, "Rabbi, we know that thou art a teacher come from God," in 3:2. Jesus is not simply a teacher come from God; Jesus IS God! Jesus rebuked the rich young ruler who came to Him saying "good master." Jesus said, "Why callest thou me good? None is good save one, that is God." Jesus was not a good master, not a good teacher, unless He was God. He insisted on being called God and received as God. Read again John 8:23 and 24.

There is no way for any one to be saved unless he accepts the Lord Jesus as the very Son of God. Remember that that is what the book of John was written for—to show that Jesus is the Son of God and get people to trust Him for salvation (20:30,31).

But again Jesus escaped, for His time is not yet come. No man can kill Jesus until God's appointed hour.

VERSES 40-42:

40 And went away again beyond Jordan into the place where John at first baptized; and there he abode.
41 And many resorted unto him, and said, John did no miracle: but all things that John spake of this man were true.
42 And many believed on him there.

Back to the Place of Baptizing

Jesus went back to the place where John had been baptizing *"at first"* (vs. 40). In the account in Matthew we are simply told that John was preaching in the wilderness of Judaea and baptized people in Jordan. In Luke 3:3 we are told, "And he came into all the country about Jordan, preaching the baptism of repentance for the remission of sins." One would suppose that was on the west bank of Jordan since He preached in the wilderness of Judaea. In John 3:23 we are told that "John also was baptizing in Aenon near to Salim, because there was much water there." We suppose this is the place to which Jesus retreated beyond the Jordan River to the eastern bank. Even there many followed Him and they remembered the witness of John who had baptized Jesus. John had done no miracles but he was obviously a prophet of God and they believed "all things that John spake of this man" (vs. 41), and that beyond Jordan many more people were saved, believing on Him (vs. 42).

Reader, above all, make sure that in your deepest heart you are trusting only in Jesus for forgiveness, salvation and eternal life.

John 11

NOW a certain *man* was sick, *named* Lazarus, of Bethany, the town of Mary and her sister Martha.

2 (It was *that* Mary which anointed the Lord with ointment, and wiped his feet with her hair, whose brother Lazarus was sick.)

3 Therefore his sisters sent unto him, saying, Lord, behold, he whom thou lovest is sick.

4 When Jesus heard *that*, he said, This sickness is not unto death, but for the glory of God, that the Son of God might be glorified thereby.

5 Now Jesus loved Martha, and her sister, and Lazarus.

6 When he had heard therefore that he was sick, he abode two days still in the same place where he was.

7 Then after that saith he to *his* disciples, Let us go into Judæa again.

Beloved Lazarus, Mary, Martha

If you remember the specific purpose of the book of John, as inspired by the Holy Spirit and written for us in John 20:30 and 31, you will see why we are told of the raising of Lazarus from the dead in the book of John, but it is not told in the other Gospels. The "signs" (miracles) in John prove that Jesus is the Son of God.

Bethany, the village where lived the two sisters, Mary and Martha and brother Lazarus, is on the Eastern backside of the Mount of Olives fifteen furlongs (vs. 18), perhaps nearly two miles from Jerusalem.

". . . *the town of Mary and her sister Martha*" (vs. 1). Did nobody else live there? Oh, yes; but the heart of Jesus turned like a homing pigeon to the place where He had been loved and fed, where Martha would do any service to please Him, where Mary with eager eyes sat and gazed in His face while He talked of heavenly things. Oh, to Jesus the town of Bethany was "the town of Mary and her sister Martha."

Would it not be blessed if when the Lord Jesus thought of your town, He always thought of it as the place where you live and where He is loved and welcomed, as at that home in Bethany!

There is a cave here which tradition says is the one where

Lazarus was buried. However, the lower entrance has been closed up and sight-seers now go down nineteen steps into the cave. Catholics have built a church nearby.

Martha seems to be the older of the two sisters. Luke 10:38-42 tells how Martha received Jesus and that she seems to be in charge, cumbered about much serving to Jesus and the twelve apostles, while Mary, so eager for spiritual truth, sat at Jesus' feet. Martha entreated Jesus for Mary to help. But Jesus said, "Mary hath chosen that good part, which shall not be taken away from her," and He would not send her away.

It seems that Jesus stayed often in this home while in the Jerusalem area. Matthew 21:17 says, "And he left them [the priests], and went out of the city into Bethany; and he lodged there." In the early morning He and the disciples would walk into the city of Jerusalem where He would teach during the day and return at night to Bethany.

"It was that Mary which anointed the Lord with ointment" (vs. 2). That anointing is discussed in the next chapter, but remember only Matthew had written this story; Mark had many years before, but did not name Mary. Tradition says the Gospel of Matthew was written in the year 37. Dr. Scofield thinks Mark was written between A. D. 57 and 63. But this Gospel of John was not written until somewhere between 85 and 90 A. D. So for many years readers of the Gospel had known of some unnamed woman who had anointed Jesus at Bethany. Now this verse identifies which Mary this was. The occasion of the anointing is given, since it had already, when the book of John was written, become well known throughout all that country, as Jesus promised that it would be (Mark 14:9; Matt. 26:13). That was the best known thing that this Mary ever did.

In verse 4, Jesus makes it clear that the sickness came upon

Lazarus for the specific purpose of glorifying God, that is, that Jesus might be glorified as the miracle-working Son of God.

"Now Jesus loved Martha, and her sister, and Lazarus" (vs. 5). That seems at first a little strange. Does not Jesus love everybody? Yes, "God so loved the world," and Jesus died for the sins of the whole world. And this love of Jesus for all us poor sinners reminds us, "Greater love hath no man than this, that a man lay down his life for his friends" (15:13). But this love for all mankind is of grace, undeserved.

But Jesus says in John 14:21, "He that hath my commandments, and keepeth them, he it is that loveth me: and he that loveth me shall be loved of my Father . . . ." So Jesus promised to those who keep His commandments, ". . . and I will love him, and will manifest myself to him." So one, by loving effort to please God and do His will, is more loved by Christ personally. That is love replying to love, and the love of fellowship added to the love of Christ.

John also calls himself "the disciple whom Jesus loved" once when John was leaning on the breast of Jesus at the Last Supper. The only other person for whom a special love of Christ is mentioned is the rich young ruler who had labored so hard to keep the commandments but yet went away sorrowful, unsaved. "Then Jesus beholding him loved him" (Mark 10:21).

Lazarus was sick but *"this sickness is not unto death, but for the glory of God, that the Son of God might be glorified thereby,"* Jesus said (vs. 4). Lazarus would die but death was only a passing shadow, and those four days in the grave were no more than if he had visited a nearby town four days.

Does this mean that the dear Lord Jesus knew and planned the death of Lazarus? Yes. And now knowing that Lazarus was sick and near to death, Jesus deliberately abode two days still in the same place where He was. Jesus was over beyond the Jordan River, John 10:40 tells us. The messenger would be a day or more coming, and Jesus a day or two in arriving after He had waited two days! In other words, Jesus waited for Lazarus to die.

Death seems a shocking, unwelcomed visitor, more terrible than war and famine to most people. But here we learn that death is in the will of God, not an accident, and not a matter of circumstances unrelated to God's loving care. If God notes the fall of every sparrow and counts the very hairs of our head, then we may be sure that every sickness, every seeming tragedy, every death, is in the hand of God. Indeed, it can be and is intended to be for the glory of God.

When death threatens in our homes, can we not look up to the Lord Jesus and ask His help but without panic, without undue fret, knowing that God has His hand on the whole affair? Remember, "the earth is the Lord's, and the fulness thereof; the world, and they that dwell therein" (Ps. 24:1).

But now Lazarus is dead, and Jesus is ready to go and manifest His mighty power again, before He goes to the crucifixion.

VERSES 8-17:

8 *His* disciples say unto him, Master, the Jews of late sought to stone thee; and goest thou thither again?

9 Jesus answered, Are there not twelve hours in the day? If any man walk in the day, he stumbleth not, because he seeth the light of this world.

10 But if a man walk in the night, he stumbleth, because there is no light in him.

11 These things said he: and after that he saith unto them, Our friend Lazarus sleepeth; but I go, that I may awake him out of sleep.

12 Then said his disciples, Lord, if he sleep, he shall do well.

13 Howbeit Jesus spake of his death: but they thought that he had spoken of taking of rest in sleep.

14 Then said Jesus unto them plainly, Lazarus is dead.

15 And I am glad for your sakes that I was not there, to the intent ye may believe; nevertheless let us go unto him.

16 Then said Thomas, which is called ˋDĭd-́ў-mŭs, unto his fellow-disciples, Let us also go, that we may die with him.

17 Then when Jesus came, he found that he had *lain* in the grave four days already.

Jesus Goes Back to Bethany

The disciples were concerned, frightened. In the last chapter, verse 31, "the Jews took up stones again to stone him," and then again in verse 39, "they sought again to take him," but He had slipped away and escaped. Now will He go back to the area of Jerusalem where they certainly planned to kill Him? Thomas did not have much faith but he had great loyalty. He said, *"Let us also go, that we may die with him"* (vs. 16).

But Jesus knew He would not die until He gave Himself to die, would not die until the appointed time when the passover lambs were dying and when the Scripture would be fulfilled by His death on the cross. So in verse 9 Jesus is saying that there are some twelve hours of daylight and a man who walks in the light would not stumble, and the Lord Jesus is saying, 'I know what I am doing, and I am not walking in darkness.'

What a lesson for us! Every Christian can have light on his pathway daily. He can know what to do, where to go, what to say. If he is arrested for Jesus' sake, he need not fret about what he should say; it will be given him in that hour.

Now Jesus tells His disciples, *"Lazarus sleepeth; but I go, that I may awake him out of sleep"* (vs. 11). What a wonderfully sweet word this is for the Christian's death! It is not death but only the shadow of death. The body sleeps for a little while, while the spirit goes immediately to be with God.

> **"Asleep in Jesus—blessed sleep.**
> **From which one never wakes to weep."**

The Christian may say with sweet confidence and assurance as does Paul, speaking of the resurrection, "O death, where is thy sting? O grave, where is thy victory? . . . But thanks be to God, which giveth us the victory through our Lord Jesus Christ" (I Cor. 15:55, 57).

Lazarus is only asleep. Jesus used the same word about the daughter of Jairus when He said, ". . . the damsel is not dead, but sleepeth" (Mark 5:39). They laughed Him to scorn but Jesus raised the maiden at once. Oh, death has lost its sting for a Christian in the will of God!

Again the disciples thought Lazarus was simply resting and would awake, and Jesus told them plainly, *"Lazarus is dead"* (vs. 14). Jesus knew all the details about Lazarus, even though He was absent. And He told them that intentionally He had left Lazarus to die *"to the intent ye may believe"* (vs. 15).

Verse 16 is pathetic: *"Then said Thomas . . . Let us also go, that we may die with him."* That Thomas loved the Lord, there is no doubt, since he was willing to die with Jesus, but his lack of faith was pitiful. In this connection, see John 20:24-29. In John 20:20 Jesus teaches that it is far better to believe the Lord without waiting for proof. There had been plenty of evidence to show that Jesus knew what He was about.

Dr. H. A. Ironside says with quaint application about verse 16: " *'Then said Thomas* [we call him doubting Thomas], *which is called Didymus . . . .'* Didymus means 'twin.' Who was the other twin? Perhaps if you look into the mirror you will see him. Thomas, the twin, *'said. . .unto his fellowdisciples, Let us also go, that we may die with him.'* Thomas was loyal to his Master, even when he could not understand."

And then Jesus and the twelve came across the Jordan up a steep road toward Jerusalem and arrived at Bethany, on the Mount of Olives.

VERSES 17-27:

17 Then when Jesus came, he found that he had *lain* in the grave four days already.

18 Now Bethany was nigh unto Jerusalem, about fifteen furlongs off:

19 And many of the Jews came to Martha and Mary, to comfort them concerning their brother.

20 Then Martha, as soon as she heard that Jesus was coming, went and met him: but Mary sat *still* in the house.

21 Then said Martha unto Jesus, Lord, if thou hadst been here, my brother had not died.

22 But I know, that even now, whatsoever thou wilt ask of God, God will give *it* thee.

23 Jesus saith unto her, Thy brother shall rise again.

24 Martha saith unto him, I know that he shall rise again in the resurrection at the last day.

25 Jesus said unto her, I am the resurrection, and the life: he that believeth in me, though he were dead, yet shall he live:

26 And whosoever liveth and believeth in me shall never die. Believest thou this?

27 She saith unto him, Yea, Lord: I believe that thou art the Christ, the Son of God, which should come into the world.

Jesus Comforts Martha

Many friends of Mary and Martha came out to Bethany to comfort them. It is sweet to have the love and consolation of those dear to us in a time of trial. At many a funeral and graveside I have known the bereaved, with choked voice, to thank God for friends and to say that one of the great blessings brought by the sorrow of death is the sweet, loving fellowship of friends.

But these are not enough. Only Jesus has the answer to the problems of death and suffering. Only Jesus can answer the question, Why? Why? Why? So Martha, when she heard Jesus was coming, went to meet Him. And now she must express the question of her heart, 'Why, Jesus, didn't you come? *If thou hadst been here, my brother had not died'* (vs. 21). But Martha was not in rebellion nor in despair. Surely Jesus still will have the answer, for Martha said, *"But I know, that even now, whatsoever thou wilt ask of God, God will give it thee"* (vs. 22).

And now here is the blessed answer: *"Thy brother shall rise again"* (vs. 23). Oh, Martha said, *"I know that he shall rise again in the resurrection at the last day"* (vs. 24). But Jesus reminds her, *"I am the resurrection, and the life"* (vs. 25).

Jesus can have a resurrection anytime He wishes. And in a time like this, there can be no comfort and assurance unless it is that the loved one has believed on Jesus, and *"whosoever liveth and believeth in me shall never die"* (vs. 26). Not at this time, for Lazarus is only sleeping. And not at a future time for the Christian. For a Christian may go through the Valley of the Shadow of Death, but the monster Death is tamed. Yes, Lazarus will rise again now, but, thank God, he already has everlasting life. Martha, do you believe that? Yes, gladly she believed it. *"Yea, Lord: I believe that thou art the Christ, the Son of God, which should come into the world"* (vs. 27).

VERSES 28-37:

28 And when she had so said, she went her way, and called Mary her sister secretly, saying, 'The Master is come, and calleth for thee.

29 As soon as she heard *that*, she arose quickly, and came unto him.

30 Now Jesus was not yet come into the town, but was in that place where

Martha met him.

31 The Jews then which were with her in the house, and comforted her, when they saw Mary, that she rose up hastily and went out, followed her, saying, She goeth unto the grave to weep there.

32 Then when Mary was come where Jesus was, and saw him, she fell down at his feet, saying unto him, Lord, if thou hadst been here, my brother had not died.

33 When Jesus therefore saw her weeping, and the Jews also weeping which came with her, he groaned in the spirit, and was troubled,

34 And said, Where have ye laid him? They said unto him, Lord, come and see.

35 Jesus wept.

36 Then said the Jews, Behold how he loved him!

37 And some of them said, Could not this man, which opened the eyes of the blind, have caused that even this man should not have died?

Jesus Comforts Mary

And now with a lighter heart Martha runs to tell Mary, *"The Master is come, and calleth for thee"* (vs. 28).

They had so anxiously watched for Jesus' coming. And someone saw Him way down the hill before He reached Bethany and told Martha. And there outside the town Mary runs to meet Jesus.

Do you note here the tender heart of Mary? She is not as matter of fact as Martha; perhaps more emotional, more affectionate, and we suppose more broken with grief than her sister whom we assume was older.

Mary's friends were with her in the house. She may have been so prostrate with grief they had not told her the Saviour was approaching until Martha tells us, "The Master is come, and calleth for thee." So the Jews, Jerusalem friends with her in the house, saw her grief. They thought she was fleeing to the grave to weep there; but down the trail she went to Jesus, and there fell at His feet. Mary was more the mystic; Martha the businesslike housekeeper. It may be the overflowing love of Mary is illustrated best of all in her offering of the alabaster box of ointment in the next chapter.

In verse 33 the Scripture says Jesus *"groaned in the spirit, and was troubled."* Verse 35 says, *"Jesus wept."* Verse 38 says again, *"Jesus therefore again groaning in himself cometh to the grave."* Three times we are told that Jesus wept. He wept here at the grave of Lazarus. Then on the Mount of Olives He wept over

Jerusalem (Luke 19:41-44). But we learn also that He wept in Gethsemane, for Hebrews 5:7 must refer to that time and place when it says that He "in the days of his flesh . . . offered up prayers and supplications with strong crying and tears unto him that was able to save him from death, and was heard in that he feared." I am sure Jesus must have wept many times besides these mentioned, for Psalm 69:8,10 speaks of Jesus surely: "I am become a stranger unto my brethren, and an alien unto my mother's children . . . When I wept, and chastened my soul with fasting, that was to my reproach." Verse 9 of Psalm 69 is quoted in John 2:17, referring to Jesus.

So the broken heart of Jesus pressed on to the cross. He must have wept many times over sinners, and since the Scripture mentions a number of times that Jesus was "moved with compassion," we may well imagine a tear in His pure eye that represented a sorrow and compassion in His heart.

Why did Jesus weep? He knows that in a few minutes He will call Lazarus out of the grave. He could not be weeping in personal sorrow over the death of Lazarus, for He Himself planned it for the glory of God. Oh, but He weeps for the tears of Mary and Martha and others. He weeps with all the broken hearts in the world. He weeps with every mother who loves her baby, every husband who stands at the casket of his wife. He weeps with every mother or father who weeps in the night over a prodigal boy or wayward girl.

We are commanded to rejoice with them who do rejoice, and to weep with them who weep. We cannot think that Jesus would do less than we are commanded to do. What a wonderful truth that Jesus weeps with us over all our sorrows!

The Jews said, *"Behold how he loved him!"* (vs. 36). Oh, yes; He loved Lazarus. But those tears are for me, too, and for you and for all who have trouble and sorrow in this world. Jesus planned for Himself to be tempted in all points like as we are, yet without sin.

So He is troubled with our troubles. He bears stripes with our punishment. He enters into every sorrow. And that means that if we let Him have His way, the sorrow will turn to joy. And if we

really believe that Romans 8:28 is true, we can "glory in
tribulation" as Paul did, and we can "take pleasure in
infirmities, in reproaches, in necessities, in persecutions, in
distresses for Christ's sake: for when I am weak, then am I
strong" (II Cor. 12:10).

All this funeral crowd know about the marvels wrought by
Jesus. Could not He have caused that even this man not die?
Yes. They asked a good question.

VERSES 38-44:

38 Jesus therefore again groaning
in himself cometh to the grave. It
was a cave, and a stone lay upon it.
39 Jesus said, Take ye away the
stone. Martha, the sister of him that
was dead, saith unto him, \Lord, by
this time he stinketh: for he hath
been *dead* four days.
40 Jesus saith unto her, Said I not
unto thee, that, if thou wouldest
believe, thou shouldest see the glory
of God?
41 Then they took away the stone
from the place where the dead was
laid. And Jesus lifted up *his* eyes, and
said, Father, I thank thee that thou
hast heard me.
42 And I knew that thou hearest me
always: but because of the people
which stand by I said *it*, that they
may believe that thou hast sent me.
43 And when he thus had spoken,
he cried with a loud voice, Lazarus,
come forth.
44 And he that was dead came
forth, bound hand and foot with
graveclothes: and his face was bound
about with a napkin. Jesus saith unto
them, Loose him, and let him go.

Lazarus Is Raised From the Dead

Jesus will raise Lazarus. He will work the miracle. But they
must have a part in it. *"Take ye away the stone"* (vs. 39). Do you
want to see a soul saved? Then you must take him the Gospel.
You must see that the unsaved are brought to the house of God.
You must use human means. The miracle of regeneration the
Lord Jesus must do, but He never saves anybody without the
help of some human instrument, some witness. "How then shall
they call on him in whom they have not believed? and how shall
they believe in him of whom they have not heard? and how shall
they hear without a preacher?" (Rom. 10:14).

I am sometimes invited to speak, and the pastor says, "Our

auditorium will seat three hundred. And if we have more than that, we can seat them in the basement and use a loudspeaker." We never have a crowd in the basement. God doesn't force crowds on preachers who do not make an effort to get crowds. If you are not willing to get the people, seek the people, God will not send them. If you want God to raise the dead, then you must roll away the stone that closes the door of death.

It is Martha who protests, *"Lord, by this time he stinketh: for he hath been dead four days"* (vs. 39). Mary seems to have had more faith.

It is hard for us to believe that God is just as able to give life to a decaying body as to a sound one. It would be hard for us to believe God could just as easily set fire to the wet wood and sacrifice on Mount Carmel, where they pour twelve barrels of water, as to make a fire with dry wood, but He could. It is just as easy for God to save a hardened sinner as to save a little child. Don't doubt, Martha. Let the men roll back the great stone from the door.

Jesus thanks God for the miracle before it happened. Actually there is no past and future with God, but always the present. For Jesus knew about the resurrection of Lazarus as well before it happened as afterward. And Jesus said, *"I knew that thou hearest me always"* (vs. 42). And here He thanks God openly before the miracle so the people may believe it. And then with this prayer and thanks, Jesus cried out with a loud voice, *"Lazarus, come forth"* (vs. 43). I think D. L. Moody first said that if Jesus had not called Lazarus by name, all who were in the graves might have come forth. Oh, that voice of power some day will be heard, and all the dead in Christ will come forth. That day in Bethany He singled out one person, but one day all who are in the graves will hear His voice and every Christian will rise with a glorified body.

Can you imagine Lazarus coming forth *"bound hand and foot with graveclothes"* (vs. 44)? His face covered with a napkin? Then Jesus said, *"Loose him, and let him go"* (vs. 44). Jesus can give life and He can make the dead live, but others must help the living to come forth.

The Lord Jesus saves sinners, but we then are to nourish and teach them "to observe all things whatsoever" Jesus taught others. The strong are to help the weak. Babes in Christ are to be fed on the milk of the Word. As Christ washed the disciples' feet, so we are to wash one another's feet, for we walk in a tainted world.

When a baby is born, the baby is supposed to come home with Mother from the hospital. When a sinner trusts Christ, then Christians are to take them into their homes and hearts, are to love them, are to encourage them, are to lead them to make public professions, are to encourage them to be baptized, are to teach them the Word. *"Loose him, and let him go."*

[In connection with this raising of Lazarus, I suggest you study the entire 15th chapter of I Corinthians about the resurrection. It does not seem that Lazarus was given a glorified body, but that the body he had before was simply raised and his spirit returned to it. As far as we know, Lazarus died again later. It will not be so in the resurrection, but our bodies will be changed; our bodies will be made like the resurrected body of Christ (Phil. 3:21).]

VERSES 45,46:

45 Then many of the Jews which came to Mary, and had seen the things which Jesus did, believed on him.

46 But some of them went their ways to the Pharisees, and told them what things Jesus had done.

Friends of Mary Converted

Does it seem strange to you that it was the friends of Mary who came to the house of sorrow, not especially those of Martha? Does it seem strange to you that she, the most ardent in her love for Jesus, was the one who had friends saved? They had seen the marvel, the miracle. They had joined in tears of sorrow with Mary. Now they rejoice with her and believe in this wonderful Saviour themselves.

This miracle and the conversion of many others through saving faith will distress the Pharisees and Jewish leaders who want to kill Jesus.

VERSES 47-57:

47 ¶ Then gathered the chief priests and the Pharisees a council, and said, What do we? for this man doeth many miracles.

48 If we let him thus alone, all *men* will believe on him: and the Romans shall come and take away both our place and nation.

49 And one of them, *named* Câi-ă-phăs, being the high priest that same year, said unto them, Ye know nothing at all,

50 Nor consider that it is expedient for us, that one man should die for the people, and that the whole nation perish not.

51 And this spake he not of himself: but being high priest that year, he prophesied that Jesus should die for that nation;

52 And not for that nation only, but that also he should gather together in one the children of God that were scattered abroad.

53 Then from that day forth they took counsel together for to put him to death.

54 Jesus therefore walked no more openly among the Jews; but went thence unto a country near to the wilderness, into a city called E-phră-im, and there continued with his disciples.

55 ¶ And the Jews' passover was nigh at hand: and many went out of the country up to Jerusalem before the passover, to purify themselves.

56 Then sought they for Jesus, and spake among themselves, as they stood in the temple, What think ye, that he will not come to the feast?

57 Now both the chief priests and the Pharisees had given a commandment, that, if any man knew where he were, he should shew *it*, that they might take him.

Pharisees Plot to Put Jesus to Death

Every miracle of Jesus gets more attention from the multitude. Every miracle convinces more people that He is the Messiah. So the priests and Pharisees gather in a council to plan. They think if Jesus continues His ministry, *"all men will believe on him"* (vs. 48). And since the Jews were especially looking for the restoration of Israel as a nation under God and for the Messiah, the Son of David, to rule as a king on David's throne, they think that the success of Jesus means rebellion against Rome. We suppose King Herod thought the same thing when he killed all the boy babies in Bethlehem, hoping to kill the Baby Jesus. But Jesus had said, "My kingdom is not of this world," by which He meant not of this present world system and world organization.

His kingdom will be on this earth, but not until the rapture and tribulation and His literal return with saints and angels to destroy the kingdoms of this world and set up His kingdom.

But note they were concerned not just about the nation. They said, *"Romans shall come and take away both our place and nation"* (vs. 48). They feared to lose their priestly jobs, their great prestige, their rich income. The truth is, in their hearts they hated Jesus and wanted Him to die. So they tried to justify themselves to themselves.

And here Caiaphas the high priest speaks a prophecy from God that one Man should die for the nation, and not for that nation only but for the world (vss. 50-52). This wicked man did not know he prophesied Christ's atoning death. Just as God made Balaam prophesy good for Israel instead of the evil that he wished to speak, so this Caiaphas, thinking only to save his place and his people from the Romans, prophesied the death of Christ for sinners.

We are reminded that in the future God has promised, "That at the name of Jesus every knee should bow, of things in heaven, and things in earth, and things under the earth; And that every tongue should confess that Jesus Christ is Lord, to the glory of God the Father" (Phil. 2:10,11). So it is not surprising now that He makes Caiaphas prophesy the death of Jesus. God will influence Pilate to offer the opposing choices of Barabbas or Jesus. The Scripture says, "Surely the wrath of man shall praise thee" (Ps. 76:10). So the wicked charges of the ungodly will cause Paul to be given a free rein to Rome.

Before these Jews had been moved with sudden anger from time to time and boiling hatred; now they start a systematic plot to put Jesus to death. So now Jesus *"walked no more openly among the Jews"* (vs. 54), that is, people in the Jerusalem area, but went away into Ephraim.

But it is about time for another annual passover season. This is the third mention in John. The first was in John 2:13; the second in John 6:4. And every male of Israel is supposed to come to Jerusalem and present himself before the Lord at this time. Will Jesus come? The crowds gather from everywhere days ahead to purify themselves and get ready for this, the most important feast of the year. And the Pharisees send out word everywhere that any man who knows the whereabouts of Jesus is to report it.

John 12

THEN Jesus six days before the passover came to Bethany, where Lazarus was which had been dead, whom he raised from the dead.

2 There they made him a supper; and Martha served: but Lazarus was one of them that sat at the table with him.

3 Then took Mary a pound of ointment of spikenard, very costly, and anointed the feet of Jesus, and wiped his feet with her hair: and the house was filled with the odour of the ointment.

4 Then saith one of his disciples, Judas Iscariot, Simon's *son*, which should betray him,

5 Why was not this ointment sold for three hundred pence, and given to the poor?

6 This he said, not that he cared for the poor; but because he was a thief, and had the bag, and bare what was put therein.

7 Then said Jesus, Let her alone: against the day of my burying hath she kept this.

8 For the poor always ye have with you; but me ye have not always.

Supper With Lazarus at Bethany

F. B. Meyer mentions that between the last verse of chapter 11 and verse 1 here, many weeks had passed. At first Jesus took refuge in Ephraim, then He crossed to Perea. He mentions that these few weeks were omitted by John but fully recorded by the other three.

Here is a good illustration of the wisdom of God in having the four Gospels written concerning the life of Christ. John gives the name of the woman—Mary; and of the objector—Judas Iscariot; while neither Matthew nor Mark give their names, but they both give the name of the host—Simon the leper, which John does not give.

This supper is recorded in Matthew 26:6-13 and in Mark 14:3-9. It is not the same supper as that in Luke 7:37,38, and the woman there is not Mary, but a fallen woman.

The supper is in the house of Simon the leper (we suppose a healed leper, now not segregated), in Bethany; though evidently it is to honor Jesus and Lazarus. And Lazarus, raised from the dead, is naturally the center of attention. It was in another home but "Martha served." Bless her heart—that was her long suit! But Mary is more occupied with Jesus than with serving or with eating; so she brought a pound of ointment of spikenard, very costly. It was in an alabaster box, no doubt carved very delicately out of alabaster stone and sealed so the precious ointment or perfume would not evaporate or spill. Such an alabaster box of ointment was found, sealed in a pharaoh's grave and is now in the Cairo Museum.

It may be that Mary, Martha and Lazarus were well-to-do. They probably had a large house if they could entertain Jesus and the twelve disciples. Martha was evidently a distinguished hostess, and so was asked to serve here at the house of her neighbor, Simon the leper. This ointment was poured on the feet of Jesus but Mark 14:3 and Matthew 26:7 also say that she "poured it on his head."

It may well be that Mary had gotten the idea from the sweet, intimate ceremony from the event when Jesus was in the house of Simon the Pharisee and a woman known as a sinner, we suppose a prostitute or at least a fallen woman, brought "an alabaster box of ointment . . . and began to wash his feet with tears, and did wipe them with the hairs of her head, and kissed his feet, and anointed them with the ointment" (Luke 7:36-39). Jesus was so pleased with that sweet and loving gift and anointing that doubtless Mary knew of it and determined to bring a like gift with the holy purpose of anointing Jesus for His burial.

It seems that some special spiritual understanding had been given to this devoted woman. She seemed to know that Jesus would die and this ointment was like the sweet spices in which the body would be wrapped.

It pleased the Lord Jesus so much that He promised, "Verily I say unto you, Wheresoever this gospel shall be preached in the whole world, there shall also this, that this woman hath done, be told for a memorial of her" (Matt. 26:13; Mark 14:9). The ointment was "very costly" John says, and Matthew and Mark say it was "very precious." It could have been sold for "three hundred pence." The pence here represented the coin denarius, used for a day's wages (Matt. 20:2).

Judas Iscariot protested. He did not like to see this "waste" just to please and anoint Jesus symbolically, a picture of loving care, of faith in His death for sinners. But Judas did not love Christ and he "was a thief, and had the bag" and out of the common purse which he gathered, he took for himself what he could.

Jesus was so pleased that He promised this woman should be made a memorial in history because the story would be printed in the Bible and go around the world to all generations. F. B. Meyer said, "Not even Judas would have called this act waste, could he have seen the love it has kindled and the acts to which it has led. It has been spoken of in all the world for a memorial of her."

Is it a waste to sacrifice for Jesus? John and Betty Stam went as missionaries to China. They were brilliant in mind, wholly devoted and well-trained. Alas, when they were soon murdered by communist bandits in China, some people cried out, "What a waste!"

But no life laid down for Christ is wasted. No money or expense or provision for Him but is worthwhile and blessed. And the loss of father, mother, wife, children, brothers or sisters and lands also, for Jesus' sake, are not a loss but great gain (Matt. 19:29).

Should the money have been given to the poor? No, "for the poor always ye have with you; but me ye have not always." So it is true that often we should give to the poor, but giving to the poor, or CARE packages to the distressed or other nations, or support of orphan homes for destitute children—these are not on a par with giving to get out the Gospel and getting people saved.

Dr. Meyer says that once, at the close of a missionary meeting, he proposed to the Christians gathered that they present to the Lord some special article which they held valuable, as a token of their personal love for Him. He says that in response to this appeal, many gave jewels and ornaments and costly articles, which amounted to a great sum for the Lord's use. He said, "We called them alabaster boxes of very precious ointment; and it was sweet to give them." Dr. Meyer said that afterwards he received a letter from a widow, who said that she had long withheld her consent for her daughter to become a missionary, but that she would stand in her way no longer. "She gave her daughter to Him as her priceless offering," he said.

VERSES 9-11:

9 Much people of the Jews therefore knew that he was there: and they came not for Jesus' sake only, but that they might see Lazarus also, whom he had raised from the dead.

10 ¶ But the chief priests consulted that they might put Lazarus also to death;

11 Because that by reason of him many of the Jews went away, and believed on Jesus.

Must Lazarus Die, Too?

Can you imagine the gawking crowds, not only the invited guests but all who could draw near the crowded patio where we suppose the supper was held? They came, not only to see Jesus but to see Lazarus who had been dead but was now alive and was sitting at the table eating with others!

And now the chief priests had greater concern yet. Miracles like the raising of Lazarus would make more friends for Jesus. The chief priests wanted to put Lazarus to death to stop the influence of this miracle. Oh, many were saved, believing on

Christ, when they saw Lazarus in the midst of his loving and happy friends and family.

VERSES 12-15:

12 ¶ On the next day much people that were come to the feast, when they heard that Jesus was coming to Jerusalem,

13 Took branches of palm trees, and went forth to meet him, and cried, Hosanna: Blessed *is* the King of Israel that cometh in the name of the Lord.

14 And Jesus, when he had found a young ass, sat thereon; as it is written,

15 Fear not, daughter of Sion: behold, thy King cometh, sitting on an ass's colt.

The Triumphal Entry to Jerusalem

This account is given also in Matthew 21:1-11, in Mark 11:1-11, and in Luke 19:29-38. John does not tell about how the young donkey colt was secured, as Matthew does. Check up the four records and see the things that each one tells that the others omit.

The Synoptic Gospels tell how Jesus sent two disciples into the village, Bethphage (with Bethany nearby), where they would find a colt tied. And Matthew says, "Ye shall find an ass tied, and a colt with her." The "colt" on which never man sat seems to have been perfectly docile and as if controlled by the Spirit of God. So they went to bring both to Jesus and if there was a protest they were simply to say, "The Lord hath need of them" and the owner would gladly send them.

It is now the week of the passover (vs. 1). And the people hear that Jesus is coming from Bethany into Jerusalem and they "took branches of palm trees" and Luke says "they spread their clothes in the way." And Matthew says that not only their clothes but they "cut down branches from the trees, and strawed them in the way."

That reminds us that in those days there were many trees all about Jerusalem. It is not so now. When Titus destroyed Jerusalem in A. D. 70 it is said that every tree within miles was cut down if it could make a cross on which to crucify a Jew. It is very likely the deforestation of hundreds of square miles in the Middle East has tended to make the climate much drier, the rainfall less, and the land that was once "flowing with milk and honey" now semiarid and much of it too barren and dry to cultivate.

They brought the colt to Jesus and threw garments on it so Jesus could sit unsoiled on the lowly beast. Now was fulfilled the prophecy of Zechariah 9:9, "Rejoice greatly, O daughter of Zion; shout, O daughter of Jerusalem: behold, thy King cometh unto thee: he is just, and having salvation; lowly, and riding upon an ass, and upon a colt the foal of an ass."

When Jesus rode down the descent of the Mount of Olives toward the Brook Kidron and the walls of the city, "the whole multitude of the disciples began to rejoice and praise God with a loud voice for all the mighty works that they had seen; Saying, Blessed be the King that cometh in the name of the Lord: peace in heaven, and glory in the highest" (Luke 19:37,38).

The praise to Jesus was hateful to the Pharisees. They wanted Jesus to rebuke the disciples. Oh, no! If He must be hated and crucified, He is due the praise of the multitude of common people who love and trust Him. And Jesus said, "I tell you that, if these should hold their peace, the stones would immediately cry out" (Luke 19:40).

Oh, I am always impressed with the stones everywhere in the Jerusalem area, the houses built of stone, stones outcropping everywhere. If the stones in Palestine ever began to shout the praises of Jesus, that would be louder praise than He has ever received!

VERSES 16-19:

16 These things understood not his disciples at the first: but when Jesus was glorified, then remembered they that these things were written of him, and *that* they had done these things unto him.

17 The people therefore that was with him when he called Lazarus out of his grave, and raised him from the dead, bare record.

18 For this cause the people also met him, for that they heard that he

had done this miracle.
19 The Pharisees therefore said among themselves, Perceive ye how ye prevail nothing? behold, the world is gone after him.

How Slowly the Disciples Understood!

When you come to consider the evidence of the resurrection of Jesus Christ, one of the most overwhelming proofs is that all these disciples were convinced of it. They did not believe in the resurrection. The two on the road to Emmaus had thought that Jesus would redeem His people but they had given up their hope. All these miracles of people being raised from the dead, of feeding the thousands, of opening blind eyes, of raising up the paralyzed and even raising Lazarus from the dead, left the disciples with a very faint and partial understanding of the deity of Christ, the need for His death, the certainty of His return to reign. *"These things understood not his disciples at the first"* (vs. 16). But after His resurrection, when He was glorified, then they remembered a hundred happenings and a hundred statements of Jesus that they had not before understood.

But all the people were telling it. They said, "I will tell you, I was there when He called Lazarus to come forth and he came out alive!" And the jubilant witnessing of these people grieved the Pharisees even more. They saw they could prevail nothing. They said, "The world is gone after him."

VERSES 20-22:

20 ¶ And there were certain Greeks among them that came up to worship at the feast:
21 The same came therefore 'to Philip, which was of Bĕth-să-́ĭ-dă of Galilee, and desired him, saying, Sir, we would see Jesus.
22 Philip cometh and telleth Andrew: and again Andrew and Philip tell Jesus.

Some Greeks Would See Jesus

The Greeks here are Grecian Jews, doubtless those who had come to Jerusalem for the feast of Pentecost as they had from so

many nations, as we read in Acts 2:8-11. These Grecian Jews
came to Philip to plead with him to intercede. They said, *"Sir,
we would see Jesus"* (vs. 21). So Andrew and Philip reported the
matter to Jesus. Dr. Scofield thinks Jesus "does not receive these
Gentiles."

In the first place, we do not know that they were Gentiles. Why
should Gentiles from Greece come to Jerusalem for the passover?
In the second place, if they had been Gentiles, why would Jesus
turn them away? He did not turn away the Canaanitish woman
who pleaded for her devil-possessed daughter. He responded to
the plea of the Roman centurion who wanted his servant to be
healed. It is a mistake to make Jesus a dispensationalist,
preaching only to Jews, offering a different plan of salvation to
the Jews.

Did these Greeks want to be saved? That is possible. It is
possible that, like the great multitude of others, they were
excited at the reports of His miracles and wanted to see Him,
even as King Herod, with Jesus about to be crucified, was anxious to see Him and ask for a miracle (Luke 23:8,9). But
whatever their heart motive, it gave an occasion for Jesus to insist that His purpose was to die for sinners and that He was not
to be known primarily as a teacher or healer, but as a Saviour.

VERSES 23-30:

23 ¶ And Jesus answered them, saying, The hour is come, that the Son
of man should be glorified.

24 Verily, verily, I say unto you,
Except a corn of wheat fall into the
ground and die, it abideth alone: but
if it die, it bringeth forth much
fruit.

25 He that loveth his life shall lose
it; and he that hateth his life in this
world shall keep it unto life eternal.

26 If any man serve me, let him
follow me; and where I am, there

shall also my servant be: if any man
serve me, him will *my* Father
honour.

27 Now is my soul troubled; and
what shall I say? Father, save me
from this hour: but for this cause
came I unto this hour.

28 Father, glorify thy name. Then
came there a voice from heaven,
saying, I have both glorified *it*, and
will glorify *it* again.

29 The people therefore, that stood
by, and heard *it*, said that it thun-

dered: others said, An   angel spake to him.

30 Jesus answered and said, This

voice came not because of me, but for your sakes.

The Seed Must Fall Upon the Ground and Die to Bring Forth Fruit

Verse 23 says, *"Jesus answered them."* So His answer was referred to these Greeks who would see Jesus and perhaps to all the multitude who crowded about Him.

Now the crucifixion approaches. *"The hour is come, that the Son of man should be glorified"* (vs. 23). This hour! This hour had been in His mind and heart from the beginning of His ministry, and now it was upon Him. His ministry would not be done except He should die. The life alone of Jesus never saved anybody. Following Jesus as a pattern is good for born-again Christians, but it has no meaning for the unconverted heart. Even the birth of Jesus is not the great climactic center of Christ's incarnation. It is His death. My Christmas song says:

> **Jesus, Baby Jesus,**
> **There's a cross along the way.**
> **Born to die for sinners, born for crucifixion day!**

"Except a corn of wheat fall into the ground and die, it abideth alone: but if it die, it bringeth forth much fruit" (vs. 24). He means simply that He must die in order to purchase salvation. He cannot reign before He suffers; nor can we. Says Macaulay: "The cross is the way of harvest, as it is the path of glory. So Jesus said of Himself: out of His dying multitudes should rise into life eternal. Redeemed men are the harvest of His suffering and death, not of His teaching and example."

Would these about Him follow Him? *"He that loveth his life shall lose it"* (vs. 25). And, to hate this life in this world and to think lightly of it or disregard life itself in this world would mean eternal rewards, not life eternal (vs. 25). If Jesus is to die, His servants should humble themselves to follow that kind of a Saviour. Elsewhere Jesus said, "If any man will come after me, let him deny himself and take up his cross daily, and follow me" (Luke 9:23). And if Jesus is to be persecuted and the world is to hate Him, then Jesus reminds us:

"If the world hate you, ye know that it hated me before it hated you. If ye were of the world, the world would love his own: but because ye are not of the world, but I have chosen you out of the world, therefore the world hateth you. Remember the word that I said unto you, The servant is not greater than his lord. If they have persecuted me, they will also persecute you; if they have kept my saying, they will keep your's also."—John 15:18-20.

Jesus is here discouraging a thoughtless and lighthearted decision for discipleship just as He did before when He told a would-be disciple, "The birds of the air have nests; but the Son of man hath not where to lay his head" (Luke 9:58).

But the awesome impending torture and misery is already pressing on Jesus. He says, *"Now is my soul troubled"* (vs. 27). He had said before, "I have a baptism to be baptized with; and how am I straitened till it be accomplished!" (Luke 12:50). He does not seek to avoid the cross. He has come to it deliberately in Gethsemane when He prays, "If it be possible, let this cup pass from me: nevertheless not as I will, but as thou wilt" (Luke 26:39). He did not pray to miss the cross but that He might not die in Gethsemane prematurely and in vain. He was praying in the will of God, not against the will of God. So here He does not pray, "Save me from this hour." No, but in a holy exaltation He faces this glorious climax of His life, *". . . but for this cause came I unto this hour"* (vs. 27). So He prays, *"Father, glorify thy name"* (vs. 28). And the Father answers from Heaven, *"I have both glorified it, and will glorify it again"* (vs. 28). Jesus is to glorify the Father in His crucifixion and then in His resurrection.

Once in THE SWORD OF THE LORD I wrote, "The dearest thing to the heart of God is to save sinners." And I mentioned that the good shepherd, when he found his sheep, put it on his shoulders rejoicing. A good woman wrote me from St. Louis saying, "I think soul winning is all right, but I think the dearest thing to God is to exalt and honor Jesus Christ." But I reminded her that the Father gladly gave His Son and glorified Him in a crucifixion and the torment and broken heart of Gethsemane and Calvary.

Oh, Father and Son unite in gladly providing this infinite and eternal sacrifice to pay for man's sin and to save sinners!

People heard the voice of God. Some said it thundered. Some said an angel spoke to Him (vs. 29). Perhaps they did not hear the words but only the sound. But Jesus told them that the voice came as a witness and evidence to them. So we suppose they may have heard the very words.

VERSES 31-36:

3. Now is the judgment of this world: now shall the prince of this world be cast out.

32 And I, if I be lifted up from the earth, will draw all *men* unto me.

33 This he said, signifying what death he should die.

34 The people answered him, We have heard out of the law that Christ abideth for ever: and how sayest thou, The Son of man must be lifted up? who is this Son of man?

35 Then Jesus said unto them, Yet a little while is the light with you. Walk while ye have the light, lest darkness come upon you: for he that walketh in darkness knoweth not whither he goeth.

36 While ye have light, believe in the light, that ye may be the children of light. These things spake Jesus, and departed, and did hide himself from them.

The Crucified Saviour Draws All Men

Jesus, looking forward to the cross, looks beyond that to His own exaltation in the judgment of this old world. Isaiah 53:11 tells about all our sins being laid on Jesus and with His stripes we are healed. But in that same connection the Lord reminds us, "He shall see of the travail of his soul, and shall be satisfied: by his knowledge shall my righteous servant justify many; for he shall bear their iniquities." The 22nd Psalm gives us the clearest picture of the heart of Jesus on the cross and what He thought. It starts with Christ crying, "My God, my God, why hast thou forsaken me?" Then, after 21 verses, the Psalm enters into the praise and victory and, "All the ends of the world shall remember and turn unto the Lord: and all the kindreds of the nations shall worship before thee. For the kingdom is the Lord's."

The crucifixion is a means to an end. It is not the end of the story. Jesus, facing the cross, thinks of the millions of people who will be saved because of it and of the final destruction of Satan.

Verses 32 and 33 are of tremendous importance. They say a glorified Saviour will have a drawing impact on every person who lives. Hyper-Calvinists insist that man is fallen, depraved, dead in trespasses and in sin. That is all true. They say that a sinner, unaided, cannot turn to Christ, and that is true. But they ignore and fail to see this other great truth. Every lost sinner in the world is called, is attracted, is moved, so that he could repent and be saved.

Jesus is "the true Light, which lighteth every man that cometh into the world" (1:9). Men have the call of a universe about them showing there is a mighty God to whom they must give account:

"Because that which may be known of God is manifest in them; for God hath shewed it unto them. For the invisible things of him from the creation of the world are clearly seen, being understood by the things that are made, even his eternal power and Godhead; so that they are without excuse."—Rom. 1:19,20.

So Jesus is potentially "the Saviour of the world." And "he is the propitiation for our sins: and not for our's only, but also for the sins of the whole world" (I John 2:2).

When God "commandeth all men every where to repent," then men can repent. No man who goes to Hell can blame God that he was not called, moved, convicted, attracted in some sense and in some measure so that he could have turned toward the light, could have had more help, could have been saved. God gave him a created world as witness. God gave him a conscience to remind him. Everybody who wants to see God can find Him. The crucified Saviour is a call to every person in the world to be saved.

Here is a great seeming conflict between a Saviour who must die and a Saviour who must live forever. The people remind Him in verse 34 that according to the Old Testament, *"Christ abideth for ever"* (Ps. 72:17; 102:23-27; Isa. 9:7). Oh, the resurrection of Christ is the answer. He is the suffering Saviour who must die.

But He is also the Son of David who must come to sit on David's throne and who will abide forever.

Again, Jesus gives them warning. They had best listen today. The hour fast approaches when the unsaved multitude will hear His voice no more. So He says, *"While ye have light, believe in the light"* (vs. 36), and with this solemn warning, Jesus slipped away and hid Himself.

"These things spake Jesus, and departed, and did hide himself from them" (vs. 36). Says Macaulay: "That departing and that hiding were a final judgment on the persistent unbelief of the Jews. In that act our Lord abandoned them to their unbelief, to reap the awful and long harvest of it."

"While the candle holds out to burn
The vilest sinner may return."

VERSES 37-43:

37 ¶ But though he had done so many miracles before them, yet they believed not on him:

38 That the saying of E-ṡaî-ăs the prophet might be fulfilled, which he spake, Lord, who hath believed our report? and to whom hath the arm of the Lord been revealed?

39 Therefore they could not believe, because that E-ṡaî-ăs said again,

40 He hath blinded their eyes, and hardened their heart; that they should not see with *their* eyes, nor understand with *their* heart, and be converted, and I should heal them.

41 These things said E-ṡaî-ăs, when he saw his glory, and spake of him.

42 ¶ Nevertheless among the chief rulers also many believed on him; but because of the Pharisees they did not confess *him*, lest they should be put out of the synagogue:

43 For they loved the praise of men more than the praise of God.

Unbelief Despite Many Miracles

Two things amaze us here. One is the continued, persistent, wicked unbelief of those who heard all His teachings, saw all His miracles, yet would not believe. The other amazing thing is the patient persistence of Jesus in repeating that He is God's Son, that He is Manna from Heaven, that He is the Bread of Life and there can be no salvation except as one trusts in Him. Jesus knows that this is a fulfillment of the words of Isaiah 53:1, "Who hath believed our report? and to whom hath the arm of the Lord been revealed?" And again, as Isaiah said, "He hath blinded their eyes, and hardened their heart; that they should not see with their eyes, nor understand with their heart, and be converted, and I should heal them. These things said Esaias, when he saw his glory, and spake of him" (See Isa. 53:1; 6:10).

But, praise the Lord, among those hardened chief rulers, also many believed on Him, although the Pharisees were so threatening that these did not confess Him. They loved the praise of men more than the praise of God. Because one is saved does not guarantee he will be brave. Those who trust Christ may be secret disciples for a time, like Joseph of Arimathaea.

Were these secret disciples really saved? According to John 3:16; 5:24; Acts 16:30,31 and many other passages, they most certainly were.

Remember, the joy of the witness of the Holy Spirit in our hearts that God is pleased with us and claims us, depends on our confessing and claiming Him. Matthew 10:33 does not say that "Whosoever does not confess me before men . . ." but "Whosoever shall deny me . . . ." Jesus means that one who accepts Him is saved, while one who rejects Him is lost. One, however, who accepts Jesus without publicly claiming Him will miss much of the joy and comfort which God has for His people. However, no doubt many of these "secret" disciples later claimed Jesus publicly among the multitudes at Pentecost and thereafter.

VERSES 44-50:

44 ¶ Jesus cried and said, He that believeth on me, believeth not on me, but on him that sent me.

45 And he that seeth me seeth him that sent me.

46 I am come a light into the world, that whosoever believeth on me should not abide in darkness.

47 And if any man hear my words, and believe not, I judge him not: for I came not to judge the world, but to save the world.

48 He that rejecteth me, and receiveth not my words, hath one that judgeth him: the word that I have spoken, the same shall judge him in

the last day.

49 For I have not spoken of myself; but the Father which sent me, he gave me a commandment, what I should say, and what I should speak.

50 And I know that his commandment is life everlasting: whatsoever I speak therefore, even as the Father said unto me, so I speak.

Jesus and the Father and God's Word, All Will Judge Men

Jesus said it again, so let us never forget it. To trust in Christ is to trust the Father (5:24). To come to Christ is to come to the Father. Jesus is God and is the only way to God. He is "the way, the truth, and the life" and "no man cometh unto the Father, but by me" (John 14:6). One who sees Jesus, sees the Father. Jesus is the Light in a dark world. And to believe in Him is to live in the light.

Does some man refuse to hear, refuse to believe? Oh, Jesus reminds him that He did not come to judge but to save. It is true that the Father has given all judgment to the Son. It is Jesus who will judge Christians at the judgment seat of Christ. It is Jesus who will judge the living Gentiles left alive when He sits on His throne as King at Jerusalem. It is Jesus who will sit on the great white throne and judge the unsaved dead and have them cast into the lake of fire.

But remember, He did not come to judge, He came to save. He takes no pleasure in the death of the wicked. And it is not Jesus alone who judges but the Father who joins in judgment and the eternal Word of God who will witness against every Christ-rejecting sinner, also. Oh, the very words of Jesus will come to face every Christ-rejecting sinner!

Jesus now speaks not for Himself as a prophet in Galilee, but for God His Father. And, oh, how gladly Jesus followed every commandment, said every word, did everything the Father wanted done.

We can see the urgency on the heart of the Lord Jesus giving these last messages before His arrest, trial and crucifixion.

John 13

NOW before the feast of the passover, when Jesus knew that his hour was come that he should depart out of this world unto the Father, having loved his own which were in the world, he loved them unto the end.

Jesus Before the Passover

All this last week Jesus has been facing the crisis. Now this passover approaches. The afternoon before they eat the passover lamb, lambs will be slaughtered and roasted with fire, then eaten with bitter herbs after sundown when the high Sabbath of the passover begins. That afternoon Jesus must die. He must fulfill the type of I Corinthians 5:7, "Christ our passover is sacrificed for us."

The book of John impresses us again and again with this last passover season in the life of Jesus. We are warned in John 11:55 that it was approaching. In John 12:1 we are told that it was six days away. In John 12:28 Jesus indicates that some set time is at hand for Him to be crucified. There must be some connection with the time that was previously set in the plan of God and the passover supper which pictures the death of the Lamb of God.

With that in mind, look again at John 12:31 and 32. The rest of the 12th chapter showed us that Israel had now completely rejected their Messiah and King. Look at the quotations from Isaiah mentioned in John 12:38-40. Notice the words about judgment in that chapter and the special warning about rejecting Christ in verse 48.

Now in the 13th chapter of John we find the passover mentioned again. It is important to notice that Jesus here specifically mentions the passover time as the time when He is to depart out of this world. Christ is God's Passover Lamb and is to be sacrificed at the regular time for the killing of the lamb, as first commanded in the 12th chapter of Exodus and practiced for centuries by Israel.

The Scofield Bible heads this verse: "The Last Passover," which is misleading. It was His last passover season. In the accounts of the supper by Matthew, Mark, Luke and John, nothing is said about a lamb. All they had was bread and wine. This was evidently a preliminary meal the night before the passover night.

. From Exodus 12:19 we learn that Jews were not even allowed to have leavened bread, that is, bread made with yeast, in their houses through the entire seven days of the feast of unleavened bread, beginning with the passover supper. In the time of Jesus, the whole period, including both the passover supper and the feast of unleavened bread, took the name of the passover, as you see in Luke 22:1. You see from John 11:55 that Jews were accustomed to come to Jerusalem several days ahead of time, do away with all leaven, and make themselves ceremonially clean, or purified, before the passover supper itself. The supper which Jesus ate with His disciples was a preliminary supper the day before the passover supper. It seems certain that the afternoon the passover lambs were killed, Jesus died on the cross, fulfilling perfectly the type. The word "passover" in verse 1 seems clearly not to mean the same as the word "supper" in verse 2. The supper was before the feast of the passover. John 13:29 shows that the feast was still in the future.

The time approaches. Jesus' love for His own burns as bright as ever. Some people are thoughtful of others, patient in tribulation, just as loving and kind when they are sick or in pain or under great provocation or stress as when surroundings are serene and untroubled, but that is rare. In pain or stress or crisis it is easier to think of self than to pour out love for others. But Jesus did that rare thing—*"He loved them unto the end"* (vs. 1).

He loved Peter, whom He knew would deny Him. He loved Thomas, who would doubt His resurrection. He loved all these, though of the confrontation in Gethsemane it will be written, "Then all the disciples forsook him, and fled" (Matt. 26:56).

Jesus never changes, thank God! On the cross He made provision for His mother. He prayed for forgiveness for His murderers.

He stopped dying long enough to save the penitent criminal nailed beside Him. And our hopes would wither if we could not depend on Jesus to love His own unto the end.

We can say with Romans 8:38,39, "For I am persuaded, that neither death, nor life, nor angels, nor principalities, nor powers, nor things present, nor things to come, Nor height, nor depth, nor any other creature, shall be able to separate us from the love of God, which is in Christ Jesus our Lord."

VERSES 2-5:

2 And supper being ended, the devil having now put into the heart of Judas Iscariot, Simon's *son*, to betray him;

3 Jesus knowing that the Father had given all things into his hands, and that he was come from God, and went to God;

4 He riseth from supper, and laid aside his garments; and took a towel, and girded himself.

5 After that he poureth water into a bason, and began to wash the disciples' feet, and to wipe *them* with the towel wherewith he was girded.

The Saviour Washes the Disciples' Feet

"And supper being ended. . . ." (vs. 2). The supper, we understand, was a preliminary meal the night before the passover supper itself. Exodus 12:19 commanded of the combined feasts of the passover and the unleavened bread, "Seven days shall there be no leaven found in your houses . . . ." So for this, the most important feast of the year, when every male must present himself before the Lord and when people came days early to these feasts, it would be customary, no doubt, to have a preliminary day as part of the season, and feast. When we say, "Last Christmas I did so and so," we do not necessarily refer to Christmas Day but to the Christmas season. So here, the passover season has begun with a preliminary day of preparation, putting out the leaven.

"Christ our passover is sacrificed for us . . ." (I Cor. 5:7). So, to fulfill the type, Jesus must die on the day the passover lambs were being killed for all Israel. The Lord would not have insisted

that a lamb should be killed on a certain day "between the evens," that is, mid-afternoon, unless His blessed Passover Lamb was to die on that day.

The supper then included unleavened bread and a "sop" of gravy or vinegar or, perhaps, possibly more, but not the passover lamb. That would be the following day after sundown.

"The devil having now put into the heart of Judas Iscariot, Simon's son, to betray him . . ." (vs. 2). Jesus knew it and had no word of scorn or shame. How could both God and Satan plan the crucifixion of Jesus? For it was "by determinate counsel and foreknowledge of God" that Jesus was delivered to die (Acts 2:23). The chief priests, Pilate, Herod, and Judas, all had bad motives, but God makes the wrath of men to praise Him (Ps. 76:10).

Men, with hatred for Christ, and God, with love for men, work together to bring about the atoning death of Christ. God sometimes lets wicked men do wrong, but He overcomes it and works it, with all the attending circumstances, for good (Rom. 8:28).

Jesus *"laid aside his garments"* (vs. 4). He did that before this, when He laid aside the garments of deity to be born a Man-Child of Mary. Christ is God. He never ceased to be God by becoming a man, but He ceased to appear as God.

On the Mount of Transfiguration Jesus appeared in His proper glory, as He will be at the Second Coming (Matt. 16:28; II Pet. 1:16-18). John saw Him when Jesus gave him the Revelation, and at His glory John "fell at his feet as dead" (Rev. 1:17). That glory Jesus had laid aside; these heavenly garments for those of earth; the outward manifestation of deity for the appearance of a man. Later, at the cross, the Lord Jesus laid aside His garments a second time. He was stripped naked, and soldiers cast lots for the seamless garment woven in one piece.

That symbolized the perfect righteousness of Christ. He appeared a naked sinner that we might put on His righteousness.

But now Jesus acts as a servant. Girded by the towel, He has laid aside garments that would present Him as a teacher or rabbi, to look and work like any common slave or servant. Jesus had said, "Whosoever of you will be the chiefest, shall be servant of all" (Mark 10:44). He had said, "For even the Son of man came not to be ministered unto, but to minister . . ." (Mark 10:45).

J. C. Macaulay, in mentioning this passage, says: "Our Lord stooped to the menial act of washing the feet of His disciples. None of them had volunteered this courtesy . . . . so the Master did it for them. You would not expect men who habitually argued among themselves who should be accounted greatest in the kingdom of God, to bemean themselves by washing one another's feet! . . ."

Is it not the glory of a mother to work, to cook, to teach and comfort her own? Many a woman, who washes diapers, scrubs floors, carries out garbage for her own, would not have done for money what she does gladly for love. Oh, blessed it is to be a servant!

John the Baptist did not feel worthy to baptize Jesus. To these disciples, secretly arguing who should be first, it seemed shocking that the Lord Jesus Himself washed their feet like a common servant.

VERSES 6-11:

6 Then cometh he to Simon Peter: and Peter saith unto him, Lord, dost thou wash my feet?

7 Jesus answered and said unto him, What I do thou knowest not now; but thou shalt know hereafter.

8 Peter saith unto him, Thou shalt never wash my feet. Jesus answered

him, If I wash thee not, thou hast no part with me.

9 Simon Peter saith unto him, Lord, not my feet only, but also *my* hands and *my* head.

10 Jesus saith to him, He that is washed needeth not save to wash *his* feet, but is clean every whit: and ye are clean, but not all.

11 For he knew who should betray him; therefore said he, Ye are not all clean.

Walking in a Dirty World, We Need Our Feet Washed Often

Peter did not understand, and so at first rebelled. "No sir," he thought, "Jesus must not wash my feet!" (vs. 8). But you remember when Peter was first called to preach and he saw that astonishing net full of fishes that filled the whole boat, he said, "Depart from me; for I am a sinful man, O Lord" (Luke 5:8). He felt his unworthiness. So now he felt unworthy to have Jesus wash his feet. But, Peter, if Jesus does not wash your feet, you have no part with Jesus! For when the Lord Jesus saves one, He obligates Himself to keep that one, to chasten him as needed, to reprove and then restore joy and fellowship with daily confessing and daily cleansing. We are clean but we walk in a dirty world and so need our spiritual feet washed daily.

They are clean—all but Judas. That is, in the sense of salvation, their sins are forgiven and those sins are all blotted out and forgotten as far as working against their salvation is concerned. In the sense of salvation, all our sins are laid on Jesus, past, present and future, and are counted paid. But God still hates sin and must punish the impenitent, so He "scourgeth every son whom he receiveth" (Heb. 12:6). A child of God who cannot lose his everlasting life can lose the daily fellowship. So, we need to come daily to plead, "Forgive us our debts, as we forgive our debtors" (Matt. 6:12).

Daily walking in the light and daily cleansing are the way to daily fellowship with God and each other. The footwashing pictures a born-again Christian getting daily renewal of fellowship and daily cleansing.

VERSES 12-17:

12 So after he had washed their feet, and had taken his garments, and was set down again, he said unto them, Know ye what I have done to you?
13 Ye call me Master and Lord: and ye say well; for *so* I am.
14 If I then, *your* Lord and Master, have washed your feet; ye also ought to wash one another's feet.

15 For I have given you an example, that ye should do as I have done to you.
16 Verily, verily, I say unto you, The servant is not greater than his lord; neither he that is sent greater than he that sent him.
17 If ye know these things, happy are ye if ye do them.

Christ Sets Us an Example to Wash One Another's Feet

Some have thought that Jesus was here setting up an ordinance and an official church ceremony of public footwashing to show our humility. But several arguments deny that. First, the command was that they were to *"wash one another's feet"* (vs. 14). Not a mass footwashing, but personal service. It was not to be a church mass ceremony, and we know that the apostles did not understand it to be so, and there is no record of any New Testament church having a footwashing ceremony.

Besides, that would miss the spiritual meaning Jesus gave here. It is as Galatians 6:1 commands: "Brethren, if a man be overtaken in a fault, ye which are spiritual, restore such an one in the spirit of meekness; considering thyself, lest thou also be tempted." We are daily to uphold one another, pray one for another, forgive one another. "We then that are strong ought to bear the infirmities of the weak, and not to please ourselves" (Rom. 15:1). We should help each other to have daily revival, daily renewal. We are to "bear ye one another's burdens, and so fulfill the law of Christ" (Gal. 6:2).

We are not greater than Jesus. No one could sin against us as we have sinned against our dear Saviour. If He can forgive us, then we can forgive each other. He is our Example for brotherly love and forgiveness.

VERSES 18-30:

18 ¶ I speak not of you all: I know whom I have chosen: but that the scripture may be fulfilled, He that eateth bread with me hath lifted up his heel against me.

19 Now I tell you before it come, that, when it is come to pass, ye may believe that I am *he*.

20 Verily, verily, I say unto you, He that receiveth whomsoever I send receiveth me; and he that receiveth me receiveth him that sent me.

21 When Jesus had thus said, he was troubled in spirit, and testified, and said, Verily, verily, I say unto you, that one of you shall betray me.

22 Then the disciples looked one on another, doubting of whom he spake.

23 Now there was leaning on Jesus' bosom one of his disciples, whom Jesus loved.

24 Simon Peter therefore beckoned to him, that he should ask who it should be of whom he spake.

25 He then lying on Jesus' breast saith unto him, Lord, who is it?

26 Jesus answered, He it is, to whom I shall give a sop, when I have dipped *it*. And when he had dipped the sop, he gave *it* to Judas Iscariot, *the son* of Simon.

27 And after the sop Satan entered into him. Then said Jesus unto him, That thou doest, do quickly.

28 Now no man at the table knew for what intent he spake this unto him.

29 For some *of them* thought, because Judas had the bag, that Jesus had said unto him, Buy *those things* that we have need of against the feast; or, that he should give something to the poor.

30 He then having received the sop went immediately out: and it was night.

"Lord, Who Is It?"

Someone will betray Jesus: one of the twelve! Who could it be? Matthew 26:22 tells us, "And they were exceeding sorrowful, and began every one of them to say unto him, Lord, is it I?" Everyone? That tells us two things. First, they did not suspect Judas. Like many another pretended Christian, he outwardly appeared a good man. Jesus knew he was unsaved, knew the covetousness that corroded his soul, but the disciples did not. Judas "had the bag, and bare what was put therein" (12:6). And he took from this common purse for himself a fee, but the disciples knew it not. He was a thief, but the disciples knew it not. It may be that by common consent they selected him to be responsible for their meager income and the dispersal of it. They may have thought his protest honest—that Mary's expensive ointment should have been sold and the money given to the poor.

Religious people are not always Christian people. Judas was not.

And the most urgent question of all, perhaps the most frightening question, was, *"Lord, is it I?"* (vs. 25). But every one of the disciples asked it. That frightening question indicates, too, their consciences warned them they might fall into terrible sin.

The truth is, in every Christian "the flesh lusteth against the Spirit." Moses, the meekest man who ever lived, once lost his temper and publicly dishonored God in the second smiting of the rock. David, "a man after his own heart," committed adultery and murder. Solomon worshiped the idols of his heathen wives. Peter cursed and swore aloud, denying Christ and quitting the ministry. Jonah deliberately disobeyed God and ran away from duty. A Christian must remember that the heart is deceitful above all things, and desperately wicked. "Keep thy heart with all diligence; for out of it are the issues of life" (Prov. 4:23).

Having a little inkling of their deceitful hearts, these disciples asked Jesus, "Lord, is it I?"

It is Judas who will fulfill Psalm 41:9, "Yea, mine own familiar friend, in whom I trusted, which did eat of my bread, hath lifted up his heel against me."

Jesus was *"troubled in spirit"* (vs. 21). The sorrow caused by a friend who proves unfaithful and becomes an enemy is very great. The tender heart of Jesus had few very close friends like Mary, Martha and Lazarus. He was hailed as a wonder-worker, but hero worship is not the same as tender affection. Do you suppose the dear Lord Jesus who was "tempted in all points like as we are" did not suffer the betrayal, the false friendship, even more than we would?

Shakespeare says about ingratitude:

> **Blow, blow, thou winter wind,**
> **Thou art not so unkind**
> **As man's ingratitude;**
> **Thy tooth is not so keen**
> **Because thou art not seen**
> **Although thy breath be rude.**
>
> **Freeze, freeze, thou bitter sky,**
> **Thou dost not bite so nigh**
> **As benefits forgot;**
> **Though thou the waters warp,**

Thy sting is not so sharp
As friend remember'd not.

John was *"one of the disciples, whom Jesus loved"* and he *"was leaning on Jesus' bosom"* (vs. 23). I wonder if John, seeing the broken heart of Jesus over the betrayal that Jesus said would come, did not then move his cot nearer and if he was not, in this caressing gesture, expressing his sympathy and love? At meals the custom was to lie on couches, lean on an elbow and eat with one hand; so that made it easy for John to lean over on Jesus' bosom.

I want for myself to see here the hungry heart of Jesus for our affection and how freely we may approach to Him, even as our Best Beloved, without being rebuffed or turned away!

I heard a Pentecostal woman praying and she addressed her prayer, "Dear, sweet Jesus"! I thought it pleased the Lord and it touched me.

When my daughters were very small, each one loved to stand by me in the car seat, sometimes holding my ear, sometimes patting me on the back of the head and saying, "My sweet Daddy! My sweet Daddy!" That was sweet to me. Do you think the Lord Jesus, who groaned and wept with Mary at Lazarus' grave, did not so crave affection and tender understanding?

"The disciple whom Jesus loved" (vs. 23) must have been John. Perhaps he was led to write it down but to modestly omit his name. In John 20:24 John will acknowledge that he is the one. But, oh, that gives you and me a right to say, "Jesus loves me! He delights in me! He wants me to be happy! He will never leave me!"

But the betrayal must come out. Jesus said, *"He it is, to whom I shall give a sop"* (vs. 26). Then He gave it to Judas. Judas had already planned to sell Jesus to the priests. And now he became devil-possessed. Jesus said, *"That thou doest, do quickly"* (vs. 27). You see, tomorrow must be the day of the crucifixion and all the events of it were pressing hard on Jesus. He knew it must be right away.

"And it was night" (vs. 30). The evening meal, the instruction, the washing the disciples' feet—all passed the evening by, now,

"it was night." Yes, the blackest night this world ever saw! After the teaching of chapters 14,15 and 16, and after the high priestly prayer of chapter 17, there will be Gethsemane, the bloody sweat and Jesus about to die in the Garden, when He would say, "My soul is exceeding sorrowful, even unto death." Then the mob, led by Judas, men with swords and staves, will come to arrest Him. There will be the infamous traitor's kiss and then the Saviour will be hustled off to the high priest's palace, there to be blasphemed, to have spittle in His face, to be beaten and condemned and kept a prisoner for a trial before Pilate the next morning.

Dr. Macaulay says verse 30, *"He then having received the sop went immediately out: AND IT WAS NIGHT,"* suggests the pall of eternal darkness coming down upon this man who had sold himself to sell the Son of God. "Whoever goes out from the presence of Christ goes out into the night, but whoever abides with Him dwells in eternal day."

Oh, sad the night!

VERSES 31-35:

31 ¶ Therefore, when he was gone out, Jesus said, Now is the Son of man glorified, and God is glorified.in him.

32 If God be glorified in him, God shall also glorify him in himself, and shall straightway glorify him.

33 Little children, yet a little while I am with you. Ye shall seek me: and as I said unto the Jews, Whither I go, ye cannot come; so now I say to you.

34 A new commandment I give unto you, That ye love one another; as I have loved you, that ye also love one another.

35 By this shall all *men* know that ye are my disciples, if ye have love one to another.

The Mark of a Disciple—Love for the Brethren

Jesus said, *"Now is the Son of man glorified"* (vs. 31). He sees one thought, the crucifixion, the long-planned atonement finished, the resurrection in power accomplished.

In John 7:39 "Jesus was not yet glorified," by which we understand to mean glorified in His resurrection. But the whole of Christ's life is coming now to a climax, and it glorifies Christ and glorifies the Father. This same night Jesus will pray:

"I have glorified thee on the earth: I have finished the work which thou gavest me to do. And now, O Father, glorify thou me with thine own self with the glory which I had with thee before the world was."—17:4,5.

Jesus had prayed before, "Father, glorify thy name. Then came there a voice from heaven, saying, I have both glorified it, and will glorify it again" (John 12:28).

Now the last words of counsel and command are to be given. Jesus addresses the disciples tenderly, *"Little children"* (vs. 33). A few hours here to counsel and fellowship, then the agony of the cross and the good-bye to these years of walking with Him daily wherever He went.

So now, *"a new commandment"* He gives (vs. 34). Let us say a new statement of the command to love our neighbors as ourselves. Now the stress is not on sacrifices, on Sabbaths, on feast days, on ceremonies; the emphasis is on love, a heart-love for other Christians. And here is the mark by which all men can recognize a Christian—if ye have love one to another (vs. 34). First Corinthians, chapter 13, says that all the gifts and services are nothing but sounding brass if there is not love. Preachers, preach the truth, however strict it be, but preach it in love!

A young preacher years ago came to me in distress. He said, "I feel a constant pressure to preach about Hell and judgment. The older preachers around criticised me saying that is too harsh, the subject is too painful to mention often. Shall I stop warning people about Hell and urging them to repent?"

In answer, I asked him a question, "Do you preach with tears? Are you brokenhearted that people are in danger of Hell?"

He replied, "Yes, I weep all through the sermon and they criticise that, too."

"Well," I said, "go ahead and preach about Hell as long as you can weep about it."

I know that many think it is unloving to be against sin. Modernists, unbelievers, who do not believe the Bible or the historic Christian faith, profess that we do not love modernists when we say they are unconverted infidels denying the historic, Christian faith. But love for Christ must still be true. Christ loves every sinner who goes to Hell and does not want him to go. And we Christians, after we are to witness the last judgment of Revelation 20 and every unbeliever cast into Hell, will then need the comfort of God wiping away our tears in Revelation 21:4.

A father who whips his child, as the Scripture commands, loves him more than the unprincipled father who does not! Proverbs 13:24 says it sharply: "He that spareth his rod hateth his son: but he that loveth him chasteneth him betimes." So love with an outgoing concern, teach with a loving intercession, but love must still do right. "Let love be without dissimulation. Abhor that which is evil; cleave to that which is good" (Rom. 12:9). Love is to "rejoice with them that do rejoice, and weep with them that weep" (Rom. 12:15).

VERSES 36-38:

36 ¶ Simon Peter said unto him, Lord, whither goest thou? Jesus answered him, Whither I go, thou canst not follow me now; but thou shalt follow me afterwards.

37 Peter said unto him, Lord, why cannot I follow thee now? I will lay down my life for thy sake.

38 Jesus answered him, Wilt thou lay down thy life for my sake? Verily, verily, I say unto thee, The cock shall not crow, till thou hast denied me thrice.

Peter Will Deny Christ

Simon Peter said, *"Lord, whither goest thou?"* (vs. 36). Dr. Meyer says:

> To that question our Lord might have given a direct answer: "Heaven! The Father's bosom! The New Jerusalem! The City of God!" but . . . He says in effect: "It is a matter of comparative indifference whither I go . . . . *Whither I go, thou canst not follow Me now; but* thou shalt follow Me afterwards"—words which our Lord caught up and expanded for the comfort of them all; for now for the first time they realized that they were about to be parted from Jesus, and were almost beside themselves with grief: "Let not your heart be troubled" (14:1).

How strange that Peter would be the one to publicly deny the Lord Jesus! The list of the apostles starts off, "The first, Simon, who is called Peter" (Matt. 10:2). It was Peter who boldly answered, "Thou art the Christ, the Son of the living God" (Matt. 16:16). And that was special revelation from God and it pleased the Saviour very much.

It was Peter who was given "the keys of the kingdom," which Dr. Scofield thinks means he was to preach first to the Jews at Pentecost and be the first to preach to the Gentiles in Acts, chapter 10. No doubt he was the most vigorous, determined, dedicated Christian of the lot. And when he said, *"I will lay down my life for thy sake"* (vs. 37), I, for one, believe he meant to do that and possibly did later.

There is no truth, however, in the Roman tradition that Peter died at Rome, and that he was crucified head downward. Peter was never in Rome and there is abundant evidence of that. He was not there when Paul wrote to some twenty-eight persons and families in Romans 16. He was not there to meet Paul when Paul arrived in Acts, chapter 28. He was not there when Paul wrote letters to the Philippians, to Philemon, to Colossians and II Timothy. In fact, Paul said, "Only Luke is with me." Peter was not mentioned. No, Peter went to the dispersed Israelites, to the circumcision. Paul had agreed he was to go to the Gentiles. So Peter preached to the dispersed Jews in the Babylon area, and both his letters traditionally are marked as I and II Peter from Babylon.

But Peter surely loved the Lord. Peter was a great Christian. How did he fall into such sin?

Well, we are to remember that all of us alike are weak, frail Christians. If Peter had watched and prayed as he ought, he would not have denied Christ. No Christian is so strong as not to need to watch and pray. Satan "as a roaring lion, walketh about, seeking whom he may devour" (I Pet. 5:8). Let us think of Peter with love and pity and of all who in time of great temptation may fail, and let us "restore such an one in the spirit of meekness; considering thyself, lest thou also be tempted" (Gal. 6:1).

Peter was selected by Satan for a special attack, "Satan hath desired to have you, that he may sift you as wheat" (Luke 22:31). Satan had selected Job for an attack as Job, chapter 1, tells us. Peter was allowed to be tempted, but he was not compelled to fall into such sin, for "there hath no temptation taken you but such as is common to man: but God is faithful, who will not suffer you to be tempted above that ye are able; but will with the temptation also make a way to escape, that ye may be able to bear it" (I Cor. 10:13). It may be that the other disciples were as cowardly as Peter but had not so boldly put themselves in the company where they would be challenged.

I have a sermon on the fall of Peter and the sin and his restoration with this outline. I use the Scriptures Luke 22:31-34, 45, 46, and 54-62.

For an introduction we remember that 80 verses of the New Testament are used to tell of Peter's sin and his restoration—15 verses in Matthew, 15 in Mark, 15 in Luke and 25 in the 21st chapter of John.

I HOW BAD WAS PETER'S SIN?

1. The sin included lying, cursing, denying Jesus, quitting the ministry.

2. Peter was then the best Christian in the world, perhaps, and the best preacher. What a shock to Christians!

3. It was the worst time to go back on Jesus and a time of awful stress when the world was against Him, when Christians ought to stand true.

II WHAT WERE THE ELEMENTS THAT LED TO PETER'S SIN?

1. He was the object of special temptation by Satan.

2. He had an old carnal nature as we all have, with a constant down pull.

3. He slept when he should be praying. He should have prayed through for victory.

4. He sat by the fire for an hour or two with the wicked soldiers who would crucify Jesus. Bad company is the way to ruin.

III WHAT ARE THE ELEMENTS THAT BROUGHT PETER BACK TO FELLOWSHIP?

1. He had a new nature, too. He went out and wept bitterly over his sin.

2. Jesus had prayed for him. "I have prayed for thee, that thy faith fail not" (Luke 22:32).

3. Jesus went after him personally, as we see in John 21.

4. God's instruments: fishes and a rooster were used to bring Peter back.

John 14

L ET not your heart be troubled: ye believe in God, believe also in me.

2 In my Father's house are many mansions: if *it were* not *so*, I would have told you. I go to prepare a place for you.

3 And if I go and prepare a place for you, I will come again, and receive you unto myself; that where I am, *there* ye may be also.

"Let Not Your Heart Be Troubled"

No doubt the apostles had need for some reassurance. They had just had it pressed upon them that the Lord Jesus was going on to the crucifixion and was leaving them.

They had just been warned that one of the twelve would betray Him, and that all of them would flee that night!

They are bound to have felt some sense of danger. If the Lord Jesus was to be killed, those close to Him were in danger also. Now is a good time for comfort; so Jesus tells them, *"Let not your heart be troubled: ye believe in God, believe also in me"* (vs. 1).

Could they trust the Lord Jesus to bring everything out right? Could they believe that literally everything in this world was in the hand of Christ and all the Father would do, Jesus would do.

They have confidence in the Lord Jesus and will rest in Him, without doubting.

"In my Father's house are many mansions" (vs. 2). Heaven awaits them and Jesus Himself is going to prepare a place for all of them and us. "Oh," He says, "you cannot possibly ask or expect more than God has provided!" Would there not be enough room in Heaven for all God's people? Oh, never fear. If there had been any lack, the Lord Jesus would have told it (vs. 2).

If the Lord Jesus had limited atonement for a select group of people, He would have said so. After He had said so many times, "Whosoever will," and "Ho, every one that thirsteth," and "If any man thirst, let him come unto me, and drink," and "Him that cometh to me I will in no wise cast out," you may be sure that the Lord Jesus had no "fine print" in the contract, limiting His love, limiting His invitation, limiting the room He has in Heaven. Oh, no! "Where sin abounded, grace did much more abound." Where the Lord Jesus did not expressly state some limits on His love and provision and on the glad welcome to Heaven, no one else should contrive or imagine any limits.

How much comfort the Bible has for trouble and sorrow! The shepherd Psalm promises that the Lord, our Shepherd, would lead us beside still waters and make us to lie down in green pastures. And we need not be afraid if we go through the valley of the shadow of death.

Yes, "in the world ye shall have tribulation," Jesus said, "but be of good cheer; I have overcome the world" (16:33).

It is true that premature death and martyrdom will come for some of these. James will be beheaded by Herod (Acts 12:2). But why should they fret? That will only be an earlier promotion to the glories of Heaven!

"My Father's house"—isn't that a lovely and intimate picture of Heaven? It is not just the place but the relationship to the Father. If it is my Father's house, then it is my house, too!

"It was father's house, though it was only a shepherd's shieling; he dwelt there, and mother, and our brothers and sisters. And where they dwell, or where wife and child dwell, there is home. Such is Heaven," says F. B. Meyer.

In my boyhood, my earthly father's house was always "our house."

Heaven ought to have an attraction for the people of God. An old song says:

> **Oh, sing to me of Heaven**
> **When I am called to die.**

We sing:

> **There is a land that is fairer than day,**
> **And by faith we can see it afar;**
> **For the Father waits over the way,**
> **To prepare us a dwelling place there.**

Again an old hymn goes like this:

On Jordan's stormy banks I stand,
And cast a wishful eye
To Canaan's fair and happy land,
Where my possessions lie.

In Revelation 22 the Lord tells us of that Heavenly City, the New Jerusalem, coming down from God out of Heaven, prepared as a bride adorned for her husband. Then, about that Heavenly City prepared for us, He says, "The Spirit AND THE BRIDE say, Come." Heaven is calling. There is room enough. Christ has prepared it.

My father had a wedding ceremony for two deaf young people in West Texas. On a note pad he wrote to the groom, "You have caught the bird; now what about a nest for her?"

With gleaming eyes, he proudly wrote, "I have the nest all ready! I have built a new house!"

Ah, yes! So we will not be strangers, we will not be outcasts, we will not be in poverty. In the Father's house are many mansions.

Again F. B. Meyer reminds us that though there are many mansions, yet there is room. "As age after age has poured in its crowds, still the cry has gone forth, There is abundant room! The many mansions are not all tenanted. The orchestra is not full."

With that in mind, Jesus said, *"Let not your heart be troubled."*

The Lord Jesus Himself is going to prepare the place (vs. 2). Why? He will come again and receive us to Himself.

He talks now not only about Heaven as the home of the soul, but as the home for resurrected bodies, for He speaks here of the Second Coming to receive Christians. He speaks now of I Thessalonians 4:16,17:

"For the Lord himself shall descend from heaven with a shout, with the voice of the archangel, and with the trump of God: and the dead in Christ shall rise first: Then we which are alive and remain shall be caught up together with them in the clouds, to meet the Lord in the air: and so shall we ever be with the Lord."

Here He speaks of that wonderful return for His own as told in

I Corinthians 15:51,52:

"Behold, I shew you a mystery; We shall not all sleep, but we shall all be changed, In a moment, in the twinkling of an eye, at the last trump: for the trumpet shall sound, and the dead shall be raised incorruptible, and we shall be changed."

The Lord is coming for His own.

We will not step out into the dark when we leave this world. But as the lost sheep feels so secure on the shepherd's shoulder, so all God's children are clasped safely in the hand of Christ and no one can take us away from Him. He wants us to be with Him.

One of the most wonderful things about Jesus and perhaps one that is hardest for us to understand is how He wants our company, our fellowship, our communion. Even in Heaven the Lord Jesus needs us to make Him completely happy. "That where I am, there ye may be also" (vs. 3). He wants to prepare a place so that when He comes, we will be with Him in the same place. Wonderful comfort!

VERSES 4-6:

4 And whither I go ye know, and the way ye know.
5 Thomas saith unto him, Lord, we know not whither thou goest; and how can we know the way?
6 Jesus saith unto him, I am the way, the truth, and the life: no man cometh unto the Father, but by me.

Jesus, the Way to Heaven

Jesus had said so many things about how to be saved, but our poor, blinded eyes do not see it so easily. We feel we must earn our way. We feel guilty because of our sins, and so we lack assurance. With all the talk of Jesus about receiving Him, about being born again, about the believer having no condemnation but everlasting life, would not they know that trusting Jesus is the way to Heaven? But Thomas said, *"Lord, we know not whither thou goest; and how can we know the way?"* (vs. 5). Well, Thomas, Jesus will say it again. The Lord Jesus Himself is *"the way, the truth, and the life: no man cometh unto the Father, but by me"* (vs. 6).

Let us say it again for Jesus has said it again: this is an exclusive way to salvation. The Lord Jesus has no rivals, He has no peers. This is the one absolutely unique way of going to Heaven. No one can ever get to Heaven without coming by faith in Jesus Christ. It may be that the Holy Spirit will reveal the thing through types and the shadows in the Old Testament so that Abraham would trust the Lord and, believing, it would be counted to him for righteousness. By faith Abel would know to offer a more excellent sacrifice; but the faith is in Jesus Himself, this "seed of the woman" who has been promised to bruise the serpent's head.

I am saying that there is no salvation without Jesus—Old Testament or New Testament. No other system or religion will ever do. Every poor soul in this world who does not come to trust Christ for salvation after the years of responsibility, must go to Hell. Jesus is the ONLY WAY TO Heaven.

He is "the way." He is "the truth" and all other plans of salvation are false. He is "the life," that is, He Himself has the everlasting life to give and He is the resurrection. All the life that every poor sinner can ever have must come through Jesus.

There is no coming to the Father except one comes to Jesus. There is no faith in God that does not mean faith in Jesus Christ the Saviour.

There is no room here for the idea that any religion is good just so you are sincere. No, no! There is no room here for the silly proverb, "We are all going to the same place, we just have different roads." No, if you have any road besides Jesus Christ, you will not get to God's Heaven. He is the only way to be saved.

An Englishman has written that what the world needs is for fundamentalists and modernists to get together and combine forces in brotherly love. No; as long as any man is a modernist, not accepting the deity of Christ, His blood atonement, the verbal inspiration of the Bible and these other great essentials of the Gospel, he has a false plan of salvation, and to mix good with evil means less than the truth.

Some foolish people would urge us to join with the heathen religions and get whatever good there is in all religions. But that is of Satan, not of God. That is the general principle of Bahaism. It is the general position of the humanists and the religious liberal. But all that is wrong. The one fundamental essential is Jesus Christ as Saviour. He is the only way to Heaven.

VERSES 7-11:

7 If ye had known me, ye should have known my Father also: and from henceforth ye know him, and have seen him.

8 Philip saith unto him, Lord, shew us the Father, and it sufficeth us.

9 Jesus saith unto him, Have I been so long time with you, and yet hast thou not known me, Philip? he that hath seen me hath seen the Father; and how sayest thou *then*, Shew us the Father?

10 Believest thou not that I am in the Father, and the Father in me? the words that I speak unto you I speak not of myself: but the Father that dwelleth in me, he doeth the works.

11 Believe me that I *am* in the Father, and the Father in me: or else believe me for the very works' sake.

Jesus and the Father

Jesus continues what is stressed throughout the Gospel of John. He and the Father are one. If you know Jesus, you know the Father.

In India a missionary asked a Hindu how did he feel toward God.

The Hindu replied, "I do not know what God is like. How would I know?"

The missionary replied, "God is like Jesus Christ."

"Oh," said the Hindu, "then I could love a God like that and serve Him!"

Thomas, if you know Jesus, you know the Father. If you pray to the Father, you pray to Jesus. If you trust in the Father, you trust in Jesus. "He that . . . believeth on him that sent me . . ." gives the same promise as, "He that believeth on the Son" (5:24 and 3:36). If you come to Jesus, you come to the Father. If you pray to Jesus, you pray to the Father. If you believe in Jesus, you believe in the Father. If you have Christ, you have the Father.

But Philip wanted the Father to be revealed. Jesus tells him He is already revealed in Jesus. If you have seen Jesus, you have seen the Father. Jesus is in the Father and the Father in Him. What Jesus speaks, the Father speaks. What works Jesus does, the Father does. Oh, then, you must accept the absolute deity of Jesus Christ.

Jesus spoke of Himself as "the Son of man which is in heaven" (3:13). He said again, "No man hath seen God at any time; the only begotten Son, which is in the bosom of the Father, he hath declared him" (1:18). Jesus on earth was in the bosom of the Father. The tie, the perfect understanding, the perfect knowledge and oneness of Christ and the Father was not hindered by His incarnation. He was not less God because He was man. He was not less in Heaven because He was on earth. We do not understand all of deity in God the Father, so we need not be surprised if there is some infinite wisdom about Jesus and infinite knowledge and holiness about Him that is beyond our comprehension. But, it is true that if you know Jesus, you know the Father.

VERSE 12:

12 Verily, verily, I say unto you, He that believeth on me, the works that I do shall he do also; and greater *works* than these shall he do; because I go unto my Father.

We Believing Christians Are to Do the Same Work as the Lord Jesus

Verse 12 is an amazing verse. How little we believe it! How little we claim it! One who believes in the Lord Jesus can do the very works Jesus did on earth. The one limitation is the measurement of our faith.

And the Lord Jesus was cut off after about three and one-half years of public ministry, and any man who lived beyond thirty-three, if his faith were adequate, could do even greater works than the Lord Jesus.

So D. L. Moody preached to greater crowds than Jesus, and had more people saved than the Lord Jesus had in His earthly ministry. So, no doubt, have some others. We know that the Lord Jesus is Saviour, but as far as being an instrument of getting out the Gospel, other men who have faith may do the very works of Jesus and greater.

We must remember that in the high priestly prayer Jesus said, "As thou hast sent me into the world, even so have I also sent them into the world" (John 17:18). And when He is raised from the dead He will breathe on the disciples and say to them, "Receive ye the Holy Ghost: Whose soever sins ye remit, they are remitted unto them; and whose soever sins ye retain, they are retained" (20:22,23).

In John 8:12 Jesus said, "I am the light of the world." In John 9:5 He said, "As long as I am in the world, I am the light of the world." Ah, but in Matthew 5:14 He said, "Ye are the light of the world."

It is not, as Dr. A. T. Pierson said, that Christ is the only light and we are simply like the moon; it gives no light, but reflects the light. That is not an adequate illustration, for I have Christ in me, the hope of Glory. I have life in myself. And God has so made it that the ordaining hand of the Apostle Paul on the head of Timothy will give him some amazing gift of power that he should stir up and use (I Tim. 4:14; II Tim. 1:6).

Peter was so filled with the power of God that they lay the sick by the roadside that his shadow might fall upon them and they would be healed, and they were (Acts 5:15). Peter and John at the Beautiful Gate of the Temple could say to the lame man who had never walked a step, "Such as I have give I thee: In the name of Jesus Christ of Nazareth rise up and walk" (Acts 3:6). He rose and walked and leaped and praised God!

For the work that Jesus did, He had the mighty power of the Holy Spirit. We can have the same fullness of the Spirit Christ had.

We remember that when Jesus was baptized and praying, the Holy Ghost came on Him in visible form like a dove. We are told, ". . . God anointed Jesus of Nazareth with the Holy Ghost and

with power: who went about doing good, and healing all that were oppressed of the devil; for God was with him" (Acts 10:38). Jesus chose to take the limitation of a man as far as service is concerned. So Isaiah 61:1 says, "The Spirit of the Lord God is upon me; because the Lord God hath anointed me to preach good tidings unto the meek; he hath sent me to bind up the brokenhearted, to proclaim liberty to the captives, and the opening of the prison to them that are bound."

We, too, can have the fullness of the Spirit and we, too, can do the work of Jesus.

Paul could say, "We pray you in Christ's stead, be ye reconciled to God" (II Cor. 5:20). Paul could stand in the place of Christ and could invite people with Christ's own authority to come and be saved. Jesus is the only Saviour, but as far as a preacher or a witness, every Christian can have the same kind of power and get the same kind of results.

VERSES 13,14:

13 And whatsoever ye shall ask in my name, that will I do, that the Father may be glorified in the Son.

14 If ye shall ask any thing in my name, I will do *it*.

Prayer in Jesus' Name

The Christian world is very much at fault in that we have made little cliches, little routine ceremonies of closing prayers, "For this we ask in Jesus' name," and that is wrong.

In the model prayer, Jesus told us that we are to pray after a certain manner. And He did not say that we should close the prayer, "In Jesus' name." He was not setting out a little ceremonial form that we should follow. He was telling us how to pray.

Asking in Jesus' name is a particular, special way of prayer. What does it mean? It means that when I come to pray in His name I am simply signing His name as authority. I am saying, "Jesus wants this and I am simply asking it for Jesus."

My executive secretary for many, many years signs my checks. I have many things to do. I am traveling for the Lord Jesus somewhere nearly every week. So there is an agreement with the bank that she can sign my name to checks. But she signs checks only for the things I have authorized! She does not decide what she would like to spend the money for or how she thinks would be best. When she has my authority, she signs my name to a check. She keeps the checkbook.

In the same way, if I come to a genuine assurance that a certain thing is what Jesus impressed me to ask and if I am asking in a sense that I know Jesus wants it and the only reason I want it is that He wants it, then I can say, "In Jesus' name."

But note that this is a very specific and definite way of praying, and the promise is, *"And WHATSOEVER ye shall ask in my name, that will I do, that the Father may be glorified in the Son. If ye shall ask ANY THING in my name, I will do it"* (vss. 13,14). So any time you add this nice little ceremonial cliche to your prayer, "And this we ask in Jesus' name," and you don't get it, then you may know that you lied to God. You were not asking in Jesus' name or you would have gotten what you asked. The Scripture plainly says so.

Someone says, "But I love to honor the Lord Jesus." Yes, but you would not honor me, for example, by forging my name to checks and getting things you were not authorized to get with my money. A lawyer once forged the signature of my father when he was sick and had a legal instrument to give him the power of attorney. On my father's forged signature, he sold an expensive bit of property and took the money. That was crooked. He went to the state penitentiary for it.

And it is crooked for you or me to pretend that we are coming in the name of Jesus and asking only for Him when it is our own desire and our own plan, not necessarily God's plan.

For example, when Jesus taught us to pray for daily bread, it is not Jesus who is hungry but it is bread for us and our family. When we come to ask for daily forgiveness as we forgive others, it is not Jesus who is guilty and needs forgiveness, it is we. So in the Lord's model prayer we were not taught to say, "In Jesus' name."

It is a great sin to allow our relationship with God to be expressed only in little routine, formal ceremonies without any heart attention.

A young pastor where I held a revival campaign was troubled and he said, "Dr. Rice, you embarrass me. Sometimes you pray, "In Jesus' name," and sometimes you do not. I have taught my people always to pray, 'In Jesus' name.' " And he gave as proof text verse 6 above: "No man cometh unto the Father, but by me."

"Yes," I said, "when you come to God you must come by way of Jesus Christ. But I have already come to God. I am already in the family, and now I can ask for Jesus if I know what He clearly wants and have assurance from Him I can represent Him in the prayer, or I can pray in my own name because I am in the family of God." As Dr. Bob Jones, Sr., used to say, "I am no outsider. I am a member of the family of God. I can just pull up my chair to the table and say, 'Pappy, please pass the biscuits.' "

How these poor, carnal minds of ours love to have little ceremonies! We get the form of godliness without the power. We get the incidentals but not the essentials. So, when you pray, do not say you are asking "in Jesus' name" unless you are asking on authority from Him. And in that case, you may know absolutely you get the answer, for God answers every prayer that comes with the authority of Jesus Christ.

This promise of asking in Jesus' name is repeated in John 16:24, "Hitherto have ye asked nothing in my name: ask, and ye shall receive, that your joy may be full."

VERSES 15-26:

15 ¶ If ye love me, keep my commandments.

16 And I will pray the Father, and he shall give you another Comforter, that he may abide with you for ever;

17 *Even* the Spirit of truth; whom the world cannot receive, because it seeth him not, neither knoweth him: but ye know him; for he dwelleth with you, and shall be in you.

18 I will not leave you comfortless: I will come to you.

19 Yet a little while, and the world seeth me no more; but ye see me: because I live, ye shall live also.

20 At that day ye shall know that I *am* in my Father, and ye in me, and I in you.

21 He that hath my commandments, and keepeth them, he it is that loveth me: and he that loveth me shall be loved of my Father, and I will love him, and will manifest my-self to him.

22 Judas saith unto him, not Iscariot, Lord, how is it that thou wilt manifest thyself unto us, and not unto the world?

23 Jesus answered and said unto him, If a man love me, he will keep my words: and my Father will love him, and we will come unto him, and make our abode with him.

24 He that loveth me not keepeth not my sayings: and the word which ye hear is not mine, but the Father's which sent me.

25 These things have I spoken unto you, being *yet* present with you.

26 But the Comforter, *which is* the Holy Ghost, whom the Father will send in my name, he shall teach you all things, and bring all things to your remembrance, whatsoever I have said unto you.

The Holy Spirit, Our Comforter

"If ye love me, keep my commandments. And I will pray the Father . . ." (vss. 15,16). That leaves the impression that only those who keep His commandments will have the indwelling of the Holy Spirit. However, the American Standard Version makes that clearer, "If you love me, you will keep my commandments." And it is stated the same way in Charles B. Williams' translation of the New Testament, the Berkeley Translation, the New International Version, and others.

So, keeping Christ's commandments is not simply a way to earn the indwelling of the Holy Spirit. Here are two simply connected facts. One who is saved will keep His commandments and will have the Holy Spirit dwelling within, sent from the Father to take the place of Jesus.

We know from positive statements in the Scriptures that the indwelling of the Holy Spirit is for every Christian. First Corinthians 6:19,20 says:

"What? know ye not that your body is the temple of the Holy Ghost which is in you, which ye have of God, and ye are not your own? For ye are bought with a price: therefore glorify God in your body, and in your spirit, which are God's."

Romans 8:9 says, "But ye are not in the flesh, but in the Spirit, if so be that the Spirit of God dwell in you. Now if any man have not the Spirit of Christ, he is none of his."

So every Christian has the Holy Spirit dwelling within. Jesus is simply stating a fact—that born-again people have a change in heart. However imperfectly, they are Christ's sheep who follow Him (10:27). Though not always sharply defined nor obviously apparent, every born-again Christian walks "not after the flesh, but after the Spirit" (Rom. 8:4). So it is not a conditional promise that the Lord Jesus may pray the Father and the Father may give Christians another Comforter, the Holy Spirit. Here is a solemnly stated eternal fact. Jesus has prayed the Father and He has sent the Holy Spirit to abide forever in the body of every Christian.

Note the time element in verse 17, *"ye know him; for he dwelleth with you"* before the resurrection of Christ. The Holy Spirit was simply with Christians, not in them. *". . . and shall be in you,"* that is, after the resurrection of Christ the Holy Spirit would be within every Christian's body as in a temple. And that promise was certainly fulfilled for these disciples in John 20:19-22, and we believe it was fulfilled for every Christian in the world. At that time and since then the Holy Spirit came in and now comes in at conversion, regeneration, and abides forever with us.

Note the Father will send *"another Comforter"* (vs. 16). The Greek term here for Comforter is *Paraclete,* which means one called alongside to help. And it is to be another like Jesus. In I

John 2:1 the word "advocate" is the same word in the original. Oh, wonderful, ever-present Holy Spirit who represents Jesus living within us! Oh, how these poor, distraught, bereaved disciples needed Someone else to comfort them, to take the place of the Lord Jesus with whom they had walked and talked daily for these nearly three years! Well, the idea is not simply a Comforter but another of the same kind, One taking the place of Jesus.

Jesus said, *"I will not leave you comfortless: I will come to you"* (vs. 18).

On this verse F. B. Meyer gives us this comforting thought: "He comes when we need Him most. When the storm is high, and the water is pouring into the boat; when the house is empty because the life that made it home has fled; when Jericho has to be attacked on the morrow, and the Jordan crossed; when lover and friend stand aloof; when light is fading before dimming eyes, and names and faces elude the grasp of the aged mind; when the last coal is turning to grey ash; when the rush of the river is heard in the valley below—Jesus says, I come . . . ."

I was asked to conduct a funeral for a fifteen-year-old girl. My heart was heavy as I thought on what I should do. It was in the deepest depression. The father had abandoned the family since he could not get a job. The mother had toiled and slaved until her body was worn out, then she took tuberculosis and was bedfast. Now her beloved little daughter was dead. We must take this dear woman in our arms so she can look down in the casket to view the child for the last time, for her last good-bye. I thought, "What shall I say?"

But when I came to her bedside to talk with her, she said with tears, yet with joy, "Brother Rice, Jesus said, 'I will not leave you comfortless: I will come to you,' and, Brother Rice, He came! He came!"

Oh, no Christian need go without the comfort of the Holy Spirit!

Then the comfort of the Holy Spirit is so real because through Him, Christ Himself and the Father come to abide within us.

You say, "I let Jesus come into my heart." What you really did was to trust Christ to save you, then the Holy Spirit moved into your body and thus He manifests the Father and the Son.

Now, the manifestation of God's blessing and the sweetest fellowship of the Holy Spirit depend somewhat on how we keep His commandments. If with heart's love we earnestly keep God's commandments and abide in His love, then the sweet Spirit of God will make Christ and the Father very real and the fellowship with Father, Son and Holy Ghost will be continuous.

Note the plain condition here. Our obedience is the thermometer that shows the temperature of our love. There is no sincerity in the love that does not set out to please God and keep His commandments. Then more and more God and Christ will be real to us, manifested by the sweet Holy Spirit.

This Comforter is "the Holy Ghost" sent in Jesus' name and sent to represent Jesus and He "will teach you all things," He will "bring all things to your remembrance, whatsoever I have said unto you." So, the Holy Spirit is a Comforter, a Teacher, a Reminder, He is a constant Witness to Christ within us and will reveal the will of God to us.

Romans 8:26,27 tell us also that the sweet Holy Spirit is our Prayer Helper:

"Likewise the Spirit also helpeth our infirmities: for we know not what we should pray for as we ought: but the Spirit itself maketh intercession for us with groanings which cannot be uttered. And he that searcheth the hearts knoweth what is the mind of the Spirit, because he maketh intercession for the saints according to the will of God."

VERSES 27-31:

27 Peace I leave with you, my peace I give unto you: not as the world giveth, give I unto you. Let not your heart be troubled, neither let it be afraid.

28 Ye have heard how I said unto you, I go away, and come *again* unto you. If ye loved me, ye would rejoice, because I said, I go unto the Father: for my Father is greater than I.

29 And now I have told you before it come to pass, that, when it is come to pass, ye might believe.

30 Hereafter I will not talk much with you: for the prince of this world cometh, and hath nothing in

me.
31 But that the world may know that I love the Father; and as the Father gave me commandment, even so I do. Arise, let us go hence.

They Can Have Peace About Christ's Departure

Again, the sweet promise, *"Peace I leave with you, my peace I give unto you: not as the world giveth, give I unto you. Let not your heart be troubled, neither let it be afraid"* (vs. 27). So the chapter began and the sweet assurance is repeated for our so-easily-troubled hearts.

Christ has the answer of the troubled heart. He promises peace.

What a contrast there is between the unrest in this old troubled world and the heart of ungodly men and the peace of a Christian!

Isaiah 57:20,21 says, "But the wicked are like the troubled sea, when it cannot rest, whose waters cast up mire and dirt. There is no peace, saith my God, to the wicked."

Jesus said, speaking about the whole age and not simply the closing days of the age, "And ye shall hear of wars and rumours of wars: see that ye be not troubled . . ." (Matt. 24:6).

Oh, nation shall rise against nation, kingdom against kingdom, famine, pestilence, earthquakes—that is the course of this age. Wicked men cannot stop wars, cannot stop crime. All the remedies that worldly men try fail. As Jesus said to the woman at Sychar, "Whosoever drinketh of this water shall thirst again," so all the satisfactions and enjoyments and remedies that this world gives fail. The Scripture says, "Even in laughter the heart is sorrowful; and the end of that mirth is heaviness" (Prov. 14:13). And Job 14:1 says, "Man that is born of a woman is of few days, and full of trouble."

The lost man has the fear of death. He has to deal all the time with the wages of sin. The way of transgressors is hard. He has to deal with the unrest of conscience. All the psychiatrists in the world cannot fix the heart of a lost man. And there is the fear of death, there is the disillusionment with the world, there is the failure of faithless friends.

But even Christians face the troubles in this world. Jesus said, "In the world ye shall have tribulation: but be of good cheer; I have overcome the world" (16:33).

Jesus said, "Think not that I am come to send peace on earth: I came not to send peace, but a sword. For I am come to set a man at variance against his father, and the daughter against her mother, and the daughter in law against her mother in law" (Matt. 10:34,35). And we are promised that Christians will suffer persecution. The servant is no better than his lord, and if the world hates Christ, it will hate those who are near Him, dear to Him, and like Him. Ah, but in the midst of every kind of trouble, a Christian can have sweet peace. Jesus promised it. He said: "Come unto me, all ye that labour and are heavy laden, and I will give you rest. Take my yoke upon you, and learn of me; for I am meek and lowly in heart: and ye shall find rest unto your souls. For my yoke is easy, and my burden is light" (Matt. 11:28-30).

In Philippians 4:6,7 are these sweet instructions and this glowing promise: "Be careful for nothing; but in every thing by prayer and supplication with thanksgiving let your requests be made known unto God. And the peace of God, which passeth all understanding, shall keep your hearts and minds through Christ Jesus."

Ah, sweet instruction in I Peter 5:6,7: "Humble yourselves therefore under the mighty hand of God, that he may exalt you in due time: Casting all your care upon him; for he careth for you."

And again the Scripture says, "In returning and rest shall ye be saved; in quietness and confidence shall be your strength" (Isa. 30:15). Again, "Thou wilt keep him in perfect peace, whose mind is stayed on thee: because he trusteth in thee" (Isa. 26:3). Ah, "Yea, though I walk through the valley of the shadow of death, I will fear no evil: for thou art with me; thy rod and thy staff they comfort me" (Ps. 23:4). Yes, "Many sorrows shall be to the wicked: but he that trusteth in the Lord, mercy shall compass him about" (Ps. 32:10). And we are invited, "Cast thy burden upon the Lord, and he shall sustain thee: he shall never suffer the righteous to be moved" (Ps. 55:22).

The Apostle Paul found: "We are troubled on every side, yet not distressed; we are perplexed, but not in despair; Persecuted, but not forsaken; cast down, but not destroyed" (II Cor. 4:8,9). And again Paul was inspired to write of himself, "As unknown, and yet well known; as dying, and, behold, we live; as chastened, and not killed; As sorrowful, yet always rejoicing; as poor, yet making many rich; as having nothing, and yet possessing all things" (II Cor. 6:9,10).

Oh, the Christian who does not have peace is missing the great blessing offered freely. "Let not your heart be troubled."

> Oh, the peace my Saviour gives,
> Peace I never knew before,
> And the way has brighter grown
> Since I've learned to trust Him more.

Are they sad that Jesus is going away? Oh, they ought to be glad. In the first place, they ought to be glad for the Lord Jesus to go back to the Father. Oh, His heart may be lonely for the streets of gold, the plaudits of angels, and the glory that He had with the Father before. They ought to be glad for His sake.

Yes, and we ought to be glad for our sakes, too. For now, instead of having Jesus in one body whom we might occasionally see or speak to for a moment, we can have the sweet Holy Spirit living within us, to be our constant Companion, Guide, Comforter, Teacher, Reminder and Prayer Helper all the time. It is better for me to have Christ with me through the Holy Spirit in my body everywhere I go, whatever I do, than to have Christ in a human body somewhere on earth whom I could see occasionally and with whom I could have a hasty bit of fellowship and teaching.

Jesus says in verse 30, *"the prince of this world cometh."* We remember that Satan is "god of this world." He is the "prince of the power of the air." We know that Satan is continually trying to take over the rule of this world. "For the mystery of iniquity doth already work: only he who now letteth will let, until he be taken out of the way. And then shall that Wicked [Man of Sin] be revealed" (II Thess. 2:7,8).

And the rule of Satan will culminate one day in the Man of Sin who, after the Lord's people are taken out at the rapture and when the combined influence of the Holy Spirit and the lives of millions of people are removed, then the Man of Sin can appear. Satan has long tried to bring it about but could not. Charlemagne wanted to rule the world. So did Kaiser Wilhelm of Germany. So did Adolph Hitler. So did Mussolini. So have some of the popes. Yet all of them have failed and will fail until after the rapture when God's people, temples of the Holy Spirit, are taken out and thus His mass influence and the Christian influence is relaxed and the Man of Sin can take over.

But this evil world ruler, Satan, who will be manifested in the Man of Sin, the Antichrist, will see all the kingdoms of this world smitten by the great Stone cut out of a mountain that will hit the image, representing the kingdoms of this world, on his feet and grind them to powder (Dan. 2:34,35).

It is said about the Lord Jesus, "For of a truth against thy holy child Jesus, whom thou hast anointed, both Herod, and Pontius Pilate, with the Gentiles, and the people of Israel, were gathered together" (Acts 4:27). And He said this is the fulfillment of the 2nd Psalm, verses 1 and 2.

This world is not a good world. It is under a curse. The mass of men are the servants of sin. So Christians should expect that Satan "as a roaring lion, walketh about, seeking whom he may devour" (I Pet. 5:8).

In verse 31 Jesus is explaining the whole pattern of His coming to live and then to die, that He will tomorrow go to the cross, that the shame and spitting, the scourging, the nails in hands and feet, the scoffing of the multitude, would all be because Jesus loved the Father and was pleasing Him. He was obeying the commands of the Father gladly.

Then He said, "Arise, let us go hence" (vs. 31). So they left the place where they had been gathered together.

John 15

I AM the true vine, and my Father is the husbandman.

2 Every branch in me that beareth not fruit he taketh away: and every *branch* that beareth fruit, he purgeth it, that it may bring forth more fruit.

3 Now ye are clean through the word which I have spoken unto you.

4 Abide in me, and I in you. As the branch cannot bear fruit of itself, except it abide in the vine; no more can ye, except ye abide in me.

5 I am the vine, ye *are* the branches: He that abideth in me, and I in him,

the same bringeth forth much fruit: for without me ye can do nothing.

6 If a man abide not in me, he is cast forth as a branch, and is withered; and men gather them, and cast *them* into the fire, and they are burned.

7 If ye abide in me, and my words abide in you, ye shall ask what ye will, and it shall be done unto you.

8 Herein is my Father glorified, that ye bear much fruit; so shall ye be my disciples.

Abiding in Christ

Remember that chapters 13 and 14 of John occur on the night that Jesus was betrayed and in the upper chamber where they ate the last supper together and where the Lord's supper was given and where Jesus washed the disciples' feet.

In John 13:28 they were still at the table, and in verse 30, Judas Iscariot went out and Jesus was left alone with the eleven disciples who were truly converted.

Thus He began the marvelous discussion which ran through the entire 14th chapter of John. This discussion all took place in the Upper Room. It is clear from John 14:31, the last sentence, "Arise and let us go hence," that at this point the Lord Jesus left the Upper Room. Notice Mark 14:26 which evidently occurred after the words of Jesus recorded in the 14th chapter of John. Remember that no one of the Gospels claims to give every detail of what happened. The record given is all correct, but not all of the record is given.

That is made clear from John 20:30 and John 21:25. Mark 14:26 and John 14:31 mean that they arose from the table and went out toward the Mount of Olives. On the way the conversation of Jesus as recorded in John, chapters 15 and 16, and the prayer of chapter 17, took place. Notice in John 18:1 that they then crossed the brook Cedron (or Kidron) which separates Jerusalem from the Mount of Olives. Remember that the 15th. chapter of John was given them as Jesus walked with His disciples, or as they lingered on the way from the Upper Room somewhere in Jerusalem, to the Garden of Gethsemane. Gethsemane was on the lower slope of the Mount of Olives. Jesus went there often to pray.

* * *

Wonderful intimacy of a Christian with Christ is indicated here. He is the True Vine. We are branches of that Vine. We are part of Christ. And if we have Christ, we have everything:

"Therefore let no man glory in men, For all things are your's; Whether Paul, or Apollos, or Cephas, or the world, or life, or death, or things present, or things to come; all are yours; And ye are Christ's; and Christ is God's."—I Cor. 3:21-23.

We are held closely in Christ's hand and none can take us from Him. So the normal thing is for the Christian to be in touch with Christ every day, have His joy, His power, know His will and have our prayers answered daily.

But Christians do not always live and abide in Christ as we should. What Christ has in mind is that His mighty power of the Holy Spirit flowing from Christ through us is to win souls.

To understand this passage you must remember that the subject here is fruit bearing. Note:

"Every branch in me that beareth not fruit . . . ."—Vs. 2.

"As the branch cannot bear fruit of itself . . . ."—Vs. 4.

". . . the same bringeth forth much fruit."—Vs. 5.

"Herein is my Father glorified, that ye bear much fruit."—Vs. 8.

Do not get away from what God is talking about here and emphasizing so greatly. The Christian is to bear fruit, and not to bear fruit is a sad failure.

Do not confuse the teaching about the fruit of a Christian in this passage with the fruit of the Spirit in Galatians 5:22, 23. The "love, joy, peace, longsuffering, gentleness, goodness, faith, Meekness, temperance" mentioned there are those graces wrought by the Spirit Himself, the ornaments that He puts upon a Christian character. But the fruit of the Spirit is one thing, and the fruit of a Christian is another thing.

So here in verse 16 Jesus says, *"Ye have not chosen me, but I have chosen you, and ordained you, that ye should go and bring forth fruit, and that your fruit should remain: that whatsoever ye shall ask of the Father in my name, he may give it you."*

Proverbs 11:30 says, "The fruit of the righteous is a tree of life; and he that winneth souls is wise." The Christian is sometimes likened to a palm tree (Ps. 92:12). But here the fruit of a Christian tree is not just the coconuts on the tree. So the fruit of the coconut palm tree is not just to bear coconuts but to bear coconuts and plant them and so grow some more coconut-bearing palm trees. In other words, the work of a Christian is to get people saved and train them to win souls.

That is exactly what the Great Commission commands. The disciples were to go and win souls (as we are) or make disciples, then baptize them, get them lined up and committed, then "teaching them to observe all things whatsoever I have commanded you." Not just teaching them doctrine but teaching them to do the things that God commanded the apostles. In other words, all who got saved under these apostles were to be baptized, and then they were taught to do the same kind of work. So the fruit of a Christian is getting people saved and teaching them to win souls, too.

The fruit of a Christian? That is illustrated in Psalm 126:5,6, "They that sow in tears shall reap in joy. He that goeth forth and weepeth, bearing precious seed, shall doubtless come again with rejoicing, bringing his sheaves with him." The fruit here, of the reaper, is the sheaves he brings.

And Jesus says in John 4:35,36:

"Say not ye, There are yet four months, and then cometh harvest? behold, I say unto you, Lift up your eyes, and look on the fields; for they are white already to harvest. And he that reapeth receiveth wages, and gathereth fruit unto life eternal: that both he that soweth and he that reapeth may rejoice together."

The fruit of a Christian is to win souls.

No so-called "deeper life" can take the place of obeying Christ on this soul-winning matter.

In the parable of the sower we are told that the good seed is the Word of God and it is going with the Scriptures to win souls and so bear fruit.

Every Christian is commanded to win souls. Revelation 22:17 says, ". . . let him that heareth say, Come."

We talk a good deal about the "call to preach." Actually, in the New Testament there is very little about a preacher's being called to preach. There is a great deal about every Christian going out to preach or to witness, to win souls, in the Great Commission. Mark 16:15 says, "Go ye into all the world, and preach the gospel to every creature." Not a learned minister preaching to a congregation, but a convert going out to preach to individuals. "Every creature" is God's plan. In that sense every Christian is called to preach, called to bear fruit, called to bring in sheaves.

And there is a sadness here in verse 2, *"Every branch in me that beareth not fruit he taketh away."*

Verse 6 says, *"If a man abide not in me, he is cast forth as a branch, and is withered . . . ."* Notice that as far as a fruit-bearing branch of the vine is concerned, man may be cast out.

I knew a man who had been greatly used of God as a preacher. He is a graduate of a great university, a graduate of a great theological seminary. He was used in wonderful revivals in winning thousands. But his family was growing. His wife was from a well-to-do family and wanted better clothes. He wanted his children to have better things in life than he had had.

The West was developing rapidly and he found he could invest in wheat lands in the Panhandle of Texas, and in two or three great crop years in the midst of World War I, he could lay aside a great deal of money and thus his wife could have the fine clothes, and his boys could go to college without earning their way. And so he did it.

Oh, but sadly, he lost all touch with the churches. Now he got no calls to preach and no invitations to become pastor. He spoke to me with great burden, wanting me to recommend him. Somebody did recommend him to a church, but some way his power was gone, the church soon split and he was rejected.

I think that, although he was saved and loved the Lord still, of course, and he still had everlasting life because God had promised it and nothing can separate us from the love of Christ, he was *"cast forth as a branch"* (vs. 6).

God will not always take second place and continue to use a man. A Christian cannot be a continuous soul winner if he has no burden and if it does not have a priority in his life. So, sometimes a Christian, as far as the fruit-bearing branch is concerned, is cast aside and withered.

How worthless is such a withered vine! Let us imagine again: Here is a branch of the grapevine but some way it is so pinched and perhaps as it is tied tightly up to some support that the sap cannot flow through it and the branch withers away. It is so fruitless that those kinds of branches men prune off and cast into a fire and burn them.

The other day in Palestine I saw a woman with a great package of twigs on her head. They were the prunings from grapevines, withered and dry, and she would use them to heat the oven and bake bread.

Do not think God is here contradicting all the things He said so plainly and so often in the book of John. One who receives Christ is born of God. One who believes in Christ shall never perish. One who puts his trust in Christ "hath everlasting life, and shall not come into condemnation; but is passed from death unto life" (5:24). Christ's sheep hear His voice and follow Him and He gives "unto them eternal life; and they shall never perish . . . ." So, God is not here contradicting what He said elsewhere. The subject here is fruit-bearing. The sad fact is that many a Christian withers away and becomes powerless and fruitless and thus a failure in his Christian life.

This is illustrated in the parable of the sower. Some seed fell among the thorns and sprang up, Jesus said. But it was choked and did not bring any fruit to perfection. And Jesus explained that "the care of this world, and the deceitfulness of riches, [and other things] choke the word, and he becometh unfruitful" (Matt. 13:22).

But here is a wonderful truth in verse 2, *"Every branch that beareth fruit he purgeth it, that it may bring forth more fruit."* Someone may think we should give great attention first to getting young converts taught in the Word and to living a separated, godly life. No; get them to winning souls first and then you will have no trouble getting a man to quit his cigarettes or to quit the dirty moving picture shows, or getting him to turn away from covetousness and malice and anger. God purgeth every branch that bears fruit so it can bear more fruit.

It is a wonderful thing to get all Christians to winning souls so they will not let anything come between them and this power to win souls. God purges those who bear fruit. The best way to get Christians to live a godly life is to get them doing what God said to do, so He can help purge them and cleanse them for soul winning.

Notice that there is no way for the branch to bear fruit *"except it abide in the vine"* (vs. 4). This soul-winning business is not primarily a matter of skill, not a matter of talent, not a matter of personality; it is being in touch with Christ in the sense that the Holy Spirit flows abundantly through us and the fountain flows all the time. We should sow the precious seed, and we should sow in tears (Ps. 126:5,6), but we must sow in the power of the Holy Spirit if we are to bear fruit.

It is rather suggestive and sweet that here the power of the

Holy Spirit is pictured by the sap flowing through the vine, so Christ and the Holy Spirit are not separated; the fullness of the Spirit means having Christ's power, too, for the Holy Spirit is "the Spirit of Christ" (Rom. 8:9).

So, people may not know all about the doctrine of Holy Spirit power, but if one is really abundantly absorbed in Jesus and with all the concern Jesus has for sinners, and all the power Jesus has is given to us, that is just another way of saying Holy Spirit power.

Yes, and we must remember that the one big thing that glorifies the Father is bearing fruit. That is the way to be a disciple.

Remember that in the parable in Luke 14 the man who made a great supper and bade many, "sent his servant" out to get the crowd to the supper. The only servant in that parable is the man knocking on doors and inviting people to the Heavenly Banquet.

So it is in Matthew 22 when the king made a marriage for his son; he sent his servants out to invite people. If you are not inviting people to Heaven you are not a servant of Christ. If you do not win souls you are not bearing fruit in the sense of this Scripture and the thing so dear to God.

The power of the Holy Spirit is pictured by one's connection with Christ so that the very life of God flows through Christ to us.

In Luke 24:46-49, the disciples have this command, then the promise:

"And said unto them, Thus it is written, and thus it behoved Christ to suffer, and to rise from the dead the third day: And that repentance and remission of sins should be preached in his name among all nations, beginning at Jerusalem. And ye are witnesses of these things. And, behold, I send the promise of my Father upon you: but tarry ye in the city of Jerusalem, until ye be endued with power from on high."

The Lord said the same thing in Acts 1:8. "But ye shall receive power, after that the Holy Ghost is come upon you: and ye shall be witnesses unto me both in Jerusalem, and in all Judaea, and in Samaria, and unto the uttermost part of the earth."

It is clear from all these Scriptures that a Christian must have
the power of the Spirit of God upon him to make him the soul
winner he should be.

A Marvelous Prayer Promise

Verse 7 is so remarkable, I beg you to memorize it and analyze
it and set out to live by it: *"If ye abide in me, and my words
abide in you, ye shall ask what ye will, and it shall be done unto
you."* Several things that verse says: First, you are to ask
anything you wish. That is also what Psalm 37:4 says: "Delight
thyself also in the Lord; and he shall give thee the desires of thine
heart." That is also what Mark 11:24 says: "Therefore I say unto
you, What things soever ye desire, when ye pray, believe that ye
receive them, and ye shall have them."

Evidently God wants us to ask whatever we desire. Some people have foolishly said that we are to pray only for what we need
and not what we want. But the Lord loves us as a father loves his
children and He wants us to have not merely the bare sustenance
of life, but the joys and blessings besides that love can give.

But the conditions are very simple and all-important: First, we
are to abide in Jesus (vs. 7). We are to be wrapped up in Jesus;
we are to be living in Jesus, and that is in the sense of one who
has the power of Christ flowing through him—that is, the sap
flows through the vine and to all the branches if you are living in
the fellowship and in the power and in the joy of Christ and, so,
wholly given over to pleasing Him.

The other condition is if *"my words abide in you"* (vs. 7). You
may love Christ ever so much, but if you are not concerned about
the Bible, you will not know what will please Christ. There is no
way to have the faith we ought to expect as we constantly are
open to the truth of the Bible. Romans 10:17 says, "So then faith
cometh by hearing, and hearing by the word of God." Oh, but if I
am so wrapped up in Christ and so absorbed and delighted in the
Bible, I will want what Jesus wants. And since I am to know the
Scripture so well and delight in the Scriptures, then I will know
what Jesus wants. That means I may have whatever I want.

And, of course, this means also that when I come to pray, if I am really wrapped up in Christ and in the Word of God, I will come with this understanding: If "for what I will" to ask is not the will of God, I will find it and I will change my prayer and make it acceptable because I will want what God wants as soon as I know it.

That is the way it was with Paul and his pleading with God (three separate times of impassioned prayer) that his thorn in the flesh might be removed. But he learned it is far better to have a weak Paul and a great God, and so he changed his prayer. And when God promised, "My grace is sufficient for thee: for my strength is made perfect in weakness," then he could say, "Therefore will I rather glory in my infirmities, that the power of Christ may rest upon me. Therefore I take pleasure in infirmities, in reproaches, in necessities, in persecutions, in distresses for Christ's sake: for when I am weak, then am I strong" (II Cor. 12:9,10).

I think we should note also that God has different conditions of prayer. That does not mean we must set out to meet every condition at one time. No. Any one promise of God can stand alone. I can take God's promise and cash in on it if I simply meet the requirements there mentioned.

There are at least five approaches that a Christian might choose in prayer.

1. If one does the will of God and keeps His commandments, then he may pray, knowing he will have whatsoever he asks (I John 3:22). It is only fair to say that we do not always meet that requirement. But wait, there are other ways.

2. We can ask when two are agreed perfectly as to what they ask (Matt. 18:19). That means that if two Christians have the same burden, not simply agree with each other that they will pray but have a heart agreement about the matter, that agreement is evidently wrought by the Spirit of God and two can have what they ask. And these can have what they ask. But sometimes one does not have that perfect agreement of heart burden with someone else and needs to pray alone.

3. Then one may ask in Jesus' name, as John 14:13,14 and John 16:24 tell us. But that would mean that I have a clear under-

standing that I am asking what Jesus wants and I feel certain definite authority from Christ to ask in His stead. And always, if one is truly asking in Jesus' name, he will get the answer. So do not trifle and do not deceive yourself on this matter.

When we were invited to ask for daily bread, that prayer was not supposed to close, "In Jesus' name." It is not Jesus who eats the daily bread we ask for.

4. And if we can ask in faith, what wonderful, wonderful things are available!

"All things, whatsoever ye shall ask in prayer, believing, ye shall receive."—Matt. 21:22.

"If thou canst believe, all things are possible to him that believeth."—Mark 9:23.

"Therefore I say unto you, What things soever ye desire, when ye pray, believe that ye receive them, and ye shall have them."—Mark 11:24.

God gives the faith, He will certainly give the answer. And in praying for the sick, "the prayer of faith will save the sick." It is not always God's will to heal. One cannot arbitrarily swing faith around to demand of God what He does not give the faith for.

But faith is a wonderful condition of prayer. In matters where God's Word has clearly stated what He wants, it would be a sin not to believe Him. A sinner would be very guilty not to trust Christ for salvation and not to have faith for that, since the promise is so clear that an honest heart would rely upon it. But in other things, God must give the faith if he claimed this promise.

Remember in Acts, chapter 12, the people prayed and prayed and Peter was delivered out of jail and they did not believe it when he came knocking at the door. God answered their prayer, not because of great faith but because He loved them and they prayed.

5. Another great condition of prayer is better than all these others. That is persistence in prayer. In the parable of the unjust judge in Luke 18, the widow got what she asked for, as that unjust judge said, "lest by her continual coming she weary me," or, as the American Standard Version has it, "lest she wear me out

by her continual coming." Persistence in prayer worked with that wicked old judge; how much more will it work with our beloved Father in Heaven!

In Ephesians 6:18 we are encouraged: "Praying always with all prayer and supplication in the Spirit, and watching thereunto with all perseverance and supplication for all saints." Again in Luke 11:8 the man begged bread for a hungry visitor. Jesus said, "Though he will not rise and give him, because he is his friend, yet because of his importunity he will rise and give him as many as he needeth." It is clear that importunity gets results when all the other qualities of pleasing God are not successful.

Isaiah 40:29-31 says:

"He giveth power to the faint; and to them that have no might he increaseth strength. Even the youths shall faint and be weary, and the young men shall utterly fall: But they that wait upon the Lord shall renew their strength; they shall mount up with wings as eagles; they shall run, and not be weary; and they shall walk, and not faint."

Wait upon the Lord.

Second Chronicles 7:14 says, "If my people, which are called by my name, shall . . . seek my face . . . ." Here are great words: Wait upon the Lord, seek God's face, importunity, supplication! Persistent prayer is the way to get things from God. Matthew 7:8 says, "For every one that asketh receiveth . . . ." But the word "asketh" there is the translation of a Greek word which really means in the present tense, "continued asking." So the honest way to take that verse is that everyone who persistently asks and asks and asks receives.

It is good to be familiar with the promises of God. If one does not find one door open he may go to another. If you cannot meet one condition, then meet another. If you feel you cannot meet any of these other conditions, at least you can persistently wait on God, and that is the best way of all to get your prayers answered.

VERSES 9-16:

9 As the Father hath loved me, so have I loved you: continue ye in my love.

10 If ye keep my commandments, ye shall abide in my love; even as I have kept my Father's commandments, and abide in his love.

11 These things have I spoken unto you, that my joy might remain in you, and *that* your joy might be full.

12 This is my commandment, That ye love one another, as I have loved you.

13 Greater love hath no man than this, that a man lay down his life for his friends.

14 Ye are my friends, if ye do whatsoever I command you.

15 Henceforth I call you not servants; for the servant knoweth not what his lord doeth: but I have called you friends; for all things that I have heard of my Father I have made known unto you.

16 Ye have not chosen me, but I have chosen you, and ordained you, that ye should go and bring forth fruit, and *that* your fruit should remain: that whatsoever ye shall ask of the Father in my name, he may give it you.

Friends of Jesus Should Show Their Love

A Christian is to continue in the love of Christ, that is, one must consciously fan the fires of love for Christ in his own heart and thus he will come more and more to abide in Christ and want what Christ wants and be able to get whatever he asks because he is asking what God wants to give. We are to love Christ and we are to abide in His love.

Oh, how wonderful it is that Christ loves us all, that He takes delight in us, and wants to make us happy, and wants to care for our needs! The very hairs of our head are numbered, and so we should abide in His love and fan our own love for Him.

That is the way to have joy, verse 11 says. That will mean joy for Christ and joy for us.

We remember that when the shepherd found the lost sheep, "he layeth it on his shoulders, rejoicing." The Lord rejoices when a sinner is saved. He has joy also in the Christian who continually tries to please Him. So while we make Jesus happy, we can be happy ourselves. The way of joy is to love Jesus Christ and be wrapped up in Him and in His work.

And Christ reminds us that His love is the greatest of all, for He lays down His life for us and calls us His friends! We are not strangers. We are friends.

It is remarkable how many pictures the Bible gives us of our relationship to Christ. We are children of God, born of God (1:11-13). We are brethren of Christ, for "he is not ashamed to call them brethren" (Heb. 2:11). We are the branches of the vine abiding in Christ, says this chapter.

In one parable we are pictured as the bride; in another we are pictured as the bridesmaids. Oh, you see, all these pictures are not enough really, to say how wonderfully we are a part with Christ and all of our future destiny and happiness and usefulness is bound up in Him. So we should abide in Him. Christ is not only our Master, our Teacher, our Saviour, our King, our Elder Brother, He is our Friend.

The intimate relationship of Jesus with us who are saved is a never-ceasing marvel of sweetness! He reveals to us His whole heart! We have recorded His prayer, His tears, His prophecies so clearly and so much in detail that every one of us can know the very heart of Jesus.

In John 20:21 we are told that He sends us exactly like the Father sent Him. He said in John 14 that we should do the very works that He did. The relationship is so intimate that we are given such authority (vs. 16) that we may pray and ask for things in the name of Jesus! His Word is so clear, and His Holy Spirit reveals His mind to us so clearly, if we ask it, that we may come to the Father and say, "Father, this is what Jesus wants. He has revealed it all to me, and I want You to do this because it will please the Lord Jesus, Your Son and my beloved Saviour"!

We pretend to ask in Jesus' name many times when we are asking for our own selfish things; but Christians have a right to find the mind of Christ when we pray and ask for those things which are pleasing in His sight.

This is the lost secret in most of our praying. That is one reason we have no more faith, no more certainty of answer to our prayers. First John 5:14,15 tells us that "this is the confidence" that a Christian may have—the certainty of answered prayer when we ask according to His will.

Servants? It would be a joy to be a servant for Christ! And it is true that we are servants if we do well what He commands us. Ah, but a servant taken into the family, a servant who becomes a son, a servant who becomes a dearest friend, is the way the relationship with Christ grows.

You see, He has chosen us, He has ordained us and He did it that we should go and bring forth fruit. So He wants us to abide in His love and never be out of touch with the Vine, nor ever be without the power of the Holy Spirit flowing through us and so bringing forth fruit. That makes Him happy, always.

"Ye have not chosen me, but I have chosen you."—Vs. 16.

Dr. H. A. Ironside comments on this passage as follows:

Did not they choose Him? Did not you choose Christ? Yes, but not before He chose you.

> 'Tis not that I did choose Thee,
> For, Lord, that could not be;
> This heart would still refuse Thee,
> But Thou hast chosen me.

> 'Twas the same love that spread the feast,
> That gently forced me in,
> Else I had still refused to come,
> And perished in my sin.

". . . and ordained you" (vs. 16).

And then when it is a question of service, it is He who chooses for this or that special work . . . .

Many people are troubled about ordination. Folks ask, "Has any one a right to preach who has not been ordained?" In the Bible you do not read of people being ordained to preach the Gospel. You never get the world "ordination" connected with the actual setting apart of a man to preach the Gospel. What about Timothy? The word "ordained" was not used in Timothy's case. "Well," you say, "did you forget about Paul and Barnabas?" No, but they had been preaching a long time in Antioch before the elders laid their hands on them . . . . He said, "I have chosen you, and ordained you, that ye should go and bring forth fruit." The word "ordained" means "set apart." . . . All the elders or others can do is to recognize what God has done already . . . .

The last part of verse 16 is like John 14:13 and 14. Underline *"whatsoever"* in these verses, then since the Saviour repeats it for emphasis in John 14:14, underline *"any thing."*

VERSES 17-27:

17 These things I command you, that ye love one another.

18 If the world hate you, ye know that it hated me before *it hated* you.

19 If ye were of the world, the world would love his own: but because ye are not of the world, but I have chosen you out of the world, therefore the world hateth you.

20 Remember the word that I said unto you, The servant is not greater than his lord. If they have persecuted me, they will also persecute you; if they have kept my saying, they will keep your's also.

21 But all these things will they do unto you for my name's sake, because they know not him that sent me.

22 If I had not come and spoken unto them, they had not had sin: but now they have no cloke for their sin.

23 He that hateth me hateth my Father also.

24 If I had not done among them the works which none other man did, they had not had sin: but now have they both seen and hated both me and my Father.

25 But *this cometh to pass*, that the word might be fulfilled that is written in their law, They hated me without a cause.

26 But when the Comforter is come, whom I will send unto you from the Father, *even* the Spirit of truth, which proceedeth from the Father, he shall testify of me:

27 And ye also shall bear witness, because ye have been with me from the beginning.

A Good Christian Must Be Willing to Suffer Persecution

The Lord Jesus had been talking about how He loves us and we should love Him. Now He said we must love one another, too (vs. 17). And that is the great sign that we are Christians, Jesus said in John 13:35: "By this shall all men know that ye are my disciples, if ye have love one to another." How can you love God and not love those dear to His heart?

That is one reason we must pay special attention in our hearts to "Christ's other sheep," for He says, "Other sheep I have, which are not of this fold" (John 10:16). And if they love Christ and He loves them, we must love them, too. That means born-again Christians who believe the Bible and love Christ but who differ with us on minor matters, or who are separated by miles, or in different organizational connections—we must love the people Christ loves and have part with Him. And then, what a happy, glad time when we all gather in Heaven around the Saviour! We are to love one another.

And if the world hate us, we need not be surprised. The world

hated Jesus and if we pleased the world, the world would love its
own.

But if we are like Christ and are chosen "out of the world" (vs.
19), then the world will not like us. This world that crucified
Jesus Christ will not take too kindly to Christians if we are
enough like Christ. If we are red-hot in rebuke of sin, earnest,
tearful and pleading with sinners; if we are "other worldly-
minded" and not too much absorbed in the teachings, convictions, amusements and unbeliefs of this world, then the world
will hate us.

We are in good company in enduring the world's hatred. Our
Lord says, *"If the world hate you, ye know that it hated me
before it hated you"* (vs. 18).

J. C. Macaulay says:

> If the world had nothing better than a cross for Jesus, it will
> not have a royal carriage for His followers: if only thorns for
> Him, there will not be garlands for us.
>
> Four centuries before Christ, the great philosopher Plato ex-
> pressed a belief which proved to be prophetic: "I am of opinion
> that the truly righteous man, if he were to appear in the world,
> would be scourged, would be thrown into fetters, would be
> hanged." He came, and it so happened to Him.
>
> But, someone says, the attitude of the world is very different
> from what it was when Jesus was here on earth. The world has
> learned His worth; and if He were to come back now, He would
> be received with mighty ovations, and heralded as the world's
> Saviour and Sovereign!
>
> But would He? Thomas Carlyle said, "If Christ came to
> London today, they would take Him to Newgate and hang
> Him."
>
> Jesus Christ would make such an exposure of the sin which
> goes unchecked all around us, even as He tore the mask off the
> Pharisees of that other day, that He would not long be endured.
> We are in enemy territory: let us not expect the treatment of
> friends.

But *"the servant is not greater than his lord"* (vs. 20). If they
persecuted Jesus, they should persecute us, when we are enough
like Jesus. If they kept Jesus' way, they would keep our way. Ah,
but the world is against Christ and against His born-again, fervent, Spirit-filled people because it does not know God and it

does not feel at home with Christians.

A Christian be persecuted? Yes. Check again those sweet beatitudes in Matthew 5:1-12. You will notice that the other beatitudes take from nine to fifteen words, but the last and the climax is the one on persecution. In verses 10 to 12 there are sixty-three words, "Blessed are they which are persecuted for righteousness' sake: for their's is the kingdom of heaven. Blessed are ye, when men shall revile you, and persecute you, and shall say all manner of evil against you falsely, for my sake. Rejoice, and be exceeding glad: for great is your reward in heaven: for so persecuted they the prophets which were before you." Ah, Christians ought to be good enough to be persecuted.

Someone has said, "If there came a great time of persecution, and they were putting to death everybody who was a good Christian, would you qualify?"

Those who hate Christ, hate God the Father also.

Now all those who rejected Him were guilty of wicked sin, because they had evidence beyond any dispute of His deity. They saw His miracles, they heard His teaching, they still hated Him, and that was deliberate sin. But it is true of them, as Psalm 38:19 and Psalm 69:4 say, "They hated me without a cause."

Christian, do not be discouraged. The Comforter will be yours. Oh, there is never so dark a night but that He is there, never so great a need but that He is guiding and can provide it. The Spirit of truth will be with us and Christians will have a witness, and these particular twelve apostles will have a special witness because they have been with Him from the beginning of His ministry (vs. 27). So in Acts, chapter 1, they must elect another man who had been with them from the baptism by John to the resurrection of Jesus, a twelfth man to bear witness to Christ (Acts 1:21-26).

Oh, sweet Spirit! Oh, sweet Comforter! Sweet Spirit of Truth! Sweet Guide in the dark night! Sweet Witness within us who helps us to witness!

John 16

THESE things have I spoken unto you, that ye should not be offended.

2 They shall put you out of the synagogues: yea, the time cometh, that whosoever killeth you will think that he doeth God service.

3 And these things will they do unto you, because they have not known the Father, nor me.

4 But these things have I told you, that when the time shall come, ye may remember that I told you of them. And these things I said not unto you at the beginning, because I was with you.

Jesus Warns of Persecution

Bear in mind that this is a part of the same discussion which began at the last supper of Jesus with His disciples in the Upper Room. John 14:31 shows that at the close of the 14th chapter they arose and left the Upper Room. Remember from Mark 14:28 that after a hymn, they departed toward the Mount of Olives. The Garden of Gethsemane was in the Mount of Olives, and John 18:1 tells that following the 17th chapter, they arrived in this garden.

It is important to notice the purpose of Jesus in these last words of counsel and teaching before His crucifixion. He gives His reason for the discussion several times. For instance, John 14:29; 15:11; 16:1, 4 and 33. The purpose: that the disciples "might believe"; that their "joy might be full"; that they "should not be offended" (or stumble); that they might "remember that I told you of them"; and that in Him they "might have peace."

So why the warning? Lest they should be offended, or discouraged, and disheartened by the certain persecutions that will follow good Christians! It seems incredible, to a young convert perhaps, that just because one loves the Lord and is true to Him, others should hate Him. Yes, the religious people would put them out of the synagogue. Yes, and the time comes again and again when *"whosoever killeth you will think that he doeth God service"* (vs. 2). The most awful persecution in this world is religious persecution.

We remind you that Jesus was killed, not by drunkards, not by sex perverts and lawless criminals, but by religious people who had very strict standards of doing right. They were Pharisees, and their religion was superficial but their persecution was religious persecution because Christ claimed to be the Son of God, and insisted on breaking down their traditions. So John 5:16 says, "And therefore did the Jews persecute Jesus, and sought to slay him, because he had done these things on the sabbath day." Jesus was convicted on the basis that He was blaspheming and claimed to be the Son of God (Matt. 26:65). Pilate himself saw that that claim did not justify Christ's crucifixion, but "the Jews answered him, We have a law, and by our law he ought to die, because he made himself the Son of God" (19:7).

Jesus had warned the disciples, "All ye shall be offended because of me this night: for it is written, I will smite the shepherd, and the sheep of the flock shall be scattered abroad" (Matt 26:31). In the Garden of Gethsemane He knows what will be true—that "all the disciples forsook him, and fled" (Matt. 26:56).

Oh, there is great danger that in the time of persecution Christians will be so discouraged they will fall away from active discipleship and following Jesus! So Paul wrote from jail to Timothy, "Be not thou therefore ashamed of the testimony of our Lord, nor of me his prisoner: but be thou partaker of the afflictions of the gospel according to the power of God" (II Tim. 1:8). Paul said that some had made shipwreck of the faith, because they had not held on to a good conscience: "Of whom is Hymenaeus and Alexander" (I Tim. 1:19,20). And Paul reminded Timothy, "This thou knowest, that all they which are in Asia be turned away from me; of whom are Phygellus and Hermogenes" (II Tim. 1:15). And sadly from his dungeon in Rome, Paul writes, "Do thy diligence to come shortly unto me: For Demas hath forsaken me, having loved this present world . . ." (II Tim. 4:9,10).

So if Paul's friends forsook him, and the disciples of Jesus failed Him in the crisis of Gethsemane and Calvary, we may know that persecution dismays and offends young Christians who are not well grounded in the faith, and though they are God's children, they do not stand true as they should.

The most awful persecution is religious persecution. Remember the Spanish Inquisition that murdered millions of people under the command of the papacy and Rome.

Even communist persecution, the most immoral and godless perhaps, is a kind of a religious persecution because communism is the religion of atheism and humanism.

So Jesus warns the disciples of persecution to come.

Oh, Christians should be willing to rejoice in persecution if they suffer wrongfully. So we should boldly follow in the steps and example of Jesus because He suffered for us: "Christ also suffered for us, leaving us an example, that ye should follow his steps" (I Pet. 2:21).

In Hebrews 11, saints of God of the past are held up as faithful, joyful witnesses. They were willing to suffer for God and righteousness. We are told of those who,

"Quenched the violence of fire, escaped the edge of the sword, out of weakness were made strong, waxed valiant in fight, turned to flight the armies of the aliens. Women received their dead raised to life again: and others were tortured, not accepting deliverance; that they might obtain a better resurrection: And others had trial of cruel mockings and scourgings, yea, moreover of bonds and imprisonment: They were stoned, they were sawn asunder, were tempted, were slain with the sword: they wandered about in sheepskins and goatskins; being destitute, afflicted, tormented; (Of whom the world was not worthy:) they wandered in deserts, and in mountains, and in dens and caves of the earth."—Heb. 11:34-38.

All this was "that they might obtain a better resurrection." Those who suffer for Jesus will reign with Him later. Paul says, "If we suffer, we shall also reign with him" (II Tim. 2:12).

VERSES 5-11:

5 But now I go my way to him that sent me; and none of you asketh me, Whither goest thou?

6 But because I have said these things unto you, sorrow hath filled your heart.

7 Nevertheless I tell you the truth; It is expedient for you that I go away: for if I go not away, the Comforter will not come unto you; but if I depart, I will send him unto you.

8 And when he is come, he will reprove the world of sin, and of righteousness, and of judgment:

9 Of sin, because they believe not on me;

10 Of righteousness, because I go to my Father, and ye see me no more;

11 Of judgment, because the prince of this world is judged.

We Are Comforted by the Blessed Holy Spirit's Presence

The disciples' hearts were filled with sorrow. We cannot blame them. Although they could not immediately see it, it was expedient that Christ should go away. Oh, the plan must be fulfilled and the blessed Holy Spirit must come, abiding in us and enduing us with power, being our Comfort, our Guide, our Teacher, our Prayer Helper. And so it is better that we will have Christ represented by the Holy Spirit literally living within us, than to have a physical Christ on earth whom we can only see occasionally.

The disciples were sad that Jesus was going away, but they ought to have been glad. He says, *"It is expedient for you that I go away"* (vs. 7). That really means that, "You would be better off with Me gone than if I were here." Hard to understand, and hard to believe, but true.

The disciples were happier at Pentecost and after Pentecost than they had ever been in the presence of Jesus in the flesh. Certainly they won more souls, had more power, better understood the Scriptures, were not as selfish, had more Christian graces, after Jesus went away than they had while He was here in the flesh.

Christians sometimes wish they could have seen Jesus, could have been with Him here as He healed the sick, as He preached, as He taught. But we are far better off as it is, for now every one of us has the Holy Spirit abiding in our bodies and we can have more power, more joy, more Christian fruit than we could have if Jesus lived in the flesh here in our own homes.

Now He literally lives IN our bodies, and we can call upon Him for power and comfort. When He was here in the flesh, He could speak to only a few at a time; and if He was in one home, He could not be in other homes. Many times the ears of people heard Him but their hearts did not hear nor understand what He said. On the contrary now: now He speaks to the heart, not the ears; now He can be in every home—or, better still, live in every heart and body. Check up carefully here I Corinthians 3:16, 17; 6:19,20; II Corinthians 6:16; Romans 8:9; I John 2:27.

Christ does live in the body of every Christian and has since Christ's resurrection. This Comforter who came in John 20:19-22, according to promise, began a new era of power and joy for Christians. And Pentecost could not have come until after Jesus was crucified and ascended (7:37-39).

And since we are warned of persecution, then we are glad to know that the Holy Spirit *"will reprove the world of sin, and of righteousness, and of judgment"* (vs. 8).

Compare verses 7 and 8. To the Christian, the Holy Spirit is a Comforter; to the world, He is a reprover! Many times preachers have stressed the work of the Holy Spirit in reproving the world, but have not stressed His work in comforting Christians. Far more is said in the Bible about the work of the Holy Spirit in a Christian than about His work in convincing and reproving lost people.

The word "of" in verses 8 to 11 might be translated "concerning." The Holy Spirit convicts the world *concerning sin* because people do not believe in Christ. That is the greatest sin, and the heart of all sin, and back of all sin (vs. 9). The Holy Spirit reproves the world *concerning righteousness,* because Jesus will be gone, and His righteous example and teaching before the world will be taken away—so the Holy Spirit must take His place in this respect. *Concerning judgment,* since that wicked generation had judged and crucified Jesus, Jesus promises that even the Devil himself will be brought to judgment. How little hope any lost man has to escape it!

"Of sin, because they believe not on me," Jesus said (vs. 9). The Holy Spirit takes the place of Jesus as Comforter and

Teacher and Guide, and so He takes the part of Jesus against this wicked world which rejected Him and crucified Him. He will reprove the world *"of sin, because they believe not on me."* All sin—but particularly deliberate sin—because they believe not on Jesus. The Jews and all of mankind have sin coming from our fallen, deceitful hearts. That may be the secret sin referred to in Psalm 19:12, the sins that people did not intend and perhaps are not even conscious of. But rejection of Christ is "presumptuous sin" as that Psalm puts it, a certain willful sin.

And the sin against Christ is the greatest of all sins because it is against God most manifest, that is, in Jesus Christ. It is a sin against such mercy, such compassion, such righteousness. To reject Christ and refuse to trust in Him is the summing up of all sin.

The Jews who rejected Christ sinned so greatly "that the blood of all the prophets, which was shed from the foundation of the world, may be required of this generation; From the blood of Abel unto the blood of Zacharias, which perished between the altar and the temple: verily I say unto you, It shall be required of this generation" (Luke 11:50,51).

That rejection of Christ by the people of Chorazin and Capernaum was worse than the sin of Tyre and Sidon and Sodom, Jesus said. And after being exalted by seeing the mighty works of Jesus, they would be cast down to Hell. And where the disciples went and preached Christ, if people would not hear, the disciples were to shake the dust off their feet as they departed, and God would hold the city accountable at the judgment.

In 1936 I went to Binghamton, New York, for a revival which, after a week, at the entreaty of a group of pastors, was moved to the Binghamton theater seating seventeen hundred. Hundreds were saved, but among modernistic pastors there was a furious response to my preaching against sin.

I preached on "Sodom, Gomorrah and Binghamton," and told of wickedness there. A newspaper reporter brought me news of a giant sex orgy that took place in the city with one hundred prostitutes brought in from New York City, and with drunkenness and fights and breaking up the furniture, and that surely was like Sodom and Gomorrah. I preached about the unbelief of modernists, and preached on the wickedness in rejecting Christ. The pastors of modern churches responded in the newspapers indignantly. "Why, Binghamton was the city of churches and colleges! It was the Athens of the State of New York! How could any sensational preacher liken a beautiful and scholarly and religious Binghamton to Sodom and Gomorrah!"

But the crowds kept coming and many, many were saved in a marvelous revival. When the revival closed after five weeks, and I took my family in the car to leave the city, I stepped out on the packed snow, shook the "dust" off my feet and asked God to hold the city accountable for the preaching they had heard and the marvelous conversions they had seen.

We drove toward New York City. The sun came out hot and snow began to melt. At Binghamton the snow had piled up to nineteen inches, and in one day in that valley the snow melted and came down the river in a flood that flooded all the area. Millions of dollars of damage was done, and some people died. I feel God was carrying out His plain promise to the disciples. Oh, it is a terrible sin to reject Christ! It brings judgment.

The Holy Spirit will come to judge *"of righteousness"* (vs. 10). That is, Christ had been so plain in His preaching about righteousness; now the sweet Holy Spirit comes to rebuke sin and reprove it. He comes to reprove all the self-righteousness, all the Pharisaical righteousness, all the ceremonial righteousness, all the religion without Christ. For we remember that the Jews to whom Jesus talked did as they did with Paul: "For they being ignorant of God's righteousness, and going about to establish their own righteousness, have not submitted themselves unto the righteousness of God" (Rom. 10:3). And we remember how Jesus, when He was here, cried out, "Woe unto you, scribes and Pharisees, hypocrites . . . ."

That kind of human righteousness is an abomination. Any so-called righteousness that leaves out Christ and the blood is a human, manufactured righteousness that will not stand up before the all-seeing eye of a holy God.

And so the Holy Spirit is to carry on in His condemnation of any righteousness without God, any morality without the fundamentals of the Faith and trusting Christ as God's atoning Saviour.

And the Holy Spirit is to convict the world *"of judgment."* Why? *". . . because the prince of this world is judged"* (vs. 11). The world that crucified Jesus has to come to judgment. The world that made that pure and Holy One like a criminal must come to the bar of judgment and its wickedness must be revealed. All who take sides against Christ, all who helped in His shame and trouble, have a sad and terrible judgment coming. To take sides against Christ means that this Holy Spirit of God takes sides against you and passes judgment on wicked men who turn down Christ.

VERSES 12-15:

12 I have yet many things to say unto you, but ye cannot bear them now.
13 Howbeit when he, the Spirit of truth, is come, he will guide you into all truth: for he shall not speak of himself; but whatsoever he shall hear, *that* shall he speak: and he will shew you things to come.

14 He shall glorify me: for he shall receive of mine, and shall shew *it* unto you.
15 All things that the Father hath are mine: therefore said I, that he shall take of mine, and shall shew *it* unto you.

More Truth to Be Revealed by the Holy Spirit

The Old Testament is the Word of God. But God is not done with the revealing truth. And so while there were many sweet and wonderful truths the Lord would have the disciples know, they were not ready for them yet (vs. 12). People need the Old Testament as they approach the New Testament. And the New Testament will be written book by book—some of it by those in this little band, Matthew and John, and a little later by others who will be inspired by the Spirit to write the New Testament.

Is verse 13 a prophecy that other books of the New Testament would be written? *"Howbeit when he, the Spirit of truth, is come, he will guide you into all truth: for he shall not speak of*

*himself; but whatsoever he shall hear, that shall he speak: and
he will shew you things to come."* Evidently it is; but much more
than that. Remember that some books of the New Testament
were written by others who were not with the disciples that
night. Remember Paul, Luke, John Mark, Jude. The promise
certainly was to others besides those present that night.

Certainly it was for us also. Not that any of us can add to the
Word of God—all of that has been given that will ever be given
(Rev. 22:18,19). As the Holy Spirit gave the Bible to writers back
yonder, so He will help us to understand the Bible. Verse 13
specifically promised that He will help us to understand
prophecy about the future. The Holy Spirit will bring to memory
the words of Jesus (14:26; 16:4).

The most important element in memorizing the Bible is
dependence on the Holy Spirit. Notice carefully verses 14 and 15,
and depend upon the Holy Spirit to show you the things of
Christ.

And verse 13 is a statement of that clear Bible doctrine of the
verbal, word-for-word inspiration of the Scriptures. The Holy
Spirit in this matter will not simply be the spirit of man but the
Spirit of God and will be speaking for Christ and for God the
Father.

We know that revelation of the Scriptures is finished now. It
was finished with John when he wrote in Revelation 22:18, "For I
testify unto every man that heareth the words of the prophecy of
this book, If any man shall add unto these things, God shall add
unto him the plagues that are written in this book."

But more than that, God has much to reveal to His people in
the Word already written. Oh, the riches that are in the Word of
God! Some of them obvious riches and seen on the surface;
others are found by the earnest heart who waits on God, delights
in the Word and meditates in it. Oh, but as the years go by, I go
back to this Mine of Truth and find marvels and riches and sweet
powerful truths that I never saw before. Yes, the Holy Spirit
reveals more truth than we knew to one who loves the Bible.

It is a marvel how, if one is wholly committed to the Bible and
does not bring to it preconceived opinions and bias—a marvel

how much God shows, even to the humblest child of God. How often I have read in the English Bible a Scripture and I felt that the wording was not the best translation, at least, after the language of the Scriptures has grown and the words have come to have slightly different meaning!

I read Revelation 22:14 in the King James Scripture which said, "Blessed are they that do his commandments, that they may have right to the tree of life, and may enter in through the gates into the city." I studied it. It could not surely mean that people earned their way to Heaven. I felt there was some mistake in copying or in translation. How easily I found that this verse in the American Standard Version corrected the translation: "Blessed are they that wash their robes, that they may have the right to come to the tree of life, and may enter in by the gates into the city."

I am saying that the sweet Spirit of God works with the Scriptures and reveals the Scriptures to the humble, contrite mind who comes lovingly and willing to take anything God says.

I read Hebrews 4:11, "Let us labour therefore to enter into that rest, lest any man fall after the same example of unbelief." We are to "labour" to enter the heavenly rest? In my own heart the Spirit of God said it meant something else—to give attention or give diligence. And when I went into the Greek form I found that is exactly what it really is saying: Let us "take heed," or "give diligence" to enter into the heavenly rest. You do not labor to get to Heaven. You give earnest attention and pay earnest heed to "make your calling and election sure."

I am saying, the Holy Spirit will help the Christian who has a humble, contrite heart and earnestly loves and meditates on the Scripture. He is a Teacher. Oh, better than any teacher in seminary or college is the sweet Holy Spirit!

I think it is well for people to get all the help they can from godly men, but always with the reservation that the Bible itself is the authority and the Holy Spirit Himself is the principal Teacher above all teachers. So the Holy Spirit will *"guide you into all truth,"* Jesus said in verse 13.

The clause in verse 13 has been misinterpreted, *"For he shall not speak of himself . . . ."* Some have said this means we should not be studying what the Bible teaches about the Holy Spirit but only about Jesus, and that it is wrong to give attention to the matter of the fullness of the Spirit. Not so. In the first place, that is not what the Scripture here says. In the second place, it would be folly for anybody to take the attitude that what the Scripture says does not mean what it says and you should not pay attention to any subject the Scripture discusses. What it says here is that the blessed Holy Spirit within us comes to talk about Jesus and comes to reveal the Lord Jesus and what He as our sweet Comforter would do if He were here.

And so the Holy Spirit glorifies Christ (vs. 14). His will is Christ's will, His message Christ's message. You cannot separate the blessing of the Holy Spirit from the presence and truth of Christ.

I have read where some modernists, liberals in the National and the World Council of Churches speak of "the Holy Spirit leading" in making their organizations ecumenical, etc., taking in saved and lost, believers and unbelievers, Christians and infidels. No! The Holy Spirit does not lead in that. It is the spirit of men, not the Spirit of God. And that zeal they have, when it would lead to sin and wrong, is not from God but Satan.

The Lord insists He has an identity with the Spirit and with the Father and you cannot know one without knowing the other.

VERSES 16-22:

16 A little while, and ye shall not see me: and again, a little while, and ye shall see me, because I go to the Father.

17 Then said *some* of his disciples among themselves, What is this that he saith unto us, A little while, and ye shall not see me: and again, a little while, and ye shall see me: and, Because I go to the Father?

18 They said therefore, What is this that he saith, A little while? we cannot tell what he saith.

19 Now Jesus knew that they were desirous to ask him, and said unto them, Do ye enquire among yourselves of that I said, A little while, and ye shall not see me: and again, a little while, and ye shall see me?

20 Verily, verily, I say unto you, That ye shall weep and lament, but the world shall rejoice: and ye shall

be sorrowful, but your sorrow shall be turned into joy.

21 A woman when she is in travail hath sorrow, because her hour is come: but as soon as she is delivered of the child, she remembereth no more the anguish, for joy that a man is born into the world.

22 And ye now therefore have sorrow: but I will see you again, and your heart shall rejoice, and your joy no man taketh from you.

Jesus Speaks Again of His Death and Resurrection

"A little while" and Jesus would be gone and they would not see Him. Oh, but after His resurrection He would appear to them again and again for forty days. Then Jesus would ascend to the Father.

They did not understand His ascension. I think the day Jesus rose from the dead He ascended to Heaven in His role as High Priest presenting the sacrifice. In John 20:17 Jesus said to Mary, "Touch me not; for I am not yet ascended to my Father." A little later Matthew 28:9 tells about some who "came and held him by the feet." Dr. Scofield suggests, as a favored view, "That Jesus speaks to Mary as the High Priest fulfilling the day of atonement (Lev. 16). Having accomplished the sacrifice, He was on His way to present the sacred blood in heaven, and that, between the meeting with Mary in the garden and the meeting of Mt. 28.9, He had so ascended and returned: a view in harmony with types."

But when Jesus in verse 16 said, *"I go to the Father,"* we think He referred principally to the ascension that would come forty days after His resurrection. He would be in the grave three days and nights and they would not see Him. Then He would appear to them and they would handle Him and see Him eat and would hear Him talk, then one day out on the Mount of Olives they would see Him ascend to Heaven. But that was a strange and marvelous thing that they did not just at this time understand.

Note verse 20. Can you imagine the sorrow of the disciples after the crucifixion when Christ is in the grave and they give up hope? The two men on the way to Emmaus said, "But we trusted that it had been he which should have redeemed Israel" (Luke 24:31). They had trusted—past tense. And the women had come and told that they had seen the resurrected Jesus, but the other disciples did not believe it. Those emotional women and their ideas! Oh, they had sorrow! The bottom had dropped out of all their hopes. The Light of the world had gone out. What would they do?

They should weep and lament, but the world would rejoice. They would be sorrowful, but their sorrow would be turned to joy in the glory of a resurrected and then of an ascended Saviour (vs. 20).

You see, the great things of God often come with travail and sorrow as a woman in childbearing; *"but as soon as she is delivered of the child, she remembereth no more the anguish, for joy that a man is born into the world"* (vs. 21). Now they had sorrow, but, oh, for all the happiness in the world for Christians there had to be this sorrow! Christ must die if the Gospel is to be preached. A corn of wheat must fall into the ground and die if it is to bring forth fruit.

Ah, blessed promise! There are great things in the future for those who trust in Jesus.

VERSES 23-30:

23 And in that day ye shall ask me nothing. Verily, verily, I say unto you, Whatsoever ye shall ask the Father ³in my name, he will give *it* you.

24 Hitherto have ye asked nothing in my name: ask, and ye shall receive, that your joy may be full.

25 These things have I spoken unto you in proverbs: but the time cometh, when I shall no more speak unto you in proverbs, but I shall shew you plainly of the Father.

26 At that day ye shall ask in my name: and I say not unto you, that I will pray the Father for you:

27 For the Father himself loveth you, because ye have loved me, and have believed that I came out from God.

28 I came forth from the Father, and am come into the world: again, I leave the world, and go to the Father.

29 His disciples said unto him, Lo, now speakest thou plainly, and speakest no proverb.

30 Now are we sure that thou knowest all things, and needest not that any man should ask thee: by this we believe that thou camest forth from God.

They Are to Enjoy the Father as Well as Christ

Here is an oft-recurring theme in the Gospel of John. Jesus and the Father are One. What Jesus does is what the Father told Him. The words He says are from the Father. And now He is going to the Father and He reminds them that He and the Father are so perfectly identified and so perfectly agreed that they could go to the Father if they know the will of Christ and ask in His name.

That is a very intimate thing. It does not mean, surely, just to mention the name of Christ, but it means when we want what Christ wants and we are so close to Him that the Spirit of God reveals what Jesus wants, then we can ask with boldness, knowing that God always gives what His Son desires. If we have the authority from Christ to come and ask a matter, then the Father will honor that immediately. We should not use "in Jesus' name," as a meaningless little ceremony, a cliche; but only as we know we speak for Christ, and then we can expect a perfect answer every time when we represent Christ truly in asking what He wants.

One need not try to argue himself into believing that what he wants is what Christ wants. There ought to be a clear understanding: I am speaking for Christ, He has authorized me to ask this of the Father.

Now they are Christ's. Jesus does not tell them "that I will pray the Father for you." No, for the Father Himself loves them and loves us and we should be just as free to come to the Father as to Jesus. And one who loves Jesus and believes on Christ as Saviour has all the love and fellowship of the Father, too. When Jesus leaves this world He will go immediately to the Father, and their prayers to Jesus and to the Father are the same and they should have perfect freedom. They are in the family now.

Dr. Bob Jones, Sr., used to say, "I am not a stranger. I am a member of God's family. I just pull up my chair to the table and say, 'Pappy, please pass the biscuits.' " Now, after having it stated so many times the disciples are beginning to understand it! Now they see the wisdom and deity of Christ more fully. They know now that He *"came forth from God"* (vs. 27). It is strange they had not fully understood that before. Now it is clear as never before.

VERSES 31-33:

31 Jesus answered them, Do ye now believe?

32 Behold, the hour cometh, yea, is now come, that ye shall be scattered, every man to his own, and shall leave me alone: and yet I am not alone, because the Father is with me.

33 These things I have spoken unto you, that in me ye might have peace. In the world ye shall have tribulation: but be of good cheer; I have overcome the world.

Another Warning

Jesus cannot leave these disciples without another solemn warning. The awful days ahead, with Christ's trial and crucifixion and the murderous hate of the Jews against Christ and His people, mean that they will *"be scattered, every man to his own"* (vs. 32). They had followed Jesus as a little body throughout the province of Galilee and down to Jerusalem and back again and again. But now they will be scattered and leave Christ alone.

There is a sense in which Jesus must die alone. Oh, the lonely Christ can do what none of us can ever do with Him! He wants us to take up our cross with Him; He wants us to be persecuted with Him; He wants us to join in with Christ in everything; but the atoning death of Jesus on the cross is that of the one perfect Substitute, the one Lamb of God who only can take away the sin of the world.

But Jesus warned them, *"Ye shall have tribulation."* Yes, *"but be of good cheer; I have overcome the world"* (vs. 33). That verse is a marvelous promise which every Christian should memorize. The discussion started out in John 14:1 with, "Let not your heart be troubled." It ends with the promise that in Jesus we may have peace! Jesus, facing His crucifixion, could say to His disciples, "Be of good cheer"—be happy, be cheerful, do not be troubled! The reason for all of our happiness is that Christ has overcome the world. And this world, with all of its treasure, with all of its hatred of the Lord Jesus and His people, cannot do away with the sweet peace which we may have from God through the Lord Jesus Christ.

John 17

THESE words spake Jesus, and lifted up his eyes to heaven, and said, Father, the hour is come; glorify thy Son, that thy Son also may glorify thee:

2 As thou hast given him power over all flesh, that he should give eternal life to as many as thou hast given him.

3 And this is life eternal, that they might know thee the only true God, and Jesus Christ, whom thou hast sent.

4 I have glorified thee on the earth: I have finished the work which thou gavest me to do.

5 And now, O Father, glorify thou me with thine own self with the glory which I had with thee before the world was.

Leaving Gethsemane, Jesus Prays

This prayer of Jesus seems to have been uttered somewhere on the road from the upper room to the Garden of Gethsemane. John 14:31, the last sentence, shows that they had left the upper room, and John 18:1 shows that they had not yet arrived in the garden.

In a quiet street, in the night, while the city slumbered about them, or it may be outside the city gate, they halted in the dusty road and with the disciples waiting about Him and listening, with what fervent interest we may well imagine, Jesus prayed this prayer to His Father.

The recorded public prayers of Jesus are not many. In John 11:41 and 42 Jesus prayed aloud in the presence of other people at the grave of Lazarus.

In John 12:27 and 28 Jesus, preaching to the Pharisees at Jerusalem, stopped and prayed aloud, and the Father answered from Heaven.

In Matthew 11:25 and 26 Jesus, after upbraiding Capernaum, thanked His Father aloud because "Thou hast hid these things from the wise and prudent, and hast revealed them unto babes . . . ."

In the Garden of Gethsemane, following this prayer of the 17th chapter of John, Jesus prayed again three different times the same words. Whether any of the disciples heard Him or not, we do not know; but the words of His prayer are given (Matt. 26:39,42,44).

There are three prayers recorded which Jesus prayed audibly while hanging on the cross. The first was evidently immediately after He was nailed to the cross: "Father, forgive them; for they know not what they do" (Luke 23:34).

A second prayer of Jesus on the cross was several hours after the crucifixion, about three o'clock in the afternoon: "My God, my God, why hast thou forsaken me?" (Matt. 27:46).

The third prayer on the cross was when Jesus prayed, "Father, into thy hands I commend my spirit" (Luke 23:46). This was just at the moment of His death.

Besides these, we are told several times that Jesus returned thanks, or blessed the food which He ate. For instance, see Luke 24:30, John 6:11, and Mark 8:6.

It is important to notice that in every recorded prayer of Jesus save one, He addressed the prayer to God as "Father." The one exception was when He prayed on the cross, "My God, my God, why hast thou forsaken me?" In that particular case Jesus, in the midst of the sufferings of the crucifixion, was taking the place of a lost sinner, dying, away from God. He suffered all the torments that sin could bring, and that prayer illustrates how perfectly He bore our sins. He must speak to God like any human being could do. Later when the suffering was finished and He was ready to die, He again said "Father."

There has been much discussion which prayer should be called the Lord's Prayer—this in John 17, or the model prayer beginning, "Our Father which art in heaven." The Scripture does not give that particular name to either, and it seems unwise to quibble about it. Since the model prayer, given as an example, is generally known as the Lord's Prayer, there is certainly no harm in calling it that. He did give it, and it is truly His, though it is not a prayer which He could pray for Himself, in every detail, since He never needed to say, "Forgive us our debts [or sins]," since He never sinned.

This 17th chapter of John is truly the Lord's Prayer, but it is not the only one, and is no more His than the other prayers which we have mentioned.

Dr. Scofield calls attention to seven requests in this prayer of Jesus: "(1) That Jesus may be glorified as the Son who has glorified the Father (vs. 1; Phil. 2:9-11); (2) for restoration to the eternal glory (vs. 5); (3) for the safety of believers from (a) the world (vs. 11), (b) the evil one (vs. 15); (4) for the sanctification of believers (vs. 17); (5) for the spiritual unity of believers (vs. 21); (6) that the world may believe (vs. 21); (7) that believers may be with Him in Heaven to behold and share His glory (vs. 24)."

Jesus has been teaching His disciples so that their joy might be full, and to prepare them for His crucifixion and later His resurrection and ascension. Now His prayer is for His disciples. Later, in the Garden of Gethsemane, Jesus will feel compelled to pray for Himself, but just now all of His thought seems to be for His disciples, including the eleven with Him then in the garden and all others who should later be converted (vs. 20). This is a prayer of Jesus for His disciples.

"The Hour Is Come"

"The hour" Jesus speaks of means the time of His crucifixion and the whole wonderful package of His resurrection and glorification. So *"the hour is come"* (vs. 1).

As we study through the Gospel of John, we have found increasing pressure on the mind of Jesus. This is coming to His mind all the time. Concerning the fragrant ointment that was poured upon Him by Mary, He said in John 12:7, "Let her alone: against the day of my burying hath she kept this." Ah, His burial.

In John 12:23 He said, "The hour is come, that the Son of man should be glorified."

Read John 13:1: ". . . when Jesus knew that his hour was come that he should depart out of this world unto the Father." In John 13:31 when Judas had gone out now to betray Jesus, Jesus said, "Now is the Son of man glorified, and God is glorified in him."

And John 14:2: "I go to prepare a place for you."

In John 14:12 Jesus said, ". . . because I go unto my Father."

Again He said in John 14:28, "If ye loved me, ye would rejoice, because I said, I go unto the Father."

So we can see that the growing pressure and holy urgency of this goal was on Jesus' mind all the time and more and more as the day approached. Now He says, *The hour is come.*

We remember that Jesus said, "I have a baptism to be baptized with; and how am I straitened till it be accomplished!" (Luke 12:50).

In Isaiah 50:6,7 this attitude in the dear heart of the Saviour was foretold:

"I gave my back to the smiters, and my cheeks to them that plucked off the hair: I hid not my face from shame and spitting. For the Lord God will help me; therefore shall I not be confounded: therefore have I set my face like a flint, and I know that I shall not be ashamed."

Yes, He had set His face like a flint toward the crucifixion.

In this high priestly prayer He is somewhat reporting to the Father on the accomplishment of His incarnation, and He reminds God that the Father had given Him power *"over all flesh, that he should give eternal life to as many as thou hast given him"* (vs. 2). Oh, the saving of sinners is what Jesus had in mind.

"And this is life eternal, that they might know thee the only true God, and Jesus Christ, whom thou hast sent" (vs. 3).

Getting people saved is the one burden on the heart of Jesus. It is the one purpose of His coming: "This is a faithful saying, and worthy of all acceptation, that Christ Jesus came into the world to save sinners" (I Tim. 1:15).

Some Bible teacher says, "I feel that my calling is to 'feed the sheep,' " that is, to teach Christians. Then your calling and that of Jesus is not the same! The only ones who are going Jesus' way are those who are working to save sinners.

Does someone have a yen for "the deeper life"? Well, the deepest life in the world is that of the Lord Jesus, and the greatest burden is His burden to save sinners, and the greatest joy for Christ and for Christians is to win souls. Yes, and the greatest reward in Heaven is: "They that be wise shall shine as the brightness of the firmament; and they that turn many to righteousness as the stars for ever and ever" (Dan. 12:3).

What joy the Saviour has to remember that everything He has done on earth has been to glorify the Father. Jesus never failed the Father in one thing. Always He perfectly represented the Father; now He can say, *"I have finished the work which thou gavest me to do"* (vs. 4).

We understand, of course, that Jesus has finished the work of His public ministry, but more than that, there is a sense in which the whole thing of His life and ministry and death and resurrection is involved here. Already the teaching, the miracles, healing people on the Sabbath, the claim of deity and representing the Father perfectly have set in courses the furies of the Sanhedrin that will lead to His death. Already Judas Iscariot has been sent out with instructions: "That thou doest, do quickly." He has gone, to sell the Saviour for thirty pieces of silver and to lead the mob with swords and staves to his tryst in the Garden of Gethsemane!

There is a sense that with Christ and the Father there is no future but all is present. Jesus knows the future and has done His duty about the future just as definitely as He has done it in the past. So in the mind of Jesus Christ it is finished. It is all planned, it is all accepted, it is all put in form. The predetermined death, burial and resurrection are already settled in the mind of Jesus.

Would it not be wonderful if every one of us, when we face death or the rapture, could say as Jesus did, *"I have glorified thee on the earth: I have finished the work which thou gavest me to do"* (vs. 4)? There is a little of that in the triumphant declaration of Paul in II Timothy 4:6,7, "For I am now ready to be offered, and the time of my departure is at hand. I have fought a good fight, I have finished my course, I have kept the faith."

Said Dr. Ironside: "He had not one regret. If anyone doubts the Deity of our Lord, let him think of Christ's record. He lived down here and never had one regret, never said one word He had to apologize for, never did one thing He later wished He hadn't done, never made one mistake, never stumbled once on all the rocky pathway from the manger of Bethlehem to the cross of Calvary. How different from ourselves!"

And now, after suffering comes the glory! All the other glory has been minor beside the great glory when Jesus goes back to the Father with all the glory of His manifest deity as He had before the world began.

VERSES 6-12:

6 I have manifested thy name unto the men which thou gavest me out of the world: thine they were, and thou gavest them me; and they have kept thy word.

7 Now they have known that all things whatsoever thou hast given me are of thee.

8 For I have given unto them the words which thou gavest me; and they have received *them*, and have known surely that I came out from thee, and they have believed that thou didst send me.

9 I pray for them: I pray not for the world, but for them which thou hast given me; for they are thine.

10 And all mine are thine, and thine are mine; and I am glorified in them.

11 And now I am no more in the world, but these are in the world, and I come to thee. Holy Father, keep through thine own name those whom thou hast given me, that they may be one, as we *are*.

12 While I was with them in the world, I kept them in thy name: those that thou gavest me I have kept, and none of them is lost, but the son of perdition; that the scripture might be fulfilled.

"Here Is the Result of These Years
With My Disciples"

The Lord Jesus manifested the Father's name unto these disciples God had given Him. The Father gave them to Jesus and He had diligently taught them and they have kept His Word. These disciples now know that all Jesus said and did came from the Father.

The words Jesus gave are the Father's words, and these disciples had been taught and have received them and now they are sure, after many, many repeated statements, that Jesus and the Father are one and He was sent by the Father.

The Lord Jesus is interceding for them: *"I pray for them: I pray not for the world"* (vs. 9). Jesus is not only expressing that prayer in John 17, but He is expressing an eternal business He has as our Intercessor. He is "an high priest over the house of God" (Heb. 10:21; 9:11). And "he ever liveth to make intercession" for us (Heb. 7:25).

We remember that Jesus told Simon Peter, when he was to be so severely tempted and was to fall into sin, "I have prayed for thee, that thy faith fail not" (Luke 22:32). The Devil could not get Peter. He could cause him heartbreak and trouble, cause him to fail, but he could not take him away from Christ.

Remember Jesus said, "I knew that thou hearest me always" (11:42), and so when He prayed for Peter, Peter was safe forever. So He prays for us and we, too, are saved forever if we have been given to Jesus Christ and have taken Him as our Saviour.

Christ is glorified in us, verse 10 says.

It is wonderfully sweet that seven times in this chapter the Lord Jesus speaks of believers as given to Him by the Father: in verses 2, 6 (twice), 9, 11, 12, 24. Dr. Scofield reminds us:

Jesus Christ is God's love-gift to the world (John 3:16), and believers are the Father's love-gift to Jesus Christ. It is Christ who commits the believer to the Father for safe-keeping, so that the believer's security rests upon the Father's faithfulness to His Son Jesus Christ.

Now lest there be a great separation, Jesus says, *"And now I am no more in the world, but these are in the world, and I come to thee"* (vs. 11). In John 8:12 Jesus said, "I am the light of the world." In John 9:5, "As long as I am in the world, I am the light of the world." By that Jesus was reminding Himself and the Father and us that we are left to do the work of Christ.

Now we are to entreat people in Christ's stead, "Be ye reconciled to God" (II Cor. 5:20). Oh, but again the Lord Jesus repeats it. The Father, in loyalty to His Son Jesus, must *"keep through thine own name those whom thou hast given me"* (vs. 11). That means there will be a happy, eternal reunion when we are gathered together with all the saints of God, all the sheep Christ has of other folds.

Dr. Macaulay says:

> No mother ever prayed for her boy on the battlefield, nor wife for her fisherman husband in the storm, more passionately or tenderly than our Lord for His own whom He sent into the world.
>
> Several years ago, while in Kentucky, my wife and I were taken to see that famous horse, Man o' War. He probably was the most valuable horse in the country at that time. The coloured Baptist deacon who was his keeper was loud in his praises. Among other items of information he gave us this, that never for a minute, night or day, was this horse without a human eye upon him.
>
> Will not the holy Father, then, watch His children to preserve them? "The eyes of the Lord are upon the righteous." "I will guide thee with Mine eye upon thee."

Safe in Jehovah's keeping, held by His mighty arm:
God is Himself my refuge, a present help from harm.

Christ kept the disciples when He was here. None of them are lost. Judas Iscariot, the son of perdition, was never saved. All these others of the twelve were saved and are kept. Judas Iscariot, "that the scripture might be fulfilled," had been included in the twelve, though unsaved.

VERSES 13-19:

13 And now come I to thee; and these things I speak in the world, that they might have my joy fulfilled in themselves.

14 I have given them thy word; and the world hath hated them, because

they are not of the world, even as I am not of the world.

15 I pray not that thou shouldest take them out of the world, but that thou shouldest keep them from the evil.

16 They are not of the world, even as I am not of the world.

17 Sanctify them through thy truth: thy word is truth.

18 As thou hast sent me into the world, even so have I also sent them into the world.

19 And for their sakes I sanctify myself, that they also might be sanctified through the truth.

Father, Care for the Hated Disciples

These last hours are meant for the comfort and joy of the disciples. How He loved them and us! The world would hate them, *"because they are not of the world"* (vs. 14). In John 8:23 and 24 Jesus said:

"Ye are from beneath; I am from above: ye are of this world; I am not of this world. I said therefore unto you, that ye shall die in your sins: for if ye believe not that I am he, ye shall die in your sins."

"We must be left here 'in the world' but 'not of the world,' to accomplish our mission to the world . . . . The divine method of preservation is not isolation from the diseased world, for we are the Great Physician's attendants to carry the sin-cure to the sick all around us. Physicians and nurses cannot be isolated from the contagion of disease, but they are inoculated with antitoxins in order to keep them from it. We are 'strengthened with might by His Spirit in the inner man' against the attacks of sin, and so secured from the domination of the evil one" (J. C. Macaulay).

Christians are not of this world, but are "born from above." "Born again" in John 3:3 is literally "born from above," the Greek word *anothen.* One born of God is different. He has a new nature. He has the Holy Spirit abiding within him. He has "now received the atonement." He is "partaker of the divine nature." All the talk of Arminians about losing salvation ignores the fact that the believer is now "not of this world," is born from above, is literally God's child. Here Jesus said, *"Sanctify them through thy truth"* (vs. 17). The word "sanctify" means literally "set apart for God." And so the word holy. It never means sinless. "The Holy City" refers to Jerusalem. Jerusalem is set apart for

God although with sinful people. "My holy mountain" does not mean that the mountains have quit sinning: it means mountain set apart for God, or by God.

In the Bible sanctification is progressive. First, all who are saved are sanctified or set apart for Heaven. Hebrews 10:14 says, "For by one offering he hath perfected for ever them that are sanctified." So when the Scripture says, "saints," it means saved people who are set apart for Heaven. In that sense saints are sanctified.

But sanctification progresses as one loves and learns and follows the Word of God. He is progressively "sanctified" by the Word. Jesus is praying that His people will more and more study the Word of God and be more and more set apart for God and like God.

Calvin remarks, "As the apostles were not destitute of grace, we ought to infer from Christ's words that sanctification is not instantly completed in us on the first day, but that we make progress in it through the whole course of our life."

So Paul in Acts 20:32 told the elders of Ephesus gathered with him at Miletus, "I commend you to God, and to the word of his grace, which is able to build you up, and to give you an inheritance among all them which are sanctified." Oh, blessed Word of God! How it builds up and changes and makes people different, sets them apart for God!

And, of course, this process of sanctification is never completed, and we never reach sinlessness and perfection until the rapture and the resurrection, when we awake in Christ's likeness.

Jesus says that He sends the disciples and us into the world (vs. 18). We are sent just as the Father sent Jesus. In John 20:21 Jesus said, ". . . as my Father hath sent me, even so send I you."

Oh, we are to be like Jesus. Jesus is the Light of the world and so we are the light of the world. We are to take up our cross and follow Jesus. We are to be persecuted as He was. We are to be Spirit-filled as He was. For all the personal ministry of Jesus— His preaching, His miracles, His witnessing—were done in the power of the Holy Spirit. In Acts 10:37,38 we read:

"That word, I say, ye know, which was published throughout

all Judaea, and began from Galilee, after the baptism which John preached; How God anointed Jesus of Nazareth with the Holy Ghost and with power: who went about doing good, and healing all that were oppressed of the devil; for God was with him."

In Luke 4:16-19 we are told how Jesus came into the synagogue at Nazareth and read to them the Scripture from Isaiah 61:1:

"*The Spirit of the Lord is upon me, because he hath anointed me to preach the gospel to the poor; he hath sent me to heal the brokenhearted, to preach deliverance to the captives, and recovering of sight to the blind, to set at liberty them that are bruised, To preach the acceptable year of the Lord.*"

And He said, "This day is this scripture fulfilled in your ears" (Luke 4:21). Ephesians 5:18 commands us, ". . .be filled with the Spirit."

Acts 2:16-18 quotes Joel's prophecy:

"*And it shall come to pass in the last days, saith God, I will pour out of my Spirit upon all flesh: and your sons and your daughters shall prophesy, and your young men shall see visions, and your old men shall dream dreams: And on my servants and on my handmaidens I will pour out in those days of my Spirit; and they shall prophesy.*"

We are to do the very works that Jesus did, for John 14:12 says, "Verily, verily, I say unto you, He that believeth on me, the works that I do shall he do also; and greater works than these shall he do; because I go unto my Father."

Oh, the dear Lord Jesus sanctified Himself. That is, He set Himself apart for the blessed saving business, and so we are to be set apart for Him or sanctified for that through the truth, the Word of God.

VERSES 20-23:

20 Neither pray I for these alone, but for them also which shall believe on me through their word;

21 That they all may be one; as thou, Father, *art* in me, and I in thee, that they also may be one in us: that the world may believe that thou hast sent me.

22 And the glory which thou gavest me I have given them; that they may be one, even as we are one:

23 I in them, and thou in me, that they may be made perfect in one; and that the world may know that thou hast sent me, and hast loved them, as thou hast loved me.

These Disciples Represent All of Us— God's People

The concern of the Lord Jesus for these eleven disciples was for all others who should believe on Christ through their words. If He prayed for Peter, "I have prayed for thee, that thy faith fail not" (Luke 22:32), He prayed for me. If these eleven were "not of this world," neither are we of this world when we have been converted, born again.

Christ wants all of His people to *"be one"* (vs. 21). All are to be one in the Father and in the Son. Then this is not a prayer or a wish for all of us to be in one supercolossal organization. No church, no World Council of Churches can answer this prayer. No denominations, no religious organizations besides the local congregations of Christians are taught in this Scripture. It is being united in heart-love for Christ and for the truth and for His saved people that Christ here prays for.

Nor does Christ here pray for a unity of creedal statements. Of course, He wants us all to hold the truth, but He does not seek a breaking down of holy convictions so that all can come to some common denominator, some general agreement, without concern for doctrine.

Christ prays that our prejudices, our bias, our self-seeking pride or denomination or cult, may be superseded by an outgoing love for all who love and trust the Lord Jesus. Can one not love Christ with all his heart, and love all the Scriptures, and yet love those who love Christ in some different group and with some little incidental convictions?

Christ would not claim an unbeliever, a liberal who denies the essentials of the Gospel as one of His sheep (I Cor. 15:3,4). He does not wish any believer to call infidels Christians nor to yoke up with unbelievers which is strictly forbidden (II Cor. 6:14-18; II John, verses 9-11).

Different Christians may have different gifts.

"Now there are diversities of gifts, but the same Spirit. And there are differences of administrations, but the same Lord. And there are diversities of operations, but it is the same God which worketh all in all."—I Cor. 12:4-6.

The members of Christ's body are not all alike.

"For the body is not one member, but many. If the foot shall say, Because I am not the hand, I am not of the body; is it therefore not of the body? And if the ear shall say, Because I am not the eye, I am not of the body; is it therefore not of the body? If the whole body were an eye, where were the hearing? If the whole were hearing, where were the smelling?"—I Cor. 12:14-17.

Cannot those who have been won by Apollos love those who have been won by Paul or Peter? Cannot those who observe a certain day love those who do not observe the same day? Cannot those who eat meats love and have patience with those who do not eat meat? Cannot we who baptize by single immersion love our brethren who believe in triune immersion? And if a brother who loves the Lord Jesus and is born of God, was sprinkled for baptism and thinks he is baptized, can we not love him, even if we understand that he is mistaken?

Romans 14:1 says, "Him that is weak in the faith receive ye, but not to doubtful disputations." Psalm 119:63 says, "I am a companion of all them that fear thee, and of them that keep thy precepts." There can be a oneness of heart among all those who love the Lord Jesus and trust in His atoning blood, and earnestly seek to please Him, and those who love God's Word and try to follow it.

In Korea, I stood barefooted on a pillow in a Presbyterian church and preached through an interpreter to Koreans sitting cross-legged on a polished floor. Oh, I loved those men and they loved me! I preached in India through an interpreter, and my heart was so drawn to the converts in India and many of the saintly men there. Before I left they gave me a dinner, and with holy devotion these gray-haired men kissed me on each cheek and hugged me to their bosoms.

O God, make us one at heart with all the people of God.

George Newton remarks on this verse, *"I in them, and thou in me"*: "If Christ is in you, let me give you this caution: let Him live quiet in your hearts. Do not molest Him and disturb Him; do not make Him vex and fret. Let it not be a penance to Him to continue in you. But labour every way to please Him, and give Him satisfaction and content, that so the house He hath chosen may not be dark and doleful, but delightful to Him."

VERSES 24-26:

24 Father, I will that they also, whom thou hast given me, be with me where I am; that they may behold my glory, which thou hast given me: for thou lovedst me before the foundation of the world.

25 O righteous Father, the world hath not known thee: but I have known thee, and these have known that thou hast sent me.

26 And I have declared unto them thy name, and will declare *it:* that the love wherewith thou hast loved me may be in them, and I in them.

Jesus Wants Us All in Glory

Peter, James, John, did you see marvels in the ministry of Jesus on earth? Oh, but you will see Him at last in the glory which He had with the Father before the world began! Nathaniel, did you believe on Jesus because He had seen your seeking heart as you knelt under a fig tree? Well, Nathaniel, you will see Heaven open and angels of God ascending and descending upon the Son of man. For all God's children will behold His glory. We will all see how the Father loves the Son and will rejoice, greater than those at His triumphal entry at Jerusalem, when they shouted, "Hosanna to the Son of David: Blessed is he that cometh in the name of the Lord" (Matt. 21:9).

"For now we see through a glass, darkly; but then face to face:

now I know in part; but then shall I know even as also I am known."—I Cor. 13:12,13.

That is what Jesus prayed for and what will happen. And as these disciples had known Jesus, they will know the Father and see God Himself face to face in a way no man can now see Him and live (Exod. 33:20).

And when we wake in His likeness and are satisfied, we will love as the Father loves and be one with both the Father and the Son. H. H. Halley says, "He closes His tender farewell by commending them to God, praying both for Himself and for them, as He turns away to tread the winepress ALONE."

John 18

WHEN Jesus had spoken these words, he went forth with his disciples over the brook Çē-drŏn, where was a garden, into the which he entered, and his disciples.

2 And Judas also, which betrayed him, knew the place: for Jesus ofttimes resorted thither with his disciples.

Jesus Arrives in Gethsemane

From Matthew 26:36-46 and from Mark 14:32-42 and from Luke 22:39-46, we learn of the events which took place between John 18:1 and John 18:2. John does not give the story of the prayer which Jesus prayed the three times in the Garden of Gethsemane, "O my Father, if it be possible, let this cup pass from me: nevertheless not as I will, but as thou wilt" (Matt. 26:39). In John we are not told of the bloody sweat (Luke 22:44), nor of the angel from Heaven which appeared to Him, strengthening Him (Luke 22:43).

This period of time between verses 1 and 2 of John 18 must have been several hours in length for these events to have taken place. It is evident that the first period of secret prayer in the garden when Jesus left the main group of disciples, taking Peter, James and John, then going farther and praying alone, must have taken about an hour (Matt. 26:36-40). The disciples went to sleep, then later after He had aroused them, He found them asleep again (Matt. 26:43). The third time Jesus allowed them to sleep on (Matt. 26:45).

It is probable that Jesus arrived at the garden at 10:00 or 11:00 p.m., and that Judas Iscariot, with the mob and officers, came about 1:00 or 2:00 in the morning, or later. We do not know why the Holy Spirit did not tell John to write down these matters, too, but it is likely that they were omitted because they would not add to the proof that Jesus was the Son of God, which was the purpose of the book of John.

The garden is Gethsemane, Matthew 23:36 tells us. They went over a Brook Kidron "to the mount of Olives," says Luke 22:39. There is now a room called "The Upper Room," in the southern area of Old Jerusalem, outside the walls, on the south. It is not the Upper Room but was made to represent it. It was built, we think, by the Crusaders, in a church building. The Crusaders were in Palestine from 1099 to 1291. The Upper Room was somewhere in the city (Luke 22:10-12).

But across the Brook Cedron to the Garden of Gethsemane *"Jesus ofttimes resorted"* (vs. 2). That is where Jesus went in John 8:1. Here Jesus probably often slept on the ground. To this He referred, we think, when He said, "Foxes have holes, and birds of the air have nests; but the Son of man hath not where to lay his head" (Luke 9:58).

Now, in the Garden of Gethsemane Jesus prays, and there Judas will lead the servants of the high priests and officers to take Him.

In this garden Jesus asked Peter, James and John to go with Him aside to pray. Here He was about to die and said, "My soul is exceeding sorrowful, even unto death." He went further and prayed three different times. The disciples went to sleep. He warned them, particularly Peter, "Watch and pray, that ye enter not into temptation: the spirit indeed is willing, but the flesh is weak" (Matt. 26:38,40,41). Jesus then prayed "with strong crying and tears unto him that was able to save him from death, and was heard in that he feared," says Hebrews 5:7.

Jesus was about to die under Satan's pressure who wanted Him to die outside the will of God and contrary to the prophecies in the Gospel. Remember the saving Gospel is: ". . . how that Christ died for our sins according to the scriptures; And that he was buried, and that he rose again the third day according to the scriptures" (I Cor. 15:3,4). So, if Jesus had died at the wrong time or in the wrong way, without dying on the passover day, without dying on the cursed cross, without having His hands and feet pierced, without the scourging, without making His grave with the wicked, as the Scriptures had prophesied, then He could not save anyone. But an angel came and strengthened Him (Luke 22:43).

Let us not think that Jesus was praying against the will of God; He was not praying to avoid Calvary. You and I know from reading the Scriptures that Jesus was to die at a certain time and way and He knew it, too. There is no shrinking in Him. He had set His face like a flint toward Calvary. He had a baptism to be baptized with and how was He straitened until it was accomplished! He was praying that the cup might pass over until tomorrow and that He would die in the right way and at the right time in order to fulfill the Scriptures. And God heard His prayer.

"Judas then, having received a band of men and officers from the chief priests and Pharisees, cometh thither with lanterns and torches and weapons."—Vs. 3.

Judas had left Jesus and the other disciples, early in the evening, in the Upper Room, after Jesus had given him the sop, indicating that he would betray Jesus. Notice that it is particularly stated that Satan entered into him (13:24-30). Matthew 26:14-16 shows that Judas had already plotted with the chief priests before this time to betray Him. However, he was deceitful. And in Matthew 26:25 he asked, "Master, is it I?"

From the other Gospels we learn that Judas, on coming to Jesus in the garden, betrayed Him by a kiss which he had promised to the officers as a sign that it was Jesus (Matt. 26:48,49). Jesus called him "friend," though it seems clear that Judas hated Jesus. We know that Jesus said he was a devil and it seems certain that Judas had never trusted Jesus as his Saviour (6:64,70). Since every man must love or hate Jesus, must cling to or depise Him, we know that Judas must have hated Him and despised Him.

Here comes Judas with soldiers and servants of the high priest. Judas knew where Jesus often went to be alone, where He spent the night in Jerusalem when not at the home of Mary, Martha and Lazarus or not invited elsewhere.

VERSES 3-9:

3 Judas then, having received a band *of men* and officers from the chief priests and Pharisees, cometh thither with lanterns and torches and weapons.

4 Jesus therefore, knowing all things that should come upon him, went forth, and said unto them, Whom seek ye?

5 They answered him, Jesus of Nazareth. Jesus saith unto them, I am *he*. And Judas also, which betrayed him, stood with them.

6 As soon then as he had said unto them, I am *he*, they went backward, and fell to the ground.

7 Then asked he them again, Whom seek ye? And they said, Jesus of Nazareth.

8 Jesus answered, I have told you that I am *he:* if therefore ye seek me, let these go their way:

9 That the saying might be fulfilled, which he spake, Of them which thou gavest me have I lost none.

The Betrayal and Arrest of Jesus

The high priest, acting as head of the Sanhedrin, was allowed by the Roman governor to have authority in civil cases and in some criminal cases. He had many officers and many servants. There was Jewish government within the Roman government.

Jesus offered Himself willingly for the arrest. But how can God, the Creator, the Sustainer of all things, be arrested, tried, tormented and murdered by sinful men? It must be made obvious to all that it is not the power of the high priest and of Rome that takes Him prisoner and to the cross. No, He freely gives Himself.

So His mighty power thrusts these men backward (vs. 6), helpless for a moment before that power that had stilled storms of wind and waves at sea, that created food for thousands, that cleansed the leper and made blind eyes to see, at a word! So they fell backward; so it was clear that He gave Himself simply and willingly to die, or they could not have taken Him.

He told the disciples He could in a moment have twelve legions of angels deliver Him had He chosen. Jesus is giving His life for others; no man takes it from Him. He lays it down as He will.

"Let these go their way," He says in verse 8. The mob from the high priest may have intended to take the disciples, too, but amazed and frustrated by His power they know they must do as He said—and the disciples go free! So when we read in Matthew

26:56, "Then all the disciples forsook him, and fled," they were only doing what Jesus planned for their safety, no doubt. Jesus, at the arrest, can still take care of His own and so His statement of chapter 17, verse 12, is true: none of them is lost or dead.

Matthew 26:48-50 tells us that Judas had an arrangement with the servant of the high priest that he would kiss Jesus to identify Him. And Jesus said, "Friend, wherefore art thou come?" When Peter would hinder Him from going to the cross, Jesus said, "Get thee behind me, Satan," but when Judas will betray Him to the death prophesied for sinners and to which He freely gave Himself, Jesus called him "Friend."

VERSES 10,11:

10 Then Simon Peter having a sword drew it, and smote the high priest's servant, and cut off his right ear. The servant's name was Măl- chŭs.

11 Then said Jesus unto Peter, Put up thy sword into the sheath: the cup which my Father hath given me, shall I not drink it?

Peter With a Sword to Defend Jesus

Before they came into the Garden of Gethsemane, Jesus had told them, "He that hath no sword, let him sell his garment, and buy one . . . And they said, Lord, behold, here are two swords. And he said unto them, It is enough" (Luke 22:36,38). And later in the garden the disciples said, "Lord, shall we smite with the sword?" and then Peter used his sword and cut off the ear of one of the servants of the high priest.

Here Jesus tells them:

"Put up again thy sword into his place: for all they that take the sword shall perish with the sword. Thinkest thou that I cannot now pray to my Father, and he shall presently give me more than twelve legions of angels? But how then shall the scriptures be fulfilled, that thus it must be?"—Matt. 26:52-54.

We are sure that when Jesus spoke of swords He was solemnly warning them that their lives would be ones of trial and danger and He wanted them to take to heart the fact that He would be arrested and tried and would die on the cross. He did not mean that at that particular time they were to have swords and defend Jesus and try to avoid the crucifixion. He meant, surely, that they and all of us must expect a life of trial, and stress, trouble, fighting and sometimes dying for the truth and for the Gospel.

In this chapter we are not told of that other miracle of Jesus' replacing the right ear of Malchus, which Peter cut off. But see Luke 22:51. The other Gospels do not tell that it was Simon Peter who cut off the ear of the young man, and they do not tell the name of Malchus.

"... the cup which my Father hath given me, shall I not drink it?"—Vs. 11.

Never will the Father give you and me a cup half so bitter as that which He put to the lips of His well-beloved Son. The cup for us may contain a few drops of gall at times, but His was all wormwood.

> Death and the *curse* were in our cup;
> O Christ, 'twas full for Thee!
> But Thou hast drained the last dark drop;
> 'Tis empty now for me:
> That bitter cup—love drank it up;
> Now blessing's draught for me!

Ah, the Lord Jesus must drink the cup which the Father had given Him, and He gladly took it.

VERSES 12-14:

12 Then the band and the captain and officers of the Jews took Jesus, and bound him,

13 And led him away to Annas first; for he was father in law to Cāī-á-phăs, which was the high priest that same year.

14 Now Cāī-á-phăs was he, which gave counsel to the Jews, that it was expedient that one man should die for the people.

Away to the High Priest's Palace

To Annas first, the father-in-law of Caiaphas, a very

influential man, then to Caiaphas, the actual high priest, "where the scribes and the elders were assembled," waiting for Judas and the band to bring Jesus (Matt. 26:57).

Note: ". . . *the captain and officers of the Jews*" (vs. 12). Caiaphas had unwittingly been inspired to prophesy the atoning death of Jesus for others, as we read in John 11:49-52.

What seemed to be the remains of the palace of the high priest was found across the valley of Cedron on the hill Ophel, and what is now south and without the walls of Jerusalem. There is built over the ruins a Catholic church, "The Church of the Crowing Cock." There were underground cells for a prison, for the high priest could have people arrested, tried and imprisoned. There, we think, he kept Jesus the rest of the night after His trial and abuse before taking Him to Pilate for judgment the next morning.

We are told that here were found weights and measures such as would be used to measure the Temple money and other things distinctively fitting the Temple. The language of Mark 14:66, "And as Peter was beneath in the palace," seems to fit this place. It was built on a steep hillside, with a patio and servants' quarters on a lower floor and with cells and storage below that.

VERSES 15-27:

15 ¶ And Simon Peter followed Jesus, and *so did* another disciple: that disciple was known unto the high priest, and went in with Jesus into the palace of the high priest.

16 But Peter stood at the door without. Then went out that other disciple, which was known unto the high priest, and spake unto her that kept the door, and brought in Peter.

17 Then saith the damsel that kept the door unto Peter, Art not thou also *one* of this man's disciples? He saith, I am not.

18 And the servants and officers stood there, who had made a fire of coals; for it was cold: and they warmed themselves: and Peter stood with them, and warmed himself.

19 ¶ The high priest then asked Jesus of his disciples, and of his doctrine.

20 Jesus answered him, I spake openly to the world; I ever taught in the synagogue, and in the temple, whither the Jews always resort; and in secret have I said nothing.

21 Why askest thou me? ask them which heard me, what I have said unto them: behold, they know what I said.

22 And when he had thus spoken,

one of the officers which stood by struck Jesus with the palm of his hand, saying, Answerest thou the high priest so?

23 Jesus answered him, If I have spoken evil, bear witness of the evil: but if well, why smitest thou me?

24 Now Annas had sent him bound unto Câî-ă-phăs the high priest.

25 And Simon Peter stood and warmed himself. They said therefore unto him, Art not thou also *one* of his disciples? He denied *it*, and said, I am not.

26 One of the servants of the high priest, being *his* kinsman whose ear Peter cut off, saith, Did not I see thee in the garden with him?

27 Peter then denied again: and immediately the cock crew.

Peter Denies the Lord

Remember that Peter was clearly a saved man and had trusted and publicly claimed Christ as his Saviour (Matt. 16:16). Remember that according to the words of Jesus, Satan had planned to tempt Peter, evidently more than the other disciples, but Jesus knew that Peter trusted Him and Jesus had prayed for him that his faith would not fail (Luke 22:31,32). "Converted" in that passage does not refer to getting saved, but to turning back to service. We need not blame Peter alone, for the other disciples did not do much better—all deserted Him.

A fire was made against the chill of the early spring night *"for it was cold"* (vs. 8). It was probably made on the stone floor of the courtyard. Peter and "another disciple" (vs. 15)—perhaps John himself—had followed Jesus. John was known to the high priest and his servants and was allowed to enter; and he then brought in Peter. The girl at the door knew John, so she surely knew he was a disciple of Jesus and was with Jesus. Then was not Peter, with John, also a disciple? But Peter quickly denied it! We suppose John stayed as close as he could to Jesus. Peter, trying to appear a stranger, stood with the servants of the high priest and warmed by their fire. Then he "sat with the servants, to see the end" (Matt. 26:58).

"Peter, once in the place of danger, actually courted temptation—not intentionally, but with the idea, probably, that the best way to escape suspicion was to mingle with the crowd . . . . The fact is that he acted his denial of Christ before he spoke it. Nothing lowers Christian morale so much as keeping company with the world *on its level,"* says Dr. Macaulay. That is what Peter did. He warmed himself at the fire of Christ's enemies . . . .

"It can't happen to me!" we think about Peter's sin.

> "So it was with Peter, boastful in his self-sufficiency. 'Though all forsake thee, yet will not I! . . . I am ready to go with thee, both into prison, and to death! . . . If I should die with thee, I will not deny thee in any wise! . . . I will lay down my life for thy sake!' Thus spake Peter instead of giving humble, earnest heed to the loving warnings of His Lord, and arming Himself against the hour of temptation. 'When I am weak, then am I strong,' declared Paul, conscious of his own deficiencies but armed with the whole armour of God. Peter stands as a lasting witness to the converse proposition, 'When I am STRONG, then am I WEAK.' Let him that thinketh he standeth take heed, lest he fall."—J. C. Macaulay.

Peter sat there for some time and denied Jesus again and then, "About the space of one hour after . . ." (Luke 22:59), sitting with the enemies of Christ, he denied Him again.

"Then began he to curse and to swear, saying, I know not the man. And immediately the cock crew. And Peter remembered

the word of Jesus, which said unto him, Before the cock crow, thou shalt deny me thrice. And he went out, and wept bitterly.''—Matt. 26:74,75.

> Return, O wanderer, return,
> And seek an injured Father's face;
> Those warm desires that in thee burn
> Were kindled by reclaiming grace.
>
> Return, O wanderer, return,
> And seek a Father's melting heart;
> His pitying eyes thy grief discern,
> His hand shall heal thine inward smart.
>
> Return, O wanderer, return;
> Thy Saviour bids thy spirit live;
> Go to His bleeding feet, and learn
> How freely Jesus can forgive.
>
> Return, O wanderer, return,
> And wipe away the falling tear;
> 'Tis God who says, "No longer mourn";
> 'Tis mercy's voice invites thee near.
>   —Unknown.

VERSES 28-32:

28 ¶ Then led they Jesus from Cái̇̀-ă-phäs unto the hall of judgment: and it was early; and they themselves went not into the judgment hall, lest they should be defiled; but that they might eat the passover.

29 Pilate then went out unto them, and said, What accusation bring ye against this man?

30 They answered and said unto Him, If he were not a malefactor, we would not have delivered him up unto thee.

31 Then said Pilate unto them, Take ye him, and judge him according to your law. The Jews therefore said unto him, It is not lawful for us to put any man to death:

32 That the saying of Jesus might be fulfilled, which he spake, signifying what death he should die.

Jesus Brought Before Pilate

"Then led they Jesus from Caiaphas unto the hall of judgment" (vs. 28), that is, to the Fortress of Antonia where Pilate had his judgment hall. It was in the eastern part of Jerusalem, north of the Temple area.

We suppose that with Jesus spending some time in the Upper Room at the Last Supper, washing the disciples' feet, and then with the teachings of chapters 14, 15, 16, and with the high priestly prayer in chapter 17, and then to the Garden of Gethsemane where He prayed for a long time, then after He was arrested and taken to Caiaphas and there abused and tried and condemned by the Sanhedrin, it may have been into the early morning hours. And it may be Jesus got no rest at all but was taken immediately to trial, as soon as they could get Pilate to the judgment hall early in the morning.

Of that Fortress of Antonia nothing now remains but what seems to have been "the Pavement" (in the Hebrew, "Gabbatha"). It seemed to have been the ground floor of that fortress, with heavy stones and with some of the stones scored so that horses bringing in chariots would not slip. And there were some cisterns underneath. There is good reason to believe this is the actual pavement on the ground floor of the palace, and it may be the very place where Jesus was tried. Scratched on the stones are the outline of games which the soldiers played. And there are ruts where the chariot wheels ran.

Of that Fortress of Antonia in the judgment hall, Queen Helena, the mother of Emperor Constantine, in 324 came to Jerusalem and tradition says she took the 28 steps of that judgment hall to Rome and that they are the steps now in the Church of the Holy Stairs on which people climb on their knees and are promised certain indulgences. That is only a tradition, with no historical evidence to back it up. But we think the pavement there in Jerusalem is authentic.

"*It was early*" (vs. 28). How early we do not know. From the preceding verse, the time the rooster crowed we would suppose to be before daylight.

The last phrase in verse 28, ". . . *but that they might eat the passover,*" shows that Jesus had not eaten the Passover Supper the night before but a preliminary meal; these Pharisees expected to eat the Passover lamb that night. Jesus would die on the cross while the Passover lambs were being slain, fulfilling the type.

This was the day when passover lambs were being killed, and that evening after sundown these high priests wanted to be purified and to eat the passover lamb, so they dare not defile themselves by entering into the judgment hall. So Pilate went out to them to ask what accusation they brought against Jesus.

Pilate instructed them, *"Take ye him, and judge him according to your law"* (vs. 31). For they had the power to bring people to court, to try them and imprison them. However, they did not have the power to pronounce the death penalty. They did, in fury, stone Stephen and perhaps could have stoned Jesus and gotten away with it, but God had a plan that Jesus must not die by being stoned by the Jews. He must be condemned in a way that would fulfill Psalm 2:2, "Kings of the earth set themselves, and the rulers take counsel together, against the Lord, and against his anointed [literally "his Christ"], saying . . . ." And Peter said in Acts 4:24-28:

"And when they heard that, they lifted up their voice to God with one accord, and said, Lord, thou art God, which hast made heaven, and earth, and the sea, and all that in them is: Who by the mouth of thy servant David hast said, Why did the heathen rage, and the people imagine vain things? The kings of the earth stood up, and the rulers were gathered together against the Lord, and against his Christ. For of a truth against thy holy child Jesus, whom thou hast anointed, both Herod, and Pontius Pilate, with the Gentiles, and the people of Israel, were gathered together, For to do whatsoever thy hand and thy counsel determined before to be done."

Herod and Pontius Pilate and the chief priests all united as rulers to put Jesus to death. And Jesus must die on the cross, for "cursed is every one that hangeth on a tree" (Gal. 3:13). He must have His hands and His feet nailed, for it was promised that "they pierced my hands and my feet" (Ps. 22:16; Zech. 12:10). And when Christ returns to reign and the nation of Jews will have their blindness taken away and they will then see Jesus, they will say, "What are these wounds in thine hands?" (Zech. 13:6). And the things that are foretold in Psalm 22 must be fulfilled and could only be fulfilled as Jesus died on a Roman cross.

So God did not allow Jews to stone Jesus, but He must die according to the Scriptures.

VERSES 33-38:

33 Then Pilate entered into the judgment hall again, and called Jesus, and said unto him, Art thou the King of the Jews?

34 Jesus answered him, Sayest thou this thing of thyself, or did others tell it thee of me?

35 Pilate answered, Am I a Jew? Thine own nation and the chief priests have delivered thee unto me: what hast thou done?

36 Jesus answered, My kingdom is not of this world: if my kingdom were of this world, then would my servants fight, that I should not be delivered to the Jews: but now is my kingdom not from hence.

37 Pilate therefore said unto him, Art thou a king then? Jesus answered, Thou sayest that I am a king. To this end was I born, and for this cause came I into the world, that I should bear witness unto the truth. Every one that is of the truth heareth my voice.

38 Pilate saith unto him, What is truth? And when he had said this, he went out again unto the Jews, and saith unto them, I find in him no fault *at all.*

Jesus, King of the Jews

The Jews had accused Jesus of claiming to be the King of the Jews. Oh, yes, Jesus is to be the King of the Jews, but not at His first coming. So He answered, *"My kingdom is not of this world"* (vs. 36), that is, not of this present world system in competition with the other kingdoms. It is true that Jesus is to be King and sit on David's throne, as the angel plainly announced to Mary in Luke 1:32,33. Isaiah 11 tells how Christ, a Branch from the stump of David, will come to set on David's throne and reign after the rapture, after His return to this earth with saints and angels, after the battle of Armageddon, but it is not of this present world system.

But Pilate pressed the matter, *"Art thou a king then?"* (vs. 37). Jesus could not deny it. But perhaps it was not worth taking time to explain to Pilate all the details of His wonderful millennial reign on this earth. And Pilate someway understood that Jesus, in some sense far beyond that present time, was to be

King. And so over the head of Jesus, on the cross, he had it written in Latin, Hebrew and Greek: "JESUS OF NAZARETH THE KING OF THE JEWS."

Did Pilate understand? Only a little perhaps. He knew that Jesus was innocent of the charges. He knew that it was for envy that they had delivered Him. Pilate felt it wrong to condemn Jesus to die. But Jesus said, "Every one that is of the truth heareth my voice." Wonderful truth that Jesus is King now in our hearts, but one day will come to reign.

> "Jesus shall reign where'ere the sun
> Does his successive journeys run."

One of my songs says:

> Sorrow and sighing shall flee away,
> When Jesus comes to reign.
> Eyes of the blind will be opened then;
> Tongue of the dumb shall sing.
>
> Raptured with Christ, then a honeymoon
> With Him in gloryland.
> With Him to earth, when the angels bring
> Israel to Holy land.
>
> Lame men shall leap as an heart, for then
> All sickness gone, all sore,
> Deserts will bloom and the thorns, and briars
> Shall curse the earth no more!
>
> Kingdoms shall fall, and old Satan's rule
> Shall end with all its tears.
> Righteousness fill all the earth, and peace
> Reign for a thousand years.
>
> We pray, dear Lord, may Thy Kingdom come,
> On earth Thy will be done.
> But we have now all Thy peace and joy
> And in our hearts Thy throne.
>
> Sorrow and sighing shall flee away!
> Flee away that glory day!
> Garden of Eden restored that day!
> When Jesus comes to reign.

Now Pilate would have released Jesus, saying, *"I find in him no fault at all"* (vs. 38).

Pilate tried to get some easy way out. First, he declared Jesus innocent. Then he offered to give them a choice of setting free Barabbas or Jesus, to celebrate the passover. But the crowds wanted Barabbas and cried for Jesus to be killed. Then he offered to scourge Jesus and let Him go. But that would not satisfy them. Then he washed his hands and disclaimed all responsibility. Poor Pilate!

VERSES 39,40:

39 But ye have a custom, that I should release unto you one at the passover: will ye therefore that I release unto you the King of the Jews?

40 Then cried they all again, saying, Not this man, but Barabbas. Now Barabbas was a robber.

Jesus Condemned; Barabbas Released

Matthew 27, Mark 15, and Luke 23 give more details of this release of Barabbas than does John.

I think we may safely say that Pilate, unsaved as he doubtless was, was yet inspired of God to put the question of deciding between Barabbas and Jesus. It was a decision between right and wrong; between the criminal, wicked sinner, and murderer, and the dear sinless Saviour. It is a choice for Heaven or Hell, for God or the Devil. God surely put it in Pilate's heart to do that.

And it must have been God who put it in Pilate's heart to question, "What shall I do then with Jesus which is called Christ?" (Matt. 27:22). Certainly God inspired Matthew to write it down. God wants every man to face Jesus Christ. He is the unavoidable Saviour.

And every sinner who turns down Christ is accepting some Barabbas. It may be some particular sin. It may be just your own self-will, not wanting to surrender to anybody. It may be heeding the specific influence of Satan.

Always it is Jesus or Barabbas.

John 19

THEN Pilate therefore took Jesus, and scourged *him.* 2 And the soldiers platted a crown of thorns, and put *it* on his head, and they put on him a purple robe, 3 And said, Hail, King of the Jews! and they smote him with their hands.

Keep the Attention on Jesus, Not Others Present

Only God could give the account of the crucifixion of Jesus as it is so marvelously given in the Gospels. The language is so temperate, so mild, so exact, with no attempt to move the feelings, yet it is the most profoundly moving story that any human ear ever heard, or any eye ever read.

No attempt is made in the gospel story to show the terrible wickedness of any particular heart. For instance, Barabbas is simply called a robber by John, while Mark and Luke say that he was a murderer but in simple terms, without elaboration.

These gospel accounts do not dwell at length on the shameful cowardice of Peter, the compromising insincerity of Pilate, the brutality of the soldiers, the horrible frenzy of the mob, nor the satanic hate of the scribes and Pharisees! No, in all this account, Jesus must remain the central figure. He moves through these events as only God could move so that we, when we read it, must say with the centurion, "Truly this was the Son of God!"

God had no reason to arouse our indignation against individuals as we pursue this terrible story.

In the account of the passion of Christ, from the Garden of Gethsemane to His death on the cross, there is no word of praise for any man, and in the light of these gospel accounts, every man and woman shows up to be what they are—painful, terrible sinners, as compared with the sinless and perfect Lamb of God.

Elsewhere in the Gospel good words have been said about Peter, about John, about Mary Magdalene and Mary, the sister of Lazarus, etc.—not here. Surely it must have been God's plan to show us, in the account of the crucifixion, the attitude of an entire race of sin-cursed and guilty beings, taking part in the condemnation and crucifixion of God's Son, our Saviour. We may be sure that in the sight of God, every man who has not accepted Christ as his Saviour is as guilty as this mob who chose Barabbas instead of Jesus; as guilty as Pilate who scourged and condemned Him; as guilty as the soldiers who drove the nails into His hands and the spear into His side, as guilty as the mob, soldiers and all, who bruised Him, blindfolded Him, crowned Him with thorns, spit in His dear face and mocked Him while He died. No honest heart can read the story of the crucifixion of Jesus without thinking far less of himself and much more of the Lord Jesus.

Later on, in preaching to these wicked people to bring about their conviction and conversion, Peter, Stephen and others denounced in startling words their shameful sin. See Acts 2:22,23; 3:14, 15; 4:10-12; 5:29-33; 7:51-54.

Lest there should be some bitterness in our hearts against all these wicked men as individuals, the Lord took pains to remind us of the prayer of Jesus when He was first crucified: "Father, forgive them; for they know not what they do." It does not please God for us to accuse the Jewish race of crucifying Jesus. They were no more guilty of that than were the Gentiles, and those individuals were no more guilty than every other individual in the world for whom Christ died.

Christ Was "Bruised for Our Iniquities"

We are told that Pilate scourged Jesus (vs. 1). Probably he had a soldier take the Roman cat-o'-nine-tails (or scourge), a whip with nine straps of leather and each one at the end fastened with a bit of metal or stone. Sometimes people died under the scourging.

Then Jesus was crowned with thorns.

I think that in the matter of Christ's trial and crucifixion there are a number of signs as to how He took on Himself all our infirmities, our sins, our punishment.

He was scourged. Must not the sinner be punished and whipped for his sins?

He was crowned with thorns. And we remember that God cursed the ground for man's sake and it brings forth thorns and briars. Oh, the dear Lord Jesus must have on Him the curse on all mankind.

He is to be nailed to a tree, for the law said, "Cursed is every one that hangeth on a tree" (Gal. 3:13).

On the cross He will cry out, "I thirst" (vs. 28). We remember the dissatisfaction and the thirst that sin brings into a world, with no answer for man's need, no peace for man's trouble, no comfort for man's wicked heart. As Jesus said to the woman at the well in Sychar, "Whosoever drinketh of this water shall thirst again." Yes, and so it is with all the waters of this world and all the natural comforts and satisfactions. "Even in laughter the heart is sorrowful; and the end of that mirth is heaviness," says Proverbs 14:13.

Oh, men make "cisterns, broken cisterns, that can hold no water" (Jer. 2:13). This world has "clouds and wind without rain" (Prov. 25:14). So Jesus, on the cross, will thirst.

The physical weakness of Jesus during this time is a reminder of how all mankind is beaten down with the results of sin, with the erosion of physical strength that goes with the erosion of character. Once some men lived over eight hundred years. Now man is cut down in the time he lives. Jesus, under constant pressure, then going all night without sleep, then the agony of the Garden when He sweat bloody sweat, was *"sorrowful even unto death."* He must be strengthened by an angel to be able to go on until tomorrow. That night we think He had no rest and at early morning He was taken before Pilate. They laid a cross on Him, though there is some evidence He must have fainted under that cross, and another man took it for Him.

And all the mockery on the cross surely must be some kind of picture of the mockery this world brings to all the hopes and aims of unregenerate, wicked men who go on in sin. So, we may say that Jesus took on Himself our infirmities and bore our punishments. And so with His stripes we are healed and all our iniquities are laid on Him.

The soldiers *"put on him a purple robe"* (vs. 2). A purple robe put over the scourged back, and the breaking heart, and out the Way of Sorrows to the cross! So goes the glory and the grandeur of this world!

Now we learn from Luke 23:5-15 that when His accusers said that Jesus was from the province of Galilee, Pilate thought here was a way he could escape the responsibility of putting Jesus to death. Why, King Herod ruled in the province of Galilee and he was in town today! So Pilate sent Jesus into the palace to see Herod. Herod had heard much of Jesus and wanted to see a miracle. He asked Him many questions, but Jesus "answered him nothing. And the chief priests and scribes stood and vehemently accused him. And Herod with his men of war set him at nought, and mocked him, and arrayed him in a gorgeous robe, and sent him again to Pilate" (Luke 23:9-11). Now Pilate has Jesus on his hands again.

Some more details are given about the abuse Jesus suffered in Matthew 27:26-31:

"Then released he Barabbas unto them: and when he had scourged Jesus, he delivered him to be crucified. Then the soldiers of the governor took Jesus into the common hall, and gathered unto him the whole band of soldiers. And they stripped him, and put on him a scarlet robe. And when they had platted a crown of thorns, they put it upon his head, and a reed in his right hand: and they bowed the knee before him, and mocked him, saying, Hail, King of the Jews! And they spit upon him, and took the reed, and smote him on the head. And after that they had mocked him, they took the robe off from him, and put his own raiment on him, and led him away to crucify him."

So the beating and the abuse of Jesus was carried on first by the servants and soldiers of the high priests when he was taken to the high priest's palace and condemned (Matt. 26:66-68).

Then, when He was brought before Herod, "Herod with his men of war set him at nought, and mocked him, and arrayed him in a gorgeous robe and sent him again to Pilate" (Luke 23:11). Then the soldiers with Pilate scourged Jesus and put on Him a crown of thorns, a purple robe and smote Him with their hands. The insane hate of the people, the soldiers and the mob of people around Jesus at the time of His arrest, trial and crucifixion is indicated by Isaiah 50:6. In prophecy Jesus said, "I gave my back to the smiters, and my cheeks to them that plucked off the hair: I hid not my face from shame and spitting."

In Psalm 22:13 it foretells, "They gaped upon me with their mouths, as a ravening and a roaring lion." Does that mean that they actually bit the Saviour as they beat Him about the head and face and pressed upon the crown of thorns and took time to enjoy the plucking out of His beard? We think so. It is said about those who stoned and killed Stephen, "they gnashed on him with their teeth." And Isaiah 52:14 foretold about Jesus, "As many were astonied at thee: his visage was so marred more than any man, and his form more than the sons of men." His face and head were so swollen, bruised and bloody, He hardly looked like a man. Ah, this is the only time that wicked man ever got to beat the face of God and spit upon Him and abuse Him and kill God! That is what they meant in their hatred of Jesus and it pictures this whole wicked world of Christ-rejecting sinners and Jesus bearing our sins and taking our punishment.

VERSES 4-9:

4 Pilate therefore went forth again, and saith unto them, Behold, I bring him forth to you, that ye may know that I find no fault in him.

5 Then came Jesus forth, wearing the crown of thorns, and the purple robe. And *Pilate* saith unto them, Behold the man!

6 When the chief priests therefore and officers saw him, they cried out, saying, Crucify *him*, crucify *him*. Pilate saith unto them, Take ye him, and crucify *him:* for I find no fault in him.

7 The Jews answered him, We have a law, and ¹by our law he ought to die, because he made himself the Son of God.

8 ¶ When Pilate therefore heard that saying, he was the more afraid;

9 And went again into the judgment hall, and saith unto Jesus, Whence art thou? But Jesus gave him no answer.

"Behold the Man!"

"Behold the man!" (vs. 5). Dr. Ironside says: "One would have thought the sight of that patient, suffering One standing there with the thorny crown pressed on His brow and the purple robe on Him and with a reed in His hand and blood pouring down His face would have been enough to soften the hardest heart and break down the strongest opposition. But there is that in the heart of the natural man which leads him to hate that which is holy, to hate perfect righteousness."

Pilate is awed. He knows Jesus is innocent but He claimed to be the Son of God, Pilate hears! He is called "King of the Jews," and His kingdom is "not of this world." Troubled Pilate had said, "What is truth?" And Pilate's wife had sent him word. She had slept after Jewish leaders insisted that Pilate come so early to the judgment hall; now she sent word to Pilate, "Have thou nothing to do with that just man: for I have suffered many things this day in a dream because of him" (Matt. 27:19).

So Pilate presents Jesus who is wearing a crown of thorns and a scarlet robe and Pilate says to the people, *"Behold the man!"* (vs. 5). We do not know all that was in Pilate's heart. Did any man ever before face such a situation as Pilate—to condemn the Son of God to death! Pilate will allow them to have Jesus crucified, but he insists He is innocent. They defend themselves guiltily, angry as they were in their hate. They must have felt their evidence was weak and the charges indefensible. So they said, *"We have a law, and by our law he ought to die, because he made himself the Son of God"* (vs. 7). We remember how those men who brought the adulterous woman to Jesus hoping He would say they should stone her, slipped guiltily away, their conscience accusing them.

We know how Judas the traitor, feeling so guilty, threw down the bribe money on the floor of the Temple and cried out, "I have betrayed the innocent blood," and went out and hanged himself! Oh, the torment of a soul which passes over all the bounds of hope in sin, betrayal, rejection, and yet knows he is such a sinner! The people must have felt some of that now.

Pilate was afraid. Jesus claimed to be the Son of God. After going out to the Jews who would not come into the judgment hall because this was the day for the killing of the passover, preliminary day of the passover feast, he returned to ask Jesus, *"Whence art thou?"* (vs. 9).

VERSES 10,11:

10 Then saith Pilate unto him, Speakest thou not unto me? knowest thou not that I have power to crucify thee, and have power to release thee? 11 Jesus answered, Thou couldest have no power *at all* against me, except it were given thee from above: therefore he that delivered me unto thee hath the greater sin.

Jesus Chose to Die

The hate of the Jewish leaders was wicked. Their treachery and murder were inexcusable. Judas was unsaved, covetous, moved by Satan to betray Jesus. Pilate was a compromiser, going along with the crowd he knew were wrong and did it in order to save his job and the favor of men. But God was using wicked men to do what God had planned "by the determinate counsel and foreknowledge of God" (Acts 2:23). God maketh the wrath of men to praise Him. No man took His life from Him. He laid it down Himself (John 10:18). On the cross He "gave up the ghost" at His own time and choice.

VERSES 12-16:

12 And from thenceforth Pilate sought to release him: but the Jews cried out, saying, If thou let this man go, thou art not Cæsar's friend: whosoever maketh himself a king speaketh against Cæsar.

13 ¶ When Pilate therefore heard that saying, he brought Jesus forth, and sat down in the judgment seat in a place that is called the Pavement, but in the Hebrew, Găb´-bă-thă.

14 And it was the preparation of the passover, and about the sixth hour: and he saith unto the Jews, Behold your King!

15 But they cried out, Away with *him*, away with *him*, crucify him. Pilate saith unto them, Shall I crucify your King? The chief priests answered, We have no king but Cæsar.

16 Then delivered he him therefore unto them to be crucified. And they took Jesus, and led *him* away.

"No King but Caesar"

This crowd of Jews did not have any special love for Caesar. But they did not want things disrupted so they would lose their position and their income and their prestige. So in order to condemn Jesus they insisted, "We have no king but Caesar." Here we find, as the Jews found, Pilate's weakness. He had no fear Jesus would seize the reins of government. He knew Jesus was no rebel against Rome. In fact, Jesus had said, "Render therefore unto Caesar the things which be Caesar's . . ." (Luke 20:25). Jesus would know that "the powers that be are ordained of God" and the ruler "is the minister of God to thee for good" (Rom. 13:1-4).

But Pilate saw that Caesar at Rome might be influenced by these rabid Jews if they protested that Pilate favored a rebel-king seeking a kingdom. Judaea had been a kingdom under Herod the Great; Pilate was now only a governor of the province—so to please these troublesome Jews and to avoid trouble at Rome, he consented for Jesus to be crucified. But he refused to take the blame himself. He washed his hands before the people and said, "I am innocent of the blood of this just person: see ye to it. Then answered all the people, and said, His blood be on us, and on our children" (Matt. 27:24,25).

What will *you* do with Jesus?
Neutral you cannot be!
Some day your heart will be asking—
"What will He do with me?"

"And it was the preparation of the passover, and about the sixth hour" (vs. 14). The sixth hour? The Gospel of John was written about the year A. D. 90 and Jerusalem had been destroyed and the Jews scattered to the world for many years without any center of culture and religion at Jerusalem. John uses the Roman way of counting time, we suppose, counting from midnight. So the sixth hour would be in the early morning. ". . . and it was early" (John 18:28). Mark 15:25 says, "And it was the third hour, and they crucified him," that is, it was about nine o'clock in the morning. And Luke 23:44 says at midday, "And it was about the sixth hour . . . ." But Matthew, Mark and Luke

had all been written many years before the Gospel of John, when the Jewish plan was still in vogue, counting from sunrise through the day. Matthew 27:45,46,50 says, "Now from the sixth hour there was darkness over all the land unto the ninth hour. And about the ninth hour Jesus cried with a loud voice . . . yielded up the ghost."

So according to the Roman way of marking time, here in verse 14 Jesus was before Pilate about six'clock in the morning. He was crucified, then, about nine o'clock. At noon, the sun quit shining, the darkness enveloped the earth until three o'clock in the afternoon. Soon then Jesus died after some six hours on the cross.

We suppose the mockery of the crowd, the abuse by the soldiers, perhaps the interlude when Jesus was taken before Herod and interrogated and abused, then the trip up to Calvary, was after six o'clock and then He would be crucified about nine o'clock.

Note that Pilate's judgment seat was in *"a place that is called the Pavement, but in Hebrew, Gabbatha"* (vs. 13). What appears to be that same Pavement still exists in Jerusalem, all that is left of the great Fortress of Antonia. It has the ruts made by chariot wheels; the stones are scored by horses that pulled the chariots; and it seems to be one of the few authentic remnants of the old Jerusalem of Christ's time.

VERSES 17-22:

17 And he bearing his cross went forth into a place called *the place* of a skull, which is called in the Hebrew Golgotha:

18 Where they crucified him, and two other with him, on either side one, and Jesus in the midst.

19 ¶ And Pilate wrote a title, and put *it* on the cross. And the writing was, JESUS OF NAZARETH THE KING OF THE JEWS.

20 This title then read many of the Jews: for the place where Jesus was crucified was nigh to the city: and it was written in Hebrew, *and* Greek, *and* Latin.

21 Then said the chief priests of the Jews to Pilate, Write not, The King of the Jews; but that he said, I am King of the Jews.

22 Pilate answered, What I have written I have written.

The Crucifixion of the Lord Jesus

Dr. Scofield gives the order of events from the crucifixion day as follows:

> A comparison of the narratives gives the following order of events on the crucifixion day: (1) Early in the morning Jesus is brought before Caiaphas and the Sanhedrin. He is condemned and mocked (Mt. 26. 57-68; Mk. 14. 55-65; Lk. 22. 63-71; John 18. 19-24). (2) The Sanhedrin lead Jesus to Pilate (Mt. 27.1,2, 11-14; Mk. 15. 1-5; Lk. 23. 1-5; John 18. 28-38). (3) Pilate sends Jesus to Herod (Lk. 23. 6-12; John 19.4). (4) Jesus is again brought before Pilate, who releases Barabbas and delivers Jesus to be crucified (Mt. 27. 15-26; Mk. 15. 6-15; Lk. 23. 13-25; John 18. 39,40; 19. 4-16). (5) Jesus is crowned with thorns, and mocked (Mt. 27. 26-30; Mk. 15. 15-20; John 19. 1-3). (6) Suicide of Judas (Mt. 27. 3-10). (7) Led forth to be crucified, the cross is laid upon Simon: Jesus discourses to the women (Mt. 27.31,32; Mk. 15. 20-23; Lk. 23.26-33; John 19.16,17). For the order of events at the crucifixion see Mt. 27.33, note.

Jesus left the judgment hall "bearing his cross" (vs. 17). That is all of the story that is told here. But Matthew 27:32 tells us, "And as they came out, they found a man of Cyrene, Simon by name: him they compelled to bear his cross." Mark 15:21 tells us this was "Simon a Cyrenian . . . the father of Alexander and Rufus."

We suppose that Jesus, weakened by the beating, the suffering, the sleeplessness, and the awful stresses and strains of bearing our sins and facing death, may have fainted or been unable to bear the cross, so they conscripted this Simon to bear it. Or, it may be that, in pity for Jesus' weakness, they insisted the other man bear the cross. We do not know more about Simon, but he has become immortal by the simple fact that on him was given the great honor of bearing after Jesus the cross on which the Saviour was to die.

Here Luke tells that on the way to the crucifixion a great company of people followed Him. When women wailed and lamented, He turned to them and said:

"Daughters of Jerusalem, weep not for me, but weep for yourselves, and for your children. For, behold, the days are coming, in the which they shall say, Blessed are the barren, and the wombs that never bare, and the paps which never gave suck. Then shall they begin to say to the mountains, Fall on us; and to the hills, Cover us. For if they do these things in a green tree, what shall be done in the dry?"—Luke 23:28-31.

Jesus knew that after denying and crucifying Him, these Jews would go on in sin, would rebel against Rome, the city would be destroyed and the Jews scattered all over the world; and when they said to Pilate, "His blood be on us, and on our children," Jews would be scattered and terribly persecuted through the centuries. Jesus had said, "When ye shall see Jerusalem compassed with armies, then know that the desolation thereof is nigh" (Luke 21:20). When He wept over Jerusalem He said, "Behold, your house is left unto you desolate" (Luke 13:35). The Temple will be destroyed.

Surely we should be reminded even now that Jews, scattered all over the world, are still blinded to the Gospel. The sin that caused them to be scattered is still their sin. They have not repented. The regathering to Palestine of a few Zionist Jews by force, to take other people's property and to establish a nation Israel again, is not the regathering foretold in the Bible when every Jew in the world will be regathered and circumcised in heart after Christ returns (Deut. 30:1-6). Then will come the time when the rebels will be purged out of Israel in the wilderness of wanderings as Ezekiel 20:36-38 tells us. Then will the Jews see the Saviour, see the wounds in His hands and be converted. Then ". . . all Israel shall be saved" (Rom. 11:26). I am saying that those Jews who followed Jesus weeping should have wept over the awful punishment coming on the nation Israel for their rejection of Christ.

He *"went forth into a place called the place of a skull, which is called in the Hebrew Golgotha"* (vs. 17). Luke 23:33 calls it Calvary. The place "was nigh to the city." Hebrews 13 says it was "without the camp" and "without the gate."

Our Catholic friends think that the Church of the Holy Sepulchre within the city is the place covering both the hill Calvary and the garden for the burial of Jesus and where He rose from the dead. Of course, that is based only on a very frail tradition.

Queen Helena, the mother of Emperor Constantine, came to Palestine in the year 324, and she selected three places where she had churches built. In Bethlehem there was no house, we suppose, suitable, so she selected a cave as the birthplace of the Saviour. The Bible does not mention that He was born in a cave. And when the wise men came, they found the star rested "over [the house] where the young child was" (Matt. 2:9,11). But more than three hundred years after the event and with the whole country devastated by wars again and again and Jews scattered over all the world, it is unlikely that anybody would know exactly where the Saviour was born or that the stable where He was born would remain.

In Galilee she selected a place where she thought the angel announced to Mary the coming birth of the Saviour. And a cave was selected where Mary and Joseph were supposed to have lived and where Joseph carried on his carpenter work. Again, it is doubtful that anyone would know where that was.

She selected then in Jerusalem the place for the crucifixion and burial.

We remember that Jerusalem was utterly destroyed in A. D.

70, and as Jesus had said, not one stone was left on another (Matt. 24:2). The siege was terrible. Many thousands died, then tens of thousands of Jews were sold into slavery. I think Josephus said that every tree within miles that could be made into a cross, was made into a cross to crucify Jews. They were scattered all over the world. There was nobody left to remember just where Jesus was crucified, and the whole area was destroyed.

Again Jerusalem was utterly destroyed in the year 135 and we are told it was so desolate and so utterly waste that a team of oxen plowed a furrow across the remains of the city.

So Queen Helena could not well have known the exact place which no one had identified for about three hundred years.

We believe that God did not want us to know for certain about the places where the crucifixion and burial took place lest we should worship the places. There is a sad tendency of human hearts to pay more attention to relics, things and incidentals than to spiritual truth.

But when General Chinese Gordon, an English general, was stationed in Jerusalem, he was not satisfied with the Church of the Holy Sepulchre. It did not seem to represent the place of the crucifixion and burial. The tomb there was artificially made. It was not the real tomb in which Jesus was buried. It was not much of a hill under that church. Besides, it was within the city. The Catholics reply that the wall of the city at one time left this outside. At any rate, Gordon, meditating, looked for some place outside the city that might have been called the Place of the Skull.

He saw a place just outside the city on the north which seemed to fit. The hill, Mount Moriah, is a ridge which runs through Jerusalem. At one end of it was the site of Solomon's Temple and on through the city and just outside the wall centuries before they had cut a valley through this Mount Moriah by the city wall, and now that left a jagged cliff-like face, and there were holes that looked like eye sockets and with the sun shining a certain way, it looked somewhat like a skull. That might be the place, he thought. But, if so, there would be a garden nearby, and a tomb.

They investigated further. They found a little vale filled with debris. As they dug into it, here was a tomb cut out of the rock. There were cisterns. There was a wine press. There was much evidence there had been a garden. He thought this must be the place. So that hill is now called "Gordon's Calvary." The Garden Tomb is below it. In every respect, as far as we know, it fits the circumstances, and we think it probably is the very tomb of Jesus.

Scrapings were taken from the floor of that tomb cut back into the rock and sent to chemists in England. They declared nobody had decayed in that tomb.

Let us be content that no one can know for sure, but let us rejoice that there is something that pictures and represents at least the burial and resurrection place of our Lord Jesus.

Pilate wrote a title in Latin, Hebrew and Greek. Not all the words are given here but adding them together from the four Gospels we find the title was, *"This is Jesus of Nazareth, the King of the Jews"* (vs. 19).

The chief priests were offended (vs. 21). They did not like anybody to recognize Jesus as King of the Jews. They insisted, "Put it down that as a blasphemer He claimed that He was King of the Jews." No, Pilate said, *"What I have written I have written"* (vs. 22). He would not change it. It was written in Hebrew, Greek and Latin. In the first place in Hebrew, because that represented the Jewish nation. We think now they spoke the Aramaic language, but the learned among them spoke Hebrew. It was written in Greek, we think the common *koine* Greek spoken now throughout the Roman Empire, as it had spread so rapidly during the Greek empire before it, and so, for common people everywhere. And it was written in Latin, representing Rome itself and the kingdoms of the world. Dr. Ironside said: ". . . in Hebrew, the language of religion; in Greek, the language of culture; in Latin, the language of government."

———————

VERSES 23,24:

23 ¶ Then the soldiers, when they had crucified Jesus, took his garments, and made four parts, to every soldier a part; and also *his* coat: now the coat was without seam, woven from the top throughout.

24 They said therefore among themselves, Let us not rend it, but cast lots for it, whose it shall be: that the scripture might be fulfilled, which saith, They parted my raiment among them, and for my vesture they did cast lots. These things therefore the soldiers did.

The Seamless Garment!

Those who were crucified would not need their clothes any more, so the soldiers ordinarily took them for themselves. We suppose the Lord Jesus was stripped naked as were the others crucified there. The nakedness would represent poor, wicked mankind with nothing to cover our sinful natures, for Jesus was taking the place of sinners. It was foretold in Psalm 22:18, "They part my garments among them, and cast lots upon my vesture."

But one of the garments of Jesus was a seamless garment, *"woven from the top throughout"* (vs. 23). It was not patched nor sewed together; it was made perfect, with one weaving, beautifully done by some loving hands. And what did it represent? The seamless righteousness of the Lord Jesus. Now He lays aside this garment so sinners everywhere can wear it. Jesus becomes officially a sinner (though not really a sinner) so that we might become officially righteous, recognized as righteous for Jesus' sake.

Isaiah 61:10 says:

"I will greatly rejoice in the Lord, my soul shall be joyful in my God; for he hath clothed me with the garments of salvation, he hath covered me with the robe of righteousness, as a bridegroom decketh himself with ornaments, and as a bride adorneth herself with her jewels."

Oh, those who trust Christ have the garments of salvation! Jesus told about a king who made a marriage for his son and invited everybody, bad and good.

"And when the king came in to see the guests, he saw there a man which had not on a wedding garment: And he saith unto him, Friend, how camest thou in hither not having a wedding garment? And he was speechless."—Matt. 22:11,12.

The man was cast out of the wedding because he did not have on the wedding garment. And so no sinner can enter into the wedding supper of Christ who does not have on the white robe of Christ's righteousness.

We are reminded of Paul's inspired teaching in Romans 10. How many are like the Jews who ". . . being ignorant of God's righteousness, and going about to establish their own righteousness, have not submitted themselves unto the righteousness of God" (Rom. 10:3). Ah, but Christ is our righteousness! And, thank God, His righteousness covers all our guilty nakedness, and we are clothed with the garments of salvation when we trust Christ.

I wonder if that soldier, who wore away that seamless garment that day after gambling for it, knew what was involved, what that garment pictured? "Think of that coat falling to a pagan Roman soldier who had taken part in the crucifixion of our Lord! Surely one must recognize in this a picture of the sinner being clothed with the spotless righteousness of Christ," says Dr. Macaulay. "For God hath made him to be sin for us, who knew no sin, that we might be made the righteousness of God in him."

A great novel was written on *The Robe* by Lloyd Douglas, referring to this garment of Jesus.

VERSES 25-30:

25 ¶ Now there stood by the cross of Jesus his mother, and his mother's sister, Mary the *wife* of Clē-ŏ-phăs, and Mary Magdalene.

26 When Jesus therefore saw his mother, and the disciple standing by, whom he loved, he saith unto his mother, Woman, behold thy son!

27 Then saith he to the disciple, Behold thy mother! And from that hour that disciple took her unto his own *home*.

28 ¶ After this, Jesus knowing that all things were now accomplished, that the scripture might be fulfilled, saith, I thirst.

29 Now there was set a vessel full of vinegar: and they filled a ·spunge with vinegar, and put *it* upon hyssop, and put *it* to his mouth.

30 When Jesus therefore had received the vinegar, he said, It is finished: and he bowed his head, and gave up the ghost.

Those by the Cross

I sometimes preach on the text in Matthew 27:36, "And sitting down they watched him there," and the theme is about those around the cross watching Jesus die. I found some years after I had been preaching that Dr. B. H. Carroll had a sermon on a similar theme. Those watching Jesus were:

I. Christians at the Cross.

1. There were the inner circle, His mother, Mary Magdalene and John.

2. There were the secret disciples, Joseph of Arimathaea and Nicodemus.

3. There were the quitters who left Jesus when things were

hard: "Then all the disciples forsook him and fled."

4. There was the backslider Peter. Although the Gospels do not tell us he was there at the cross, I Peter 5:1 tells us he was "a witness of the sufferings of Christ."

II. Lost Sinners at the Cross Included:

1. The scribes and Pharisees, religious but lost.

2. Pilate, who kept his job but lost his soul.

3. The crude, rough soldiers, thoughtless and wicked, but condemned.

4. The mob of people following their leaders in demanding the crucifixion.

5. The centurion, almost saved, convinced that Jesus is the Son of God, but we do not know that he was saved.

6. The poor thief on the cross who trusted Christ and was saved according to Luke 23:39-43.

How suitable it is that here by the cross stands Mary, the mother of Jesus. Catholics have made her too prominent. She was never mentioned in the New Testament after Acts 1:14 and no one gave her any special reverence, no one asked her to pray for them. She was not called the mother of God, the Bible says nothing about her being immaculately conceived, etc. All that is contrary to the Bible. But Mary was a good woman. Let us say that she stood for all the purest and best of womanhood. But beside her was Mary Magdalene out of whom Jesus had cast seven devils. Oh, by the cross of Jesus the ground is very level; the vilest sinners as well as the tenderest child can come to be saved the same.

And here was the mother's sister, strangely, also called Mary. She was the wife of Cleophas. And here was John. These are near the cross.

Who will take care of Jesus' mother? The younger sons of Mary, half-brothers of Jesus, were not even saved as far as we know up to this time (John 7:5). Their names were James, Joses, Simon and Judas (Matt. 13:55). These will be converted and join in a pre-Pentecostal prayer meeting (Acts 1:14). There were sisters, also, but these were not saved. They were all younger than the thirty-three years of Jesus. Perhaps they had no good way to care for their mother.

So Jesus turns her care to His beloved disciple, John. It is said that John lived in Ephesus in his old age and he kept Mary there until she died.

On the cross Jesus said to Mary, *"Woman, behold thy son!"* (vs. 26). And to John He said, *"Behold thy mother! And from that hour that disciple took her unto his own home"* (vs. 27). What a comfort that somebody Jesus could rely upon took care of His mother!

"After this, Jesus knowing that all things were now accomplished, that the scripture might be fulfilled, saith, I thirst."—Vs. 28.

Already Jesus had said a final good-by to His mother, committing her to the care of the beloved disciple. After this, Jesus, knowing that all things were now accomplished, that the Scripture might be fulfilled, said, "I thirst."

He was offered vinegar mingled with gall to drink and refused it (Matt. 27:34). But in the act of death He received the vinegar. "I THIRST!" was the cry of the Saviour before He died for the sins of all mankind, on the cruel cross.

All things are now accomplished! But that the Scripture may be fulfilled and that all mankind may know the torment of His sorrow, He cries out, "I thirst!" This thirst is foretold in Psalm

22:15: "My strength is dried up like a potsherd; and my tongue cleaveth to my jaws; and thou hast brought me into the dust of death." His mouth is dry. His tongue swells and sticks to His jaws. Thirst is a horrible thing. But even in His torment and His thirst the Saviour thinks of the Scripture and is set on fulfilling it. All must know that He is bearing in His own body the torments of the damned, the wages of sin for all the world, and so He cries, "I thirst!" Even in His death, Jesus pleases not Himself but the Father, and the Scripture is fulfilled.

We know, of course, that the Saviour did not expect water on the cross. When He set His face toward Calvary to die for the sins of the world, He well knew what He was giving up. He never sought to dodge it. No, no! His cry, "I thirst," is meant only to show His agony and to cause us to realize what He suffered for us. He knew He would be given vinegar and gall to torment Him further, to burn His mouth and crack His lips—the added insult from those who hated Him without a cause. The holy thirst of Jesus He could have satisfied in a moment, but He did not. For our sakes, He did not! The thirst of the Lord Jesus on the cross was my thirst. He suffered what I should have suffered. His torments were intended rightfully for me. They who offered the one altogether lovely the vinegar and gall should have given that bitter sponge to me. Let us rejoice that the holy thirst of Jesus purchased us the right to drink and drink and never thirst again.

The seven sayings of Jesus on the cross are sometimes listed as follows:

(1) "Father, forgive them; for they know not what they do" (Luke 23:34).

(2) "Woman, behold thy son! Then saith he to the disciple, Behold thy mother!" (19:26,27).

(3) "To day shalt thou be with me in paradise"—His words to the dying thief (Luke 23:43).

(4) "I thirst" (19:28).

(5) "My God, my God, why hast thou forsaken me?" (Matt. 27:46).

(6) "It is finished" (19:30).

⑦ "Father, into thy hands I commend my spirit" (Luke 23:46).

"It Is Finished" (Vs. 30)

1. The sufferings of Christ are finished. Praise the Lord!

2. The atonement is finished. Sin is paid for. Praise the Lord! "There remaineth no more sacrifice for sins," Hebrews 10:26 tells us. Now no priest's offering mass can add one fraction of an ounce to the value of the atoning blood of Jesus. Thank God, the sins of the world are paid for! "He is the propitiation for our sins: and not for our's only, but also for the sins of the whole world" (I John 2:2).

3. Finished, too, are the ceremonial laws that pointed toward Christ's coming. Jesus said, ". . . one jot or one tittle shall in no wise pass from the law, till all be fulfilled" (Matt. 5:18). But now there need be no more lambs offered as sacrifice. Christ, the Lamb of God, has died.

Now there need be no more Jewish Sabbath picturing Heaven earned by good works; that plan has failed. Now those who have ceased from their own works have entered into rest. We already have a Sabbath in our hearts when we trust Jesus, and that is pictured by that great high Sabbath day when the passover lamb was eaten (Exod. 12:14). There is not a single command in the New Testament to keep the Sabbath. Sabbath-breaking is not even mentioned in the New Testament. That was part of the ceremonial law as Colossians 2:16,17 plainly tells us.

Now there is no more requirement for circumcision. Now what God wants is circumcision of the heart which is pictured by the fleshly circumcision.

Now there is no more human priesthood except that all the saved are priests and pray for one another. But now no robed priest is needed to come to forgive sins. We have a High Priest forever interceding for us. It is finished!

———

VERSES 31-37:

31 The Jews therefore, because it was the preparation, that the bodies should not remain upon the cross on the sabbath day, (for that sabbath day was an high day,) besought Pilate that their legs might be broken, and *that* they might be taken away.

32 Then came the soldiers, and brake the legs of the first, and of the other which was crucified with him.

33 But when they came to Jesus, and saw that he was dead already, they brake not his legs:

34 But one of the soldiers with a spear pierced his side, and forthwith came there out blood and water.

35 And he that saw *it* bare record, and his record is true: and he knoweth that he saith true, that ye might believe.

36 For these things were done, that the scripture should be fulfilled, A bone of him shall not be broken.

37 And again another scripture saith, They shall look on him whom they pierced.

A Bone of Him Not Broken

The Sabbath was approaching; it would begin at sundown. So the Jews want Jesus and the two thieves removed from the cross before sundown. That Sabbath was not the regular weekly Sabbath but *"an high day,"* that is, an annual Sabbath. It is the Sabbath of Exodus 12:16, the day of the passover supper and the first day of the feast of unleavened bread, a day of "an holy convocation" and "no manner of work shall be done in them"— on the first day and the seventh day of this feast of unleavened bread. That was a high annual Sabbath.

We believe that Jesus was crucified on Wednesday. He must remain in the grave through Thursday, Friday and Saturday for He was to be there "three days and three nights." And, as Dr. R. A. Torrey said, "That must include at least seventy-two hours, and it could include more." So we believe Jesus was buried after being washed and anointed, and after the tomb was slightly enlarged to provide for the taller body of Jesus, and after the fine linen was bought and the spices and Jesus was wrapped in that. It must by then have been into the night of Thursday, after sundown, when He was buried. Then sometime Saturday night He arose. He arose on the first day of the week, so He was in the grave Thursday, Friday and Saturday, we believe.

Now the Jews planned *"that their legs might be broken"* (vs. 31). Oh, but if they should break the legs of Jesus, it would ruin all the plan of God. Remember that the saving Gospel is that "Christ died for our sins according to the scriptures; And that he was buried, and that he rose again the third day according to the scriptures" (I Cor. 15:3,4). And the Scriptures had the plain command about the passover lamb, picturing Christ our Passover, that "a bone of him shall not be broken" (Exod. 12:46; Num. 9:12; Ps. 34:20). Now for fifteen hundred years the Jews had understood that the passover lamb must be roasted whole with fire, it must not have a bone broken. That pictured Jesus our Passover Lamb, so the Jews must not be allowed to break the bones of Jesus. And when they came to Him, they found He was dead already (vs. 33).

And now a soldier, doubtless not thinking that he was fulfilling the Scriptures, took a spear and pierced the side of Jesus and *"forthwith came there out blood and water"* (vs. 34). It is the blood that makes an atonement for our souls, and so the Lord must make it obvious here.

Once I was preaching on the blood of Christ and in my heart the Lord seemed to rebuke me. "Did not you promise Me that when you came to Scripture, you would preach it all exactly like it is, the best you knew? Then why is it you preach on the blood when I said, 'blood and water'?"

I penitently said, "Lord, if You will show me what the water means, I will preach that, too."

I think that here it must mean the work of the Holy Spirit. Titus 3:5 says, "Not by works of righteousness which we have done, but according to his mercy he saved us, by the washing of regeneration, and renewing of the Holy Ghost." There, the washing must be by the Word and renewing of the Holy Ghost. But here it is the two elements of our salvation stated differently. Here is the blood of Christ to make atonement; here is the power of the Holy Spirit to regenerate us.

Water pictures the Holy Spirit also in Isaiah 44:3, "For I will pour water upon him that is thirsty, and floods upon the dry ground: I will pour my spirit upon thy seed, and my blessing upon thine offspring." So when Jesus died He provided not only atoning blood to pay for sin, but the mighty power of the Holy

Spirit which He had promised. And the Holy Spirit has a part in
working the miracle so that one is "born of the Spirit" when he is
saved.

*"For all these things were done, that the scripture should be
fulfilled."*—Vs. 36.

How careful and meticulous Jesus was that every sentence,
every line of the Scripture should be fulfilled! And the Scriptures
are so marvelously fulfilled in the birth, the life, in the trial,
crucifixion and death of Jesus that one would be foolish not to
receive the infallible proofs that Christ is very God in the flesh,
as the Scripture had said.

Psalm 22:16 had prophesied about Jesus, ". . . they pierced
my hands and my feet." That is fulfilled. But Zechariah 12:10
had prophesied about Israel, ". . . they shall look upon me
whom they have pierced, and they shall mourn for him, as one
mourneth for his only son . . . ."

So there are evidently several groups who must face the
pierced Jesus.

1. Israel must face Him. Oh, the blindness that in part has
happened to Israel will be removed after the rapture, after the
tribulation, after Christ returns and Israel is regathered to face
Him and the rebels are purged out. Then "they shall look on him
whom they pierced." That is when a nation shall be saved in a
day! Of all the great revivals in the world, that ranks as one of
the greatest of all! Jews will face the Saviour whom they
crucified.

**2. Those who had part in His trial and crucifixion must
face Him, too.** Hear what Jesus said. But when the high priest
said to Jesus, "I adjure thee by the living God, that thou tell us
whether thou be the Christ, the Son of God," then Jesus said to
him, "Thou hast said: nevertheless I say unto you, Hereafter
shall ye see the Son of man sitting on the right hand of power,
and coming in the clouds of heaven" (Matt. 26:63,64).

Those in Hell will have the lid lifted so they can see Christ
coming in power and glory. "They shall look on him whom they
pierced."

3. But is that not true about every lost sinner in the world?
Philippians 2:9-11 says:

"Wherefore God also hath highly exalted him, and given him a name which is above every name: That at the name of Jesus every knee should bow, of things in heaven, and things in earth, and things under the earth: And that every tongue should confess that Jesus Christ is Lord, to the glory of God the Father."

Oh, then, everybody in Heaven and on earth and in Hell will face the returning Jesus, and every tongue will confess that He is the Lord. Those who reject Him and are in torment will admit that He is the Saviour, the Creator, is all He claimed to be, and they will confess their wickedness.

Revelation 1:7 says, "Behold, he cometh with clouds; and every eye shall see him, and they also which pierced him: and all kindreds of the earth shall wail because of him." So, then, every eye shall see Him and they which pierced Him, and all the kindreds of the earth shall wail because of Him. The unsaved must see the Saviour and face Him and bow to Him.

Wailing? Yes, because Jesus will come to destroy the kings of this earth as pictured in that stone cut out of a mountain without hands and which smote the image picturing the world empires and broke it to pieces and the dust scattered it away. So will Christ destroy the kingdoms of the world and His kingdom shall fill the whole earth.

4. Oh, and we shall see Him, too. In Heaven, the only one to have any wounds, we think, will be Jesus. For when He arose from the dead, He invited Thomas to put his fingers in the nailprints and in the wound in His side. I suppose all of us will have all our wounds and scars of this poor old sinful life removed, but Jesus will be the only one officially who has paid for sins for us, and when I see Him . . . . .

> **When my life work is ended, and I cross the swelling tide,**
> **When the bright and glorious morning I shall see;**
> **I shall know my Redeemer when I reach the other side,**
> **And His smile will be the first to welcome me.**

> **I shall know Him, I shall know Him,**

> As redeemed by His side I shall stand;
> I shall know Him, I shall know Him
> By the print of the nails in His hand.

Oh, yes, for us it will be glorious for eternity to look on Him who was pierced for us!

VERSES 38-42:

38 ¶ And after this Joseph of Ăr-ĭm-ă-thǣ-ă, being a disciple of Jesus, but secretly for fear of the Jews, besought Pilate that he might take away the body of Jesus: and Pilate gave *him* leave. He came therefore, and took the body of Jesus.

39 And there came also 'Nĭc-ŏ-dē-mŭs, which at the first came to Jesus by night, and brought a mixture of myrrh and aloes, about an hundred pound *weight.*

40 Then took they the body of Jesus, and wound it in linen clothes with the spices, as the manner of the Jews is to bury.

41 Now in the place where he was crucified there was a garden; and in the garden a new sepulchre, wherein was never man yet laid.

42 There laid they Jesus therefore because of the Jews' preparation *day;* for the sepulchre was nigh at hand.

The Burial of Jesus

Two men now took it upon themselves to take down the poor abused body of the Saviour, emaciated so that every bone showed through, and the stripes and scars, the scourging, the nail-torn hands and feet, the spear gap in His side out of which flowed the blood and water and His face so bruised and swollen that He did not look like a man—they took that poor body down. They could not allow that the dear Saviour should be buried in a pauper's field.

Joseph is called "a counsellor" (Luke 23:50), so he was a member of the Sanhedrin and "had not consented to the counsel and deed of them" and he "waited for the kingdom of God" (Luke 23:50,51). And Nicodemus was "a ruler of the Jews" (John 3:1), so he also was a member of the 71-member Sanhedrin that ruled the Jews. Before this, Nicodemus had protested once in the Sanhedrin meeting that they ought to give Jesus a chance to prove Himself (John 7:50,51). And Joseph had been a disciple "but secretly for fear of the Jews." And now they besought Pilate for the body of Jesus.

First Pilate inquired if Jesus had been some time dead. Matthew says they "begged the body of Jesus." Mark 15:44,45 says, "And Pilate marvelled if he were already dead: and calling unto him the centurion, he asked him whether he had been any while dead. And when he knew it of the centurion, he gave the body to Joseph." I am sure Pilate was surprised that these two members of the Sanhedrin, that same Sanhedrin that condemned Him to die, should now take up tenderly the body of Jesus and bury it.

It was Nicodemus who "brought a mixture of myrrh and aloes, about an hundred pound weight," that they might wrap the body of Jesus in it and as long as possible prevent the stink of decay. But it was Joseph who "bought fine linen, and took him down, and wrapped him in the linen, and laid him in a sepulchre which was hewn out of a rock" (Mark 15:46). And right near the place of the crucifixion was a garden and in it a new tomb. It was Joseph's tomb. And Matthew 27:60 says he laid the body "in his own new tomb, which he had hewn out in the rock: and he rolled a great stone to the door of the sepulchre." So these two— Nicodemus, furnishing the hundred pound of spices as the manner of the Jews was to bury; Joseph, the fine linen cloth and the new tomb—bury Jesus.

It is interesting to think that Joseph of Arimathaea, who had the tomb made for himself, and with room for one or two others to be buried there, must have been a short man. For in the Garden Tomb now in Jerusalem we find how they had to chisel out at the foot to make more room for a longer body. So we suppose that Jesus was taller than Joseph and that they hastily chiseled out in the tomb to make more room, as they tenderly put the body there.

They hurried and laid the body there because the preparation day would begin, that is, the high Sabbath, the night when they ate the passover lamb which was already roasting and would be eaten—at sundown that day, so they hastily buried the body of Jesus and rolled a great stone to the door of the sepulchre and departed.

John 20

THE first *day* of the week cometh Mary Magdalene early, when it was yet dark, unto the sepulchre, and seeth the stone taken away from the sepulchre.

2 Then she runneth, and cometh to Simon Peter, and to the other disciple, whom Jesus loved, and saith unto them, They have taken away the Lord out of the sepulchre, and we know not where they have laid him.

3 Peter therefore went forth, and that other disciple, and came to the sepulchre.

4 So they ran both together: and the other disciple did outrun Peter, and came first to the sepulchre.

5 And he stooping down, *and look-ing in,* saw the linen clothes lying; yet went he not in.

6 Then cometh Simon Peter following him, and went into the sepulchre, and seeth the linen clothes lie,

7 And the napkin, that was about his head, not lying with the linen clothes, but wrapped together in a place by itself.

8 Then went in also that other disciple, which came first to the sepulchre, and he saw, and believed.

9 For as yet they knew not the scripture, that he must rise again from the dead.

10 Then the disciples went away again unto their own home.

Jesus Rises From the Tomb as He Promised

At what hour did Jesus rise from the dead? Matthew 28:1 says, "In the end of the sabbath, as it began to dawn toward the first day of the week . . . ." The Sabbath ended at sundown, and this Sabbath was the Saturday weekday Sabbath.

Some time in the night there was a great earthquake and the angel descended and rolled back the stone from the door and sat upon it, Matthew 28:1,2 tells us. "As it began to dawn" to us would ordinarily mean the coming of daylight, but it may simply mean the approach of the first day of the week, and the day with Jews began at sundown.

So sometime in the night Jesus rose from the dead. And *"when it was yet dark,"* Mary Magdalene came very early to the sepulchre and saw the stone taken away. Bishop Andrews beautifully describes Mary Magdalene: "She was last at His cross, and first at His grave. She stayed longest *there,* and was soonest *here.* None felt they owed so much to Christ."

Look again at verses 5 and 6: *"And he stooping down, and looking in, saw the linen clothes lying: yet went he not in. Then cometh Simon Peter following him, and went into the sepulchre, and seeth the linen clothes lie."* Dr. Ironside describes the grave as we have seen it many times:

> Today you can see this skull-shaped hill and on one side of it there is a garden where a few years back they uncovered a sepulchre cut into the face of the cliff and it answers in every detail to the tomb described in the Word of God. As you draw near, it is natural to stoop down, as John did, and look in. The entrance, originally, was very low. Near this doorway there is a little window which throws the light upon an empty crypt, plainly visible as you peer through the entrance. The crypt is about 24 inches high, cut out of the limestone rock, and in that crypt the body would have been easily seen, lying upon its bed of spices, if it were still there.

Dr. Scofield gives the order of events, combining the four narratives of the four Gospels, about the resurrection as follows:

> Three women, Mary Magdalene, and Mary the mother of Jesus, and Salome, start for the sepulchre, followed by other

women bearing spices. The three find the stone rolled away, and Mary Magdalene goes to tell the disciples (Lk. 23. 55-24. 9; John 20. 1,2). Mary, the mother of James and Joses, draws nearer the tomb and sees the angel of the Lord (Mt. 28. 2). She goes back to meet the other women following with the spices.

Meanwhile Peter and John, warned by Mary Magdalene, arrive, look in, and go away (John 20. 3-10). Mary Magdalene returns weeping, sees the two angels and then Jesus (John 20. 11-18), and goes as He bade her to tell the disciples. Mary (mother of James and Joses), meanwhile, has met the women with the spices and, returning with them, they see the two angels (Lk. 24. 4,5; Mk. 16. 5). They also receive the angelic message, and, going to seek the disciples, are met by Jesus (Mt. 28. 8-10).

Now Mary Magdalene, seeing the stone taken away, ran to Peter and John and said, *"They have taken away the Lord out of the sepulchre, and we know not where they have laid him"* (vs. 2). They did not understand that He was risen from the dead.

Peter and John ran together. John may have been younger and outran Peter and looked in the sepulchre. "What slowed Peter's feet? Not age, but a sudden shock of memory," declares Ralph Connor. "What right has he to take part in a search for the body of the Man he so deserted!" And then Macaulay adds: "But even as a panic of self-condemnation grips him, another memory arouses him. That look of recall flashes again upon his vision, and, with heart almost bursting with a passion to find his beloved Master, he renews his speed . . . till he has pushed past John hesitating at the opening of the tomb, and leapt in."

But Simon Peter went boldly into the sepulchre and there was the cloth in which Jesus had been wrapped and the napkin that was about His head, lying by itself. Then John went into the sepulchre, too, *"and he saw, and believed"* (vs. 8). Now he understood that Jesus was raised from the dead. Up to this time none of them had seemed to understand the promises that He would rise from the dead. Perhaps they had taken them in some symbolic sense.

And now the disciples *"went away again unto their own home"* (vs. 10). That meant they left Jerusalem and took the trip north up to the province of Galilee and perhaps to Capernaum or Bethsaida, and Peter went back to his fishing, as we see in the next chapter.

Mary Magdalene and the other Mary had sat and watched the grave when Jesus was buried there (Matt. 27:61). And now Mary Magdalene and the other Mary came to the sepulchre (Matt. 28:1).

VERSES 11-18:

11 ¶ But Mary stood without at the sepulchre weeping: and as she wept, she stooped down, *and looked* into the sepulchre,

12 And seeth two angels in white sitting, the one at the head, and the other at the feet, where the body of Jesus had lain.

13 And they say unto her, Woman, why weepest thou? She saith unto them, Because they have taken away my Lord, and I know not where they have laid him.

14 And when she had thus said, she turned herself back, and saw Jesus standing, and knew not that it was Jesus.

15 Jesus saith unto her, Woman, why weepest thou? whom seekest thou? She, supposing him to be the gardener, saith unto him, Sir, if thou have borne him hence, tell me where thou hast laid him, and I will take him away.

16 Jesus saith unto her, Mary. She turned herself, and saith unto him, Răb-bō-nī; which is to say, Master.

17 Jesus saith unto her, Touch me not; for I am not yet ascended to my Father: but go to my brethren, and say unto them, I ascend unto my Father, and your Father; and *to* my

God, and your God.
18 Mary Magdalene came and told the disciples that she had seen the | Lord, and *that* he had spoken these things unto her.

Jesus Appears to Mary Magdalene

Matthew 28 tells us that there was with Mary Magdalene "the other Mary." Luke 24:10 tells us that "it was Mary Magdalene,

and Joanna, and Mary the mother of James, and other women that were with them, which told these things unto the apostles."

But here we learn that Mary saw the *two angels in white apparel* (vs. 12). Luke 24:4 says "two men," that is, the angels appeared as men. They were sitting, *"one at the head, and the other at the feet"* (vs. 12). The place of Christ's burial and resurrection is dear to us, although we would be tempted to foolishly worship the spot, and so the Lord prevents the certainty of the place. "But if the Spirit of him that raised up Jesus from the dead dwell in you, he that raised up Christ from the dead shall also quicken your mortal bodies by his Spirit that dwelleth in you," says Romans 8:11. These angels seem to reverence the cold stone place in which our Saviour's body had lain; they wanted to point it out—that it was empty; Jesus had risen. Angels ere there now, but the Holy Spirit had watched over that grave until the second that that body should be quickened. So He watches over the grave of every Christian.

Dr. J. Wilbur Chapman, preaching at Dayton, Ohio, at a Bible conference of ministers and workers, said:

> I was sitting in my home in the country, reading the account of an address delivered by Dr. Moorehead at a Bible conference, and he said he believed it was true that when one became a Son of God the Spirit of God came into him to dwell, and he continued to dwell always. "I don't know but that in some way unknown to me He will continue to abide, even though in the tomb, until the resurrection morning. But," said he, "if any of my brethren deny me the privilege of this belief, I will say, when I became a son of God, the Spirit of God came into my life, and He continues to abide through life, and then if I am placed in the tomb He will still hover over me. He hovers over that tomb keeping watch until the day breaks in glorious resurrection."
>
> I could not read the closing sentences, for the tears had filled my eyes, and I told my man to hitch the horse to the carriage, and my wife and I rode out to the little grave where we had buried our firstborn boy, and as we stood there that morning we said, "Thank God, He is keeping watch," and peace filled our souls. And I shall never forget going across the country to stand beside the grave of my mother, and I said, "Thank God, thank God, for thirty years He has been keeping watch, and when the morning breaks He will lift them up, to be united by the Spirit again—the body in the grave and the spirit in His presence." That is the work of the Holy Ghost.

Then Mary saw Jesus and did not recognize Him; she thought it was the gardener. But when Jesus spoke to her and called her name, she immediately knew Him. Oh, I am sure she would have gladly laid her hands upon Him, but He said, *"Touch me not; for I am not yet ascended to my Father"* (vs. 17).

I think that, as Dr. Scofield suggests, "Jesus speaks to Mary as High Priest fulfilling the day of atonement (Lev. 16). Having accomplished the sacrifice, He was on His way to present the sacred blood in heaven, and that, between the meeting with Mary in the garden and the meeting of Mt. 28. 9, He had so ascended and returned."

Matthew 28:9 says, "And they came and held him by the feet," evidently after Mary had seen Him and the type had been fulfilled.

We are sure that Jesus ascended to Heaven. Oh, don't begrudge it! His eyes must long to see the streets of gold and the angels and the glories there "glorified with the Father." Then He will return, and from time to time for forty days will appear to the disciples.

Mary came and told the disciples she had seen the Lord. But the words of these women "seemed to them as idle tales, and they believed them not" (Luke 24:11). And the message of the angel was more than John's Gospel tells us. We read in Matthew 28:5-8:

"And the angel answered and said unto the women, Fear not ye: for I know that ye seek Jesus, which was crucified. He is not here: for he is risen, as he said. Come, see the place where the Lord lay. And go quickly, and tell his disciples that he is risen from the dead; and, behold, he goeth before you into Galilee; there shall ye see him: lo, I have told you. And they departed quickly from the sepulchre with fear and great joy; and did run to bring his disciples word."

And they told the disciples about Jesus, "Behold, he goeth before you into Galilee; there shall ye see him." Already verse 10 of John 20 tells us, "Then the disciples went away again unto their own home"; so Jesus would be there to meet them.

VERSES 19-23:

19 ¶ Then the same day at evening, being the first *day* of the week, when the doors were shut where the disciples were assembled for fear of the Jews, came Jesus and stood in the midst, and saith unto them, Peace *be* unto you.

20 And when he had so said, he

shewed unto them *his* hands and his side. Then were the disciples glad, when they saw the Lord.

21 Then said Jesus to them again, Peace *be* unto you: as *my* Father hath sent me, even so send I you.

22 And when he had said this, he breathed on *them*, and saith unto them, Receive ye the Holy Ghost:

23 Whose soever sins ye remit, they are remitted unto them; *and* whose soever *sins* ye retain, they are retained.

Jesus Appears to the Disciples

We suppose that the departure from Galilee on the part of Peter and others was to be tomorrow morning, and there has been a great excitement this first day of the week and perhaps they would not be ready without some preparation to leave. At any rate, now, this same day of the resurrection, the disciples, frightened, uneasy about what these murderous Jews would do, were in the Upper Room with the doors shut (it is the same Upper Room, evidently, where they had the Last Supper together), and Jesus appeared to them and said, *"Peace be unto you"* (vs. 19). This age-old salutation is still used among the Jews. He showed them His hands with the nailprints and His side with the gash of the spear (vs. 20). Luke 24:40 indicates that the feet also were shown. Five open wounds to witness that death is conquered and that Christ is alive.

> Five bleeding wounds He bears,
>   Received on Calvary;
> They pour effectual prayers,
> They strongly plead for me:
> "Forgive him, O forgive," they cry,
>   "Nor let that ransomed sinner die!"

And another poem sweetly reminds us:

> Lord, when I am weary with toiling,
>   And burdensome seem Thy commands,
> If my load should lead to complaining,
>   Lord, show me Thy hands,—
> Thy nail-pierced hands, Thy cross-torn hands,
>   My Saviour, show me Thy hands.

> Christ, if ever my footsteps should falter,
>   And I be prepared for retreat,
> If desert or thorn cause lamenting,
>   Lord, show me Thy feet,—

Thy bleeding feet, Thy nail-scarred feet,
My Jesus, show me Thy feet.

Read the two sentences in verse 20 carefully. *"And when he had so said, he shewed unto them his hands and his side. Then were the disciples glad, when they saw the Lord."* Read Luke 24:36-45 and you will see how hard to convince they were. The stubborn unbelief of these disciples is almost past understanding. Every detail had turned out as the Saviour promised. When the three days and three nights were finished, the grave was empty, yet they did not believe. The angels appeared to the women and then Jesus Himself appeared to Mary, yet they did not believe. The Roman seal was broken on the tomb, the soldiers were gone, the linen clothes were carefully folded in such a way as to prove that the Saviour was risen, yet they did not believe. Now when He came into their presence to speak to them, they foolishly thought He was a ghost, a spirit!

They did not believe the word of Jesus, that He would rise; they did not believe the testimony of the angels, that He was risen; nor of Mary who saw Him. Now they did not believe their own eyes. The proof which Jesus gave to them convinced every doubter among them. This ought to convince our hearts and make us all the more sure of the resurrection of Jesus. Nothing but indisputable proof, absolute certainty, convinced this group of disciples that Jesus arose from the dead. The man who denies that Jesus arose from the dead is a fool. The proof is past question.

In this connection, remember that every New Testament preacher, including all these apostles, preached continually to the public that Jesus was risen from the dead. See Acts 1:22; 2:24, 30-36; 3:15; 4:10,33; 5:30-32. In all these cases where the resurrection was preached in and about Jerusalem, it was never once denied! The reason is made clear when you read I Corinthians 15:4-8. There were over five hundred living witnesses who had seen Jesus after His resurrection! Later, when Paul preached the resurrection in far-off Athens (Acts 17:3,32), the people scoffed at it, as they did in other places many years after the resurrection. But the proof of the resurrection of Christ was so overwhelming, with so many eyewitnesses still alive during the ministry of the apostles, that no one dared to dispute it in that vicinity and time.

The disciples rejoiced when they saw the Saviour. They are now sure He is risen from the dead.

Now He repeats to them what He had said in the high priestly prayer in John 17:18: "As thou hast sent me into the world, even so have I also sent them into the world." Now Jesus says to them, "As my Father hath sent me, even so send I you."

And if they are to be sent like Jesus, then they must have the anointing of the Spirit. As Jesus was filled with the Spirit when He was baptized and praying, so the disciples must have the same Holy Spirit. Note here that *"he breathed on them, and saith unto them, Receive ye the Holy Ghost"* (vs. 22). No doubt this has in mind the dispensational change that now the Holy Spirit is to live within their bodies. That is what the Lord had foretold about the Holy Spirit, "For he dwelleth with you, and shall be in you" (14:7).

He was with the disciples that night before the crucifixion, but on the day of the resurrection He came into their bodies. This is the same thing promised in John 7:37-39:

"In the last day, that great day of the feast, Jesus stood and cried, saying, If any man thirst, let him come unto me, and drink. He that believeth on me, as the scripture hath said, out of his belly shall flow rivers of living water. (But this spake he of the Spirit, which they that believe on him should receive: for the Holy Ghost was not yet given; because that Jesus was not yet glorified.)"

Note that "the Holy Ghost was not yet given; because that Jesus was not yet glorified" in a resurrection body! Now it is time. And from this time on, as far as we know, every Christian in the world, from the time of conversion, has the Holy Spirit abiding in his body. This is the plain statement of I Corinthians 6:19,20 and Romans 8:9.

But it is implied and intended that the indwelling of the Holy Spirit is to be fruitful in the fullness of Holy Spirit power pouring out from the Christian. And that will wait for these until the day of Pentecost. After they have tarried and prayed, they will be endued with power from on High.

Keep these two things separate: the indwelling of the Holy Spirit began the day of the resurrection of Christ; the fullness of the Spirit for these disciples, a special enduement of power from on High, came at Pentecost.

Verse 23 has troubled many. Compare it with a similar statement in Matthew 16:19, addressed primarily to Peter: "And I will give unto thee the keys of the kingdom of heaven: and whatsoever thou shalt bind on earth shall be bound in heaven: and whatsoever thou shalt loose on earth shall be loosed in heaven."

But here the same promise is given: *"Whose soever sins ye remit, they are remitted unto them; and whose soever sins ye retain, they are retained."*

Our Catholic friends who think that Matthew 16:19 authorized Simon Peter to be the head of a worldwide church, the viceregent of God on earth and the founder of the papacy, ignore the fact that the same plan and promise is given to all the disciples here. We know ahead of time from many, many Scriptures that no man save Christ could forgive sins on his own authority.

On the above verse Dr. Ironside says:

> It has been claimed by some that these disciples were the first bishops of the Church, and the Lord was giving them the authority to remit sin and retain sin, and that they were to go out into the world and people were to confess sins to them and they would tell them what penance to do and thus obtain remission of their sins. I do not find anything like that here.
>
> One of the most important of the group, the Apostle Peter, was there that day and Peter went forth in the name of the Lord to proclaim remission of sins. How did he do it? Did he say, "You come to me and confess your sins to me and I will forgive them"? Did he say anything like that? Let us see. In Acts 10 we find Peter preaching the Gospel in the household of Cornelius. He tells of Christ's wonderful life: "The word which God sent unto the children of Israel, preaching peace by Jesus Christ: (He is Lord of all) . . . To him give all the prophets witness, that through his name whosoever"—confesseth his

sins to a priest—"Shall receive remission of sins." Is that right? Do you have your Bible open? What does it say? "That through his name whosoever *believeth in him* shall receive remission of sins." Believe on Jesus and you will get remission. That is the commission that every servant of Christ has . . . ."

A famous Greek scholar has said that this passage, "Whosesoever sins ye remit, they are remitted unto them," would permit the future perfect tense "they shall have been remitted." In other words, if one, with the clear leading of the Holy Spirit, knows one who has trusted Christ as Saviour, he has a right to say to him, "Your sins are forgiven." Not that he forgives them but because he knows the man has trusted Christ for forgiveness. And if one refuses to take Christ as Saviour, then the apostle or anybody else, in the power of the Holy Spirit, who knows he is refusing, has a right to say, "Your sins are retained; they are not forgiven." In other words, one in the power of the Spirit who knows one has trusted Christ, can boldly say that his sins are forgiven.

Whatever else it means, this could not mean the papacy nor that Peter nor any other priest had power to act for God in forgiving sins. Jesus plainly said in John 14:6, ". . . no man cometh unto the Father, but by me." And one who comes to Christ in his heart has his sins forgiven. So says the Spirit-filled Apostle Paul in Acts 13:38,39:

"Be it known unto you therefore, men and brethren, that through this man is preached unto you the forgiveness of sins: And by him all that believe are justified from all things, from which ye could not be justified by the law of Moses."

Believing on Christ is the only way any man gets forgiveness of sins. But a Spirit-filled Christian, knowing a sinner has trusted Christ, has the authority to tell him his sins are forgiven. And one who knows that a sinner has not trusted in Christ has the authority to tell him his sins are unforgiven.

———

VERSES 24-29:

24 ¶ But Thomas, one of the twelve, called Dĭd´-ў-mŭs, was not with them when Jesus came.

25 The other disciples therefore said unto him, We have seen the Lord. But he said unto them, Except I shall see in his hands the print of the nails, and thrust my hand into his side, I will not believe.

26 ¶ And after eight days again his disciples were within, and Thomas with them: *then* came Jesus, the doors being shut, and stood in the midst, and said, Peace *be* unto you.

27 Then saith he to Thomas, Reach hither thy finger, and behold my hands; and reach hither thy hand, and thrust *it* into my side: and be not faithless, but believing.

28 And Thomas answered and said unto him, My Lord and my God.

29 Jesus saith unto him, Thomas, because thou hast seen me, thou hast believed: blessed *are* they that have not seen, and *yet* have believed.

Thomas Sees Jesus; Is Convinced of His Resurrection

Thomas was something of a doubter. He was the one who, although he believed Jesus was going to get killed going back to the Jerusalem area, said, "Let us also go, that we may die with him" (11:16).

August Van Ryn says about Thomas:

> There were two empty seats in the Upper Room on the evening of the day when our Lord rose from the dead. Judas was not there and neither was Thomas . . . . Thomas received a nickname that day which he has never gotten rid of; for ever since he has been known as "Doubting Thomas." He typifies, I think, the unbelief of believers . . . .

August Van Ryn says:

> Thomas missed seeing the proofs of the Lord's resurrection, yet apparently he needed them more than any of the others did . . . . Thomas missed these words, "Peace be unto you." He missed the commission of being sent out in the service of the Lord (vs. 21). He no doubt received it later, but the fact remains that at least for one week he did not have his commission as the others did. He missed being breathed upon as Jesus said to His own that night, "Receive ye the Holy Ghost . . . ." We cannot afford to miss this divine unction. Thomas also missed the commission which our Lord gave in regard to church action and the exercise of church discipline, to which the commission of verse 23 undoubtedly refers . . . .

Thomas could not believe that Jesus was really risen from the

dead. He wanted more evidence. We can imagine the awful
certainty of Jesus' death. The blood poured out and the poor,
naked body hanging there dead and then taken down and buried.
It is not easy to believe one is risen from the dead. Oh, he thought
if he could only put his hands in the nailprints and see them and
feel the hole in his side, then he would believe.

So eight days later, Thomas being with them, Jesus came, the
doors being shut, and spoke, "Peace be unto you." Ah, Thomas,
you can have all the evidence you need. Isn't it a wonderful thing
that the dear Lord Jesus is willing to deal with our poor
unbelieving hearts and give further evidence? "Thomas, put
your finger in the nailprints and your hand in My side and see
for yourself!" It is still true: "Draw nigh to God, and he will draw
nigh to you." It is still true: "Then shall we know, if we follow on
to know the Lord" (Hos. 6:3).

We should remember that being saved does not make one
perfect in understanding or perfect in faith. And saved people
sometimes have very little confidence about spiritual truth and
blessing.

Ah, but blessed are those who find faith comes quickly in
Jesus! We are commanded, "Have faith in God." And it is
especially blessed to have faith in the midst of difficulties and
trouble.

VERSES 30,31:

30 ¶ And many other signs truly did
Jesus in the presence of his disciples,
which are not written in this book:
31 But these are written, that ye
might believe that Jesus is the Christ,
the Son of God; and that believing
ye might have life through his name.

Signs and Wonders in John

John's Gospel is written especially that people might trust in
Jesus Christ as the Son of God and that *"believing ye might have
life"* (vs. 31).

So many, many details of Christ's discussion about His deity are given in John. And again and again the plan of salvation so simply stated in John occurs again. In John 1:12; John 3:15, 16, 18, 36; John 5:24; John 6:37, 40, 47, and a few other times, like in Acts 10:43; Acts 13:38,39 and in Acts 16:31, the plan of salvation by simple faith in Christ is stated, but the word "believe" is the big word throughout the Gospel of John. Oh, to take it to heart, then! Remember that the Gospel of John is particularly given to prove the deity of Christ and to get people to trust Him.

There are many miracles not told in these Gospels. The world could not contain the record of all that Jesus did (21:25).

John 21

AFTER these things Jesus shewed himself again to the disciples at the sea of Tiberias; and on this wise shewed he *himself*.

2 There were together Simon Peter, and Thomas called Dĭd´-ў-mŭs, and Nathanael of Cana in Galilee, and the *sons* of Zebedee, and two other of his disciples.

The Risen Saviour Appears in Galilee

Verses 1,2: *"These things"* in verse 1 refers to the two appearances of Jesus to the disciples in a group in the Upper Room at Jerusalem, as mentioned in John 20:19,26. He had appeared to the disciples together only twice, and 21:14 shows that this chapter tells of His third appearance to a group of the disciples. He had appeared, besides this, to individuals, to Mary (20:14), to the two on the road to Emmaus (Luke 24), to Peter, and perhaps to others (I Cor. 15:5).

Jesus had commanded the disciples to go before Him into Galilee where He would see them (Matt. 28:7,10; Mark 16:7). In fact, Jesus had foretold, before His death, that He would rise and would meet them in Galilee (Mark 14:28). It was in the province of Galilee, some 80 miles north of Jerusalem, where Jesus repeated the Great Commission as given in Matthew 28:16-20. Evidently after His appearance in the province of Galilee in a mountain comes this appearance to the disciples by the Sea of Tiberias, or Galilee.

The Sea of Tiberias is the Sea of Galilee, the lake Chinnereth or Gennesaret. It is here called the Sea of Tiberias because Tiberias is a principal city on the west side of this little Sea of Galilee, about seven and a half miles wide and fifteen miles long. The Sea of Galilee is called the Sea of Tiberias. The city of Tiberias was named for Emperor Tiberias. It remains a thriving little city to this day.

It is rather strange that of all the cities and towns of Galilee Jesus never went to Tiberias, as far as the records show. That may have been because the city was built over an old cemetery and Jews thought it was ceremonially unclean. At any rate, it did not have the blessings of Christ's public ministry, it appears, and it avoided the curse that came on Bethsaida, Chorazin, Capernaum, the cities that were blessed by His ministry but refused Him and so were condemned and disappeared (Matt. 11:20-24).

At the Sea of Galilee at this time were Simon Peter, Thomas, Nathanael, James and John and two other disciples. In John 20:10 we read, "Then the disciples went away again unto their own home." If that means they went to their home in Galilee, as it probably does, then it does not mean that they left the day of the resurrection. And in John 20:26, when Jesus appeared to the disciples again, does this Scripture mean that He appeared to them in Galilee? Probably so. It would have taken several days to prepare and return by foot up to Capernaum and Bethsaida.

VERSES 3-5:

3 Simon Peter saith unto them, I go a fishing. They say unto him, We also go with thee. They went forth, and entered into a ship immediately; and that night they caught nothing.
4 But when the morning was now come, Jesus stood on the shore: but the disciples knew not that it was Jesus.
5 Then Jesus saith unto them, Children, have ye any meat? They answered him, No.

Fruitless Fishing

And now they are to go fishing.

Notice Peter's leadership: He said, *"I go a fishing"* (vs. 3). So the others straightway go with him.

Doubtless they are at loose ends. There is a great change in their life pattern since Jesus died. He has not in detail expounded to them the Great Commission. It is natural they should go back to their homes. And, natural, too, that they should set out to do some work to provide for their families.

Can you imagine the frustration when they fished all night and caught nothing? I can imagine Peter remembering all the years

he made a good living for his family here. Now there seems not to be a fish in the lake! But the Lord Jesus has planned it so. He has control of all the fish and all the lakes.

Once before when they needed tax money, He had instructed Peter to go cast in a hook, take up a fish and find a coin in its mouth with which to pay taxes. The Lord Jesus could control the cock that crowed to remind Peter of his sin. All the resources of the world were at Christ's command. We remember that when the children of Israel went into the land of Canaan, the Lord sent hornets before them to help drive out the heathen. The Scripture says, "The stars in their courses fought against Sisera" when he was defeated by the Israelites (Judg. 5:20). And at Joshua's word the movement of the sun in relation to the earth was held up for a day that victory might come.

And when Jesus went into Jerusalem at the triumphal entry, and the Pharisees would have rebuked the children and others who cried out, "Hosanna to the son of David: Blessed is he that cometh in the name of the Lord," the Lord Jesus had said, "I tell you that, if these should hold their peace, the stones would immediately cry out" (Matt. 21:9 and Luke 19:40). And we are told that when Christ returns, then "all the trees of the field shall clap their hands" (Isa. 55:12).

God could use a donkey to rebuke Balaam, and He could use fishes here to rebuke backslidden Peter. Can you imagine Peter's feelings? He feels, "I am ruined! I can't be a preacher! Who would trust a cursing preacher, one who was cowardly and denied the Saviour?" And I suppose he thought, I have a family and my mother-in-law lives with me, and I must make a living. And so through that fruitless night they pulled the net and caught nothing!

Did you know that to go fishing, or to plow a field, or to run a store without God's help and cooperation is a failing business? And Peter, the Lord has a lesson to teach you and the other disciples.

The Lord Jesus knew the sad heart, the defeated heart of Peter. When He arose from the dead, He had the angel to say to the women first at the tomb, "But go your way, tell his disciples and Peter that he goeth before you into Galilee: there shall ye see him, as he said unto you" (Mark 16:7). "And Peter"—oh, Peter, you don't count yourself a disciple, but Jesus counts you in! And the Lord Jesus not only prayed for you so that Satan could not have your soul, He not only has the cock to remind you, and the fishes to hold away to bring you back to your sense of destiny and your call as a preacher and apostle, but now Jesus comes after you personally to restore you to service.

Now Jesus *"stood on the shore"* (vs. 4). He was not recognized. Is it strange? Mary thought He was the gardener when she saw Him in the garden just after His resurrection (20:15). The two on the road to Emmaus did not recognize Jesus when He walked along beside them and opened the Scriptures until their hearts burned within them. They recognized Him only when He sat with them at supper to break bread (Luke 24:13-35). And now these disciples did not recognize Him.

No doubt it is partly because it is totally unexpected. They cannot yet realize He is risen from the dead. We see sometimes what we expect to see. We fail to notice things we do not expect and cannot believe.

Was there so much difference in the appearance of Jesus after His resurrection? I suppose that the bruises and wounds have healed. I suppose that the torment and trouble He endured does not show now in His sweet, calm, heavenly face, but we have no doubt it is the same Jesus, in the same body, only now glorified. In the sense that His ministry is finished, the sufferings are over, He is now in the glorified body. But He does not shine with all the manifestation of deity as He will later when John sees Him in Revelation 1:13-17, and as He will at His second coming and as He appeared to the disciples on the Mount of Transfiguration. But the disciples did not know Him.

Note the tender language: *"Children, have ye any meat?"* (vs. 5). They were His children. And isn't it strange they didn't recognize the voice?

Their fishing boat and nets were empty; they had caught nothing.

VERSES 6-11:

6 And he said unto them, Cast the net on the right side of the ship, and ye shall find. They cast therefore, and now they were not able to draw it for the multitude of fishes.

7 Therefore that disciple whom Jesus loved saith unto Peter, It is the Lord. Now when Simon Peter heard that it was the Lord, he girt *his* fisher's coat *unto him*, (for he was naked,) and did cast himself into the sea.

8 And the other disciples came in a little ship; (for they were not far from land, but as it were two hundred cubits,) dragging the net with fishes.

9 As soon then as they were come to land, they saw a fire of coals there, and fish laid thereon, and bread.

10 Jesus saith unto them, Bring of the fish which ye have now caught.

11 Simon Peter went up, and drew the net to land full of great fishes, an hundred and fifty and three: and for all there were so many, yet was not the net broken.

Success With Christ's Blessing

Now Jesus tells them to cast their net on the right side of the ship, and they did. What a great difference in working without God and working with Him; working without His instruction and blessing and working with His instruction and blessing! Now suddenly they have a great multitude of fish and cannot even draw the net, it is so full!

John, who seemed to be the most spiritually minded and perceptive of the apostles, had suddenly flashed back in memory. He remembered another time when he and James, Peter and Andrew were in the boats and they had caught nothing and washed their nets. But Jesus told Peter to launch out into the deep and let down his nets for a draught. He let down one net and it was suddenly full with fish; the net was breaking and he had to call James and John in another boat to help him. And there Jesus had called them to preach and said, ". . . from henceforth thou shalt catch men." Oh, John, it is Jesus!

And when he said it, Peter, too, saw the whole thing. His hungry heart must get to Jesus. He must hear words of forgiveness. He must see if Jesus still wants to use such a frail, sinning man as a preacher!

And with typical impetuosity, he put on his fisher's coat because he was naked and jumped into the sea (vs. 7). Peter, can't you wait for the boat? No, he must get to Jesus at once!

I am reminded of a revival campaign in Gary, Indiana, when I preached on Peter's backsliding. When I gave an invitation for sinners to trust Christ and for the backslidden in heart to come and lay their lives on the altar and be revived and blessed and happy and Spirit-filled again, one man came almost running down the aisle. Sobbing he said to me, "Oh, I have been a backslider for five years! That is a long time to stay away from home! Tell my wife I want her to come down and pray with me." These two rededicated their home and themselves to God. He realized he had been "away from home."

Peter knows it, too, and how eager he is to get to Jesus!

Jesus had started to cook breakfast for them and had already fish and bread, but He wants them to have part, so He said, *"Bring of the fish which ye have now caught"* (vs. 10). This is rather surprising. They had been unable to draw in that net full of so many big fish, but with abounding strength Peter seizes the net and drew it to land full of 153 big fish! My, I can imagine that

Peter sure made fish scales fly getting more fish ready for Jesus to cook on those coals!

Is it not wonderful that the Lord Jesus, even in the glorified body, was not ashamed to do the menial work of making a fire and cooking food over it! The Lord served the breakfast. Those same nail-scarred hands also spread our breakfast table. Do we give thanks to Him?

Let every woman who prepares meals think: The Lord Jesus did it, too, for those He loved, and so do I. And let every Christian remember that work is blessed, it is right, it pleases God, it is honorable and Christ-honoring.

VERSES 12-14:

12 Jesus saith unto them, Come *and* dine. And none of the disciples durst ask him, Who art thou? knowing that it was the Lord.

13 Jesus then cometh, and taketh bread, and giveth them, and fish likewise.

14 This is now the third time that Jesus shewed himself to his disciples, after that he was risen from the dead.

The Third Appearance

The disciples gathered around Jesus and the campfire. And now all of them recognize He is the resurrected Saviour. They are diffident. They are glad. They are eager for His presence. They are astonished. Yet they are waiting for instruction; and so they eat.

Jesus again took bread and fish and gave them. Oh, how He loves to feed His own people! And it is good for us to pray, "Give us this day our daily bread."

Now this is the third time Jesus showed Himself to His disciples after He had risen from the dead.

The first time was certainly the day of the resurrection. And He counts His appearance to the women at the tomb, His appearance to the two disciples on the road to Emmaus in Luke 24, and His appearance with all the disciples in the Upper Room that same day at evening (20:19-23) as one appearance. Then eight days later He appeared to the disciples again (20:26). And now this third time He appears to the disciples by the Sea of Galilee. After the resurrection of Jesus, I Corinthians 15:5-8 tells us:

". . . And that he was seen of Cephas, then of the twelve: After that, he was seen of above five hundred brethren at once; of whom the greater part remain unto this present, but some are fallen asleep. After that, he was seen of James; then of all the apostles. And last of all he was seen of me also, as of one born out of due time."

He appeared again and again for a period of forty days. Acts 1:3 says, "To whom he shewed himself alive after his passion by many infallible proofs, being seen of them forty days, and speaking of the things pertaining to the kingdom of God."

In Luke 24:39 we read that Jesus had the disciples put their hands upon Him. They saw Him eat and drink before them. In his first Epistle John reminds us of Christ manifested: "That which was from the beginning, which we have heard, which we have seen with our eyes, which we have looked upon, and our hands have handled, of the Word of life" (I John 1:1). Acts 1:3 tells us that to the apostles "he shewed himself alive after his passion by many infallible proofs, being seen of them forty days, and speaking of the things pertaining to the kingdom of God." So for forty days the Lord Jesus showed Himself to the people: once to a crowd of more than 500 and hundreds were alive even in Paul's day to give witness to it. One who does not believe in the resurrection of Christ is a fool, as Jesus Himself reminded the two on the way to Emmaus and said, "O fools, and slow of heart to believe all that the prophets have spoken: Ought not Christ to have suffered these things, and to enter into his glory?" (Luke 24:25,26).

VERSES 15-17:

15 ¶ So when they had dined, Jesus saith to Simon Peter, Simon, *son* of Jonas, lovest thou me more than these? He saith unto him, Yea, Lord; thou knowest that I love thee. He saith unto him, Feed my lambs.

16 He saith to him again the second time, Simon, *son* of Jonas, lovest thou me? He saith unto him, Yea, Lord; thou knowest that I love thee. He saith unto him, Feed my sheep.

17 He saith unto him the third time, Simon, *son* of Jonas, lovest thou me? Peter was grieved because he said unto him the third time, Lovest thou me? And he said unto him, Lord, thou knowest all things; thou knowest that I love thee. Jesus saith unto him, Feed my sheep.

Peter, if You Love Me, Back to Preaching!

How earnestly and yet how plainly Jesus pressed the matter! "The gifts and calling of God are without repentance" (Rom. 11:29). Peter is saved and will not be unsaved; he is called and will not be uncalled. He must serve the Lord.

Do you love Christ? Then you must prove it by telling others. Obedience is the measure of love. This is what Jesus said in John 14:15, 21, 23, 24. One who loves Christ shows it by the way he obeys.

Three times Jesus asked the question, *"Simon, son of Jonas, lovest thou me?"* First He said, *"Feed my lambs"* (vs. 15). Because Peter, you have been weak and frail and many another Christian will have been frail also, not mature Christians, perhaps, and they will need comfort. Tell them God has forgiven you and is using you. Feed the little lambs, Peter.

And then He said, *"Feed my sheep,"* the second and third times (vss. 16, 17).

Peter was grieved. Did Jesus not believe in his love? Oh, yes, but Peter must say so. He must decide in his own mind that, despite his failure, a compelling love for Christ makes him go on and preach the Gospel, win souls and represent Christ.

Notice what Peter is to do. "Feed my lambs" and "Feed my sheep." Evidently He refers to feeding the lost sheep of the house of Israel, for that is what he did. Soon Peter will be standing up at Pentecost and preaching to the thousands, and many will be saved. So, feeding the sheep here certainly refers to bearing fruit, getting people saved, carrying out the Great Commission, as

Peter and all the apostles had been plainly commanded.

When Jesus asked, "Peter, do you love Me more than these?" does He mean more than the other disciples love Him? Peter had said before, "Though all men shall be offended because of thee, yet will I never be offended" (Matt. 26:33). That implied that Peter loved the Lord so much that he would be faithful at any cost. Peter was the one who had the clear revelation, "Thou art the Christ, the Son of the living God."

"Peter, do you still love Me? Do you love Me more than these?" Oh, Peter makes no boast now but humbly says, "Lord, You know I love You."

Did He mean, "Peter, do you love Me more than the fish and the fishing business?" I am sure Peter did, but Jesus wanted him to openly renounce the idea of a life of making money, a secular life. Says Macaulay: "I do not think the Saviour's three questions to Peter were asked in rapid succession, but they broke in on the conversation at intervals. Between questions, the fallen but rapidly rising disciple had time to think."

And Dr. Ironside has this comment:

> The outstanding theme of this chapter is the public restoration of the Apostle Peter. He who had failed the Lord so sadly in the hour of need might have thought he would never again be recognized as one of the apostles. But he was just as tenderly loved by the Lord after his failure as before. I wish we could take that in.
>
> *   *
>
> Now I have no doubt that the Lord had actually restored Peter's soul before this public event took place. We are told that when those disciples came from Emmaus on that first Lord's Day evening they found the disciples gathered together, saying, "The Lord is risen indeed, *and hath appeared unto Simon.*" Just where that appearance took place we do not know, but there had been a secret meeting between Peter and the Lord he had denied, and as a result of this, I am sure Peter's soul had been restored.

VERSES 18,19:

18 Verily, verily, I say unto thee, When thou wast young, thou girdedst thyself, and walkedst whither thou wouldest: but when thou shalt be old, thou shalt stretch forth thy hands, and another shall gird thee, and carry *thee* whither thou wouldest not.

19 This spake he, signifying by what death he should glorify God. And when he had spoken this, he saith unto him, Follow me.

Peter to Be a Martyr

We do not know in history about the death of Peter. His two epistles are labeled as from Babylon where he went to preach to the dispersed Jews. In I Peter 5:13 he writes, "The church that is at Babylon, elected together with you, saluteth you; and so doth Marcus my son." And in II Peter 1:13,14 he wrote, "Yea, I think it meet, as long as I am in this tabernacle, to stir you up by putting you in remembrance; Knowing that shortly I must put off this my tabernacle, even as our Lord Jesus Christ hath shewed me." Then Peter seemed to know that his martyrdom was at hand, which Jesus foretold here in John.

In that, he is like the Apostle Paul who wrote in II Timothy 4:6, "For I am now ready to be offered, and the time of my departure is at hand."

F. B. Meyer comments:

> Following Christ involves almost certain suffering at first. When Peter asked what they would have, who had left all to follow Jesus, the Master did not hesitate to say that the bitter herb of suffering would mingle with all the dishes with which their table might be spread: and when James and John tried to bespeak the right and left seats of the throne, He spoke of the cup and baptism of pain. But afterwards, when the cross and grave are passed, then the fullness of joy and the pleasures which are at God's right hand forevermore!

Tradition says that Peter died in Rome but that is unreliable and untrue. The Roman Church must have Peter be in Rome or there is no excuse for the papacy, no excuse for the claims of the Roman Church to forgive sins and such matters. But Peter was never at Rome. Note the evidence:

1. When Paul wrote to Rome in Romans, chapter 16, he

named about twenty-eight families and persons to whom he sent greetings. Peter was not named because he was not there.

2. When Paul came to Rome, in Acts 28, some met him but Peter did not and the Jewish leaders there were not familiar with the Gospel. Peter was not there.

3. When Paul wrote from Rome, his epistles to the Ephesians, Philippians, Colossians, II Timothy and Philemon, in all these he never mentioned Peter as being at Rome. In fact, he expressly says in II Timothy 4:10-12:

"For Demas hath forsaken me, having loved this present world, and is departed unto Thessalonica; Crescens to Galatia, Titus unto Dalmatia. Only Luke is with me. Take Mark, and bring him with thee: for he is profitable to me for the ministry. And Tychicus have I sent to Ephesus."

So Paul would say, "Only Luke is with me," and the other good Christians who had been there are gone. Peter is not named. He was not with Paul. The Roman tradition that Peter at this time was in the Mamertine prison with Paul is unscriptural.

4. The Apostle Peter had clearly found the will of God that he was to go to the circumcision, that is, to Jews, while Paul was to go to the Gentiles at Rome and elsewhere, says Galatians 2:7-9. So Peter went to the dispersed Jews at Babylon, and never appeared at Rome.

We do not know the details of his death, but no doubt he died a martyr, and we are sure that he was glad to die for Jesus.

VERSES 20-25:

20 Then Peter, turning about, seeth the disciple whom Jesus loved following; which also leaned on his breast at supper, and said, Lord, which is he that betrayeth thee?

21 Peter seeing him saith to Jesus, Lord, and what *shall* this man *do?*

22 Jesus saith unto him, If I will that he tarry till I come, what *is that*

to thee? follow thou me.

23 Then went this saying abroad among the brethren, that that disciple should not die: yet Jesus said not unto him, He shall not die; but, If I will that he tarry till I come, what *is that* to thee?

24 This is the disciple which testifieth of these things, and wrote these

things: and we know that his testimony is true.

25 And there are also many other things which Jesus did, the which, if they should be written every one, I suppose that even the world itself could not contain the books that should be written. Amen.

What About John?

John was very close to the Saviour. Was it jealousy that made Peter inquire about John? Or, if Peter is to die as a martyr, as verse 18 indicates, what about John? Will he be martyred, too? Peter, that is none of your business. *"What is that to thee?"* (vs. 22).

John will evidently live longer than others of the disciples. The Gospel of John, the book of Revelation and the epistles were probably written about the year 90.

Jesus said, *"If I will that he tarry till I come, what is that to thee?"* (vs. 22). In other words, the disciples were to expect Jesus to return at any time. They were plainly commanded to "watch therefore, for ye know neither the day nor the hour wherein the Son of man cometh" (Matt. 25:13). And if John is to live until the rapture, that would be none of Peter's business.

We remember the disciples had argued who should be the greatest. And James and John had their mother come and plead with Jesus that they should sit on His right hand and left hand in the kingdom. They were wrong. In Matthew 20:1-16 Jesus had told the parable of the laborers in the vineyard and those who worked one hour received a penny, as well as those who worked all day. Jesus reminded the disciples that the rewards of laborers were left in the hands of the Master, and everyone would be treated fairly and all of us, thank God, treated by grace.

There went out a saying that John the beloved would not die, but that is not what Jesus said (vs. 23).

Now, in verse 24 we learn that John himself is the one He called *"the disciple whom Jesus loved"* (vs. 20; 19:26; 13:23), and John is the one who was allowed to write it that he was the disciple whom Jesus loved but modestly refrained from giving his name until here in verse 24.

Do the Gospels tell all of the life of Christ on earth? Oh, no. They tell only selected things that were needed in divine

revelation. But if everything Jesus did were told and explained *"the world itself could not contain the books that should be written"* (vs. 25), because everything Jesus said had such infinite riches, everything He did had such infinite importance and meaning, the world could not receive it all.

But, thank God, the book of John is written that we may know He is the Saviour and trust Him and love Him.